Remaking the Tasman World

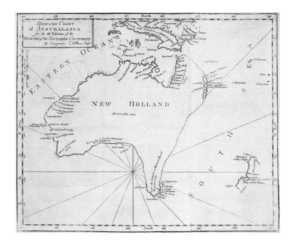

REMAKING THE
TASMAN WORLD

Philippa Mein Smith, Peter Hempenstall
and Shaun Goldfinch

with Stuart McMillan and Rosemary Baird

CANTERBURY UNIVERSITY PRESS

UNIVERSITY OF CANTERBURY
Te Whare Wānanga o Waitaha
CHRISTCHURCH NEW ZEALAND

First published in 2008 by
CANTERBURY UNIVERSITY PRESS
University of Canterbury
Private Bag 4800, Christchurch
NEW ZEALAND
www.cup.canterbury.ac.nz

Edited by Tanya Tremewan
Design and pre-press production by Rachel Scott

Cover image: *Metaphorical Proximity* by Reg Mombassa

Printed in China through Bookbuilders

CONTENTS

PREFACE

A broader mission came to an end with this book's publication. Late in 2002 the Marsden Fund of the Royal Society of New Zealand awarded us a research grant for a multi-year project entitled 'Anzac Neighbours: 100 years of multiple ties between New Zealand and Australia'. Our aim was to explore the trans-Tasman relationship on a variety of levels over the 'long' 20th century. In 2002 the New Zealand Foreign Affairs, Defence and Trade Select Committee also reported on its inquiry into New Zealand's economic and trade relationship with Australia and quoted Simon Upton: 'It is time that we made a twenty-year investment in building up a generation of New Zealanders whose fluency with Australia extends beyond good-natured insults and cut-price weekends in Sydney. The media, academic, scientific and cultural spheres need to be engaged.' We agreed, since we three authors each had a trans-Tasman history that left us puzzled at the ignorance and shallowness of knowledge on both sides of the Tasman about the real nature of trans-Tasman activity. For our research proposal we composed a series of propositions. These ranged from asking if the 'Tasman world' ended with Australian federation to identifying linkages in the 'antipodean response' to restructurings of the world economy, the transfer of ideas and policies, common experiences and culture, and the legacy of British histories. We thank the Marsden Fund for making the outcome – this book – possible.

Philippa's puzzling over the history of Australasia began in the 1980s when she moved to Canberra to undertake a PhD at the Australian National University. She was intrigued by a remark that as a student from New Zealand she belonged to the 'real Australasia'. What did that mean? The ANU itself seemed to house a significant number of closet New Zealanders; they cropped up everywhere once one started to look for them. Then there was the matter of her father's love for Australia; he spent his 'OE' in 1952 crossing the continent from Melbourne to Darwin. Consequently a stuffed baby crocodile sat on the china cabinet during Philippa's childhood, a memento acquired from a crocodile hunter in the Top End. In a typical pattern for Pakeha New Zealanders some of her forebears had migrated via Australia. In Canberra the 'fush and chups' jokes and ribbing about woolly jumpers did not last long; Philippa fitted in, becoming a dinkum Aussie by 1988 and taking up an academic post at Flinders University in Adelaide.

When Peter moved across the Tasman in 1998 he discovered it was like leaving his brothers and sisters to live with a family of cousins: the assumptions and expectations were the same, the rituals and reactions slightly off centre. As an Australian he was 'othered' on arrival in New Zealand, and, from a world where the east coast of Australia, particularly Sydney and Melbourne, was the metropolis and New Zealand rarely invoked, he entered the South Island's contrasting landscape with its own set of self-contained yet outward-looking communities. Australia was always on the radar: from the first radio news in the morning to the last TV news at night. The Tasman became more than 'the ditch': it became a meaningful place where cultures and histories and individual lives criss-crossed effortlessly, all the time.

Shaun Goldfinch crossed the Tasman in the 1990s to do a PhD in Politics at the University of Melbourne. He returned to take up a lectureship at the University of Canterbury, which is where we three met in Cafe 101 in 2002.

This Marsden-funded project began at a point when the New Zealand–Australia relationship was 'drifting apart', at least on the surface. But we were encouraged by evidence of continuing closeness. At the New Zealand Historical Association Conference in Christchurch in 2001 Jill Roe, then president of the Australian Historical Association, called for 'closer intellectual relations' to parallel 'closer economic relations'. Peter Beilharz and Trevor Hogan of the Thesis Eleven Centre at La Trobe University, Melbourne, engaged in their own exploration of what it meant to be 'antipodean', discovered our group in 2003 and we thank them and their postgraduate students for sharing questions and approaches. We organised three workshops with the Thesis Eleven Centre from 2004 to 2007. They exemplified the existence of a Tasman world of ideas and friendship as we alternated between New Zealand and Australia. One outcome was a special issue of their journal *Thesis Eleven* in February 2008 about New Zealand's various worlds.

Across diverse strands of historical scholarship there was simultaneously a pronounced shift – amounting to a conjuncture – from writing national histories towards 'world' history and 'transnational' studies of flows and connections. These trends reflect major global shifts seen in the resurgence of China and India, unparalleled since the rise of Germany and the United States in the 19th century. *Remaking the Tasman World* is a case study of a 'transnational' or connected 'Tasman world' history that illustrates the impact of global forces on Australia and New Zealand and the effects of regional dynamics. Globalisation is a segmented process, and as part of setting limits to this project we have not compared our findings about Tasman relations to other, similar relationships such as between Canada and the US. We sought to be clear in our definitions and purpose; the concepts of 'Australasia' and the 'Tasman world' proved challenging enough to untangle.

We are especially grateful to the New Zealand Ministry of Foreign Affairs and Trade for funding and support, and extend personal thanks to Secretary

Simon Murdoch, Peter Kennedy, Bede Corry, Peter Heenan and other MFAT staff for their invaluable understanding and guidance over the last five years. A grant from MFAT allowed us to recruit Stuart McMillan to research and write the chapter on defence (Chapter 9). With MFAT's blessing we were accorded delegate status to three of the Australia–New Zealand Leadership Forums from 2004 to 2006, courtesy of Kerry McDonald, the inaugural chair, who always appreciated the value of trans-Tasman history. Philippa and Peter duly established the NZAC (New Zealand–Australia Connections) Research Centre at the University of Canterbury in 2005 to fly the flag for New Zealand–Australia relations. We thank the University of Canterbury and especially then Deputy Vice-Chancellor Ian Town for supporting this initiative, which developed into the New Zealand Australia Research Centre (NZARC) in 2008. MFAT also awarded two small Historical Research Grants for primary research on trade relations and Anzac peacekeeping. We thank Chris Seed of the New Zealand Ministry of Defence for his generous and wise guidance, and Gerald Hensley, former head of the New Zealand Prime Minister's Department, who helped mightily through discussions and by making comments on the text. Brigadier Roger Mortlock threw light on the peacekeeping operation he commanded, while Australian High Commissioners Allan Hawke and John Dauth were always interested and supportive. In addition, the Australian High Commission in Wellington made a grant available for Stuart McMillan to visit Canberra for research.

One of the pleasures of this project involved working with postgraduate students. Two students awarded Marsden MA scholarships to work on the project, Vanessa Roberts and Shelley Harford, produced first-class theses, as did Rosemary Baird. It was of great benefit for Shelley and Rosemary, both Canterbury history graduates, to participate in the Building Research Capability in the Social Sciences (BRCSS) initiative established to foster future social scientists in New Zealand. Richard Bedford and Jacques Poot of the BRCSS Research College were exemplary colleagues in helping with demographic literature for Chapter 3. Postgraduates Linda Moore and Angela Findlay also made contributions to research.

Through the UC Social Science Research Centre summer studentship scheme we employed Claire Dann, Julia Macdonald and Rosemary Baird, as well as Gary Whitcher on a UC summer scholarship to work on themes commissioned for the project. Rosemary's input from her summer project is reflected extensively in the writing of Chapter 8. The final distribution of work, once Shaun moved institutions and Philippa and Peter developed research within the NZAC Centre, is shown on the contents page. We owe thanks to the University of Canterbury for a range of support, including study leave that enabled Peter to do overseas research and Philippa to complete the book. Our colleagues in the School of History, and particularly Len Richardson, were always supportive and helpful with ideas and critique.

Reg Mombassa's interest extended not merely to granting copyright permission but to sharing other artwork and to chats on the phone. Michael Leunig and Peter Nicholson provided refreshed cartoons. Doug Munro conducted research on our behalf and volunteered extra findings and ideas. Colin McGeorge wrote unsolicited an erudite report on school texts that were used on both sides of the Tasman, and read a chapter draft; David McIntyre and the late Keith Jackson read chapters; David Lee of the Australian Department of Foreign Affairs and Trade gave generous assistance; and Max Quanchi supplied cuttings on trans-Tasman events. We thank our interviewees, identified and unidentified, for their generosity, among them Alan Ward, R. Gerard Ward, Richard Barwick, Bryant Allen, Don Beaven, Benjamin Pittman and Doris Cope. Retired diplomat Paul Cotton assisted with networking and memoirs, while Gary Hawke and staff at the Ministry of Economic Development and at the Strategic and Defence Studies Centre of the Australian National University threw light on past and present attitudes and policies. We thank Hugh White, Robert Ayson, Des Ball, Paul Dibb, Ron Huisken, Derek Quigley, and also Peter Jennings and Alan Dupont.

J. G. A. Pocock clarified our thinking about British history, oceanic perspectives and what being antipodean means for New Zealanders (if not for Australians), through his correspondence from the US. He reassured us: 'I like your definition of "Australasia" as "the British world south of Asia".' Though he agreed that it would be better if the two countries 'knew, and cared, more about each other', he also had a warning: 'I suspect, however, that you should stress the ways in which they are unlike – which may at least provoke curiosity – rather than telling them they are less dissimilar than they may have thought, which may merely encourage their present indifference.' That retort persuaded us to place the discussion of differences between New Zealand and Australia as Chapter 2.

A phalanx of institutions cheerfully made resources accessible: Archives New Zealand, the National Archives of Australia, the Alexander Turnbull Library, National Library of Australia, State Libraries of New South Wales and South Australia and libraries at the Australian National University and University of Canterbury. Special thanks go to Br Dominic Obbens and his colleagues at the Christian Brothers archives of St Mary's Province in Balmain, Sydney; Rose-Lee Power at the Avondale Seventh Day Adventist College, Cooranbong, New South Wales; and Glynn Litster and Robert Dixon. Dave Small, Curator of the Cartographic Collection at the Alexander Turnbull Library, made a singular contribution by retrieving the charts reproduced in the colour section and arranging for them to be digitised. Philippa is responsible for all the illustrations with the exception of the Leunig cartoon in Chapter 2 (found by Peter). We thank the artists and copyright holders: Reg Mombassa, Bob Brockie, Laurence Clark, Allan Hawkey, Eric Heath, Jim Hubbard, Michael Leunig, Peter Nicholson, Al Nisbet, Tom Scott, Bill Paynter, Jacques Poot, Ashley Smith,

Debby Edwards, Chris Lonsdale, Ngaire Scales, the Alexander Turnbull Library, Archives New Zealand, Christchurch Art Gallery, Museum of New Zealand Te Papa Tongarewa, Museum Victoria, the Ministry of Education and the National Gallery of Victoria.

Earlier drafts of Chapters 4 and 6 drew on papers by Shaun Goldfinch ('Shared State Experiments: Policy transfer and convergence in Australia and New Zealand', *Otemon Journal of Australian Studies*, Vol. 32, 2006, pp. 61–81) and Nicholas Harrigan and Shaun Goldfinch ('A Trans-Tasman Business Elite?', *Journal of Sociology*, Vol. 43, No. 4, 2007, pp. 367–84). Thanks are due to Nicholas Harrigan and Martin Goldfinch.

Canterbury University Press provided exceptional support, editing and design. After Richard King's untimely death in March 2008, Rachel Scott stepped in as publisher. Tanya Tremewan edited the text and prepared the index. Lastly we thank family members: Philippa's Uncle Donald Crawford and especially our partners, Richard Tremewan and Jacquie Monti, who have lived with this book and tolerated our trans-Tasman enthusiasms.

Philippa Mein Smith, Peter Hempenstall and Shaun Goldfinch
2008

CHAPTER ONE

Rediscovering the Tasman World

Philippa Mein Smith and Peter Hempenstall

New Zealand and Australia were good at ignoring each other during the 20th century. This apparent lack of interest seems odd because they also persistently talk about each other as 'family', sharing the closest bonds of language, culture and historical origin. Perhaps, though, the two different behaviours are not contradictory. In families, people often go about their business ignoring one another while being highly conscious of other members. They also indulge in playful banter. That certainly has been the case between Australia and New Zealand. 'Playful banter' is naturally in the eye of the beholder. These two European settler societies have a well-practised set of stereotypes that regularly break through their apparent mutual indifference. To Australians, Kiwis are a timid people, rural hillbillies who like sheep a little too much; or they are heavily tattooed Maori gang leaders; or fun-loving singers and band members. For New Zealanders the average Australian is a brash, loud-mouthed exhibitionist, sport-obsessed, rapacious and uncultured.

In this book we examine some of these 'cartoon' images, mindful that New Zealanders use such ploys more frequently to imagine their own distinctive, desirable qualities. Our aim is to move beyond such stereotypes to begin to answer the bigger question of how New Zealand and Australian pasts are connected. We need a wider view to understand who we are, to adapt J. G. A. Pocock's plea for a new cosmology, by 'remapping the various systems within which [identity] moves'.[1] Pocock's agenda was a new British history of and by diverse peoples that could not be annulled by Britain's return to Europe; ours is a trans-Tasman history mindful of the British imprint.

In constructing their national stories history books on both sides of the Tasman have taken the more polite road of ignoring the other country's existence. On the Australian side of the 'ditch', one can comb the benchmark national histories without finding more than a cursory glance at New Zealand. From Keith Hancock's precocious little book *Australia*, published in 1930, through to the 10-volume, richly illustrated histories written for Australia's bicentenary in

1988, the Australian story has excluded any mention of a common history with New Zealand.[2] Surveys of the history-writing field in Australia have sustained that tradition. John Moses' 1979 edited collection on historical disciplines and culture in *Australasia*, while denying that historians 'here' in the south seas saw themselves as champions of national spirit, paraded a set of essays by practitioners of Australian, New Zealand, Pacific and Asian history that talked about patterns of interaction but studiously ignored those between Australia and New Zealand. The exception was Bill Gammage, who was rather dismissive of Kiwis' ignorance about national dates and symbols and their alleged disregard of the Anzac tradition.[3] Graeme Osborne and Bill Mandle's 1982 collection on new history writing in Australia maintains the silence. Though an excellent essay by Hank Nelson looks north to Papua New Guinea, no one bothered to look east across the Tasman.[4]

It may seem odd to the rest of the world, accustomed to considering Australia and New Zealand together, but ignoring one another is the norm in local historical and opinion-making circles. Journalist Paul Kelly's *End of Certainty* talks of 'the Australian Settlement' (in capitals) that endured for eight decades after federation.[5] Its five planks – 'white Australia', 'arbitration', 'protection', 'state paternalism' and 'imperial benevolence' – are represented as unique and distinctively Australian when they had their analogues or even to some extent their genesis across the Tasman. John Rickard in his 1988 cultural history of Australia claims arbitration as a distinctive Australian institution, expressive of the national psyche.[6] In 2002 the concluding volume from the Australian National University's Reshaping Australian Institutions Project reiterated that Australia was unusual for its system of tariff protection that underpinned the 'Australian Settlement'. Yet New Zealand historian Erik Olssen and others have demonstrated that these 'experiments' are central to New Zealand history, just as they are to Australian history.[7] Even social scientist Francis Castles describes industrial conciliation and arbitration as 'this most peculiar of Australian institutions' when he argues in notable earlier works that the core concepts of the 'wage earners' welfare state' and the politics of 'domestic defence' also applied to New Zealand.[8]

At the July 2002 conference in Brisbane of the Australian Historical Association – the umbrella organisation for historians in Australia – colleagues welcomed New Zealand papers, but relegated these to the 'Pacific' strand, separate from Australian history. In September 2002 a major international conference of the Association for Canadian Studies in Australia and New Zealand met in Canberra on the subject of possible converging futures, without a mention of New Zealand.[9] Similarly, the continuing ignorance of New Zealand fictional literature in Australia compared with that from India or Canada regularly draws bemused comments from reviewers.

New Zealanders are just as guilty. They have absorbed the myth that New

Zealand's 'Better Britons' are superior to Australian Britons. New Zealanders lacked the taint of convictism, they were moulded by a vigorous, cooler climate and they enjoyed relations with a superior type of 'native'.[10] New Zealand scholars have underwritten this tale of separate histories. The country's nationalist historian, Keith Sinclair, chose to focus primarily on the 19th century when writing for his edited collection *Tasman Relations*. He insisted on a 'destiny apart', especially in respect of New Zealand's better race relations.[11] Closer to our time, the *New Zealand Journal of History* chose to shape its millennium edition of 2000 around the theme for the 21st century of New Zealand in the Pacific, omitting Australia.[12] In his 2001 grand synthesis of New Zealand history, *Paradise Reforged*, James Belich re-emphasises British at the expense of Australian connections and argues that New Zealand departed its 'old, Tasman world' in 1901 for a 'recolonial' relationship with Britain.[13]

From the 1960s a small set of historians with trans-Tasman links began to show awareness of Australia–New Zealand relations as global forces drew the two closer together, though this work was treated as peripheral to both imperial and national histories.[14] In the wake of the New Zealand–Australia Free Trade Agreement (NAFTA) in 1965 certain economists and diplomats collaborated on analyses of the official relationship with a focus on trade, which remain useful for historians.[15] Foreign policy collections pinpoint cyclical flurries of interest in response to global shifts, external threats and birthdays.[16] By 2001 the centenary of federation had produced a cartoon history of trans-Tasman relations indicative of the real tone of the relationship (see Chapter 2), but federation conferences continued to lament the dearth of historical scholarship.[17]

There have been some attempts by historians to make cross-Tasman comparisons, about race relations and stock and station agents for example, but they tend to be thematic studies that share an interest in colonisation and settler societies.[18] Other publications with 'Australia and New Zealand' in their titles contrive to bring the two countries' historical experiences together but address shared issues separately.[19] The most enduring thematic analyses are by labour historians familiar with the common experience of a trans-Tasman labour movement; James Bennett's explicitly 'transnational' labour history from 1890 to 1940 belongs to this school. So does a special trans-Tasman issue of the journal *Labour History* complementary to this book, which went to press in parallel.[20]

Economic historians have contemplated the Australian and New Zealand economies' mutual influence in the late 19th century and trends in trans-Tasman trade and finance as part of a British Commonwealth economic network and the sterling area in the mid-20th century.[21] Political studies occasionally recognise that Australia and New Zealand are separate but 'path-dependent', though most do not go far beyond making comparisons.[22] Brian Galligan and Richard Mulgan stand out for their sketch of a loose 'asymmetric political association' that they imagine might combine elements of nation-to-nation and federal relations in the future, building on existing arrangements between the neighbours.[23] It was his experience of rupture in the alliance established by the Security Treaty between Australia, New Zealand and the United States of America (Anzus) in the 1980s, despite his best efforts, that impelled a former Secretary of Defence, Denis McLean, to attempt an historical explanation of the nature of the trans-Tasman relationship. In his view, a united Austral-Asia is logical but is unlikely to happen because of nationalism, which makes New Zealand and Australia a 'prickly pair'.[24] A long-term commentator, Colin James, decided the relationship by the early 21st century was of 'two asymmetric, independent, sovereign nations', emphasising their divergences despite what they had in common.[25]

Pacific historians have tackled a more regionalist agenda since the early work of C. Hartley Grattan, but his survey volumes reflected an interested American's perspective that saw the Pacific as a region that included the large rim countries and treated Australia and New Zealand as its south-western quadrant.[26] The kind of Pacific history that evolved out of the Australian National University tradition under New Zealander J. W. Davidson after the Second World War concentrated on the oceanic islands and their contact histories. It left persistent boundaries between Pacific, Australian and New Zealand history, despite the direct explanatory relevance of New Zealand to an understanding of relations between indigenous peoples and new immigrant settlers and of Australian history to the experience of Papua New Guinea.

The Blackwell History of the World volume *A History of Australia, New Zealand and the Pacific* by Donald Denoon and Philippa Mein Smith is a latter-day attempt to write about a coherent region, even though it no longer had a name, as they point out.[27] Denoon argues that 'Australasia' is a 'repressed memory', which historians have airbrushed out of both Australian and New Zealand historiographies.[28] The term Australasia had been widely used from the late 18th century. Coined by the French writer Charles de Brosses in 1756 for one division of the imagined *Terra Australis*, it entered English in 1766 as referring to the lands 'south of Asia' before Captain James Cook's voyages of discovery debunked the myth of the great south land presumed by European cosmologies.[29] By the late 19th century its parameters had shrunk to the British world south of Asia, commonly referred to as 'the seven colonies of Australasia' and Britain's sphere of influence in the near Pacific, including Papua and Fiji. Historians since have erased the word and concept of 'Australasia' from both Australian and New Zealand history, as if they wanted to forget that New Zealand and the Australian colonies were part of Australasia before 1901. Yet this imagined community was 'real', as James Belich also recognises, even if it was a bit vague or fuzzy around the edges.

Maps of Australasia

Maps assist us to avoid anachronistic thinking about the region as they chart changes in the way Europeans imposed frames of meaning. *Polus Antarcticus,*

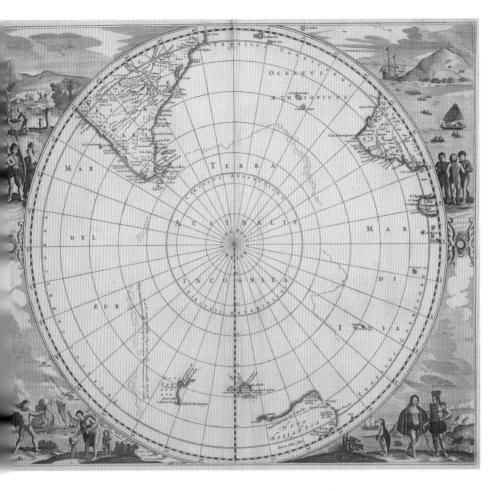

Plate 1. Polus Antarcticus: Terra Australis Incognita, De Wit, Amsterdam, 1666.

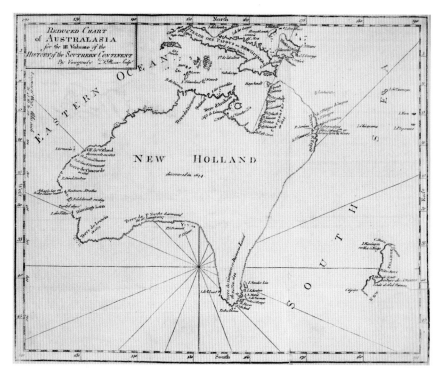

Plate 2. Robert de Vaugondy, Gilles, Reduced Chart of Australasia for the third volume of the *History of the Southern Continent*, in Charles de Brosses, *Terra Australis Cognita, or, Voyages to the Terra Australis ...*, ed. John Callander, Edinburgh, 1768.
SPC 06/729, Rare Voyages Collection, Special Printed Collections, Alexander Turnbull Library, Wellington

Plate 3. Nuove Scoperte: Fatte nel 1765, 67 e 69 nel: Mare del Sud, Presso Antonio Zatta, con privilegio dell' Ecc'mo Senato, Venezia, 1776. MapColl 800a/1776/Acc.32125, Alexander Turnbull Library, Wellington

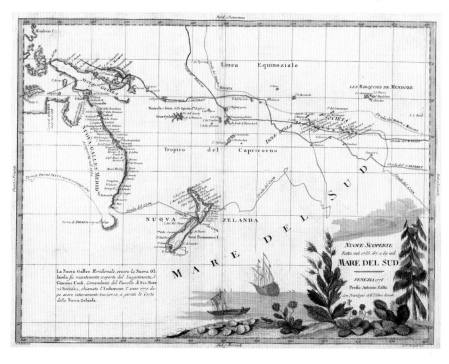

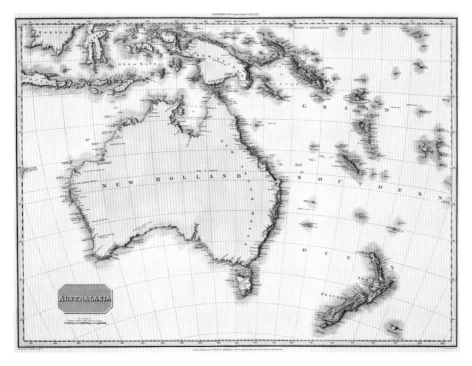

Plate 4. Australasia, Cadell & Davies; Longman, Hurst, Rees, Orme & Brown, London, 1813.
MapColl 800a/1813/Acc.1304, Alexander Turnbull Library, Wellington

Plate 5. David H. Burr, *New Holland and New Zealand*, D. Burr, New York, 1834.
MapColl 800a/1834/Acc.25703, Alexander Turnbull Library, Wellington

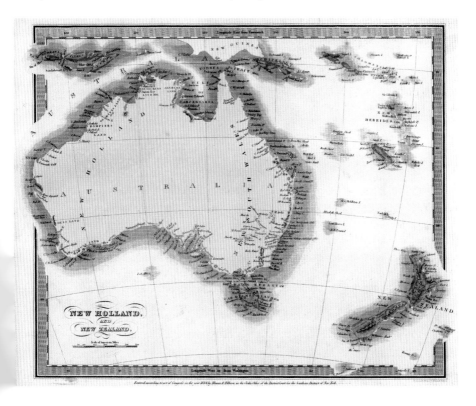

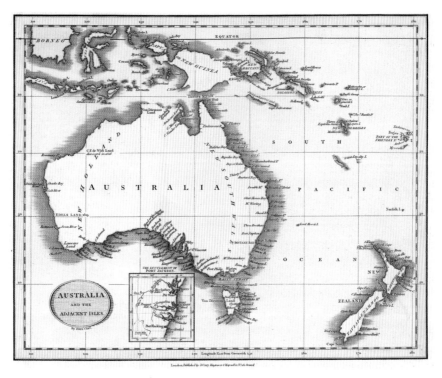

Plate 6. John Cary, Australia and the Adjacent Isles, J. Cary, London, c. 1810.
MapColl 800a/[ca. 1810]/Acc.3775, Alexander Turnbull Library, Wellington

Plate 7. Australasia, Committee of General Literature and Education; Society for Promoting Christian Knowledge, London, 1863? MapColl 800a/[1863?]/Acc.43774, Alexander Turnbull Library, Wellington

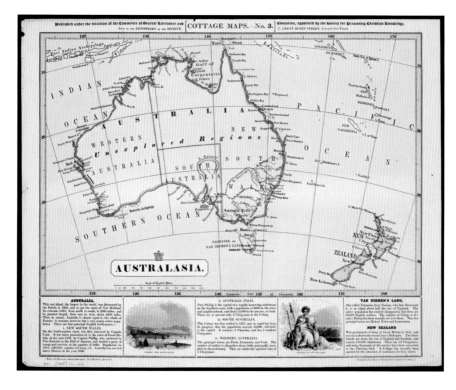

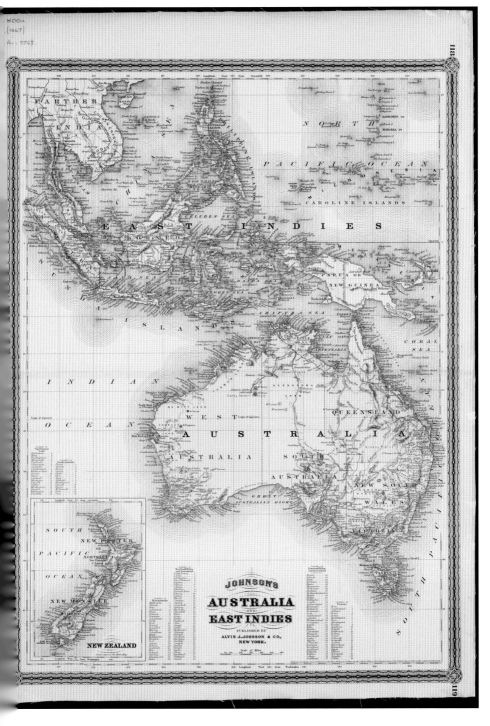

Plate 8. Johnson's Australia and East Indies, Alvin J. Johnson & Co., New York, 1867.

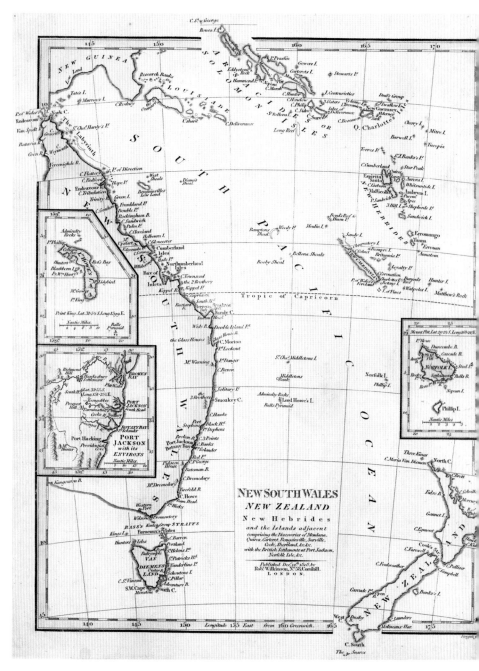

Plate 9. New South Wales, New Zealand, New Hebrides and the Islands adjacent, Robert Wilkinson, London, 1808.

Plates 10a & b. A Chart of Part of New South Wales, Van Diemens Land, New Zealand and Adjacent Islands, with the Principal Harbours, Charles Wilson (late J. W. Norie & Co.), London, 1857.

MapColl 800aj/1857/Acc.32076 and 800aj/1857/Acc.32077, Alexander Turnbull Library, Wellington

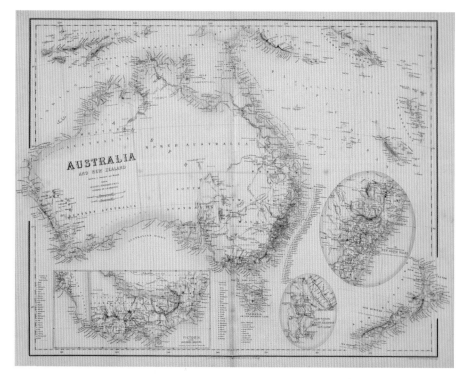

Plate 11. Australia and New Zealand according to Arrowsmith and Mitchell [Goldfields], A. Fullarton & Co., Edinburgh, London, Dublin, 186? MapColl 800a/[186-?]/Acc.3762, Alexander Turnbull Library, Wellington

Plate 12. Australasia Industries & Communications, George Philip & Son, London, 1908, from *The Harmsworth General Atlas.*
MapColl 800gf/1908/Acc.1283, Alexander Turnbull Library, Wellington (British possessions are coloured red)

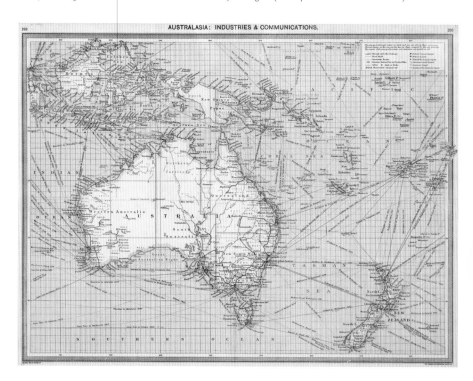

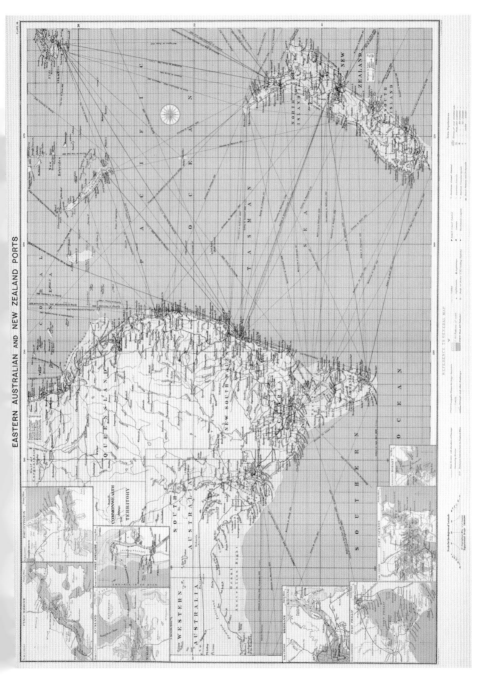

Plate 13. Eastern Australian and New Zealand Ports, George Philip & Son, London, 1918.
MapColl 800gmfs/[1918]/Acc.45905, Alexander Turnbull Library, Wellington

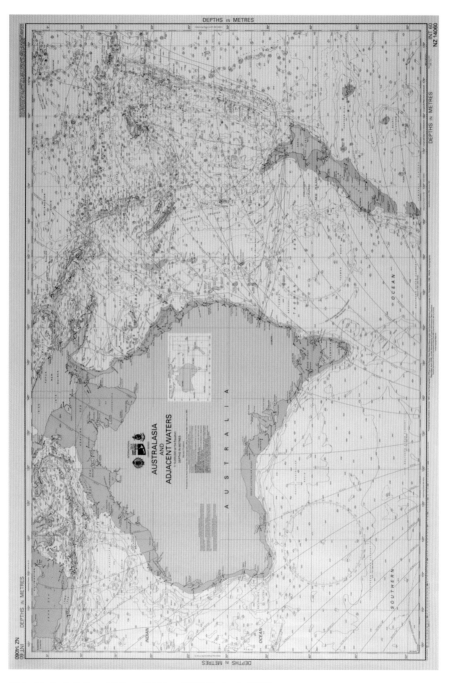

Plate 14. Australasia and Adjacent Waters, 2006 (first pub. 1987).
INT 60 NZ 14060, Land Information New Zealand

Plate 15. *Near Heidelberg*, 1890, oil on canvas, 53.4 × 43.1 cm, by Arthur Streeton, Australia (1867–1943), who lived in England 1899–1919.
National Gallery of Victoria, Melbourne, Felton Bequest, 1943

Plate 16. *Mountain Stream Otira Gorge*, 1893, oil on canvas, 136.5 × 194cm, by Petrus van der Velden, Dutch/New Zealander, 1837–1913.

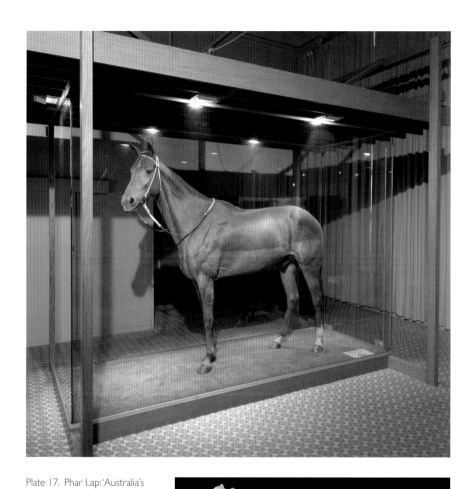

Plate 17. Phar Lap: 'Australia's
Wonder Horse'.
Museum Victoria: http://www.
museumvictoria.com.au/pharlap/

Plate 18. Phar Lap's skeleton.
Museum of New Zealand Te Papa
Tongarewa, Wellington

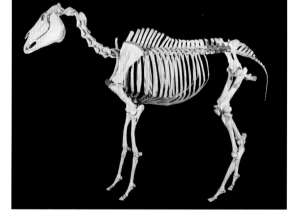

PROPOSED AUSTRALIA-NEW ZEALAND COMMON CURRENCY

THE BASIC COIN WILL
BE THE **ANZAC**, APPROX
12 CM IN DIAMETER...

IT WON'T OPERATE ALL
VENDING MACHINES...

...BUT THAT DOESN'T
MATTER BECAUSE YOU
CAN EAT THE COIN

Plate 19. Peter Nicholson, *The Australian*, 28 April 2000.
www.nicholsoncartoons.com.au, courtesy of Peter and Mary Nicholson

Plate 21.
Courtesy of Reg Mombassa, Sydney

Plate 20. A poster for Ridgway, Cole &
Ridgway's Palace Circus, Nelson, April 1912.
Eph-E-CABOT-Circus-1912–01, Alexander Turnbull
Library, Wellington

Plate 22. Tasman Empire Airways Limited travellers' certificate, Auckland to Sydney, in the flying-boat
RMA *Aotearoa*, 3 May 1941.
Eph-A-AVIATION-TEAL-1941–01, Alexander Turnbull Library, Wellington

1666 (Plate 1) shows the fragments of *Terra Australis Incognita* located by the voyages of European discovery that Dutch cartographers mapped in the 17th century. Abel Tasman's first venture into the southern ocean in 1642 added the future Tasmania and New Zealand to the bottom of this well-known map. French cartographers accepted Tasman's chart but were impatient to complete it. In the 1660s French mapmakers published several versions of *Hollandia Nova detecta*, or *decouverte*. A century later this chart bore the new name 'Australasia' (Plate 2). As drawn in 1768 Australasia extended from New Holland to Papua New Guinea – by then understood to be separated from the continent by Torres Strait – as well as east to New Zealand. But French creativity added a fake east coast of Australia, awaiting Cook's discoveries. Plate 2 is the first map of Australasia in English. Cook himself carried the French version, bound up in the French history of voyages to *Terra Australis* (and which de Brosses published in 1756), on his first voyage to New Zealand and Australia (1768–71). The impact of Cook's voyage was to dominate an Italian view of the south sea(s) from the 1770s (Plate 3), and expose the swathe of ocean as opposed to land to the east of Australia.

In Cook's wake, Australasia joined the British world from 1788 through the process of colonisation that radiated outwards from the convict port of Sydney. As settlement expanded it grew to be a British idea, shorthand for the British colonies south of Asia. Illustrating how widespread the loss of memory has been, the following maps of Australasia from the Alexander Turnbull Library in Wellington have not been used before, and the library specially digitised them for this project. They show how the idea of Australasia predated Australia, which was depicted as New Holland as late as 1813 (Plate 4) and 1834 in one United States map (Plate 5). But names were yet to settle with settlement in the early 19th century; sometimes Australasia was depicted as Australia and the adjacent islands, with New Holland relegated to western Australia (Plate 6); and sometimes, or contemporaneously, as Australia, New Zealand and the adjacent islands, or just Australia and the adjacent isles. But New Zealand consistently formed Australia's principal 'Pacific frontier'.[30] These maps confirm that Port Jackson – Sydney – was the hub of this region, and that New South Wales was the 'mother colony' of New Zealand as well as of eastern Australia.

By the 1860s Papua and/or New Guinea disappeared from British maps of Australasia (Plate 7). Although this 'cottage map', intended for use in schools, depicts the self-governing colonies that separated from New South Wales in the first half of the 19th century, along with Western Australia, it omits Queensland, which split off in 1859. Nonetheless it shows how Australasia as a rubric shrank to comprise the settler colonies of Australia and New Zealand, so that from the 1890s T. A. Coghlan, the New South Wales government statistician, published statistical accounts of the seven colonies of Australasia.[31] Alternative perspectives reinforce the Britishness of Australasia. The American view included the East

Indies (from the Second World War, Southeast Asia) as shown in a view from New York in 1867 (Plate 8). So did Chinese perspectives: the Chinese name for Southeast Asia, Nan Yang (literally South Sea), is extended by some Chinese to include everything south of China, whereas the name for Australia and then New Zealand is Xin Jin Shan (New Gold Mountain), as a result of the gold rushes of the 1850s and 1860s.[32] Even British understanding of how far Australasia extended remained ambiguous at the end of the 19th century, when Victorian statutes defined Australasia to mean the Australian mainland plus New Zealand, Tasmania, Fiji and 'any other British Colonies or possessions in Australasia.'[33]

The Tasman world

Australasia won't do any more. From where New Zealanders stand, across 2000 kilometres of ocean from Australia and a long way from the outlying islands of Asia, Australasia remains an unpersuasive geographical concept. For New Zealanders it is an unsatisfactory term for Australia and New Zealand, whereas in Australian use it means Australia, New Zealand and the Pacific Islands south of Asia.[34] The coverage suggested couples an Australia that already threatens to dominate New Zealand with a large, diffuse and alien Asia, a condition that the security crisis in East Timor and Indonesia's coolness towards Australia only reinforce. Australasia does not satisfactorily describe the *antipodean* concerns of two, separate migrant settler societies whose past, present and future are just as intimately tied together in mutual opposition to, or uneasy tension with, histories and cultural formations on the other side of the earth. Nor does Australasia any longer sum up the relationship of Australia and New Zealand with certain island groups of the southwest Pacific where small offshoots of these migrant societies exist. A new storyline is necessary, reflected in the title of this book, to position New Zealand more assuredly for the future.

A better concept for this new storyline is one that James Belich says operated as an organic entity in the 19th century but, with Australian federation, died away: the Tasman world.[35] In practice, the Tasman world never died and indeed has strengthened. New Zealand and Australia share a history that is rich and deep across a range of institutions, social structures and events. That history also accommodates communities, individuals and encounters on island Melanesian and Polynesian frontiers. Both nations began life as a common colonial entity, part of the still-expanding southern British world of the 18th century. Captain James Cook is the common ancestral cultural hero of both migrant societies; he connects the landmasses through his explorations of 1769–70 and his encounters with Maori and Aboriginal Australians. Both countries revere him, though Australia has been quicker to question whether Cook is really marginal to Australian history, given that he visited only once and showed no interest in the place thereafter; indifference has always been a cardinal sin for Australians.[36]

We understand the Tasman world to be a working region defined by a history of traffic that connects New Zealand to Australia since Cook's voyages and the establishment of a beachhead at Sydney. The Tasman world's scope is determined by the depth and range of connections, as far as the traffic extends between New Zealand and Sydney, Perth or the Northern Territory. Unlike Australasia, the Tasman world asks the viewer or participant to look *sideways* rather than northwards. The term is deliberately New Zealand-focused. New Zealand needs Australia; Australia does not need New Zealand and has not done so since 1901 when six colonies joined to create a nation, which made New Zealand relatively small.

Again, maps provide insights because they illustrate the Tasman world at work. In the early 1800s the region's defining links were formed by maritime traffic between New South Wales, New Zealand, the New Hebrides and the adjacent islands as mapped by Spanish, French and English explorers. The traffic envisaged, however, was to travel among British settlements around the Tasman Sea based on the hub at Port Jackson, as Plate 9 shows. By the 1850s that traffic was concentrated between Sydney, ports in Tasmania and northern and southern New Zealand from the Bay of Islands to Stewart Island (Plate 10). The gold rushes brought new activity and a focus on land rather than sea: on the goldfields of Victoria, New South Wales and New Zealand (Plate 11). Industries and communications shaped the links and shrank distance by 1908 across Australasia (Plate 12). The sea voyage from Hobart to Bluff took four days, and the trip from Sydney to Wellington or Auckland five days. A decade later, technology had shaved a day off the Tasman crossing, and trans-Tasman traffic was concentrated between the New Zealand main centres and the state capital cities of eastern Australia from Brisbane to Adelaide (Plate 13). By 1918 'Australasia' had disappeared from the map's title, replaced by Australia and New Zealand. Nation-building, including the transcontinental railway from Perth to Sydney, and the upheavals of the First World War encouraged its obsolescence; Australasia had become old hat.

Awareness of the Tasman world as a map of systems brings to the fore the existence of myriad *communities of interest* that traverse the Tasman, and that this book argues undercut national histories since Australian federation in 1901. In the story of New Zealand's preference for a separate destiny it is routine to quote Sir John Hall at the Australasian Federation Conference in 1890: 'Nature has made 1,200 impediments to the inclusion of New Zealand in any such federation in the 1,200 miles of stormy ocean which lie between us and our brethren in Australia.' Yet Hall went on to say: 'That does not prevent the existence of a community of interests between us.'[37] Historians have ignored Hall's addendum. Yet politicians and officials regularly adopted the language of 'community of interest' to express the idea of a real and working trans-Tasman community.[38] In the course of this book we show how governments in Australia, New Zealand and the Australian states shared policy ideas, innovations and laws, as well as people, to a remarkable degree. Within particular communities of interest and expertise, policy-makers learnt from one another in a process that political scientists call policy learning, lesson drawing, diffusion or policy transfer.

Early Tasman links

Early settlement links between New Zealand and the Australian colonies register in the historical stories of both countries. The early governors' remits in New South Wales included New Zealand, and the Union Jack united settlers on both sides of the Tasman. Most trading voyages originated in Sydney from the 1800s to the 1830s. Early traders and entrepreneurs looked back to Sydney as their prime destination: sealers in the South Island and Foveaux Strait, which was named after a minor Sydney official; Sydney shipowners who established whaling stations along the east coast; traders in timber, flax and other Maori products. As far back as 1830, 75 ships crossed the Tasman to and from Sydney: 35 to and from New Zealand, 13 from New Zealand heading elsewhere, such as Hobart, and 27 from elsewhere via Sydney to New Zealand.[39] Ships carried flax, pork and potatoes grown by Maori who displayed entrepreneurial flair and adaptive agricultural skills. Maori treated Sydney as a major link in their trading activities as well as an important source of muskets. They had a visible presence in the town as seamen, traders and students at the seminary established by Rev. Samuel Marsden at Parramatta, where chiefs learnt Christian works and agriculture.

Captain John Stewart of the brig *Elizabeth* arrived in Sydney with 30 tons of New Zealand flax in 1831, his reward for assisting Te Rauparaha to attack his Ngai Tahu enemies; the first British Resident, James Busby, was appointed from New South Wales in 1833 in response to Maori representations; while Captain William Hobson, Lieutenant-Governor, departed from Sydney for the Bay of Islands on 19 January 1840 to organise the Treaty of Waitangi. After 1840 Australia's eastern colonies helped provision the first enclaves of British settlers in New Zealand. In return, demand grew in New South Wales for grain, tallow and timber. The New Zealand sheep farming industry was beholden to the Australian colonials who provided the first merinos to stock the runs. The east coasts of both landmasses thrived together on the sheep's back in the 19th century, and inventions such as shearing combs, refrigerated transport and the stump jump plough crossed the Tasman in both directions to enhance pastoralism and agriculture. Jim McAloon demonstrates how the great farming families of Canterbury and Otago were drawn from across the Tasman, bringing cattle and the best sheep. Their experience taming the harsh new landscape and their manual and industrial skills were a form of capital to develop this easterly extension of Australia. They were a class of Australasian – we would say Tasman – capitalists. McAloon argues that the capitalist class in New Zealand has remained thus through its networks of money, family, migration and intermarriage.[40]

The gold rushes of the mid-19th century also intimately shaped both developing settler cultures. An estimated 17,000 miners poured into Otago after 1861 from Australia, and 60 per cent of the export trade in gold and wool was trans-shipped there. The movement was not just of white miners (and former convicts from New South Wales and Van Diemen's Land, often conveniently forgotten on the New Zealand side of the Tasman) but of significant numbers of Chinese. As miners followed the next rush to the South Island's West Coast, or returned to the Australian colonies, Otago businessmen and council members issued an invitation to Chinese miners in Victoria to work the Otago goldfields. By 1871 their number reached 4200 before spilling over to the West Coast. New Zealand colonists shared with Australian colonists the same suspicion of Chinese immigrants, so that the developing 'white Australia policy' influenced New Zealand's national policy from the late 19th century.

This story of trans-Tasman influences on New Zealand also encompasses the Christian churches and their missionaries, and the labour movement. Both will appear in later chapters. So will the federation of the Australian colonies into one nation state in 1901, and the decision by New Zealand not to join. Australian federation figures on both sides of the Tasman as the zero point in the 'modern' historical development of both nations, as though they veered off on totally separate national cultural paths.

Our contention is different. It may be that both countries stared past each other more frequently in the years after 1900 than previously, but both were on the same mission: to create progressive white men's nations, first within the British empire and later the Commonwealth, committed to the same social and racial goals and sharing the same values, institutions and people. They continued to operate in a shared Tasman world that was as strong, or as weak, as the globalising world to which their economies and populations related in the 20th century. Indeed, the ties that bound them together were stronger than the factors that kept them apart. New Zealand and Australia have been described as 'born modern' experiments,[41] precocious settler societies that shared a geographical region, a common heritage in the British empire and a series of bargains between the state and the private economy. The bargains were organised around a fair living wage, compulsory arbitration of industrial disputes and immigration policies that protected their Anglo-Celtic identity and restricted the entry of unwanted, low-cost labour. British institutions, British law and British education underpinned their choice of social structures. Both countries remained enmeshed in the British financial system until the 1940s.

There were, of course, periods when indifference, suspicion and irritation were more pronounced, notably between the two world wars, when the world de-globalised and uncoupled. Political relations looked north to the empire for solidarity rather than sideways in the 1920s and 1930s, even though five Australian immigrants were Cabinet ministers in New Zealand's first Labour government. Trade relations deteriorated after Australian federation and a wall of tariff protection kept the distance between the countries. But global stresses did not put paid to the Tasman world, as we shall see in Chapter 5.

Bonds of war and defence

War was the area of international activity that brought both societies together in the first half of the 20th century and made 'Anzac' the emotional cornerstone of the relationship. The Australian and New Zealand Army Corps (Anzac) experience at Gallipoli in 1915 is seen on both sides of the Tasman as the birthplace of the nations of the Southern Cross, side by side. Ever since, politicians have pronounced on the warm solidarity that binds Australians and New Zealanders together in the Anzac spirit.

This solidarity was, however, open to question at the time. New Zealand and Australian soldiers were at one another's throats from the moment they were thrown together in Egypt prior to Gallipoli. New Zealanders considered Aussies to be bumptious know-alls.[42] Aussies saw Kiwis as too subservient to British military culture, and less independent than Australian larrikins. They did share Gallipoli, but different parts of it. Ever since, each country identifies its celebration or mourning on Anzac Day with different locations on the peninsula: Chunuk Bair for New Zealanders, Lone Pine for Australians. From a cultural studies perspective, Tara Brabazon argues that Gallipoli actually fractured the relationship between Australia and New Zealand,[43] which suggests (contra Belich) there was something still there to break in 1915. Though a New Zealander is supposed to have invented the acronym Anzac, Australia introduced the Anzac Day Dawn Service; New Zealand copied its solemnity and form from 1939.[44] But in the 21st century there are subtle differences in the way Anzac Day is celebrated in each country.

The Second World War raised another question mark over Anzac togetherness. Both countries automatically declared war on Germany in support of Britain, and both fought in the same theatres of war in Europe and Africa. Both were shocked to learn that Britain could not promise a fleet to defend Singapore, whose naval base was supposed to protect the two dominions. But whereas Australia's Prime Minister, John Curtin, insisted to Churchill that his own country's soldiers must come home to defend Australian shores from Japanese invasion, New Zealand chose to follow Britain, accepting that Britain was not going to supply the weapons and aircraft New Zealand asked for to defend herself. New Zealanders and Australians ended up fighting the same war but separately. Pocock claims New Zealand's decision was really about trade, keeping her 'protein bridge' to Europe open.[45] Australians occasionally still assert that this decision let down the Anzac partnership. When Australian Prime Minister Paul Keating visited Papua New Guinea in 1992 to mark the Kokoda Track as the place where modern Australian history began, his speech writer,

Don Watson, felt a shiver of derision at an invitation to speak being extended to the New Zealand representative, as though Kiwis had contributed anything to that war front.[46] Implicit was the assumption that Anzacs should pull together in their local world.

That their local world was not other people's world did bring New Zealand and Australia closer, in the form of the Anzac or Canberra Pact of 1944 as the war turned in the Allies' favour. Though historians have subsequently differed in their assessments of this pact, it demanded recognition that the southwest Pacific was a region where both countries worked together and should be consulted about the form of any postwar organisation for the area.[47] The Anzac Pact had material descendants in the South Pacific Commission of 1947 and the Pacific Islands Forum where both countries, till today, patrol the boundaries of their mutually supportive relationship with South Pacific island nations. The Cold War also kept Australia and New Zealand close in their defence postures and strategies, working together with the United States towards regional security. Australia was head prefect in the schoolyard of the South Pacific, coordinating the two countries' response to the Anzus alliance.

There had often been voices of discomfort in New Zealand about following the Australian lead in respect to the US and her Cold War politics. That discomfort grew to estrangement when the US administration of Ronald Reagan dropped New Zealand from Anzus. That move was a result of the 1985 decision by the New Zealand Labour government under David Lange to implement a nuclear-free policy in its territorial waters. Lange made clear after his resignation that his opposition to the development of nuclear weapons through tests in the Pacific went back to 1962 when he was frightened by the remarkable glow that was caused by the testing of America's Starfish nuclear device in the upper atmosphere of the north Pacific.[48] It shocked many New Zealanders that the effect of nuclear explosions thousands of kilometres away could be seen in New Zealand. But the Anzus crisis was ironically a fillip to trans-Tasman defence cooperation. New Zealand found itself more reliant on Australia for assistance in a range of areas; the number of Kiwis attending training courses in Australia doubled and, by 1988, 70 per cent of New Zealand's overseas training was carried out in Australia. The Anzac frigate project of 1989 seemed to strengthen ties, and the term Closer Defence Relations was coined in 1991 to emphasise the increasingly integrated nature of the two countries' defence programmes (see Chapter 9).[49]

A wedge in the Tasman defence community, at least in public, appeared to widen with a minority National government's refusal to buy a third frigate in 1999; then, when New Zealand Labour returned to government, it closed down the fighter air arm that used to be integrated with Australian forces in a regional force. Most revealing of the difference in the partners' world views, New Zealand began to articulate a different approach to regional security based on a policing or peacekeeping role closer to home in the islands, leaving to Australia the big questions of security for the wider region. The signalling of this approach was represented in the media as a chasm between New Zealand and Australia on strategic policy, and in perceptions of threat to the region. The corollary was that each country possessed a different attitude to the US and a different degree of willingness to follow her into the Middle East.

In practice, at the start of the 21st century, the trans-Tasman regional security alliance was more alive and functioning than many people or the media were prepared to admit. Alexander Downer, Australian Minister of Foreign Affairs, acknowledged in 2005 that New Zealand is a foreign country that does things differently; where New Zealanders reside on the map means that they see the world differently from Australians. They have a different geopolitical perspective, reflecting Auckland's considerably greater distance from Hong Kong and the Taiwan Straits compared with Darwin's ('the distance of tyranny' to reverse Geoffrey Blainey).[50] But this difference in perspective has not stopped intimate cooperation in East Timor, during the Bougainville crisis on which New Zealand took the initiative, and in the policing of the Solomon Islands troubles through the Regional Assistance Mission to Solomon Islands (RAMSI). New Zealand and Australia enjoy today a 'complementarity' in force structure and operational behaviour that has never been so intimate.

Economic ties

Economic insecurity is the real nightmare for New Zealand, as a small country with few natural resources save for cows and sheep, and distant from the world's markets. Economics has been the foundation stone of the Tasman community of interests, and trade, financial and labour ties stretch back to the foundations of New South Wales. Before 1860 New Zealand's incorporation into the colonial Australian economy was such that she was 'merely an offshoot of her larger neighbour'.[51] New Zealand banking was from the first dominated by Australian interests, and the colonies shared financial institutions (Chapter 6). Pastoralism – still central to New Zealand exports – benefited from early Australian input in terms of capital, expertise, livestock and financial, commercial and legal frameworks.[52] Stock and station agents, themselves an invention of the trans-Tasman settlers, set up on both sides of the Tasman in the mid-19th century, and were the largest companies in both countries well into the 20th century.[53] Australian manufacturing and other business interests were somewhat reluctant to invest overseas before 1970, except in New Zealand, where Australian manufacturing, retailing, insurance, entertainment and other service industries appeared from the mid-19th century.[54] New Zealand investment moved in the other direction – albeit at a more modest level – with shipping, insurance, limited banking, stock and station and retail firms setting up in Australia. Labour, too, has flowed ceaselessly across the Tasman. Both sides have benefited, including from the 'brain exchange' of skilled labour and executive talent. New Zealand Prime Minister Robert Muldoon's (purloined) quip about the IQ of both countries going up when New Zealand labour moved to Australia works both ways when viewed in historical perspective.

Although economic and business ties have long formed trans-Tasman communities of interest, what has changed is the impetus driving them since the late 20th century. The comprehensive Australia New Zealand Closer Economic Relations Trade Agreement (CER), accomplished in December 1982 through the teamwork of Doug Anthony, the Australian Deputy Prime Minister, New Zealand Prime Minister Muldoon and officials, was a milestone for the closer integration of the two economies.[55] CER was the sequel to the New Zealand–Australia Free Trade Agreement (NAFTA) of 1965, which Chapter 5 will show was not a free trade agreement but an attempt to manage the tricky transition between old and new worlds once Britain joined the European Economic Community (EEC). If NAFTA was a learning exercise, its successor, CER, represented a whole new start. CER drove a 500 per cent increase in trade over 20 years, and propelled harmonisation or mutual recognition of commercial, consumer and other law and regulatory frameworks. In 2006–07 trans-Tasman trade amounted to NZ$15.7 billion in goods and over $6 billion in services. New Zealand was Australia's sixth-largest market and tenth-largest source of imports. Australia is New Zealand's principal trading partner and its leading source of investment. New Zealand as a key market for Australia is equivalent to a state about the size of Queensland. As if to celebrate its 'coming of age' by 2004, CER, already the world's most flexible and successful free trade agreement, set an enabling platform for work towards a single economic market.[56]

One of us, Peter, served as a delegate to the first three Australia–New Zealand Leadership Forums, begun in 2004. He watched them grow from a series of set-piece statements of position – and difference – on everything from high-level foreign policy strategy to accounting practices, into a closer-knit series of focused working parties, now working annually across the Tasman. Their focus is to remove or soften 'behind the border' regulation of the movement of goods, services, labour, capital and ideas. Advocates on both sides want integrated competition regimes, harmonised taxation policies, especially for portability of superannuation, and a seamless banking environment. The last is a matter of strife in New Zealand because of the whiff of imperialist interference with national sovereignty that is threatened by more banking control by Australia. Australian banks already own all the major banks in New Zealand, even though they run them separately from their home institutions. The forums made clear that there is already a shared Tasman business culture with big goals for a future common currency, security and defence integration, visa-free reciprocal entry and a common immigration policy (Chapter 6). The various names given to these aspirations – a single Australasian market (SAM), CER+, a Tasman economic area (TEA), or a single economic market – already imagine a real Tasman world in the economic sense. One small start of great symbolic significance is the achievement of combined Australia–New Zealand passport queue signs since 2005, first at New Zealand airports and then at airports on Australia's eastern seaboard. These signs represented a Leadership Forum victory over Canberra bureaucrats who dragged their heels for years.

A social and cultural Tasman world

The forum conversations included historical accounts of the worlds that New Zealand and Australia inhabit. That brings us to a further set of themes: the social and cultural Tasman world. New Zealanders and Australians have lived together in the antipodes for over 200 years, their histories mutually shaped and constrained by distance. They share a series of frontier zones that are often as remote from the everyday lives of their citizens as foreign countries: Australians from the east coast rarely engage with Western Australia or Tasmania; northern Queenslanders regard Brisbane as a foreign country where things are done differently. Similarly, South Islanders caricature Aucklanders as people who view everything south of its southern outskirts, the Bombay Hills, as rustic and suspect.

Between these far-flung frontiers the flow of cultural traffic both ways across the Tasman has been continual since 1788, but has been especially strong since the Second World War when, allegedly, the separate national identities were hardening. The volume of that flow was predominantly towards New Zealand from Australia. Miles Fairburn argues that whatever James Belich asserts about New Zealand's 'recolonial' relationship with Britain after Australian federation, Australian cultural influences did not diminish.[57] They were mundane but powerful influences, such as the continuing travel of New Zealanders to Australia and vice versa. We shall examine how the flow of migration from New Zealand to Australia increased from the 1960s and spiked from the late 1970s as recession bit in New Zealand, and there was genuine alarm in Wellington about the net outflow of migrants. But Australians were likewise travelling the other way to the extent that until the 1960s the net flow of migrants across the Tasman was towards New Zealand, not the other way round.

Australian tourists to New Zealand always outnumbered British tourists four to one, and in 2005 New Zealand was the most popular destination for short-term visits by Australians. Australian sportspeople and entertainers visiting New Zealand also outnumbered their British counterparts. Australia was the largest supplier of recorded music to New Zealand in most years from 1914 to 1981. New Zealand purchased more magazines, newspapers and comics from Australia than from any other country between 1949 and 1981 – the *Australian Women's Weekly*, *Pix* and *Post* were as much New Zealand as Australian publications, and acted as a conduit for features of culture such as fashion. The Canterbury

Museum has the best collection of 20th-century clothing on show in Australia or New Zealand, and many of the styles documented came from Australia via magazines like the *Women's Weekly*. Australia was the main overseas supplier for commercial radio broadcast material. Serials like *Portia Faces Life*, *Dr Paul: A story of adult love* and even *The Air Adventures of Biggles* were Australian made or adapted in Australia from British serials. The quintessential comedy radio serial was *Dad and Dave from Snake Gully*, which had a particular appeal to New Zealand's provincial farming communities. *Footrot Flats* had a similar appeal to rural audiences in Australia and was serialised in major dailies. New Zealand gifted Melbourne with John Clarke, who has become the premier comic in Australian life today. Little known in his adopted country across the Tasman is that his original character, Fred Dagg, wearing the iconic black singlet (in Australia it is blue) claimed by 'real men', was the archetypal gumbooted, towelling-hatted, slow-talking New Zealand farmer.

The trans-Tasman influence of John Clarke is a small piece of evidence that Kiwi culture has had a continuing impact of its own on Australia. This influence is growing now that half a million New Zealanders live in Australia, with their unemployment rate lower and their productivity rating higher than the average in that country. The biggest concentrations are in Sydney and the Gold Coast, where New Zealanders make up 6 per cent of the local population according to the last census. One in six or seven Maori now live in Australia, though they generally expect to come home.[58] In the meantime they are forging new tribal identities, generically named Ngati Ocker, and aspire to found marae where traditional community ceremonies can take place. The continuing presence of 60,000 Australians in New Zealand means that ties of intermarriage and kinship are growing in both countries, so that new sets of trans-Tasman genes will create a common future.

In the education sphere there has been an unheralded flow of New Zealanders into the tertiary education institutions of Australia, especially since the 1960s. Postwar New Zealand was producing more university-educated people than it could employ, just at the point when Australian universities were expanding. Consequently New Zealanders flocked into Australian teaching and research positions in the 1960s. As many New Zealanders have done so well, they made their way unobtrusively to the top. Many of the recognised academic leaders in Australia in the mid-20th century were New Zealanders – Douglas Copland, economist and adviser to Australian governments; W. D. Borrie, population researcher and director of the Research School of Sciences at the Australian National University (ANU); a run of New Zealand directors of the ANU's research schools, including geographers Gerard Ward and Max Neutze. Others include Derek Freeman, the anthropologist who took on Margaret Mead in a celebrated international controversy in the 1980s, and Rex Nan Kivell, the art collector after whom one of Australia's Pacific collections in Canberra is named.

The same patterns of influence may be traced in the worlds of journalism and the media, which contain many expatriate closet Kiwis. The large number of original 'Australasian' professional associations still operative today reflects the common culture of the Tasman world. As discussed in Chapter 7, a history of contacts and migration flows between the two countries' education systems constituted virtually a single province when it came to educational policy.

There are two other areas where Kiwi culture has brought a quiet revolution to Australia. One is perhaps not so quiet: musical entertainers, especially Maori show bands in the early days, which toured circuits of pubs and clubs for decades, plus a long lineage of postwar rock and pop artists from Johnny Devlin to Max Merritt, King Kapisi, the Finn brothers and Jenny Morris, to bands such as Dragon, Salmonella Dub, the Datsuns and Crowded House. You cannot make sense of the history of Australian rock'n'roll without New Zealand.[59]

The second area of influence culturally and economically is the sheep shearing industry. While Australians make jokes about the love affair Kiwis have with sheep, New Zealand shearers, especially close-knit Maori family units, have moved ceaselessly through the Australian landscape, following the shearing season from state to state, back to New Zealand, then on again to Australia. Their greatest impact has been in the use of the wide comb, which enables more wool to be extracted in a shorter time than the short comb used by Australian shearers. Its use initially led to large and irate union disputes in postwar Australia, as employers favoured New Zealand shearers over the local shearers organised by the Australian Workers' Union because they used the wide combs and were less union-oriented than Australians.[60] Kiwi culture had a largely unnoticed but key role to play in the class conflict that has gone on in the agricultural and livestock industries in Australia. The wide comb has become accepted, and shearing has evolved into a small business-oriented enterprise on Kiwi lines rather than the older union-organised culture that it used to be in the Australian outback.

Denis McLean argues that paradoxically Australia and New Zealand are 'divided by a common culture, common origins, common just about everything'.[61] Their stories may be related – indeed are composed of strands of a single history – but most of the time competing national narratives are at play and influence public opinion through advertising, competing goods and services, and sporting rivalry. New Zealand is different from Australia. There *is* a Kiwi culture, if we define culture as the structures, rituals, symbols and coded patterns of behaviour in a society and the meanings that people give to them. How New Zealanders relate to those elements is subtly different from the way Australians relate to them in their society, even if one can read the translations readily when crossing the Tasman either way.

The most obvious arena where we recognise this difference is in relations with the indigenous communities, their languages and their histories. But there are many other less obvious ways, such as civil society discourse, the way egalitarianism operates, activities and expectations by local governments and communities, rural class structures and behaviour patterns, and provincial life and culture. Auckland, which otherwise is a mirror of Sydney in lifestyle and behaviour, has a very different relationship with Maori and Pacific Island cultures from any place in Australia. There is an argument that the evolving joint Polynesian and Pakeha connection to New Zealand's physical world is creating a new aesthetic, a new sense of what Maori call turangawaewae, a place to stand. If Britain is the historically classical antipodes to New Zealand, then what is the antipodal point to the growing Pacific Islander and Asian communities whose numbers will drive the New Zealand economy by the middle of this century?

Australia, for all its influence on Kiwi culture, still represents something of a dark side to New Zealanders: a whiff of underarm cheats, perhaps, or a collective mean-spiritedness towards refugees and its own indigenous communities. New Zealand likes to present its culture as a morally superior package of Middle Earth, clean and green, with a more representative participatory democracy, practising a moral foreign policy in the Pacific region that shows greater sensitivity to Islander needs. This is a spurious moral superiority: scratch a Kiwi and you will find Aussie social and racial attitudes underneath. New Zealand and Australian culture have much in common. The two countries have had an interactive, if elastic, history in which Australia has been both a core concern and a blind spot for New Zealanders. The distinctive South Island braided river with its overlapping channels and differential rates of flow provides a useful metaphor to express the interaction of cross-Tasman historical influences, coming together and moving apart at different rates, in varied flow patterns as they both generally head in the same direction and produce a truly trans-Tasman culture.

Born modern

Donald Denoon sees the re-emergence of Australasia in all these developments, a region stretching from Dili to Dunedin.[62] There is a coherent region that those with a maritime outlook – the Australian and New Zealand navies – still see as Australasia (Plate 14). But our focus is sideways, across the Tasman, rather than north into the Pacific neighbourhood south of the equator; with the exception of the security analysis, that is, in Chapter 9. At the beginning of this project we set out to trace the multiple ties between Australia and New Zealand over the long 20th century, and along the way uncovered a Tasman world that is a working region defined by a history of human interactions and continual cultural traffic. The Tasman world was demonstrably part of the British world until the Second World War; Chapter 4 will show how reformers transplanted, exchanged and developed ideas from British law and policy. Australia filtered British influences on New Zealand while New Zealand provided alternatives for Australia within an imperial ambit. The Tasman world exemplified how the British empire acted as the 'principal global conveyor-belt' for ideas of civil society and social movements.[63] Over time, it has grown less and less derivative of Britain for its identity (if not its culture: a different matter). Increasingly the Tasman world reshaped a variety of United States influences.

It is not London that is now New Zealand's metropolis for culture but the eastern Australian conurbation, which stretches from Melbourne through Sydney to Brisbane. This does not mean abandoning our cultural inheritance from Europe. J. G. A. Pocock, whose home town is Christchurch, has spent his later years arguing for the force of a wider sense of the British world in which historians of the north must not leave out the edges of empire and antipodeans must know their ancestry. Mutual ignorance of the respective outer boundaries of histories – whether between Europe and Australia/New Zealand, or between Australia and New Zealand – thwarts understanding of what being modern means. Australia and New Zealand were brought into being by what C. A. Bayly writes of as 'the birth of the modern world'.[64] It is the character of that modernity and how it worked itself into both societies that urges us to construct a combined narrative about a 'Tasman world'.

CHAPTER TWO

The Cartoon History of Tasman Relations

Philippa Mein Smith

Aussie bloke: *What do you call a Kiwi with 10,000 girlfriends?*
A: *A shepherd.*
Kiwi bloke: *What do you call 15 Aussies watching the Rugby World Cup final?*
A: *The Wallabies.*[1]

Cartoons, like jokes, are a pithy source of the stereotypes that underpin the entertainment value of each country to the other. In his endearing 'cartoonists'-eye-view' of trans-Tasman relations, Ian Grant observes that 'Cartoons are the quick, gut reaction' of artists who draw 'their inspiration from popular sentiment'.[2] Grant's collection *The Other Side of the Ditch* illustrates the tenor of popular sentiment through time, predominantly from a New Zealand point of view because Australian cartoonists, like their homeland generally, can afford to take no notice of New Zealand. For the same reason, the majority of the images we have chosen for our book are from the Alexander Turnbull Library in Wellington (the exceptions are Leunig and Nicholson in this chapter). Our selection shows how cartoons are nationalistic in the way that they portray Aussies and Kiwis differently. By their nature they emphasise rivalry and differences, which are more compelling than similarities. This chapter exposes the stereotypes, and explores how they highlight some major points of divergence in the histories of Australia and New Zealand. These differences do matter considerably. But they are not the focus of this book's overall argument because differences – and the search for unique national stories and identities – obscure the persistence of the Tasman world.

Differences
Australia and New Zealand are different. Real points of divergence provide the ground for particular national stories and for poking fun. First and foremost are

the contrasts in their physical environment and the way settlers have adapted to them; for landscape carries the 'freight of history'.[3] Charles Dilke was typical of British observers when he mused in 1890 that the striking contrast between the Australian continent and New Zealand lay in the 'country', the 'scenery', the 'landscape': 'so different are the countries themselves'.[4] William Pember Reeves, then the colony's representative in London, contrasted temperate New Zealand with 'hot and dry' Australia in *The Long White Cloud* (1898). He insisted that neither New Zealand's 'contour nor climate is in the least Australian'. Distance between them mattered too: 'Only one bird of passage migrates across the intervening sea.'[5] Australia is also geologically old, its red earth ancient, whereas New Zealand is young in this sense.

The main difference between the countries is one of scale. Australia is nearly 30 times the size of New Zealand and comparable in size with the United States. When New Zealanders fly to Asia they spend half their time flying over the Australian continent. Yet, demographically, Australia is a small country separated by large distances. Geoffrey Blainey, who coined the phrase 'tyranny of distance', put it like this:

> In one unnoticed way the two countries are similar in shape. While New Zealand is a long finger of land, the Australia where eight of every ten people live is a slightly longer and wider finger stretching from South Queensland to Melbourne with a bend of the forefinger extending to Adelaide.[6]

Twenty years later that finger stretched to Queensland's Sunshine Coast and beyond. It follows that both countries faced the high costs of distance incurred in transporting people and things that Blainey identified, whereas ideas transferred cheaply, as we shall see.[7]

The vastness of the land and sky seeped into the Australian outlook, and bestowed a 'big country' perspective. But it also bred anxieties. One was the apprehension about how to hold the continent for white people. From the 1850s awareness grew that Australia's empty north happened to be in close proximity to a 'mobile, migratory Asia': India, the East Indies and China.[8] That nurtured a resolve to shut out the 'teeming hordes' of Asia – the 'yellow peril' – and to fill the empty spaces with white people, the desired builders of new settler societies. David Walker argues that Australian nationalism's 'powerful masculinising and racialising impulse' would have been weaker were it not for the geopolitical threat of an awakening Asia.[9] The same white racial impulse was at work in the new world democracies of the United States and also New Zealand, so that by 1900 all people who were non-white, non-Christian and non-European in culture were deemed 'unassimilable' by the democratic settler states around the Pacific rim.[10]

New Zealand's remoteness and smallness, however, in contrast to Australia's vast size and proximity to Asia, shaped divergent world views and perspectives on security (Chapter 9). Continental Australia looks northwards as a matter of geopolitical and historical necessity. To a lesser extent Australia also looks east, west and even south to secure its boundaries. Indonesia – not New Zealand – is Australia's nearest significant neighbour, followed by Papua New Guinea. By contrast, New Zealand is an island nation, mountainous and maritime at the same time, separated by 2000 kilometres of sea from its nearest neighbours, all far away across the South Pacific; the closest are New Caledonia and Australia, which are friends and – in the case of Australia – family, not potential threats.

Differences of climate and weather are real, shaping migration patterns, lifestyles, art and beliefs. Before air conditioning, it was accepted as medical certainty that Europeans were racially unsuited for work in Australia's tropical north and that the heat would lead to racial decay. This idea seeped into popular consciousness on both sides of the Tasman.[11] Subsequently the climate became a feature of the Australian way of life, pivotal to the beach and surf culture that developed in the 20th century, and the barbecue.

Heat and piercing light made the sun a symbol of Australia, and this status showed in art. The Heidelberg School (the first Australian school of painting), which flourished in Melbourne in the 1880s, offered striking perceptions and images of the light and landscape. Its major figures were not overtly nationalist; they may have seen themselves as shaping an Australian culture, 'but they did not see their work as nation-building'.[12] Their radicalism resided in the form and implications of their art, which came to be called Australian expressionism, and which displayed, according to art historian Bernard Smith, 'a naturalistic interpretation of the Australian sunlit landscape'.[13] The Heidelberg painters translated the quality of the sunlight to canvas. Arthur Streeton's *Near Heidelberg*, painted in their *plein air* style in the summer of 1890, is a fine example (Plate 15). Depicting the return to the city (Melbourne) after a picnic, the painting itself is a farewell to the time that the Heidelberg School artists spent together.

Art painted in New Zealand manifested different qualities. A 'gothic' style, dark – suggestive of a national colour, black – later also seen in films, caught the collective imagination. Petrus van der Velden painted the Otira Gorge, on the west side of Arthur's Pass in the Southern Alps, about the same time. He used the contrast between light and dark – black and white – to convey a sense of the romantic landscape and sublime wilderness in the alpine environment (Plate 16). The forces of nature dominate the scene: the roaring torrent of water, the dark bush on the mountainside, and the sky filled with storm clouds suggestive of a cold southerly front sweeping overhead.[14]

Taking as their starting point the shared history of Australia and New Zealand as southern, settler societies and British colonies and dominions, environmental historians Libby Robin and Tom Griffiths conclude that the 'long-term influences of very different physical environments and Indigenous inheritances' mean that the differences in environment are more important than the similarities and set the two countries on divergent paths.[15] Different resource bases are a material example, and a product, of the divergent environments. There is a marked contrast between an economy based on milk and one based on coal. While New Zealand has gold and coal reserves, it lacks the base metals that exist in abundance across the Tasman and make Australia the 'Lucky Country', where economic downturns are contained by digging holes in the ground. Environment and climate shape the structures of the economy, politics, culture, and historical possibilities. New Zealand developed grasslands at the expense of other land development strategies and used fertiliser to drive a 'grasslands revolution' in the 20th century.[16] Minerals, on the other hand, shaped Australian history to a greater degree, so that Australia is a premier mining country.[17]

Complementing the contrasts in the physical environment are the extra-ordinary differences in the indigenous plants and animals. Hopping kangaroos and sleepy koalas, brilliantly coloured birds and butterflies in Australia contrast with New Zealand's birds of more muted hue. The native emblems of kiwi and kangaroo stand in contrast, each as odd and amusing as the other. Australian animal life is also more threatening, which intensified the alien sense that Europeans first felt in Australia. Although urban Australians did not at first meet crocodiles, the whole of Australia is home to poisonous snakes and spiders. Even biting insects can kill. New Zealand lacks equivalent menace. Though the oceanic and alpine weather poses risks, virtually all the wildlife on land is harmless, most obviously the flightless kiwi.

In 2006 cartoonist Al Nisbet used this difference in threat levels to illustrate a Kiwi response to being lured across the Tasman: the Australian advertising campaign 'Where the bloody hell are ya?', and tax cuts. Australian Federal Treasurer Peter Costello played to the theme. He told ABC Radio that high-income earners would benefit from re-locating: '[I]f there are Kiwis who have skills and who want to come to Australia as skilled immigrants of course they would be welcome in Australia.'[18] The native birds of each country also sound different. Australian parrots screech, the kookaburra laughs, while tui and bellbirds sing. According to the national stereotypes the contrasts in bird life ex-tend to the people: Australians dress in brightly coloured feathers and are brash and loud, whereas New Zealanders are silent, dull or subdued, or (at best)

Press, 20 May 2006, courtesy of Al Nisbet

relatively tuneful. The colours worn by national sports teams of green and yellow, and black lightened by a silver fern, illustrate the difference.

Such distinctions affect the shape of what academics call 'imagined communities'.[19] These are the powerful sense of belonging to separate national communities with shared but distinctive values and habits. An imagined community is more encompassing than the constitutional framework or political boundaries of the nation state. Stereotypes about oneself and others' communities are the basis of national sentiment that colours the trans-Tasman relationship. New Zealanders and Australians employ such stereotyping to differentiate themselves. The classic pair are Barry Humphries' stereotypes of Australian and New Zealand women from the 1950s: the Australian housewife, Dame Edna Everage, and her elderly New Zealand bridesmaid, Madge Allsop. Dame Edna is the rainbow-coloured Australian bird *par excellence* with her mauve coiffure, diamante spectacles and vivid gowns. Garish, pushy, extroverted and loud, she is the antithesis of sour-faced Madge, who is ridiculously silent. Dame Edna is a cosmopolitan creature from suburban Melbourne, whereas Madge is from provincial Palmerston North. Dame Edna is always the star – she has her own website – while Madge plays the sidekick as the bridesmaid, a role New Zealanders tire of playing, especially before audiences such as Dame Edna's on BBC television.

The strange differences in the indigenous animal life provide rich fodder for poking fun, with animals representing the national stereotypes, and each the butt of jokes on the other side of the Tasman. Tom Scott sketched a fine example at the time of a tightening in Australian policy towards New Zealanders in 2001 (see Chapter 3). He responded to Australian headlines about Kiwi welfare bludgers by portraying the possum (opossum in New Zealand) in this light. The Australian brushtail possum, a protected 'native' in its homeland, was an exotic intruder in New Zealand. Introduced in the 19th century for its fur, it proceeded to nibble its way through tracts of native bush, the damage recognised only once Pakeha New Zealanders began to discover their own country in the 20th century. Only after 1949 was unlimited trapping and poisoning permitted.[20] Scott drew the possum as New Zealanders came to see it: an Aussie pest that cost the taxpayer; flattened as if driven over by the Kiwi bloke (in his uniform of black singlet and towelling hat), who grabs the scoundrel by the scruff of the neck and holds it aloft as a rejoinder to Aussie complaints (see page 36).

While indigenous animals represent the national types, a species introduced by European colonisation provides the ultimate symbol of trans-Tasman competition and rivalry in the 20th century. That symbol is the racehorse Phar Lap, who is hailed as 'Australia's wonder horse' by Museum Victoria, yet was born in Timaru, New Zealand, in 1926 (Plate 17). Phar Lap was raised on New Zealand grass; bought for a bargain and crated to Sydney; and won the Melbourne Cup in 1930 after surviving being shot at by a masked gunman. The first Melbourne Cup winner to be captured on 'talkie' film, he won North America's richest race

Tom Scott, *Evening Post*, 27 February 2001.
H-648-019, NZ Cartoon Archive, Alexander Turnbull Library, Wellington, courtesy of Tom Scott

in 1932, and died shortly after in suspicious circumstances. The Tasman world fights over Phar Lap because he was a hero, a home-grown movie star when people most needed one during the depression of the 1930s, who overcame adversity to win by lengths. Big and lanky, with warts on his face, he proved to be one of the greatest racehorses ever seen in Australia and New Zealand. In death, as in life, Phar Lap embodied the Tasman world. His is a trans-Tasman story, and yet national narratives fought over the pieces. Nationalism literally dismembered Phar Lap: his big heart is stored at the heart of the Australian nation in the National Museum of Australia in Canberra; his hide is on display at Museum Victoria in Melbourne (Plate 17); and his skeleton is an exhibit at the Museum of New Zealand Te Papa Tongarewa in Wellington (Plate 18). He is the most popular exhibit at all these places. Phar Lap truly belongs to all three.

From the perspective of Mambo artist 'Reg Mombassa' (the pseudonym and alter ego as artist of musician Chris O'Doherty), sport – rugby – tops the list of 10 comparisons in the 'Mambo culture clash' between Aussie and Kiwi culture (opposite). (We take sport seriously in Chapter 8.) Sheep are second, followed by Anzacs, the military heroes of the First World War, while the contrasts in scenery come halfway down the ranking of cultural components. 'Reg' drew the 'ten comparisons' as an historic monument that marks how Kiwi and Kangaroo live, fight and die together, as they vie for top position in their region of the world.

The concept of 'greater New Zealand' is an alternative to the standard map of Australasia, or greater Australia, which arguably it takes a trans-Tasmanite to imagine; for this noted Australian artist was born and raised in New Zealand. 'Reg' has publicly confessed: 'Drawing pictures for Mambo also provides the opportunity to employ the basest of toilet humours and to make unkind observations about a variety of ideas, individuals and institutions under the guise of decorating some yards of cotton.'[21] So we may happily place his art alongside selected cartoons. There is an irony in the commentary on this particular T-shirt because the ticks – one tick or two – are self-awarded by each side. It is ridiculous that Australians and New Zealanders give themselves a tick for rugby and sheep (two ticks in the New Zealand case), and even for gang warfare.

'Reg' uses his art to comment on contemporary Australian government policies. Among other aspects of the Mambo tablet of national commandments related to political and popular culture, therefore, the fourth and fifth are about race issues: attitudes to refugees, and the presence or absence of a treaty between British government representatives and the indigenous people. Here it is debatable whether New Zealanders or Australians themselves accord Australia a bad mark or cross; that depends on who is wearing the T-shirt. Either way, the choices of 'asylum' and 'treaty' suggest that the 'Mambo culture clash' can be read as a response to the *Tampa* refugee crisis and the decision by the Howard government in 2003 to join the invasion of Iraq. The tablet of 10 comparisons points to disparate histories of race relations and a contrasting racial dynamic.

Reg Mombassa, 2003

The indigenous people themselves were profoundly different from one another. A major difference was the length of settlement, and their corresponding experience of time in their contrasting physical environments. Aboriginal Australians have lived in Australia for at least 40,000 years, and more likely 60,000 or even 100,000 years, whereas New Zealand Maori are relative newcomers, arriving hundreds rather than thousands of years ago. Aboriginal ancestors walked or rafted to Australia; the eastern Polynesian ancestors of Maori sailed by outrigger canoe. Both peoples have been called 'future eaters': societies who lived unsustainably at first, like the European colonists, but who in the case of indigenous Australians dwelt on the continent for a sufficiently long time to experience many natural crises, as a result of which they adapted to living in harmony with their environment.[22] This is a lesson that indigenous Australian history suggests humanity learns with time, and that economically 'developed' societies must re-learn. By contrast, the people who became Maori had to adapt rapidly to life in their colder archipelago from as recently as 1300 AD, and to the arrival relatively soon afterwards of Europeans.

Maori were more intelligible than indigenous Australians to European senses of what was 'civilised' because Maori were like themselves: Maori were more hierarchical, settled, competitive and materialistic, and they embraced European technology and ideas. They were gardeners as well as hunter-gatherers. Aboriginal people were dismissed as nomadic, though they also practised fire-stick farming. Maori were more familiar to Europeans, including in how they fought: 'They built forts, engaged in pitched battles, and required British regiments to defeat them, reinforced sometimes by volunteers from Australia.'[23] It was an act of valour to fight warrior Maori but not to do battle with indigenous Australians.

Most puzzling of all, Aboriginal Australians did not see the world as material. It is true that Maori too 'saw the world as an organic whole where the wind, land, flora and fauna were all signs of their gods and ancestors. But for Maori gods could be challenged, mastered and even killed.'[24] The god Tane's closest ally was Tumatauenga, the god of war, and the two competed to impose order on the world. Such beliefs fostered behaviours that made more sense to Europeans, as in the story of Horeta Te Taniwha, about a small boy's meeting with Captain Cook, who gave the little boy a nail as a symbol of the newcomers' technology. By contrast, Aboriginal people rejected Cook's trade trinkets as 'terrible hard biscuits'.[25] Maori spoke a single language, which made cross-cultural talk easier. Indigenous Australians were divided into hundreds of language and dialect groups.[26] Europeans found the Australians unfathomable because they could identify nothing in common with them other than their humanity.

Yet European prejudice denied the first Australians even that fundamental quality, treating them as beasts rather than humans. As C. D. Rowley observed in *The Destruction of Aboriginal Society* (1970): 'The Maori was respected as a warrior; the Aboriginal was despised as a rural pest'.[27] Aboriginal people were judged to be more 'primitive' or 'degenerate' than Maori, who were assumed to be superior because they were warriors and gardeners. Part of the myth of 'Better Britishness' favoured in New Zealand was that 19th-century colonists enjoyed relations with a superior type of 'native'.

The different timing of the beginnings of formal British settlement also contributed to different policy outcomes on each side of the Tasman. Timing made New South Wales a penal colony in 1788. The colonisers, as convicts, were also colonised; they were prisoners consigned to exile. That affected relations with Aboriginal people and frontier violence. In New Zealand sovereignty rests – or seems to rest – upon a treaty between the British government and the indigenous people: the Treaty of Waitangi, signed in 1840 at the height of the influence of the humanitarian movement in British religion and politics. There was no treaty between the British government and the first Australians.

Divergent policies ensued of 'amalgamation' in New Zealand and 'segregation' of indigenous people on reserves in Australia. Australian states, which were responsible for Aboriginal affairs under the Australian Constitution, resorted to various strategies of control in the 20th century, among them forcibly removing children of mixed descent from their Aboriginal mothers. These policies, which produced the 'stolen generations', had the eugenic purpose of 'breeding out' Aboriginality, for which there was no policy equivalent in New Zealand. The closest were campaigns against use of the Maori language.

Australia and New Zealand also differ in their political systems, despite their shared inheritance of the Westminster system of parliamentary government. Australia is not a unitary state but a confederation. The Commonwealth of Australia comprises six states that were separate colonies before 1901 and two territories, one of which – the Northern Territory – is a proto-state that is vast yet thinly populated, while the other is the Australian Capital Territory, home of Canberra, the national capital, and national institutions, from the federal parliament and the High Court to the Australian War Memorial. New Zealand has been a unitary state since 1876 when the provincial councils were abolished. The Australian federal government and state governments are also two-tiered with upper and lower houses; the exception is Queensland, which like New Zealand (since 1950) has a single house of parliament. Both countries also developed layers of local government. The result is a greater complexity of government in Australia, and in-built checks and balances within the political system that inhibit revolutionary change. The speed and range of reforms imposed on New Zealand under the rubric of 'Rogernomics' in the 1980s and continuing into the 1990s were therefore not possible in Australia because of the institutional impediments.

History matters in understanding contemporary community attitudes. National histories by their nature are selective of things national, and relish differences. The problem is that Australian and New Zealand stories have ignored each other, when both their stories are the strands of a single history since British colonisation. New Zealand and Australia have had separate national narratives since 1901. Even the shared Anzac legends from the Great War generally ignore each other. As Ken Inglis explains:

> Anzacs together, Diggers at least in parallel, Aussies and Kiwis apart: the war had given citizens of the southern dominions two words which distinguished them from metropolitan Britons, and another pair which signalled their different nationalities.[28]

New Zealanders and Australians celebrate separate and distinctive national heroes and heroines. They read different books; the creative literatures are separate. Australia and New Zealand have a 'resistant relationship over books and readers', demonstrating national cultural boundaries.[29] The occasional crossover comes with international success: by novelists such as Janet Frame, Patrick White, Peter Carey and Elizabeth Knox.

To think in terms of traffic across the Tasman Sea offers one way to overcome the limits that national narratives impose on how communities view their worlds, or see themselves in relation to others. A shared antipodean condition of looking north rather than sideways is a reminder of how national identity and global outreach are interdependent. Yet, in foregrounding links and shared histories in the southern ocean, we cannot dismiss the identity stories that communities create for themselves.

New Zealand and Australian federation

All the prejudices and stereotypes that we are familiar with today evolved over the 20th century. These stereotypes embody perceptions of social, political and economic characteristics held by the citizens of both countries, and affect attitudes and behaviour in sport, in the military and on race issues. Nations define themselves by what they are not, and for New Zealanders the act of not joining Australia in 1901 defined their first reference point: that they were *not* Australians. William Pember Reeves expressed the general flavour of New Zealand colonial nationalism in 1901: '[O]ur colony is in no sense an offshoot or outlying province of Australia.'[30] Such insistence underlines Australia's importance to the making of New Zealand identity and a search for exceptionalism.

The vanity of nation-building politicians was integral to the invention of a distinctive colonial identity. Ashley Hunter's 1899 cartoon 'Aut Caesar aut nullus' (emperor or nothing) suggests that there was no better example than New Zealand Premier Richard 'King Dick' Seddon. Seddon would not tolerate a decline in his power or importance as a colonial leader. Asked by the premiers of the Australian colonies preparing to federate: 'Don't you want to come aboard of our ship?' he prefers to 'paddle his own little canoe' rather than relinquish his position as 'skipper' to be a 'bo'sun's mate'. Stella Allan (née Henderson), a New

AUT CAESAR AUT NULLUS
Chorus of Federalists: 'Don't you want to come aboard of our ship?'
Hon. R. S.: 'What? Give up my position as skipper of this 'ere little craft to be a bo'sun's mate along of you? No thanks!' (Proceeds to paddle his own little canoe.)
New Zealand Graphic, 8 July 1899, J-040-007, Alexander Turnbull Library, Wellington

Zealand suffragist who moved to Melbourne where she ran the women's page for the Melbourne *Argus*, observed in 1900 that Seddon felt 'from first to last' that "'our destiny as a colony lies apart and separate from the destiny of Australia'".[31]

Historian Keith Sinclair subsequently explored the history of the New Zealand wish for a 'separate destiny'. In addition to his treatise on nationalism, *A Destiny Apart* (1986), he wrote a piece for the Australian bicentenary on 'why New Zealanders are not Australians'.[32] For Sinclair, Tasman relations were a device to highlight New Zealand uniqueness and construct New Zealand in opposition to Australia. The sense of destiny on which he focused was precisely what the New Zealand story of non-federation shared with the Australian federal story. The first Australian Prime Minister, Edmund Barton, and his successor, Alfred Deakin, believed that 'God wanted Australia to be a nation' so that Australians would enjoy a better future among English-speaking peoples.[33] Federation was a 'sacred cause'. The central motive was the same: to gain identity and status.[34]

On both sides of the Tasman, hopes for a better world took the form of the pursuit of purity of race. By the beginning of the 20th century 'white Australia' and 'white New Zealand' shared a strong racial consciousness and desire to advance the 'interests of our Anglo-Saxon race'. The federal idea needed the 'white Australia' policy because the pursuit of social betterment entailed exclusion of 'Asiatics' and other undesirable groups. As Prime Minister Edmund Barton explained to New Zealand representatives who were inquiring into federation, after the event, in 1901:

> On the question of the character of the immigration which should be allowed, I take it that the ideas and sympathies of New Zealand and Australia are practically identical . . . our objections to alien races . . . are practically the same, and . . . we have the same desire to preserve the 'European' and 'white' character of the race.[35]

From an Australian perspective, the 'crimson thread of kinship' celebrated by 'federation father' Henry Parkes of New South Wales ran through all the seven colonies of Australasia.

New Zealanders, however, entertained a separate idea of 'the people'. They agreed that 'the people' comprised the British race, but they imagined differently what it meant to be British. Stella Allan ('Vesta' of the *Argus*) discerned a feeling 'that we are a "peculiar" people, just a little superior to others, and destined to lead the world in social conditions'.[36] The president of the Canterbury Trades and Labour Council, Jack McCullough, put it more bluntly: 'I think we are a better type of men than they have on the other side.'[37] He anticipated Muldoon's quip eight decades later that New Zealand migrants to Australia raised the IQ of both countries. This whiff of superiority pervades Scatz's 1900 cartoon 'How we see it'.

More concisely than words, Scatz's cartoon encapsulates why New Zealand did not join Australia. Zealandia, Britannia's daughter, is the symbolic female of classical tradition who embodies the ideals of 'civic nationalism' concerned with the principles and values of the state. Zealandia wears an indigenous cloak, which distinguishes her from her sister Australia, who is reading in the background. Civic New Zealand holds hands with the 'noble savage', a Pacific Islander rather than Maori, who is suggestive of Seddon's preferred alternative to Australian federation: a Pacific Islands federation led by New Zealand. The dominant character is the ogre, a classical threat to virtuous femininity. That ogre is convict Australia. Zealandia fends off the monster because 'those arms bear chains', and opts for a destiny of kinship with the South Pacific, untarnished by

HOW WE SEE IT

The Ogre: 'Come into these arms.'
New Zealand: 'Nay, sir, those arms bear chains.'
New Zealand Graphic, 20 October 1900, J-040-002, Alexander Turnbull Library, Wellington

the convict stain. The disreputable past of the Australian colonies obstructs a closer relationship between Zealandia and 'Australia fair', who but for convictism could advance together. Were it not for the manacled monster, moreover, the cartoon suggests that civic New Zealand might have been able to teach federated Australia something about race relations.

It was widely assumed that race relations were better in New Zealand both because white New Zealanders were descended from free, 'pioneer' immigrants and because the Maori were a superior 'native'. Captain William Russell, the leader of the opposition, outlined the common view at the first federation conference in

Melbourne in 1890: 'New Zealand politics for years hinged almost entirely on the native question.' The lesson learnt from the New Zealand Wars of the 1860s was that of 'native administration'. He went on to assert that responsibility could not be entrusted to Australians:

> [W]ere we to hand over that question to a Federal Parliament – to an elective body, mostly Australians, that cares nothing and knows nothing about native administration, and the members of which have dealt with native races in a much more summary manner than we venture to deal with ours in New Zealand – the difficulty which precluded settlement for years in the North Island might again appear ... the advance of civilisation would be enormously delayed.[38]

Although the Treaty of Waitangi had disappeared from settler conscious-ness after being declared a legal 'nullity' in 1877 and the concept of biculturalism had yet to be invented, a proto-bicultural narrative of brotherhood between Maori and Pakeha was already in place. Russell repeated his message at the second federal convention in Sydney in 1891. Native title was of 'grave moment' and settler–indigenous relations 'of the most serious importance'.[39]

A related objection concerned the probable position of Maori in a federal system. A section of the draft Australian Constitution inserted at the convention in 1891 (which became section 126 of the Commonwealth Act 1900) provided that in reckoning the population of a state, aboriginal natives would not be counted. It was thought that not counting Maori in the population would have reduced New Zealand's presence in the House of Representatives by at least one member. That would 'cast a slur upon the Native race here', even though 'full-blood' Maori were excluded from New Zealand population totals at the time.[40] Adding to the sense of difference, Maori men could vote (and women from 1893), whereas indigenous Australians were disenfranchised after the creation of a 'white Australia'. There was therefore some doubt about whether Maori would be excluded from the federal franchise.[41]

Captain Russell's view that New Zealand was likely to develop a 'different national type' was widely shared. New Zealanders like Russell were sceptical that the goal of a 'white Australia' could be achieved because northern Australia was tropical and therefore unsuited to white men's labour; it was Aboriginal, and a 'breeding ground for coloured Asiatics'.[42] Allegedly the act of federating would therefore put the purity of New Zealand 'stock' at risk. Russell suspected that, despite immigration restriction acts, the 'law of nature would be stronger than the law of the Commonwealth'.[43] The labour movement agreed that there was 'a great danger of a big influx of coloured labour coming here'.[44] Many believed that if New Zealand joined Australia the tendency of social life and morals would be downward. This claim also had a gender component. Whereas Australian suffragists supported federation to secure the vote for white women in the federal parliament in 1902, New Zealand suffragists such as Stella Allan opposed federation because they worried about losing their political influence in a larger commonwealth in their work to remove women's civil and political disabilities.

The myth of natural abundance augmented beliefs that New Zealand was an intrinsically healthy country for settlers, and that, given its 'vast natural resources', New Zealand should not sacrifice being independent.[45] The 'energy of her people' was thought to be environmentally determined by the brisk, windy weather, just as the 'severity of their climate' gave Scotsmen an advantage, or so it was said in Otago.[46] Medical theories reinforced popular belief that climate moulded character, and in New Zealand eyes there was but one trajectory for Australians: downwards, given the enervating effects of their tropical climate.[47] How could anyone do other than 'go troppo' in northern Queensland? New Zealanders and Australians were therefore already representing themselves in the world differently. Their settler populations shared in defining Asia as the 'other', but differed in their relationships with the indigenous peoples against whom they also defined themselves. Both were seeking to identify a national 'type', and Pakeha New Zealanders imagined themselves as an 'island race', as southern Britons, who were destined to be different from 'a nation for a continent' across the Tasman. William Pember Reeves expressed the prevailing attitude in 1901:

> The Maori are brown Polynesians, as different from the Australian 'blackfellows' as Abyssinians are from Namaquas. None of the Australian beasts or reptiles, only one bird, none of the eucalypts and acacias which are the conspicuous features of Australian plant-life, ever found their way across the Tasman Sea . . . The climates of the Commonwealth and the Colony are as unlike as are the landscapes, and some people think that the two branches of the Anglo-Saxon race which inhabit them are already developing different characteristics.[48]

The Rev. William Curzon-Siggers of Dunedin endorsed this view: New Zealand was 'an insular nation. Australia is a continental nation. The history of all races shows that continental races and insular races diverge further and further apart.'[49]

The Anzac legend

The use of Australians as a reference point for New Zealanders extended to the Anzac legend in the First World War. Australia and New Zealand shared the making of Anzac, which is the emotional cornerstone of the trans-Tasman relationship. It may therefore seem curious that the national histories on each side of the Tasman treat the shared Anzac tradition separately, when it is derived from an ad hoc acronym for Australian and New Zealand Army Corps, and its soldiers' ill-fated landing on the Gallipoli peninsula on 25 April 1915.[50] Anzac Day has developed into a proxy national day for both countries. The Anzac hero

Anzac Cove (Anzak Koyu) in 2008. This sacred site in Turkey is too small and steep to host the annual commemorations, which are held further north.

is a common masculine archetype of 'service, courage, commitment, endurance and mateship'.[51] That the Anzac tradition of mateship and friendly rivalry gave real strength to the men in the First World War is evident in cartoons by the soldiers themselves. Drawn on the Western Front in 1916, where the New Zealand Division fought as part of II Anzac Corps in the north of France around Armentières and on the Somme, Thompson's sketch below reflects how New Zealanders and Australians still fought and died side by side, in close partnership against the German foe.

That the 'Anzac spirit' had meaning for the men is clear later in the 20th century in photographic images from the Korean War where two Australian infantry battalions and a New Zealand artillery regiment opposed the communist advance as part of the 1st (unique) United Nations Commonwealth Division.[52] In their photograph

Thompson, 1916, from a magazine by men at the front.
John Tait Collection, courtesy of Jack Tait

of October 1951 (below), soldiers from Victoria and New Zealand pose beside the notice they erected at the edge of Anzac Park, a playing field that they built alongside forward defensive positions so that the British Commonwealth troops could play rugby, soccer, athletics and other sports. To a lad the soldiers are the 'hard man' and 'hard case', the New Zealanders indistinguishable from the Australians in their spiritedness.[53] The differences among the mates show only in their headgear: the Australians wear 'Aussie' hats.

Deeper differences evolved in the respective Anzac traditions which reflected the differences of size and perspective in trans-Tasman relations. New Zealand and Australia developed parallel yet separate Anzac legends from April 1915, both variants of a British heroic-romantic myth of the chivalric, Christian soldier.[54] There are different emphases in how the young men 'tested and proved' by war are commemorated and mourned on Anzac Day on each side of the Tasman. Joint ownership of this war story about the birth of each nation in a 'baptism of fire' at Gallipoli embraces competing as well as common claims to Anzac, driven by the pressure for uniqueness that such histories impose.

Australian and New Zealand personnel at Anzac Park, near forward defensive positions in Korea, October 1951, From left to right: Pte F. E. Marks, Victoria, Australia; Bdr L. J. Webster, Masterton, NZ; Bdr N. Miller, Christchurch, NZ; Pte E. H. Bennets, Vic; Pte E. J. Roberts, Vic.

Ian C. Mackley, K-0457, War History Collection, Alexander Turnbull Library, Wellington

The solemn, sacred word 'Anzac' denotes rivalry and difference as well as bonds of blood and battle against a common threat or foe, particularly from the perspective of the smaller partner. Histories of war and national identity show how Australians defined themselves against one reference point, the British, while the smaller force within the Anzac corps defined itself against both the British and the Australians. The First World War reinforced the New Zealand stereotype of the natural gentleman who sprang from the loins of pioneers. Mythologically the gentleman farmer contrasted with the larrikin Australian heir of the bush legend as well as the chinless, urban British soldier cartoon figure.[55]

Lieutenant-Colonel W. G. Malone, a New Zealand hero who happened to fit the gentleman farmer type and was killed on Chunuk Bair at Gallipoli in August 1915, judged the Australians negatively from the moment they joined the New Zealand convoy off Western Australia. 'They seem a slack lot,' he wrote in his diary in November 1914. 'Perhaps it is my prejudice against Australians. I have it but cannot say why.'[56] He dismissed the French as 'slack' too, while 'our men on the whole look like gentlemen and the Tommies don't'.[57] His judgement did not improve in the course of withstanding heavy Turkish shell and rifle fire at Anzac Cove. Malone wrote in May 1915:

> It is a relief to get in where war is being waged scientifically and where we are clear of the Australians. They seem to swarm about our line like flies. I keep getting them sent out. They are like masterless men going their own ways. I found one just now crawling like a big brown fly over my bivouac. I straightened him up ...[58]

As a military officer known for his fastidiousness, perhaps Malone was impatient with the stereotypical ethos of the bushman that he detected in the behaviour of the Australian troops. The Australian official war correspondent and historian C. E. W. Bean confirmed that New Zealand commanders such as Malone objected to 'drinking and slovenliness' in Cairo and encouraged 'their men to have nothing to do with the Australians, but to show by their neat dress and sobriety that there was a wide difference between the two forces'.[59] Conversely,

Australian (nd), courtesy of Max Quanchi, Queensland University of Technology

London Underground, courtesy of Doris Cope, Sydney

as the much larger force the Australians could afford not to be conscious of the smaller partner. For them the British 'Tommies', and officers, were reference points, not the 'Fernleaves' or Kiwis (a term that emerged on the Western Front).

National stereotypes

Such stereotypes persist in advertisements today. 'We take New Zealand seriously (someone has to)' is a clipping from an Australian newspaper in 2003, directed at an Australian audience, that captures a customary Aussie disdain plus cheek. The billboard on the London tube advertising Steinlager beer, on the other hand, is a direct descendant of the stereotypes embedded in the Anzac legend of the gentlemanly New Zealander compared with the larrikin Australian.[60] The two are related – the New Zealander is a 'sophisticated Australian' as opposed to not Australian – but they are also different; and the New Zealander is again a little superior, as if a convict or bushman would not drink such beer.

Tom Scott, c. 1988.

H-652-009, NZ Cartoon Archive, Alexander Turnbull Library, Wellington

An Australian stereotype of the New Zealander is of someone nondescript, quiet, boring, or the country cousin, akin to Tasmanians. Michael Leunig's comment on Australian reconciliation (page 50) makes this point. Not only must southerners and Queenslanders say sorry to one another, but the healing process involves telling jokes about New Zealanders as well as Tasmanians. The matching New Zealand stereotype of the Australian is a skite. New Zealand cartoons may represent Australian confidence as boastfulness. According to Tom Scott in 1988, for example, 'Australia invented the wheel, the radio, aeroplanes, penicillin, and the dirty great whopping fib'; or so says his Aussie bloke, whom he draws as Australians depict themselves, the archetypal bushman of *The Australian Legend*.[61] Scott's 'NZ-eye-view', however, is consciously one-eyed.

When outsiders were the reference point, the localised allusions to competition and rivalry evaporated, and the Anzac spirit presented as mateship. This was the case when the partners combined against a common enemy, as in both world wars and the Korean War. But it also applied whenever Australia and New Zealand defined themselves against Britain in the course of the 20th century as senses of nationhood developed.

The United States relationship

The critical alliance for Australia and New Zealand in the postwar era was the three-power Anzus Pact of 1951 with the United States, entered into without

Michael Leunig, *Melbourne Age* (nd), courtesy of Michael Leunig

Britain. Anzus addressed the postwar realities of power in the Asia–Pacific region; it reflected the Tasman world's 'dual dependency', that is, dependence on the United States as well as on Britain in the aftermath of the Second World War.[62] The United States emerged as the dominant superpower in the Pacific, and was poised to assume Britain's place in world affairs. Through Anzus, Australia and New Zealand gained a regular forum for privileged, high-level communication with Washington. More importantly, the United States gained its desired 'soft peace' with Japan, and a means to consolidate its strategic position in Northeast Asia by committing Australia and New Zealand to support American interests.[63] The Americans insisted on a tripartite agreement: Australia was content to exclude the Commonwealth and the North Atlantic Treaty Organisation (Nato) to strengthen wider regional security in Asia, whereas New Zealand was anxious to retain British support. The significance of the alliance grew as the Cold War intensified. The treaty became 'an instrument of co-operation', a 'formal statement of existing friendships' among three partners who had 'fought side by side'.[64]

By 1952, after a change of government to the Conservatives in Britain, there was growing disquiet there about her exclusion from Anzus. In the cartoon below, Sid Scales drew a snapshot of the Anzac partners' new alliance

Sidney E. Scales, *Otago Daily Times*, 27 September 1952.
A-311-4-001, NZ Cartoon Archive, Alexander Turnbull Library, Wellington, courtesy of Mrs Ngaire Scales

with the United States. A pipe-smoking 'Uncle Sam' is arm in arm with the young ladies New Zealand and Australia, whom he leads away from an anxious, matronly Britannia. Potentially, the cartoon suggests, 'Uncle Sam' is leading the young women astray, or at least off to have a good time, to the chagrin of their unfashionable – dowdy – perplexed mother figure. Scales drew this image at the height of the Anzus 'rumpus' in September 1952 when no British representative was invited to attend the first Anzus council meeting at Pearl Harbor.[65] The message is clear: a shared Australian and New Zealand future together with the United States, without Britain. The cartoon also captures the allure of American popular culture for Australians and New Zealanders and the glamour of Hollywood. Is it our imagination, or is Miss Australia with her fur-trimmed coat and more ostentatious necklace just a touch more glamorous than Miss New Zealand?

Thirty years later, cartoonists conveyed the rupture in the alliance after the New Zealand Labour government under David Lange refused to admit the destroyer USS *Buchanan* in 1985, which was not nuclear-powered (see Chapter 9). The Anzac relationship survived the crisis and New Zealand's suspension by the US from the American alliance, even if defence issues resurfaced as a bugbear in trans-Tasman relations in the late 20th century. Practicalities demanded that Australia still had to deal with New Zealand, while one may argue that New Zealand could afford to assert its nuclear-free status in opposition to the superpower, the United States, because it had unquestioned Australian support should it, improbably, be threatened. Officials got on with working together more closely in defence than ever before, developing a 'no surprises' policy in defence and security, as in the trade relationship, even as the differences over defence were more sharply defined.

Eric Heath illustrated the irony of closer defence relations in the aftermath of the Anzus breakdown (opposite). In 1987 the public heard that, in an agreement between Australia's Hawke Labor government and the Lange Labour government, the two would build vessels suited to the needs of both navies. The aim was to build 12 new Anzac frigates: eight for Australia and four for New Zealand, starting with an initial two ships. All the frigates were to be built in Australia, with full trans-Tasman industrial input. The Anzac ship project lifted defence collaboration and technology transfer to a new level.[66] Heath's cartoon illustrates the nationalist alarm that this news fired in New Zealand. With a smirk, the stereotype of the Aussie 'underarm' cheat switches the design of the new frigates for the New Zealand navy to nuclear-powered. The request comes from Prime Minister Bob Hawke, holding the Anzus treaty, who leads the act of one-upmanship against the Lange government. He is backed by his pipe-smoking American ally and by the Australian military/naval establishment. At a stroke, Hawke and his American and Australian henchmen realise the worst fears of the Anzac frigates' opponents: the sabotage of an independent New Zealand foreign

Eric Heath, *Hello*, 13 September 1987.
C-133-033, NZ Cartoon Archive, Alexander Turnbull Library, Wellington, courtesy of Eric Heath

policy. In this, as in other examples of New Zealand media coverage, popular sentiment dominates the practical advantages of working together.

Rivalry and competing identities

Sporting rivalry is another theme favoured by cartoonists. In this book we acknowledge sport's importance to the Tasman world by giving it a separate chapter alongside security (Chapter 8). Media coverage of sport savours intense trans-Tasman competition. Hence satirist John Clarke's concluding tip on what a union of the countries might look like when consulted by the Australian magazine the *Bulletin* in 1988: 'The new Parliament House in Canberra can . . . be turned into an all-weather sporting complex, thereby satisfying the only genuine interest of the entire population of both countries.'[67]

In the cartoon on page 54 Jim Hubbard comments on two New Zealand sore points that have become mythologised in contests and engagements between New Zealand and Australia: the infamous underarm bowling incident during World Series cricket in Melbourne in 1981, when the Australian captain, Greg Chappell, told his brother to bowl underarm to thwart a New Zealand win (see Chapter 8); and the long-running trade dispute over New Zealand apples, which Australian governments have excluded on quarantine grounds since 1924 (see Chapter 5). The conflated stories about cricket and apples, from which the stereotype of the poor sport has evolved, send a message that the archetypal Australian denies a 'fair go' to the New Zealand sport. Hubbard's Aussie poor sport, drawn in the combined guise of 'Aussie protectionism' and a test cricketer,

Jim Hubbard, *Hawke's Bay Today*, 20 October 2000.
A-350-099, NZ Cartoon Archive, Alexander Turnbull Library, Wellington, courtesy of Jim Hubbard

bowls the apple underarm as in the 1981 incident. While the historical trade dispute is theoretically over the disease fireblight, Hubbard elaborates his theme by making the bowled apple harbour a worm.

Historically, the biggest New Zealand suspicion of Australia is that closer relations with Australia will result in takeover. Eric Heath detected this misgiving during negotiations for a Closer Economic Relations trade agreement (CER) in 1979, the context for 'Chomp!' (opposite). 'Chomp!' both encapsulates and expresses nationalist fears that intimacy with an appealing Australia would spell a loss of identity and independence. Advocates of a separate destiny have resisted Australian takeover since the 1890s. Captain Russell voiced the sentiment in 1891: 'Yes, there is a disposition to be embraced; but we think it should not be a bear's hug.'[68] So did David Lange when interviewed by the *Bulletin* in 1988, purportedly on the grounds that he represented a future leader of a United States of Australasia. Asked whether a union of Australia and New Zealand was inevitable, Lange retorted:

> It is inevitable that we will move even closer and we should take advantage of that without buying into the disadvantages. At the moment it's quite nice having a mistress rather than being married to her.[69]

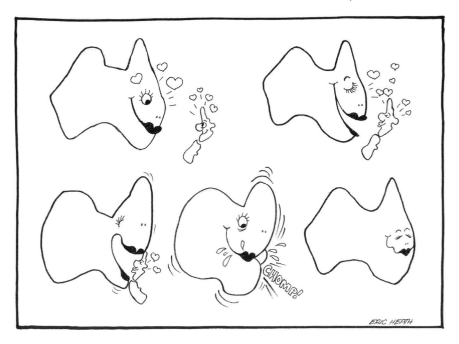

Eric Heath, *Dominion*, 17 August 1979.
B-144-573, NZ Cartoon Archive, Alexander Turnbull Library, Wellington, courtesy of Eric Heath

By the end of the 20th century trans-Tasman economic relations had evolved to a point where there was talk of a common currency or currency union.[70] 'Momentum builds for Anzac dollar,' the *Press* headlined in April 2000 when New Zealand parliament's foreign affairs, defence and trade select committee announced it would review the benefits of CER and how it might develop.[71] Peter Nicholson, cartoonist for the *Australian*, responded by suggesting the Anzac biscuit (Plate 19). Nicholson's concept of the Anzac biscuit as a common currency wittily illustrates the existence of a shared – British – heritage and a common culture.

Parallel with the pavlova, the Anzac biscuit evolved in Kiwi and Aussie kitchens from a category of biscuit known as rolled oats crispies or rolled oats biscuits that appeared shortly before the Great War.[72] The Anzac biscuit crystallised simultaneously in a range of places across New Zealand and Australia. Like the pavlova, a source and symbol of rivalry and competing identities, the Anzac biscuit is indeed a common currency. It bears witness to a shared popular culture and a history of living together.

CHAPTER THREE

Living Together

Philippa Mein Smith and Peter Hempenstall

The Anzac biscuit suggests a common culture, even if the ingredients may vary or be in different measures; and this rolled oats biscuit, sweetened with sugar and desiccated coconut, emerged as the 'national' biscuit for Australia and New Zealand in the 20th century. The pavlova performs a parallel role as the 'national' dessert of both nations, but the Anzac biscuit carries the weightier burden of symbolising the commemoration of Anzac Day and women's war effort.[1] Competing identities are only one part of the stories carried by the Anzac biscuit. Rolled oats, the basic ingredient, evoke a Scottish heritage and a broader British history. Baked in kitchens on both sides of the Tasman, the Anzac biscuit shows how the Tasman world created an evolving common culture with subregional variants. Wattleseed is a recent addition to some Australian recipes, while New Zealand culinary authority Alison Holst returned to television screens in 2008 with a version that uses less butter to adjust for the increased price of dairy products.

Lamb and potatoes are other common foods. Their sequel on the dinner table is the pavlova, the fluffy meringue cake – crisp on the outside, soft in the middle – that by the 1930s signified the wife and mother's worth as a cook and her command of the kitchen. On the furthest edges of the Tasman world, in Perth (1935), Rangiora (1933) and the pages of the *New Zealand Dairy Exporter Annual* (1929), the pavlova developed spontaneously from a tradition of dainty baking using staple ingredients. Pavlova consists of egg whites and sugar, with whipped cream as an accessory, and constitutes a festive food served at communal occasions and events.[2] Foods common to Australia and New Zealand include not just such sweet entertainment fare but the breakfast staple of Sanitarium Weetbix, advertised as good for 'Aussie kids' and 'Kiwi kids' in what has become a trans-Tasman food market. The Seventh Day Adventist Church's Sanitarium Health Food Company has also made the yeast extract Marmite (a byproduct of beer manufacture) since 1919. Its competitor, Kraft Vegemite, is a similar spread with the label 'proudly made in Australia since

1923', which expatriate New Zealanders request in food parcels. If we are what we eat, then by such means Australians and New Zealanders are extended family and neighbours.

Movement of people

Binding this common culture is a history of trans-Tasman people movement. Rollo Arnold called this two-way flow the 'Perennial Interchange', a form of 'shifting' as opposed to overseas migration.[3] Characteristically, people migrate in the hope of a better life, and from decades of research into trans-Tasman travellers in the late 19th and early 20th centuries Arnold unearthed all kinds of people who aspired to do better by shifting within this 'family of colonies': mobile professionals in banking and insurance, clergy, teachers and journalists; travelling entertainers, circus performers and shearers; miners and sawmillers; and escapees, on the run from convictism, divorce, bankruptcy, crime or mishap. General economic conditions, experiences and assessments on each side of the Tasman determined the balance of this interchange over time. Until the 1960s more people moved from Australia to New Zealand than vice versa, reflective of the relative strength of the New Zealand economy until the world economy was restructured from the mid-1960s.

This movement is different from expatriatism, which has usually been cultural rather than political or economic in Australia and New Zealand, growing from the same values that fed the cultural cringe: the need to reach back to the old world, historically London, for high culture. The Tasman world is not about high culture, although that also is a shared heritage. It is bound by common strands of popular culture, by ways of living that speak of the everyday, of getting on and getting by. Ruth Park, for example, author of classic Australian novels including *The Harp in the South* (1948), left New Zealand for Sydney in 1942 to meet and marry the writer D'Arcy Niland. In her autobiography she wrote of wanting to make a living from writing: 'As much as I loved my country, if I wished to become a professional, I would eventually have to leave.'[4] Her autobiography is divided neatly into two volumes, the first covering her New Zealand life and the other her time in Australia.

People from all walks of life participated in this interchange. At the pinnacle of power in the 19th century were the governors who represented the British Crown: from Captain Hobson, who as Lieutenant-Governor came to New Zealand in 1840 with its annexation to New South Wales; and Sir George Grey, who was at different times Governor of South Australia, New Zealand (twice) and the Cape Colony; to Frederick Napier Broome, Governor of Western Australia from 1883 to 1889, who was briefly a pastoralist in Canterbury where his wife, Lady Barker, wrote the minor classic *Station Life in New Zealand*. The governors were followed by the colonial premiers Sir Julius Vogel, who followed the gold rush from Victoria to New Zealand in 1861, and Lancashire-born

Richard John Seddon, the long-serving New Zealand Liberal Premier from 1893 to 1906. A well-known figure on both sides of the Tasman, Seddon died on board ship between Sydney and Wellington. His successor, Joseph Ward, migrated from Melbourne as a child in 1863.

Vogel, Seddon and Ward's mother were among the thousands who were ambitious to succeed and attracted by the lure of possible riches across the Tasman. A wave of adventurers followed the gold discoveries around the Pacific rim from California to New South Wales and Victoria in the 1850s, and from Victoria to the South Island in the 1860s. The southern rush began in Otago in 1861 at Gabriels Gully, named after Gabriel Read, a prospector from Tasmania. Altogether, two-thirds of the goldminers reached New Zealand from across the Tasman, while all of the 37,000 Irish migrants to the West Coast rushes from 1865 to 1867 arrived via Australia. The big population gains for New Zealand were from gold between 1861 and 1865 (45,500 people) and harder times in Australia from 1901 to 1905 (over 35,000 people). W. D. Borrie, a New Zealand demographer who himself was part of the interchange and became Professor of Demography at the Australian National University, calculated that New Zealand made a net gain of 96,000 people from across the Tasman in the 57 years from 1858 to 1915.[5]

In the 1880s, on the other hand, New Zealand lost more people than it gained to the Australian colonies. One was J. C. Watson, the third Australian Prime Minister and leader of the world's first national Labor government, who moved to Sydney after he lost his job in 1886. At the turn of the century hard times imposed by drought in Australia propelled another wave to New Zealand, including five labour movement figures who migrated between 1900 and 1907 and became Cabinet ministers in New Zealand's first Labour government from 1935. Of these five radicals, two were Victorians, two were from New South Wales, and one was from Tasmania. The last of this group to cross the Tasman was Michael Joseph Savage, New Zealand's first Labour Prime Minister (1935–40), who arrived in New Zealand on Labour Day in 1907.[6] About 5 per cent of the soldiers who joined up in New Zealand for the First World War were also born in Australia, with men enlisting on whichever side of the Tasman they happened to be at the time.[7]

At one level the indigenous histories of both countries are strands of a single history, and for some indigenous people, making the best of their lives also entailed migration. Two people of mixed descent attracted our notice for the grace with which they moved between cultural worlds. One was the suitably named Bessie Te Wenerau (Wene) Grace of Ngati Tuwharetoa in the central North Island, who was the granddaughter of the paramount chief Te Heuheu Tukino IV, Horonuku, and of the Rev. Thomas Grace. Educated at Nelson Girls' College and Canterbury College, she joined the Sisters of the Church, a Church of England order, in 1922, taking the name Sister Eudora; graduated MA with first-class honours from the University of London; and was headmistress of St Hilda's Collegiate School in London before being appointed headmistress of the Church of England Girls' Grammar School in St Kilda, Melbourne. She died of cancer in 1944.[8] The other personality was 'Queensland Harry' (1875–1957), an Aboriginal rough rider who became a 'legendary figure' in New Zealand for his buck jumping and exhibition riding of outlaw horses at circuses and shows (Plate 20).[9] Queensland Harry first toured New Zealand with Barton's Circus and won the New Zealand rodeo buck jumping championship in Invercargill in 1906. After performing in Sydney he returned to New Zealand permanently with Barton's Circus in 1914, and spent the remainder of his life travelling the Agricultural and Pastoral (A & P) show circuit and working horses on farms. Harry staged rough riding exhibitions into old age, performing his final shows at Waimate, where he died in 1957.[10] Such personalities are missing from national stories yet are central to the Tasman world.

A return flow of people continued both ways across the Tasman throughout the 20th century. But a fundamental shift in trend occurred when the predominant flow switched dramatically from eastwards to westwards from the late 1960s. The reversal of the trans-Tasman flow since then is due to Australia's superior economic performance. In the two decades up to 1984 a total of 152,000 people headed from New Zealand across the Tasman. Beginning in the late 1960s there was a mass exodus of young people faced with limited employment opportunities at home; in the 1970s two-thirds of the departing New Zealanders were between 15 and 24 years of age.[11]

Among the wave of New Zealanders who left in the second half of the 1960s was the ophthalmologist and humanitarian Fred Hollows (1929–93), who went on to become the Australian of the Year in 1990. Fred Hollows was born in Dunedin and attended Palmerston North Boys' High School. After graduating with a BA from Wellington he studied at Otago Medical School and later pursued ophthalmology work in Britain, moving to Sydney in 1965 as Associate Professor of Ophthalmology at the University of New South Wales. From there he toured remote outback settlements, and was struck by the poor state of Aboriginal health. Hollows was dismayed about trachoma, an eye infection that was a major cause of blindness in Aboriginal communities, yet could be easily treated by antibiotics if diagnosed sufficiently early. Over three years he treated thousands of Aboriginal people with the infection and performed more than 1000 operations on complicated trachoma cases, restoring eyesight; he also helped establish the Aboriginal Medical Service in Redfern. Hollows is an apt representative of a shared history because he is listed among the 'top 100' New Zealanders and the 'top 100' Australians named by Prime Television in 2005 and the Bulletin in 2006.

Another among the late 1960s exodus was Reg Mombassa (Chapter 2), whose artwork Metaphorical Proximity adorns the book cover. Nothing captures

Fred Hollows and Don Crawford, milkbar socialists debating theology and politics, Palmerston North, 1946. Fred was in his final year at Palmerston North Boys' High School. The two met at the Church of Christ.

the Australia–New Zealand relationship better than his image of the kangaroo and the kiwi chained to each other. The kangaroo may be leading the poor-sighted kiwi, but the kangaroo is the migrant in a landscape that melds central Otago with the volcanic cones of suburban Auckland. Mombassa was raised in south Auckland; his family moved to Sydney in 1968 to 'try their luck' when he was a teenager.[12] He, too, embodies the Tasman world: as a Mambo artist, a musician who performs with the band Mental As Anything, and who exhibits on both sides of the Tasman. He designed the 'heroes' segment of the Sydney 2000 Olympic Games closing ceremony in which several of his Mambo characters also played a role.[13]

After the wave of trans-Tasman migration between 1901 and 1906, the biggest of all waves in the 20th century were in the opposite direction: westwards, with New Zealanders departing in three pronounced surges to Australia in the late 1970s, the late 1980s and at the end of the century. In four years from 1977 to 1980 Australia's net gain of New Zealand-born people numbered 63,000: equivalent to 70 per cent of New Zealanders living in Australia at the time of the 1976 census and 23 per cent of Australia's net population increase from migration.[14] Since the 1970s marked fluctuations in levels of people movement as well as increased international migration flows have occurred, with migration from New Zealand to Australia more extensive and volatile than from Australia to New Zealand (see opposite page).[15]

From the 1970s, therefore, trans-Tasman migration became an issue that concerned governments. The long-term movement by New Zealanders across the Tasman peaked at over 40,000 departures per year (about 30,000 net) – around 1979–81, 1988–89 and 2001. The highest number of departures – 44,592, tempered by 11,517 people arriving from Australia – was in 1989. The first outflow was in response to the Muldoon era, peaking at 42,910 in 1980; the second, and highest, to Rogernomics, which subjected ordinary New Zealanders to economic restructuring and redundancies. The third, which peaked at 42,367 in 2001, was associated with the sluggish New Zealand economy compared with Australian growth at the end of the 1990s and the increasing pay gap. A further spike of 43,419 (29,892 net) was recorded for the year ended 31 March 2008 as this book went to press. A more precise econometric explanation for this volatility is that the movement of people soared because travel costs declined; young baby-boomers headed offshore; while real earnings and employment grew faster in Australia, but trans-Tasman difference fluctuated.[16]

Over the 30 years from 1976 to 2005 a total of 856,943 people left New Zealand for Australia. In the same time period 401,610 people left Australia for New Zealand, producing a net outflow from New Zealand to Australia of 455,333.[17] Such was the extent of this movement that by 2001 New Zealanders were the second-largest overseas-born group in Australia.[18] New Zealand began to exert a substantial influence on Australian migration flows by becoming the

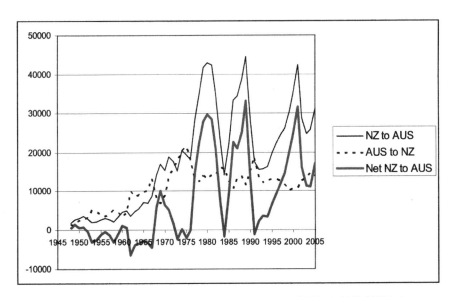

Trans-Tasman Permanent and Long-term Migration Flows, year ended 31 March 1948–2005, in Jacques Poot and Lynda Sanderson, 'Changes in Social Security Eligibility and the International Mobility of New Zealand Citizens in Australia', *PSC Discussion Papers*, No. 65, June 2007, courtesy of Jacques Poot, University of Waikato.

main source of permanent immigrants and the main destination of permanent emigrants.[19] Conversely, from a New Zealand perspective, the substantial outflow meant that by the beginning of the 21st century roughly 10 per cent of all New Zealanders (of whom a fifth at any time were living overseas) were in Australia.

For New Zealand, Australia continued to be the second source of immigrants after Britain. Australia has been one of New Zealand's top three source countries for permanent and long-term arrivals for over a century.[20] Since the 1960s the overall level of movement increased from Australia to New Zealand only, as we have noted, without the massive fluctuations evident in the other direction. There were three main groups in this smaller flow: returning New Zealanders; Australians moving within a single profession or labour market; and 'relay migrants', who moved to Australia from elsewhere and subsequently to New Zealand. About a third of Kiwis who move to Australia return home after a few years. Around 35 per cent of New Zealand citizens who left for Australia between 1978 and 2003, for example, with the intention of staying for a year or more, actually returned in that 25-year period.[21] There is a circular pattern of people movement, consistent with the 'Perennial Interchange' a hundred years ago, whereby New Zealanders live and work in Australia for a while and then return to New Zealand. Those who returned from Australia in 1999–2000 ventured across the Tasman for an average of just over five years. Circular movement is indicative of integrated labour markets; so much so that the Australian demographer Graeme Hugo considers circularity – and integrated labour markets – a defining characteristic of the flows between Australia and New Zealand.[22]

Trans-Tasman travel arrangements

A set of trans-Tasman travel arrangements that kept entry formalities to a minimum in the 20th century protected and helped to perpetuate the historical pattern of free people movement. At first the ability to move freely applied to British subjects, including Maori. Free movement as a principle operated within a broader context of racially exclusive policies – white Australia and New Zealand – from the 1880s into the 1960s. Within the constraints set by the immigration restriction acts on both sides of the Tasman, the settler populations could move freely until national governments imposed travel restrictions during the First World War.

The first formal trans-Tasman travel arrangements were introduced in 1920 as a means to dispense with the wartime controls. They reflected both the history of Tasman traffic in goods and people and the parallel immigration restriction acts. The formal arrangements had the pragmatic intent of ensuring free movement for 'white' natural-born British subjects travelling directly between the countries. Maori – but not Pacific Islanders – could enter Australia without an entry permit. In instances where the prejudice of an

New Zealand Prime Minister Sidney G. Holland and Minister of Social Security Eric H. Halstead, with an Australian representative, sign the social security agreement with Australia, December 1955.

F-177039-1/2, Morrie Hill Collection, Alexander Turnbull Library, Wellington

individual customs official obstructed the movement of a group of shearers or entertainers, one-off political intervention would put things right. Aboriginal Australians, such as Queensland Harry, could enter New Zealand at customs officers' discretion.[23] Asian migrants were discouraged by a poll tax and a language test that deliberately made no direct reference to race or colour. This mutual anxiety about 'back door' entry by 'undesirables' and 'aliens' reflected both ethnic solidarity in the white settler societies of the region and the international concern with population control on each side of the Pacific and Indian Oceans.[24]

In 1948 Commonwealth countries moved from using British passports to having their own. Consequent adjustments to the travel arrangements confirmed the existence of a Tasman world because British citizens had to present a passport to enter Australia or New Zealand once the two former colonies adopted separate Australian and New Zealand citizenships.[25] By contrast, white Australians, Pakeha and Maori could still cross the Tasman both ways without the formalities of passports or permits. Effectively, through this distinction in paperwork, the Tasman world exercised sovereignty against Britain.

After the Second World War divergent immigration policies did not immed-iately impel changes to these informal arrangements. That the travel arrangements remained steadfast for so long – until 1973 – resulted from the strength, and slow death, of the 'white Australia' policy. Only from 1973 could Pacific Islanders who were New Zealanders enter Australia under these arrangements. It was the protracted demise of White Australia that paved the way for free entry by the then few non-European, non-Maori New Zealanders who wanted to cross the Tasman. Politicians subsequently acclaimed this amendment, which the Labo(u)r prime ministers Gough Whitlam and Norman Kirk settled at their first official meeting in January 1973. The Trans-Tasman Travel Arrangement (TTTA), as it became known, allowed all the citizens of each country to visit, live and work on either side of the Tasman without a passport or visa. The previous National government of Jack Marshall also favoured 'completely free travel' because 'any Australian citizen [could] come freely to New Zealand'.[26]

In 1981, however, Malcolm Fraser's Liberal–National Country Party coa-lition insisted on passports for all travellers to Australia on the pretext of deterring terrorists and drug traffickers. The Australians imposed border controls and opted for passports when New Zealand Prime Minister Robert Muldoon rejected an alternative proposal to harmonise border procedures.[27] New Zealand followed suit by requiring passports for arriving passengers in 1987. In practice the Australian requirement for a passport to enter Australia made a passport for travel to New Zealand necessary for anyone who wanted to return to Australia.[28]

The more New Zealand migrant numbers rose in the late 20th century, the more suspicious Australians grew about 'back door' entry from the Asia–Pacific region. Was New Zealand a weak spot in border control? Demographic statistics supported such anxieties by suggesting that only three-quarters of the inflow to Australia from New Zealand consisted of people who were born in New Zealand.[29] In this context Australia, citing national interests, set new limits on the idea of free people movement, and introduced a special category visa for New Zealanders in the 1990s. Diplomats joke that this is a 'Claytons' visa because New Zealand travellers are not aware they have one. More significantly, the TTTA continued as before, allowing New Zealanders and Australians to visit, live and work in the other country without restriction.

By the late 1990s the confluence of a changed political climate and greater visibility of Kiwis in Australia created new tensions. The Howard government objected that a growing proportion of the flow from New Zealand consisted of new settlers who moved to Australia after obtaining New Zealand citizenship; Australia also complained about an imbalance of welfare payments.[30] The latter annoyance prompted a joint review of the social security agreement between Australia and New Zealand. The neighbours had signed their first social security agreement in 1948. By 1969 New Zealanders and Australians enjoyed immediate access to social welfare benefits in either country. The surge in the late 1980s of

New Zealanders moving to Australia generated a political response in the form of waiting periods for New Zealanders living in Australia and a reimbursement system in 1989 and 1994. But the joint review in 2000 returned to first principles, and drafted a new cost-sharing agreement to preserve the TTTA while removing the irritant in the relationship prompted by media reports about back-door entry.[31] Australian social welfare entitlements for future New Zealand migrants changed from June 2001: New Zealanders were no longer automatically eligible for social welfare benefits (other than the pension and for disability), regardless of how long they had lived in Australia. Nor were students eligible any longer for the Higher Education Contribution Scheme (HECS). Instead, for either of these payments, New Zealanders had first to apply for permanent residence.

Not everyone in Australia agreed with the negative media reports about Kiwi migrants and 'dole bludgers'. Statistics show that New Zealanders had higher rates of labour force participation than people born in Australia as well as migrants from other countries. Their rates of unemployment were also significantly lower.[32] Stirred by the bad press, Reg Mombassa responded by sending his 'Kengaroo' – a kangaroo with a Kiwi accent – to live in New Zealand (Plate 21). The Kengaroo had to adapt as all migrants do, especially to the different climate and environment.

The trans-Tasman travel arrangement survived the Howard government's challenge because of the trend towards closer integration under CER. The arrangement assumed a new form in 2005: that of combined Australia/New Zealand passport queues at airports, first in New Zealand and, later that year, on the Australian east coast. These directions at the border literally act as signposts to travellers that there is a Tasman world.[33]

Tourism

Shared passport queues also recognise that Australia and New Zealand are each other's largest travel markets. Nearly 4 million passengers travelled between Australia and New Zealand in the year ended December 2005.[34] New Zealand was the most popular destination for Australians, whether they were on holiday, visiting friends and relatives, or on business; over half of New Zealanders' overseas trips were trans-Tasman. The Tasman world has consituted a travel market since Union Steam Ship Company steamers visited the principal ports of New Zealand, Australia, Tasmania and the 'South Sea Islands' at the start of the 20th century, and ventured into Milford Sound. From the 1920s to the 1970s Australia was already the 'most favoured destination' for New Zealand travellers, who preferred it by three to one over Britain. Likewise, Australians made up the highest proportion of travellers to New Zealand, outnumbering the British by four to one as tourists and as visitors on business, and as sportspeople and entertainers by an even larger ratio.[35]

ANOTHER MILESTONE GONE

Neil Lonsdale, *New Zealand Observer*, 1 May 1940.

A-316-4-002, NZ Cartoon Archive, Alexander Turnbull Library, Wellington, courtesy of Chris Lonsdale

Improvements in the technology of travel transformed the Tasman travel market in the 20th century. While a full day was scythed from the time it took to cross the Tasman by sea between 1908 and 1918, the biggest transition was from sea to air travel during the Second World War. Another milestone had gone, Neil Lonsdale observed in 1940, once British flying-boats started to ply the Tasman, flown by Tasman Empire Airways Ltd (TEAL).[36] From 1940 it took hours rather than days to cross the Tasman. 'Progressive travellers' who could afford the fare took the flying-boat *Aotearoa* from Auckland to Sydney (Plate 22); those with fewer resources continued to travel by sea on the *Wanganella*. Progressive travellers included prime ministers on trans-Tasman business. Prime Minister Peter Fraser travelled secretly to Melbourne by flying-boat on a cold 10-hour flight in 1942. By 1958 it was taking Prime Minister Walter Nash five and a half hours to fly by Tasman Airways from Auckland to Sydney, and five hours to return. The trip shrank to four hours in the 1960s, with jet travel.

Both the national carriers, Qantas and Air New Zealand, launched their inaugural jet flights between Sydney and Christchurch in 1965, carrying groups of journalists and celebrities from Australia to New Zealand. While the Qantas group travelled by bus to the Marlborough Sounds and Franz Joseph Glacier, the Air New Zealand group drove by Tasman Rental car to the glacier, encountering a mixed standard of hotels, and uncertainty about where they would find meals.[37] By 1968 the new Australian Tourist Commission adapted its marketing to New Zealand's contemporary economic downturn. It focused on a plan to 'show the practicability of holidaying in Australia on the New Zealand travel allowance', which – after New Zealand's devaluation in 1967 – in Australian dollars was only $14 a day. Television commercials advertised: 'Exciting Australia, only the Tasman away.'[38] The 1960s and 1970s saw a substantial increase in short-term trips across the Tasman associated with tourism and holidays, business, and family links.

Befitting the status of the two countries as each other's biggest tourist market, the New Zealand Tourist and Publicity Department collaborated with tourist and publicity bureaux in the Australian states to promote trans-Tasman travel. It is also noteworthy that tourist bureaux, along with trade agencies, were

Australian and New Zealand tourist bureau directors' 11th annual conference, February 1960.
AAQT 6401 A60470, Archives New Zealand, Wellington

In February 1978 New Zealand hosted for the first time the Australian Ministers of Education Conference at Raukawa Marae.
AAQT 6401 B13864, Archives New Zealand, Wellington

the first New Zealand government agencies in Australia, established in Sydney and Melbourne in 1906 (see Chapter 5). New Zealand had an exhibit at the All Australian Exhibition and Trades Fair held as part of Australia's 150th anniversary celebrations in 1938. There New Zealand won a cup for the float 'March to Nationhood', which featured a Maori warrior and two maidens, a re-enactment of the signing of the Treaty of Waitangi, and early settlers. Members of the Polynesian Club in Sydney also made it possible for New Zealand to be represented at the associated 'Pageant of Nations', where they performed 'canoe poi and Samoan dances.'[39] Trade and industry interchange was also well established in the first half of the 20th century. Departments of Agriculture and stock and station agents planned tours for farmers. In the 1930s parties of 'progressive' Victorian dairy farmers visited New Zealand to see 'advanced methods', inspiring a 1933 booklet sponsored by the Victorian Department of Agriculture to proclaim: 'Two Southern lands join heart and hands and greet as kin with worlds to win.' Likewise, sheep farmers from New Zealand and South Australia undertook reciprocal tours in 1936. Farming tours were still being arranged in the 1950s.[40] Tourist bureau directors from Australia and New Zealand participated in conferences together, as did educationists and education ministers.

Living in both places

New Zealanders who move to Australia permanently or long term are much like Australians – only younger on average. This broad similarity marks them out from other migrants. A study of the main locations of New Zealanders in Australia over time confirms that the Kiwis in Australia behave like Australians. Like Australians, Kiwis have historically moved to Australia's growth states. In the early 20th century the chains of interaction across the Tasman world in the main encompassed Victoria, New South Wales, New Zealand and Tasmania. By 1976 the boundaries for this traffic had broadened: in addition to the 32 per cent of the New Zealand-born in Australia who lived in Sydney, there were significant concentrations in Brisbane, Canberra and Darwin. Tasman frontiers had shifted north and west to the mining area of the Pilbara in Western Australia and to northern and coastal Queensland.[41] By 2001 – in tandem with a pronounced movement of people within Australia – over half the New Zealanders in Australia lived in Queensland and Western Australia. More than one-quarter lived in the New South Wales coastal strip stretching north and south from Sydney, and another quarter on the Gold Coast between Brisbane and Tweed Heads.[42] These patterns show that trans-Tasman migration is much like an extension of internal migration within Australia. Moving to Australia is akin to moving inter-state.

The experience of Maori in Australia mirrors the overall trends in people movement. Maori were initiators of the Tasman world; Maori traders treated Sydney as a major hub in their business activities as well as a source of muskets, and chiefs learnt agriculture and other Christian works at Rev. Samuel Marsden's seminary, Rangihoua, at Parramatta. Like Pakeha, Maori moved to Australia in increasing numbers from the 1960s. From about one in 50 in 1966, the proportion of Maori who lived in Australia rose to one in six or seven by 2006. The two main national clusters of Maori by the early 21st century were in New Zealand and Australia. Significant communities existed in Queensland and Western Australia, as well as in Sydney. Almost all Maori now have whanau across the Tasman.[43] Maori move in pursuit of opportunities, especially economic ones; to join family already in Australia; for the lifestyle; and to enjoy the multiculturalism offered by world cities. They also move to escape problems at home such as gangs, drugs, domestic violence, perceived prejudice about Maori issues, or negativity within their own families.[44]

Maori Australians are representative of the Tasman world, not least because they retain strong links with New Zealand, links assisted by the telephone and the internet, and through the maintenance of protocol. While they maintain strong emotional ties, some cross the Tasman to experience a broader picture. Some find that being in Australia helps with the necessity of learning to move in both worlds. In turn they make a significant contribution to Australian culture. Sometimes parents would like to go back to New Zealand but their Australian-

born children say no. One issue for Maori, therefore, is whether and how to maintain the tradition of taking the dead back to New Zealand. Increasingly Maori are buried in Australia; Rookwood Cemetery in Sydney, for example, has a Maori section. A related issue is whether local bylaws allow the dead to be laid out in customary fashion. To address such questions, and the needs of Kiwi youth – Pakeha as well as Maori – without family networks, big-hearted individuals established the Maori Women's Welfare League Poihakena (Port Jackson) Inc in Sydney. This autonomous organisation, which is not a branch of the Maori Women's Welfare League in New Zealand, reinforces the idea of working side by side as family and neighbours.[45]

Maori have participated in the trans-Tasman labour market for more than 200 years and links forged from the shared experiences of a migratory workforce in general – shearers, slaughtermen, miners, seamen – extended to connected labour movements. Historically, labour is one of the most visible sectors in the Tasman world because trans-Tasman associations formed to battle capitalist and global forces attracted labour historians' interest. Many trade unions have strong historical relationships with their counterparts in the other country. Some have 'Australasia' in their titles. Perhaps best known are the Australian radicals who carried their hopes for a better future to New Zealand: from the Red Feds and Prime Minister Michael Joseph Savage to the utopian socialist William Lane. The latter walked off stage out of Australian history – and labour history – not when he departed for Paraguay to establish a New Australia in the 1890s but when he metamorphosed into a conservative who returned to live in New Zealand.[46] Free movement of activists extended to the communist parties of Australia and New Zealand.[47] James Bennett concludes that his findings on the labour movement in Australia and New Zealand 'largely substantiate' the propositions with which we began this project: to test the existence of a Tasman world after 1901.[48]

A classic case is of the Kiwi (often Maori) shearers who complicate the Australian story of shearers as the epitome of 'mateship' in the outback. The 'wide comb' dispute in the shearing industry (Chapter 1) coincided with the rise of, and was celebrated as a win for, the 'New Right' in the 1980s when the workingman's paradise was pensioned off. New Zealand shearers provided the catalyst for the dispute, which arose from an ideological and class struggle between shearers and graziers, traditional enemies in Australian national mythology. A Kiwi culture of fast shearing rather than the 'universal tally' (a maximum number of sheep sheared a day) disturbed Australian Workers' Union habits in Australia. New Zealand shearers innovated from around the edges of the Tasman world, starting in Western Australia, which became an 'enclave of New Zealand shearing culture' from the 1960s.[49]

In the late 20th century, when globalisation shifted government priorities from the worker to the consumer, the peak trade union bodies in Australia and New Zealand – the Australian Council of Trade Unions (ACTU) and the New Zealand Federation of Labour (NZFOL), later the NZCTU – developed their trans-Tasman links and sought a shared perspective on international political questions, such as apartheid and nuclear issues in the 1970s and 1980s. They also transferred policies across the Tasman in an effort to develop innovative responses to Rogernomics and parallel deregulation in Australia.[50]

Music

Perhaps more than any other form of popular entertainment culture, New Zealand-born music has reflected the binding together of the Tasman world. Both Maori and Pakeha have contributed a disproportionate weight of talent but Maori were the first to cross the ditch in numbers to make music. Known for their chorales on marae and at church and community festivals at home in New Zealand, Maori concert parties ventured to Britain during Queen Victoria's reign and Australian recording engineers came to New Zealand in the 1920s to record Maori music.[51] During the 1950s the concert party evolved into the Maori show band, first in Aotearoa, then by migration and networking in the hotels, Returned Services League of Australia (RSL) clubs, nightclubs and cabarets of Australian cities. Groups like the Maori Troubadours, the Maori Premiers, the HiQuins and Maori HiFives played to packed houses in Sydney, Melbourne and on the Gold Coast in Queensland. Every main hotel during the 1960s seemed to have a Maori group or individual Maori entertainer. They brought not just disciplined vocal harmonies but proficiency at playing a range of instruments, and added skits, impressions and slapstick comedy to their routines.

The show bands represented a hybrid mixture of Maori traditional heritage and popular middle-of-the-road songs, linking Australian and Kiwi venues with resorts and clubs throughout the Pacific islands, broadening the Tasman world's profile. The bands grouped and split on a regular basis from another mobile freemasonry of musicians – other Maori groups in both countries – adapting styles to suit the changing Tasman audiences in the 1960s and 1970s. But the lifeblood of Maori rhythm and harmony never stopped pulsing. The Quin Tikis had at least four reincarnations with new members. Mahora and the Volcanics started in a travelling circus of musical performers touring the Australian continent, often presented as 'noble savages' in a caravanserai of talent. They then honed their polished routines in Sydney and Melbourne hotels before taking on the United States.[52] The Volcanics recognised early the value of including Maori culture in their shows, a form of trans-Tasman education often neglected in the telling. Also neglected is the tale of the Australian-born children of Maori show band members who settled in Australia. The Young Polynesians started in Surfers Paradise in 1975 as a conscious effort to teach the children of Maori settlers about their heritage and culture, and launched professional entertainment careers for many as they grew.

Individual Maori made a distinguished mark. Ricky May died in Australia a much-loved performer; John Rowles was perhaps the most successful international star among Maori singers; and Howard Morrison not only toured Australia but became a spearhead for New Zealand trade and tourist commissions in other countries as well.[53]

Tex Morton was Australia's first music idol. From a beginning in the 1930s collecting folksongs and putting Banjo Paterson to music, he went on to be named in 1976 the Father of Australian Country Music and to become the first person inscribed on the Country Music Roll of Renown. In between these early and later achievements he recorded the first country music outside the United States and honed his skills as a guitar player, yodeller, whip cracker, poet and songwriter. His Stetson hat and high-heel boots set the uniform for country singers. After the Second World War Tex moved to the United States, then to Canada where he studied psychosomatic hypnosis and wrote a PhD thesis on the paranormal among Australian Aboriginal people. Dr Morton then became famous again, as the extraordinary hypnotist The Great Morton, first in the US, where he drew larger crowds than Houdini, then back in Australia. By the 1960s, as roadshows and vaudeville collapsed under the assault of television and nightclubs, Tex took his trailer and fishing gear and spent several years touring Aboriginal districts in the outback; he was inducted into several tribes. Tex Morton, writes Alan Turley,

> was Australia's first real music superstar. He was recognised as the world's leading authority on hypnosis and supernatural phenomena. He was described as the greatest showman in the world of his time but at the same time he made a serious contribution to an evolving field of medical science.[54]

Tex was also a Kiwi. Born Robert William Lane, he was a fifth-generation Nelsonian and directly descended from the first European settlers of 1842. After a childhood spent eeling and splashing about in the Maitai River, he attended Nelson College then ran away to try his hand in show business. In 1932 Tex worked his passage to Sydney, where he became the toast of a nation. He never abandoned New Zealand, touring in 1949 before leaving for the United States. In the 1970s, in the twilight of his fame, Tex Morton hosted the popular TV show *The Country Touch*. He is buried beside his parents in Nelson.

Tex Morton's story stands for the strong ties of popular culture that joined New Zealand to Australia throughout the 20th century. They shared what Miles Fairburn calls a 'bitsa' culture, with bits drawn freely together from Britain and the US.[55] More decorously, Jim Davidson argues the two countries shared 'dominion culture': a blend of magazines, radio, sport, music and social life centred on churches, Apex and Rotary clubs, stamp collecting and Scouts, derived from Britain but intersected, sometimes jarringly, by American influences.[56] This representation perhaps underplays the influence of Australia specifically on New Zealand culture. Fairburn shows how both countries shared a mixture of 'Anzac, Hollywood and Home' in their movie predilections, architecture, magazine choices and language, to the extent that, argues Fairburn, New Zealand cannot be said to have an exceptional culture in any way.[57] While his focus is on Australian influence in New Zealand, the focus of this book is on interactions both ways: on the Tasman world's shared heritage, with variants of each other's as well as American and British cultural components.

Trans-Tasman traffic in print and sound made Australia the largest supplier of recorded music between 1914 and the 1980s; made her magazines, such as the *Bulletin*, *Women's Weekly* and *Pix*, also the most popular in New Zealand; and brought a deluge of radio serials far outstripping those from Britain or the US. Hollywood came to New Zealand not just directly but sometimes via Australia. Kiwis enjoyed the emergent Australian films of the 1970s and the stereotypes embodied in television dramas from *The Sullivans* to *McLeod's Daughters*, mocking them gently in self-recognition; New Zealand soap *Shortland Street* was just the other side of the coin to Australia's *Neighbours*, while *Home and Away* reflected the joint antipodean pleasure in sand and salt water.[58]

Tex Morton also embodies the circuits in theatre and modern music that made for the 'Perennial Interchange'[59] during the 20th century. A Tasman world of theatre touring and management existed, controlled largely from Australia by a 'mobile freemasonry'[60] of magnates and producers represented predominantly by J. C. Williamson and George Musgrove. Australian and New Zealand audiences were demanding in their taste. Most plays came from Britain – Gilbert and Sullivan were eternal favourites – with local talent employed who became stars on both sides of the Tasman. New Zealand figured as part of regional Australia in the pattern of touring before the Second World War, audiences across the Tasman world expecting the best as citizens of empire and self-regarding modern cosmopolitans.

Most talent went west to Australia from New Zealand. A few adventurous Australian musicians were seen on the far side of the ditch in Kiwi shows, generally pop stars touring New Zealand in their early days before fame. But even in breaking new ground Kiwi pop stars and rock'n'roll artists were prominent in forging a trans-Tasman world.

Pop stars have been important in charting the sensitivity of the young to the imagined national community in a rapidly globalising world culture. When Johnny Devlin moved from New Zealand to Australia he changed his style of music to connect with both local and overseas trends. In the 1960s Ray Columbus and the Invaders also moved to Sydney and deliberately made up songs and jive moves to start new dance crazes, introducing Sydney's rockers and surfies to a Kiwi rock style; their song 'She's a Mod' reached number one in both countries and over the years the Invaders supported leading international acts in Australia. Max Merritt and the Meteors achieved the same, though more raunchily: they were the hottest band in Australia in the late 1960s. At another point on the spectrum, drummer and actor Bruno Lawrence introduced the multimedia presentation of review, comedy, film and jazz rock music to Australian audiences (admittedly hard-core, tolerant youth audiences) through his travelling project Blerta. The resonances of one's own country could reach across the ditch: Split Enz's song 'Six Months in a Leaky Boat' is seen as a quintessentially Kiwi song about island isolation and wanderlust but was written in Australia after the band had settled there; Tim Finn was inspired to write it after reading Geoffrey Blainey's Australian history, *The Tyranny of Distance*.[61] New Zealand musicians continued to move to Australia in the 1980s and 1990s, tailoring their music to an Austral-global market, using Australia as a bridgehead to tackle the Americas, and then the world. In the 21st century it is the turn of Kiwi-flavoured hip-hop and rap. Nurtured in an activist Pacific community that protested against nuclear testing in the Pacific and the Springbok rugby tour of 1981, composers, musicians and groups such as Che-Fu, Scribe, Supergroove, P-Money and Brotha D are connecting with Australian audiences and taking out multiple awards at Australian music ceremonies.

Gambling and horse racing

Gambling associated with a variety of 'sports' is another of the Tasman world's connecting tissues (Chapter 8). This connection did not atrophy with federation of the Australian colonies in 1901. The cultural baggage that migrants carried predominantly from the British Isles included practices and attitudes about gambling. Gentry gambling included gambling on horse racing and, often in gentlemen's cubs, card playing.[62] The vast majority of the working-class populace brought with them traditional gambling means such as cards and boxing, and fairs and local race meetings continued to be places for a flutter. Gambling was woven into the fabric of holiday events for all classes, often based on race meetings. The festivities and public holidays surrounding both the Wellington and Melbourne Cups, for example, were direct descendants of similar meetings at Newmarket, England.[63]

Some discontinuities between the Tasman neighbours did develop under separate political traditions, most evident in the differing attitudes of both countries' Labo(u)r parties. The Australian Labor Party, perhaps because of its earlier rise to power, was never anti-gambling, instead choosing to support the working man's right to gamble.[64] In contrast, the New Zealand Labour Party, perhaps due to the financial hardships of the 1930s when it rose to power, was vehemently anti-gambling, especially Prime Minister Michael Joseph Savage.[65] This divergence in political attitudes led to some legislative differences, most notably the continued illegality of bookmakers in New Zealand at a time when they were on the rise and widely accepted in Australian society. The influence these laws had on the general population, however, was arguably small. Common practices and ideas born of a shared cultural heritage continued to be transferred across the Tasman Sea between neighbours who remained culturally and socially similar.

In 1881 George Adam, proprietor of a Sydney hotel, Tattersalls, ran his first public sweep on the Sydney Cup. By 1897 the Tattersalls sweeps and lotteries had moved to Tasmania, and on main streets around New Zealand signs claiming 'We post to Hobart' became ubiquitous.[66] One of the most enduring elements of trans-Tasman gambling had been born: New Zealanders wagered on Tattersalls sweeps for Australian races, predominantly the Melbourne and Sydney Cups, but also on local races such as the New Zealand Cup. Australians in turn could participate in sweeps on high-profile New Zealand races such as the Wellington Cup. The regular lottery draws were hugely popular; Tattersalls' takings from New Zealand regularly amounted to 30 per cent of their overall figures.[67]

Tattersalls was not the only one to run sweeps on horse racing. Newspapers were often the medium of advertisement for sweeps, with both the Sydney Sprinting Club and Wellington's sweepstake operator George North using them to attract a trans-Tasman clientele. Ideas about lotteries and sweeps of other kinds also flowed between the countries. Land sweepstakes or raffles proved popular in New Zealand after their apparent success in Victoria and New South Wales. The two world wars saw Australians and Kiwis gamble together on all manner of sweeps, most notably makeshift horse racing by the cavalry. Two-up also became entrenched in New Zealand after the First World War as returning soldiers brought it home courtesy of their Australian companions.[68]

Both societies imported gambling practices and policies from each other. The Queensland Labor government from 1916, for example, adopted a policy of charitable gambling when it borrowed aspects of the New Zealand model of public maternity hospitals and baby health care in the 1920s. Queensland funded its maternal welfare schemes through the state-run Golden Casket lottery, whose large customer base extended to New Zealand.[69] Technology transfer was also frequent. The best example is the introduction and subsequent running of Totalisator Agency Boards (TAB) in New Zealand and various Australian states. In 1950 New Zealand set up the first off-course totalisator in the world.

Soon the Victorian and New South Wales governments sent people to study its establishment and operation in an attempt to ascertain how best to

"REMEMBER WHEN HE WAS A COLT IN 1951 AND WE WONDERED WHAT HIS FORM WOULD BE? NOW HE'S A TOP-CLASS STAYER."

Nevile Lodge, *Evening Post*, 1965.
J-065-069, NZ Cartoon Archive, Alexander Turnbull Library, Wellington, courtesy of Debby Edwards

appropriate this new technology. While fundamentally adopting the Kiwi model, Australia's innovative use of new bet types, advanced technologies and integrated pools saw New Zealand looking across the Tasman in the 1980s for fresh ideas.[70] This mutual development of technology culminated in the 1990s with the introduction of fixed-odds sports and racing betting via the New Zealand TAB, essentially a bookmaking service.

Towards the end of the 20th century New Zealand again turned to the Australian experience while grappling with the thorny issues of poker machines and casinos. Poker machines had been illegally imported into New Zealand as early as the 1950s, initially from the US via Australia. A much larger influx came from Australia from the late 1970s. These imports were often used by sports clubs or Returned Services' Associations, just as they were in Australia, yet their illegality confined them to an underground subculture, as opposed to the Australian experience, where they played an enormous role in financing and promoting large RSL and rugby league clubs.

Their prohibition in New Zealand was based primarily on moral objections: concerns about disreputable owners becoming rich while poorer people became addicted. The government, however, was trying to reignite its own lotteries and also realised it could use poker machines as revenue earners for its Lottery

Commission funds through taxation, as for other forms of gambling. It then turned to Australia to try to ascertain which rules and regulations had worked best for poker machines and what pitfalls to avoid.[71]

Casinos provide a similar example. They had been legalised in Tasmania and the Northern Territory under strict rules since the 1970s. In both areas they had proved government moneyspinners and great boons to tourism.[72] Again the New Zealand government used the Australian example and granted only very specific, set numbers of licences in legalising casinos.[73]

Along with gambling, as the foregoing discussion indicates, comes horse racing, and the horse racing and breeding industries can claim to be the most consistently interconnected communities across the Tasman world during the 20th century. What is it about the industry that gives it such tight connections transcending national boundaries? A sociological approach to racing culture would suggest that the industry as a whole views itself as one class, as one group of people with a shared language and traditions, along with familial ties that enable it to communicate and operate even across countries. In the case of Australia and New Zealand, it is true that the industry has similar historical events, precedents and cultural factors that have enabled a shared story to evolve outside national narratives.

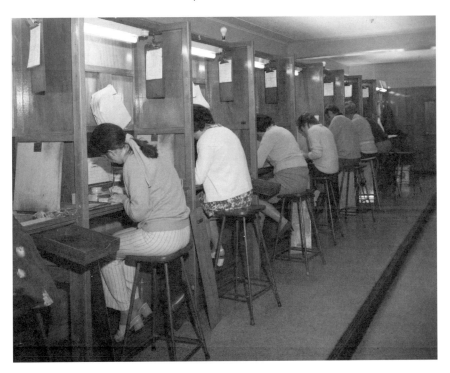

Inside a TAB office, July 1971.
AAQT 6401 A97089, Archives New Zealand, Wellington

Within a trans-Tasman gambling world, an entire culture of racing and breeding not only reinforces its own language but also patrols its own acceptable rules and boundaries of engagement. Breeders understand each other when they talk of teaser stallions, dosage principles and black type. Owners worry together over acceptance fees and a stiff ride. Trainers share gleeful tales of outstanding sectionals and woeful tales of handicappers, 'giving her 1 kilo over weight for age'. Strappers know the language of the stables, to watch for 'the boss' or to check a colt's off fore, just as jockeys grimace together about the sauna room, that dodgy hole at the third furlong or that young lad's monkey action. Such exchanges bespeak an international language and set of customs, and at the antipodes of international racing they have helped to forge a strong trans-Tasman community.

A plethora of examples illustrates the familial nature of these ties. Prominent Sydney trainer Tommy Smith's trans-Tasman connections, for example, were perpetuated across five decades. In the 1950s Smith began frequenting the New Zealand yearling sales at Trentham, Wellington. A history of Australian buyers at New Zealand sales existed before this (witness Phar Lap) but Smith became the forerunner for large-scale, regular buying of New Zealand yearlings to race in Australia. One of his first purchases became the Australian champion Tulloch, whose success reignited Australian interest in the New Zealand sales.[74] As this interest ebbed and flowed over the ensuing decades, Smith remained a constant presence at Trentham and later Karaka. When he retired, his daughter, Gai Waterhouse, took over his stable in Sydney, and also inherited his love of the New Zealand sales ring. Waterhouse briefly set up a satellite stable in Matamata, bringing her own young Australian stable foreman, Mark Walker, who stayed on to become one of the two top trainers in New Zealand.

The racing and breeding industries did not invent this common bond and language in the antipodes; they came from Britain, from centres of racing and breeding such as Newmarket and Cork. But the shared tradition stretched across the Tasman almost as soon as racing and breeding began in both sets of colonies. The New Zealand Stud Company began life in Auckland in 1883 as a deliberate attempt to breed horses good enough to compete across the Tasman.[75] Before the turn of the century New Zealand horses had already won three Melbourne Cups, and the transfer of jockeys, trainers and horses between the two countries was extraordinary given the length of the sea voyage.[76] John Chaafe, an Australian jockey, came to New Zealand in the late 1870s and turned to training, initially in Otago and later in Auckland. In the early 1880s he moved to Queensland to train before heading to Sydney. He then returned to Auckland to be a caretaker trainer for prominent Auckland trainer George Wright, who was campaigning members of his own team in Australia.

The racing class and the traditions it encapsulated did not go unchallenged. The rise of a self-made moneyed racing class in both countries produced a challenge to the gentry establishments that controlled the leading thoroughbred racing clubs. These self-made men tried to integrate within the existing racing clubs but the very forces that created a strong connected industry kept them out. They were not of the right families, and they did not know the appropriate language and behaviour. In short, they were not the 'sort' to enter the gentrified rooms of the Victorian Racing Club or the Christchurch Jockey Club. As their participation became increasingly limited through bans and underhand tactics against their horses, they moved into proprietary race clubs and eventually into harness racing.[77]

Harness racing came to the Tasman world from the US. It was not part of most migrants' shared traditions and did not fit within the existing thoroughbred world. Shut out from that environment, harness racers created a second trans-Tasman industry whereby breeders, trainers and drivers moved through a connected world in much the same way as their thoroughbred counterparts. One of its most visible products is the Inter Dominion series, run every year in either a different Australian state, or Christchurch or Auckland. The Inter Dominions had their beginnings in the 1896 Inter-Colonial Free For All, run at the new harness track, Moonee Valley, in Melbourne. Four of Australia's best took on New Zealand mare Calista, with victory going to New South Wales pacer Fritz. There was no follow-up at that stage but Western Australian administrator James Brennan revived the idea and staged the Australasian Trotting Championship in Perth in 1925. After much lobbying the Inter Dominions were established permanently in 1935 and staged for the first time in Perth in 1936.[78] The role of Perth in an expansive Tasman world is significant: areas such as Western Australia with their large, self-made and working-class populations saw the rise of harness racing in Australia. Nor is it a coincidence that harness tracks were built predominantly in working-class areas such as south Dunedin and east Perth.

The shared cultural heritage and traditions of racing, the flow of personnel and practices between Australia and New Zealand in both thoroughbred and harness racing constitute one of the clearest examples of a Tasman world that continued beyond Australian federation in 1901. This common racing world has maintained connections to its European roots but it is unusual in also incorporating significant Asian racetracks and markets in a way that reinvents an authentic sense of a new 'Australasia'. It is generally believed that the Asian market began to become strong in the 1980s and was disrupted by the 1987 sharemarket crash.[79] But a burgeoning business with Asia began as early as the 1960s. While horse exports to Canada, South Africa, the US and Australia remained higher, the New Zealand industry had steady business with Malaysia, Singapore, Japan and the Philippines in the late 1960s. From 1965 to 1969, exports to Malaysia and Singapore increased from under $1000 to $37,000. Japan and the Philippines also experienced rapid growth. In the 1980s Japanese and Hong Kong buyers became more active at the Premier Sydney Easter and

Karaka yearling sales, and auctioneering companies began to buy horses deemed 'good running types' to market in Asia.

The relationship was never simply one way, from the Tasman world to Asia. Since the early 1980s there has been a triangular transfer of personnel incorporating the region. Japan and Hong Kong in particular have become areas of immense growth in worldwide racing and now enjoy considerable esteem. The Japan Cup meeting in November and the International Meeting at Sha Tin in Hong Kong in December see the best horses from around the world invited to compete; they include New Zealand and Australian horses. The best trans-Tasman jockeys and trainers now seek licences in Asia to broaden their skills and compete against stronger international competition. Asia has become part of the wider circuit of racing that used to stretch only from Sydney to Melbourne and across to Auckland or Christchurch.

A second example of Asia's dynamic role is the case of shuttle stallions: horses that serve mares in both hemispheres as each spring breeding season finishes. They represent a further integration of the Australian and New Zealand breeding communities, focused particularly in the Hunter Valley in Australia and the Waikato region in New Zealand. A tradition of using Irish or American bloodlines already existed but certain individuals, such as John Messara at Arrowfield Stud in the Hunter Valley, began to introduce Japanese bloodlines into Australia and New Zealand. Messara made arrangements with the owners of Japan's greatest stallion, Sunday Silence, to send Australian mares to Japan. These mares were then transported back to Australia to foal and their yearlings fetched million-dollar prices at auction. To complete the picture, Sunday Silence's owners sent mares to Australia to be covered by Messara's own stallions. New Zealand's Java Lodge was also an early innovator of Asian connections in the breeding arena, importing a son of Sunday Silence to stand at stud. Many of these yearlings returned to Japan or Hong Kong after being bought at auction by Asian buyers. As the shuttle stallion phenomenon has grown, trans-Tasman studs have stood increasing numbers of Japanese horses.

It is fitting, then, that Phar Lap's body parts are distributed between museums in Melbourne, Canberra and Wellington, as we saw in Chapter 2. Phar Lap is the hero horse in Tasman world popular culture. All three museums – two national, one state – advertise Phar Lap on their websites. Phar Lap embodies the 'bitsa' culture. A history of living together explains why his bits are the Tasman world's most popular exhibits.

CHAPTER FOUR

Shared State Experiments

Shaun Goldfinch and Philippa Mein Smith

The Tasman world shared state experiments at the very time that Australasia was dismembered at the beginning of the 20th century. New Zealand and the Australian colonies exchanged policies and people to a remarkable degree, and after 1901 so did New Zealand and Australian state and federal governments. The patterns of policy sharing, learning and innovation grew from a history as British colonies, which shared an English constitutional heritage and British law, both statute and common, explicitly borrowed from metropolitan sources but also from other colonies, including Canada. The self-governing colonies discussed and adapted this constitutional inheritance through exchanges at imperial (later Commonwealth) conferences well into the 20th century.[1] Common state institutions constituted a major feature of British cultural baggage and a form of 'coercive' policy transfer.[2] An easy informality in fact marked such exchanges, as officials understood the nature of their association to be that of equal partners within an 'empire of liberty'.[3] The knowledge sharing and copying, built on familiarity and trust, saved time and resources: an important factor for reformers and nation-builders in Britain's antipodes. Positioned as far as was possible from the imperial centre – at the ends of maritime links – the 'seven colonies of Australasia' shared patterns of state development in a complex process involving agency and institutional frameworks.

In London, for example, Agents-General and other visitors from the Australasian colonies met regularly with and formed delegations to the Secretary of State for the Colonies. Colonial representatives broached diverse topics such as jealousy between Victoria and New South Wales, land laws, taxation, colonial democracy, emigration, the rabbit plague, federation, tariffs, trade unions, indigenous people, and the annexation of Pacific islands to protect British interests.[4] Similar concerns – especially the last – preoccupied intercolonial conferences in Australia, which New Zealand representatives attended in 1873, 1881 and 1883. The colonies cooperated on issues such as a joint naval squadron in 1887, and an intercolonial royal commission into the rabbit problem in the same year.

Once federation of the Australian colonies looked likely in the 1880s and 1890s, New Zealand was invited to and took part in the constitutional conferences of 1890 and 1891. Regular intercolonial and imperial conferences and the federal movement all helped to build links and friendships among the colonies, assisting the development of consensus and the sharing of ideas.[5]

Into the 20th century, officials and professionals met as regional communities. New Zealand police attended inter-state meetings of police commissioners.[6] New Zealanders also participated in meetings of railways commissioners and about postal and telegraph services. The colonies debated in particular issues of technology, transport and communications, which were vital to colonial progress and connected the empire. The telegraph facilitated information and news sharing across the British empire and the world, with Australia linked to London via Singapore in 1872, and New Zealand to Australia by trans-Tasman submarine cable in 1876, completing the All Red Route. But telegrams were expensive; most from New Zealand only went as far as Australia.[7] From 1886 the New Zealand United Press Association – an alliance of regional and city papers – largely took its international news from Australian press combinations, while Tasman world audiences received a reasonably uniform diet of international news, with an empire slant. New Zealand remained reliant on Australian sources into the 1920s.[8]

The 'Tasman settlement'

This family of colonies established similar models of economic development in the later 19th century. Paul Kelly's 'Australian Settlement' – consisting of 'White Australia, Industry Protection, Wage Arbitration, State Paternalism and Imperial Benevolence'[9] – was an Australasian or Tasman 'settlement', with key elements originating in New Zealand. This project encompassed early democracy and the vote for women; dispossession of indigenous people; aspirations to land and home ownership for settlers; and embryonic welfare states. The seven colonies were the 'showcase of progressive politics in the 1890s',[10] and their state experiments attracted the attention of reformers as far away as the United States of America.[11] The Australasian Progressives of the late 19th and early 20th centuries, and the British liberal thought they adopted, provided a welcome environment for policy innovations that could fit, or be made to fit, preconceived ideas of what new world countries should be like.[12] As Sidney Webb enthused in 1898, their efforts to reproduce a 'brighter Britain' were of 'special interest' because the antipodes tackled problems shared by the English 'in a peculiarly English way'.[13] The components assembled by such Progressives as William Pember Reeves in New Zealand and Charles Kingston in South Australia were 'not "merely isolated experiments, devised to meet particular emergencies", but "parts of a definite, systematic, far-reaching policy of social re-organization"'.[14] Together this social and economic reordering constituted a strategy of 'domestic defence',[15] or a 'settler contract'[16] that ostensibly balanced the demands of an export-led economy, exporting food and wool to Britain. As Fairburn points out, however, this ideal society was often just that – an ideal – and life was often grimmer than mythology allows.[17] One can also question whether the 'settlement' was more an aspiration than an achievement.

While the Tasman traffic in ideas was circular, New Zealand's role as an innovator was central.[18] As Davis noted in 1971, although 'modern Australian writers are . . . reluctant to admit the fact, Australian state and Commonwealth governments at the turn of the century looked continually to New Zealand for precedents.'[19] This tendency was strongly evident in Tasmania. The Hobart to Bluff steamer carried ideas and people, while conservative and radical papers, politicians and policy entrepreneurs referred to New Zealand regularly, either as a positive or negative lesson. Debate centred on New Zealand's agrarian legislation, land tax issues, and the moves to break up large estates. Tasmanian Labor members saw experience in New Zealand as a qualification for office. Politicians visited from both sides: Premier Seddon in 1897 when he defended New Zealand's loans to rural settlers, and New Zealand member of Parliament A. W. Hogg in 1904 when he evangelised the New Zealand tax on unimproved land; and the Tasmanian Tax Commissioner when he examined the tax's operation in New Zealand. A form of the tax on unimproved land was later taken up by the Fisher Commonwealth Labor government (1910–13).

A central aspect of this settler contract or 'domestic defence' was compulsory arbitration, where industrial (including wage) disputes between unions and employers were settled in a tribunal before a judge, with compulsory reference to an arbitration court, and rulings binding on both parties. To the American Progressive Henry Demarest Lloyd in 1900, compulsory arbitration was one of Australasia's 'advanced institutions': not merely a 'novelty in a subordinate field of legislation' but 'a new growth of the living organism of modern society.'[20] New Zealand adopted compulsory arbitration in 1894, followed by Western Australia (1900), New South Wales (1901), the Commonwealth of Australia (1904), and Queensland and South Australia (1912). In the new federal Australia, proponents also tied arbitration explicitly to the concept of New Protection that became the orthodoxy for the rest of the century. This link allowed local industries, particularly manufacturers, to accommodate themselves in the arbitration system by linking trade protection to social protection for workers, with the promise of protection from foreign competition for firms that paid 'fair and reasonable' wages. This direct state intervention in and regulation of the labour market would be an aspect of New Zealand and Australian society into the late 20th century. It formed a key component of what Castles terms the 'workers' welfare state', where welfare in a full-employment society was delivered through a regulated labour market that guaranteed a 'living wage.'[21]

The adoption of compulsory arbitration showed the importance of imperial elite networks and policy transfer; it was an experiment that the Australasian colonies shared, and was exceptional to them.[22] William Pember Reeves was the main force behind New Zealand's Industrial Conciliation and Arbitration Act 1894. Reeves held the post of Minister of Labour in the Liberal government from 1892 until 1896. The New Zealand act itself was similar to Charles Kingston's earlier and unsuccessful 1890 South Australian bill, with an almost identical full title; so much so that Kingston later accused Reeves of intellectual plagiarism.[23] Reeves certainly borrowed from Kingston, but also noted the influences of arbitration initiatives across the world.[24] The majority of the Australian colonies and federal Australia studied the New Zealand legislation and its effects, noted problems and attempted to correct them. New Zealand directly influenced the Western Australian model.[25] The New South Wales Backhouse Royal Commission in 1901 toured New Zealand to study the operation of the act in detail,[26] before New South Wales adopted its own compulsory arbitration mechanism that incorporated lessons learnt. In turn, New Zealand borrowed ideas and policies from Australia, particularly from the federal arbitration system. Policy-makers appreciated that arbitration courts could play a central role in setting wages and conditions by the turn of the century.

Policy transfer among government statisticians and other officials mirrored the growth of Australasian approaches to state development. Colonial statisticians constituted one such Tasman community of expertise and interest, who conferred with metropolitan Britain and among themselves in order to devise uniform statistics to market the colonies as well as meet imperial requirements.[27] Official statistics both promoted entrepreneurial state activity and highlighted the aspirations to build a New World, revealed in appeals to 'White Australia', the 'workingman's paradise' and 'Better Britain'. Colonial statisticians made the connections that were fundamental to state-making through conferences, correspondence and irregular visits. The colonial statists first met in London in 1860, when the Fourth International Statistical Congress included British colonial representatives so that they might learn by example. The Australasian colonies presented a joint report to the congress, 'prepared with great care and ability', on the 'Irregularity of the Statistical Phenomena Observable in the Australian Colonies since the Gold Discovery of 1851'.[28] Australian statisticians followed up with their own meeting in Melbourne in 1861, organised by the Victorian statist, W. H. Archer. His successor, H. H. Hayter, visited New Zealand on a 10-week holiday in 1873. In Wellington, Hayter prepared a report for the Registrar-General on New Zealand statistics and census-taking and suggested improvements.[29] Political demands also mounted for statistical uniformity. The intercolonial conference attended by colonial secretaries and treasurers from all seven Australasian colonies in 1873, for example, prompted a second local meeting of statists in Hobart in 1875, although New Zealand, Queensland and Western Australia did not attend because the invitation failed to arrive in time.[30]

The statists published a surge of statistical material in the late 19th century.

Victoria published the region's first yearbook in 1874, which earned international acclaim.[31] New Zealand's Premier, Sir Julius Vogel, issued an *Official Handbook of New Zealand* in 1875; New South Wales issued its first yearbook, *The Wealth and Progress of New South Wales*, in 1887. From 1890 New South Wales statistician T. A. Coghlan produced an Australasian version, *A Statistical Account of the Seven Colonies of Australasia*, which after federation was renamed (in 1902–04) *A Statistical Account of Australia and New Zealand*. As modern societies, the Tasman world elevated the status of the male breadwinner, with the statisticians agreeing in 1890 to a new occupational classification that separated breadwinners from dependants, and relegated a large number of wives to the 'dependent' category.[32]

The Tasman world was also 'born suburban' and demanded a new type of urban environment.[33] Reformers shared innovations in town planning: driven by imperialism and evangelical reform, the influence of the British garden cities and town planning movement traversed imperial networks in the early 20th century. Charles Compton Reade, an 'Anglophilic New Zealand journalist' and self-trained planner, proved a key conduit.[34] Initially accompanied by English-man William Davige, Reade conducted a grand 16-month 'Australasian Tour', beginning with a lecture in Auckland on 6 July 1914 and continuing across Australia to late 1915. On the way he delivered numerous lectures and advised state and local governments, before finally ending up as government town planner in Adelaide. Before he left Australia in 1920 Reade was instrumental in initiating the South Australian Town Planning and Development Act 1920, which established a department to monitor and develop suburban plans and com-munities. Other planning enthusiasts were connected across the Tasman through venues such as the Australian planning conference in 1918.[35]

New Zealand and the Australian states shared health and social policy innovations throughout the 20th century, with influence flowing back and forth across the Tasman. The infant welfare movement represented an international response to health transition in the developed world, and the Plunket Society (named for the New Zealand Governor's wife), established in Dunedin in 1907, was widely studied in Australia and elsewhere. After leaving New Zealand Lady Plunket summoned its founder, Dr Frederic Truby King, to Britain during the First World War, and her sister, Lady Munro Ferguson, the wife of the Australian Governor-General, invited Truby King to Australia on his way home in 1919.[36] Health reformers in the eastern states were interested in the Plunket Society's appeal to well-to-do women and called for the establishment of similar organisations in Australia.[37] In the wake of the First World War New Zealand became the model for infant welfare – to varying degrees in different states – especially for positions of Director of Infant Welfare in Victoria, New South Wales and Queensland in the 1920s. But some Australian doctors dismissed Plunket and its devotees as a 'religious cult'.[38] Australian preschool child health and welfare initiatives to promote all-round child development in turn influenced

New Zealand, with visits to Australia in the 1930s and 1940s. Plunket New Zealand's car child restraint programme in the early 1980s was 'copied in several parts of Australia, and in England and Scotland', while 24-hour phone services in South Australia and Western Australia provided the model for Plunketline, which was launched in 1994.[39]

Good relations in occupational health between health officials in Sydney and Wellington in the 1950s and 1960s led to invitations for New Zealanders to have observer status at the National Health and Medical Research Council's Industrial Hygiene Committee meetings in Australia. After attending a meeting in Sydney in July 1965, Dr J. F. Copplestone, Assistant Director of Public Health in the New Zealand Department of Health, reflected: 'The two-way exchange is of undoubted assistance to both sides and I find that our point of view is now being sought. This is the result of regular attendance at these meetings.'[40] Anti-tobacco policies in both countries in the late 20th century, including legislation and anti-smoking campaigns, were extensively shared. New Zealand Department of Health officials visited Australia in the 1980s, while the Victorian Tobacco Act 1987 inspired similar legislation in New Zealand.[41] Repeated health restructuring in the New Zealand 'reform laboratory' during the 1980s and 1990s provided some lessons for Australia on how *not* to carry out health reform, as Australian Minister of Health Tony Abbott noted in 2005.[42]

Parallel patterns of transplant or copying are discernible in case law. From the interwar years, encouraged by a shortage of resources, New Zealand judges paid more attention to Australian sources. The number of Australian citations – always dominant from the 1870s to the 1970s – shot up in the depression, making another leap in the 1960s. The volume of citations showed that Australian law 'had a different position in the use of precedent in the New Zealand courts', while the count of cited Australian cases confirmed the impact that Australian case law had on the development of New Zealand law.[43]

The great depression

During the depression, economic ties strengthened between Britain and the dominions with the beginning of the Sterling Bloc in 1931 and through the agreements made at the imperial Ottawa conference in 1932, when Britain abandoned free trade for a system of preferential tariffs ('imperial preference'). Although the great depression in the Tasman world, and particularly in New Zealand, lacked the severity experienced in the northern hemisphere, the stresses of the era prompted the southern dominions to cooperate, sometimes presenting joint policy positions to the imperial authorities in London, such as in debates over shipping lines.[44]

The depression era again saw a period of state experiments for Labo(u)r parties. In some cases the parties diverged. Under Labor Prime Minister Scullin the Australian federal government's continued reliance on the protective devices of the 'wage earners' welfare state' from 1929, its failure to deal with the difficulties of the depression, commitment to the orthodoxy of neoclassical economics, targeted welfare measures and its defeat in 1931 all provided a lesson for New Zealand's first Labour government, elected in 1935. As Bennett argues, Scullin's policy failures were a factor in the move away from economic orthodoxy and the adoption of the universal provisions contained in the New Zealand Social Security Act 1938, which introduced universal health care, free maternity care, means-tested pensions, universal superannuation and the unemployment benefit, as well as increasing other welfare payments. For a while this legislation established New Zealand as a welfare leader. It reflected American influences, but also important were British experts who visited New Zealand in 1936 and advised on superannuation and a national health scheme after a similar visit to Australia.[45] Additionally, New Zealand policy-makers studied the Australian superannuation scheme.[46] Measures unsuccessfully sought by Labor in Australia, such as a central reserve bank, were introduced in New Zealand, where Labour converted the Reserve Bank – established in 1934 – to 100 per cent public ownership.[47] The Australian Reserve Bank Act 1959 separated Reserve Bank functions from Commonwealth savings bank functions.

The policies of the New Zealand Labour Party and its financial and social reform attracted considerable attention and discussion in Australia, although this interest did not always lead to policy change. Labour's financial policies allowed cheaper credit for housing and public works, although its main contribution was to subsidise public housing. In 1939 both sides of faction-ridden Australian Labor appealed to New Zealand examples, which assisted a Labor victory in a New South Wales by-election.[48] When the Tasmanian Labor Treasurer visited New Zealand in 1939 he claimed 'a real and quite unique affinity between New Zealand and Tasmanian Labor parties'.[49] Both parties shared a fleeting dalliance with Douglas ideas of 'social credit'. New Zealand Labour provided examples for Labor parties across Australia well into the 1940s, from education spending and racial issues to price stabilisation schemes and the end of wartime rationing. As Davis notes, 'Australian Labor politicians were distinctly less coy than Australian historians in tacitly accepting the existence of an Australasian identity'.[50] New Zealand Labour also provided negative lessons for Australia, such as over the potential for tension between 'socialist' and other aims of the Australian Labor Party. In 1941 the Western Australian Minister of Health rejected an item that urged 'full hospital and medical attention' as in New Zealand, on the basis that it was irrelevant to the Western Australian experience and would scare away doctors from the state.[51] Queensland's Labor government, on the other hand, copied the New Zealand model of free public hospital care.[52]

War and postwar

During the Second World War most democracies centralised their economies and imposed price, wage and other controls, often with great success, and

Australia and New Zealand were no different. The war and the success of planning proved for many that the state could provide a vital and positive role in the economy, while Keynesian economics provided a theoretical justification.[53] Both central Labo(u)r governments declared their postwar commitment to full employment,[54] reflecting an international consensus that macroeconomic variables could be manipulated to realise this aim.[55] Full employment was to be achieved within the system of fixed exchange rates and Sterling Area capital controls (New Zealand introduced some capital controls in 1938) and the Bretton Woods Agreement from 1958 when sterling became convertible. New Zealand remained sceptical about the Bretton Woods institutions and did not join the International Monetary Fund (IMF) until 1961; Australia joined in 1947.[56] The New Zealand Labour government nationalised the Bank of New Zealand in 1945 and the internal air services in 1946; but the High Court defeated the Australian Labor government's attempt to nationalise private banks in 1948. Both Labo(u)r parties were swept from office by national elections in 1949. An era of conservative government lasted until the election of short-lived Labo(u)r governments in 1972, apart from a brief Labour interlude in New Zealand between 1957 and 1960.

In the 1950s, when politicians and public worthies were preoccupied with the effects of mass media (American) culture on young people, New Zealand authorities looked across the Tasman for how to control 'pernicious literature'. By that they meant glossy magazines, comics and cheap paperbacks, often American in origin, printed under licence in Australia. New Zealand's Mazengarb committee, set up by the Holland National government in 1954, followed an inter-state conference held in Australia in 1953 to tackle the 'comic book menace', and the ensuing legislation. The Mazengarb committee and the New Zealand Indecent Publications Amendment Act 1954 copied sections from South Australia's legislation of December 1953, Victoria's Police Offences (Obscene Publications) Act 1954, and Queensland's Objectionable Literature Act 1954. By such means, the Australian states mediated the effects on New Zealand of postwar American culture and its youthful appeal.[57]

The postwar era, maligned as an era of stagnation and over-regulation by economists spouting the fashionable market liberal economics of the 1980s and 1990s, was in fact a period of reasonable prosperity, low unemployment and some liberalisation.[58] Both countries expressed alarm at Britain's first attempt to join the European Economic Community (EEC) in 1961, although Australia was not as economically tied to the British market as New Zealand was.[59] Both resented Britain for subsidising its domestic agriculture and for not preventing dumping of food by non-Commonwealth countries.[60] Australia renegotiated the Ottawa Agreement in 1956 and both New Zealand and Australia gradually moved from a dependence on Britain as a source of imports, exports and capital, well before Britain's successful membership application to the EEC in 1973. The change in focus was accompanied by some relative decline from the heights of prosperity of the mid-20th century, but this decline was gradual and occurred against the background of rapid, unprecedented economic recovery and a technological 'catch-up' by the rest of the Organisation for Economic Cooperation and Development (OECD) in the 1950s and 1960s, with Australia above and New Zealand at the average OECD per capita GDP in 1984.[61]

The New Zealand Australia Free Trade Agreement (NAFTA) was signed in 1965, but subsequent events showed it to be a bit of a misnomer (Chapter 5), and haggling over trade protection continued.[62] Some of the stranger shared traditions unwound, such as six o'clock closing (where pubs closed at 6pm), which was finally abolished in South Australia and New Zealand in 1967. Both countries experimented with policy settings in the face of the economic difficulties and stagflation of the 1970s and early 1980s.[63] Australia fought long and hard over trade liberalisation in the 1960s. The Whitlam Labor government cut tariffs by 25 per cent in July 1973 but in the face of economic difficulties introduced further import protection in the form of quantitative controls. The Fraser government, despite rhetoric otherwise, shied away from large reductions in protection and actually increased protective measures in some areas.[64] New Zealand reduced its reliance on import licensing (a quantitative import control); by 1981 import licensing covered only 18 per cent of New Zealand imports, compared with 75 per cent in the mid-1960s. Gradual trade liberalisation proceeded, although as Prime Minister Robert Muldoon observed in 1979, progress 'has been disappointingly slow'.[65] Governments undertook financial liberalisation and other reforms, albeit in a manner that seemed slow and tentative, and often inconsistent, by the standards of the late 1980s and 1990s.[66]

Economic reform and policy convergence

A period of rapid economic liberalisation in the 1980s and 1990s replaced the moderate, stop-start liberalisation of the postwar era. Initially, under ostensibly social democratic Labo(u)r governments elected in Australia in 1983 and in New Zealand in 1984, both countries adopted a broad range of policies that drew on then fashionable neoclassical economics and neo-liberal thought. Changes included floating the exchange rate; extensive liberalisation of financial, capital and other markets; reduced trade protection; fiscal restraint and monetary deflation; changes to the machinery of government; corporatisation and sale of some government assets; and broadening the tax base. Changes to industrial relations frameworks included the development of an incomes policy through the Accord in Australia, and radical liberalisation of the labour market in New Zealand. As in the 1890s and 1930s, the Tasman world became a centre of attention for its 'state experiments'.[67]

Both periods of reform drew on international trends, particularly the growing influence of market liberal ideas in the economics discipline and in the Anglo-American policy world. Similarities between the economic developments in the two countries are therefore unsurprising. There were direct links: New Zealand officials visited Australia to examine the float of the Australian dollar in December 1983 before floating the New Zealand dollar in March 1985. (They had done the same before introducing decimal currency in the 1960s.) The Australian Secretary to the Treasury, John Stone, a noted and occasionally forceful advocate of economic liberalisation, visited New Zealand. The Australian Campbell Report on financial liberalisation, published in 1981, influenced New Zealand financial reform.[68] There was also some sharing of people. Roger Kerr, from 1986 chief executive of the New Zealand Business Roundtable, worked for the Australian Commonwealth Industry Commission (also known for its hard-line stance) for three months from late 1984 to 1985. He later employed former Industry Commission officials in the Business Roundtable. Australian and New Zealand Treasury officials negotiated a staff exchange under what became CER in the early 1980s. Networks were also formed indirectly. A number of senior Australian and New Zealand officials, many influential in the reforms of the 1980s and 1990s, were seconded to international organisations such as the OECD, IMF and World Bank. These organisations, many of which had a strong neo-liberal agenda, were important influences on policy directions and significant avenues for consensus building among international policy elites.[69] Similarly, neo-liberal think tanks, again with interweaving memberships, provided important avenues for consensus building. For example, strong links formed between the Centre for Independent Studies in Sydney and New Zealand policy and business leaders, with former New Zealand Finance Minister Ruth Richardson (1990–93) a board member, and former State Services Commissioner Roderick Deane a frequent visitor and board member. There was also a short-lived attempt to establish a New Zealand-based Centre for Independent Studies.

While sharing similarities, the periods of economic reform in Australia and New Zealand from 1983 to 1994 were also different in a number of ways. In New Zealand reformers imposed rapid economic policy changes, sometimes in the face of public opposition, often in secret and despite explicit election promises to the contrary. In Australia the Labor government introduced a more gradual process of change. Skilful at building and maintaining support for the new policy directions, the Hawke government cajoled and used the symbols and rhetoric of consensus, and incorporated key interest groups in policy-making. Australia's economic reforms also lacked the ideological and theoretical purity of New Zealand's reforms. This difference in outlook was particularly evident in the Accord, the corporatist-type arrangement between the Australian Council of Trade Unions and the federal government that survived eight incarnations from 1983 to 1996.[70] The divergence in the labour market grew pronounced after the introduction of New Zealand's Employment Contracts Act 1991, which introduced a radical system of individual contracts in employment, overturning the state sponsorship and regulation of labour that had lasted since the late 19th century. As in the 1940s, the radicalism of some of the New Zealand reforms provided negative lessons. As Davis notes, 'New Zealand GST and industrial legislation was used, with some success by Paul Keating in 1993, to show reluctant Labor voters in Australia the dire consequences of a local Liberal–Country Party government.'[71]

Despite Australia's successful period of reform and significantly stronger economic performance from the mid-1980s, which created a trans-Tasman performance gap, New Zealand's reforms remained a model for some policy and business elites.[72] The 'purity' of the reforms, their comprehensiveness and their derivation from (then) cutting-edge neoclassical economics continued to be attractive.[73] From the mid-1990s, and after the election of the federal Coalition government in Australia in 1996, there was further convergence. The New Zealand Fiscal Responsibility Act 1994 required the government to formulate and report its fiscal policy objectives to parliament and how it would meet them. With some divergences, this act provided a model for the Australian Charter of Budget Honesty Act 1998.[74] Australian parliamentary select committees discussed the New Zealand model at length, with submissions by such luminaries as the former New Zealand Treasury Secretary Graham Scott and Ruth Richardson, the self-proclaimed originator of the New Zealand act.[75] The Commonwealth National Commission of Audit of 1996 recommended legislation along New Zealand lines.[76] International organisations such as the OECD promulgated similar moves for best practice.[77] The IMF saw New Zealand's act as the 'benchmark piece of legislation'.[78] The so-called $8 billion 'Black Hole' budget deficit left by the outgoing Labor government in 1996 provided the necessary impetus and language of crisis.

Australian states also adopted fiscal responsibility legislation in the Victorian Financial Management Act 1994, the Queensland Charter of Social and Fiscal Responsibility Act 2004, the New South Wales Fiscal Responsibility Act 2005 and the Western Australian Financial Responsibility Act 2000, all of which showed remarkable similarities to the New Zealand statute. The Commonwealth adopted a goods and services tax (GST), so the Labor opposition claimed that GST in New Zealand had led to problems with 'losers out of this tax package . . . As we saw in New Zealand, it was the compensation package that went quickly out the back door'.[79] Public management showed some convergence, including the adoption of accrual accounting in 1999, and a greater focus on 'outputs' for government goods and services, with New Zealand models cited in discussion.[80]

In 2005 the Howard government passed legislation amending the Workplace Relations Act 1996 so that it moved Australia closer to the model of industrial relations established in New Zealand by the radical anti-union Employment Contracts Act 1991, including the latter's focus on individual contracts. This policy was transferred across the Tasman, even though the

Employment Contracts Act was associated with falling productivity growth and was replaced in 2000 by the more moderate Employment Relations Act.[81] New Zealand examples were used in parliamentary debates both to support and to attack the new bill.[82] Western Australia had already introduced similar legislation. The greater economic success of Australia since the mid-1980s is often cited to support greater economic liberalisation and tax cuts in New Zealand. Such arguments are ironic given that the Australian economic reforms were less doctrinaire than New Zealand's, and that divergence from Australian economic performance largely followed the reforms of the late 1980s and 1990s.[83]

Possibly the most dramatic policy transfer was between Victoria and New Zealand in the early 1990s. New Zealand's state-sector reforms along 'New Public Management' lines are often cited as exemplars.[84] But few jurisdictions adopted them to the extent that Victoria did. Introduced following the election of the Victorian Liberal government in October 1992, these reforms borrowed heavily from the New Zealand model in regard to privatisation, corporatisation, fiscal responsibility, reporting requirements, managerialism and individual contracting in employment, even to the extent of copying the titles and large sections of New Zealand statutes. Just six days after the election, the process of transfer had begun when the Victorian premier initiated a Commission of Audit. Its subsequent report drew clear parallels between the economic climates in Victoria and New Zealand. A number of key policy entrepreneurs, consultants and innovators from New Zealand were recruited into the Victorian public service. Visits of Victorian ministers and officials to New Zealand were common, while New Zealand policy entrepreneurs also visited Melbourne. Think tanks provided another important link. Writings and books from New Zealand were important, as were New Public Management tracts.[85] It was not only the content of legislation that was borrowed from New Zealand. The 'crash through' approach to reform – where policies where introduced in large packages with little discussion or debate – was also evident in their introduction in Victoria.[86]

The most fundamental trans-Tasman policy convergence occurred after CER was established in 1983. This agreement promoted the increasing harmonisation and coordination of policy, as well as the mutual recognition of each other's different regulatory and legislative regimes, and increasing talk of a single market, with all the convergence and harmonisation of law that implies. Mechanisms for cooperation multiplied, from joint committees to regular ministerial meetings. A host of trans-Tasman memoranda and agreements appeared. In 1986 New Zealand adopted competition law that reflected Australian examples, and in 1988 a protocol eliminated the application of anti-dumping laws.

The Trans-Tasman Mutual Recognition Arrangement (TTMRA), signed in 1996 and activated in 1998, is another example of a mechanism that emerged through CER. It allows any goods legally sold in one country to be sold in the other. Any person registered to practise an occupation in one jurisdiction may register to practise in the other without further tests or examinations. The aim was to allow goods and people to meet one set, rather than two or more sets of standards. Doctors are the exception (in this case specialist medical colleges perform the gatekeeping). In 2000 the two countries approved a Memorandum of Understanding on the Coordination of Business Law, updating an earlier 1988 memo, which a ministerial forum affirmed in 2003. Ministers signed the Open Skies Agreement, confirming a single aviation market, in 2002. In 2004 a Trans-Tasman Accounting Standards Group was established, with representatives from various accounting agencies, professional groups, the Australian Treasury and the New Zealand Ministry of Economic Development, to establish similar accounting standards. In February 2005 New Zealand Finance Minister Michael Cullen and Australian Treasurer Peter Costello endorsed the Australian Productivity Commission's recommendation to integrate further the countries' competition and consumer regimes. In 2006 there were further moves towards mutual recognition and the harmonisation of banking regulation, consumer regulation, business taxation and securities law, as well as towards coordinating the New Zealand Reserve Bank and the Australian Prudential Regulation Authority 'especially in times of financial crisis'. A common currency is not ruled out as integration proceeds; nor is a common border for customs and quarantine.

A new Tasman settlement?

The Tasman world's historical ties, cultural and institutional similarities, and strong social and organisational links provide a field for sharing policy innovations, lessons, successes and failures. A common British and Westminster heritage assists this process. But there is more to the trans-Tasman traffic in ideas and policies than a shared British history. New Zealand's small size, lack of institutional density, and relative lack of checks and balances in the political system make it comparatively easy for governments to experiment with rapid policy change. Indeed, the notion of New Zealand as a social laboratory – particularly in the 1890s, 1930s and 1980s – is ingrained in national myth. It taps into the insecurities of a small nation on the edge of the planet as somehow leading the world, despite its insignificance in terms of both economic might and political power. But this notion is also occasionally accepted elsewhere: sometimes explicitly by Australia, where New Zealand's similarities provide a test case that is as close as is possible outside a controlled laboratory environment.

New Zealand policy innovations therefore provide a cognitive shortcut for Australian policy-makers. Similarly, the different jurisdictions of the Australian states and territories provide lessons for New Zealand policy-makers, as does the Commonwealth of Australia. It is easy to look – and fly – across the Tasman in either direction to find solutions to similar problems. Again, insecurities make New Zealand policy innovators keen to promote their new solutions, and there are certainly financial incentives to sell themselves as consultants.

This borrowing is not simply a problem-solving activity. Reforms may appeal for ideological reasons, despite their questionable success in practice. Ironically, New Zealand's neo-liberal reforms of the 1980s and 1990s remained an exemplar for some Australian elites, despite the greater success of the more moderate Australian reforms and, in the case of the Employment Contracts Act 1991, despite its abandonment by New Zealand. The New Zealand Labour Party's dalliance with social credit monetary policies in the 1930s attracted attention – both positive and negative – across the Tasman well after Labour had jettisoned them. The Keating Labor government used New Zealand examples to demonise GST and other proposals of the Hewson Liberal Party in the 1993 election, despite Paul Keating's advocacy of a GST system akin to New Zealand's in the mid-1980s. Failures can also provide useful policy lessons: the limited success of the Scullin Labor government provided examples for New Zealand's Savage Labour government from 1935. Similarly, the shambolic, ill-considered New Zealand health reforms of the 1980s and 1990s supplied examples of what *not* to do in Australia. In the 1930s the Australian 'left' envied the relative lack of institutional constraints on executive power in New Zealand, which allowed a Labour government to implement its social agenda without the delays imposed by a federal government, the complexities of a federal system and the constraints of a written constitution. In the 1980s and 1990s the left reassessed the value of checks and balances on an executive, as successive Labour and National governments implemented radical neo-liberal policies in New Zealand, while more complex and constrained Australia pursued a more moderate programme of economic liberalisation. Australia and New Zealand have sometimes competed to be seen as the most orthodox of countries undertaking neo-liberal reform.[87]

Policy success and failure, of course, are political and social constructs. People on different sides of a debate have often pointed to and/or misrepresented Australia (or New Zealand or another state) to support quite different conclusions. Examples range from compulsory arbitration debates in Western Australia in the late 19th and early 20th centuries, and the reforms of the 1930s and 1940s, to each country's restructuring of the 1980s and 1990s, public-sector reforms in Victoria, and debates about the Australian Work Choices legislation, which contributed to the Howard government's demise in 2007.[88]

Mechanisms of policy transfer are myriad and multi-layered. They have included inter-colonial and imperial conferences; professional conferences and meetings; social and family networks; the interchange of personnel ranging from prime ministers and other politicians to bureaucrats, consultants, business elites, and policy activists and entrepreneurs. Visits from political leaders at state and federal level to and fro across the Tasman have been common and regular since the mid-19th century, and have increased with improvements in the technology of transport and communications, especially since air replaced sea travel. Documents and legislation have flowed across the Tasman. Formal structures have facilitated other links. Joint investigations superseded inter-colonial conferences and commissions in the late 20th century. Examples include the joint reviews of trans-Tasman shipping by the New Zealand Ministry of Transport and the Australian Bureau of Transport Economics in 1978, 1980 and 1987, and the large number of inter-governmental and other committees related to CER and harmonisation issues. New Zealand has long been committed to the 'habit of consultation' with Australia; by the late 1980s its representatives participated in over 20 standing committees of federal and state ministers, and meetings between select committees of the respective parliaments.[89]

Importantly, the Council of Australian Governments (COAG), established in 1992, led to the development of a number of inter-governmental agreements and consequent legislation by the six states, the two territories, the Australian Commonwealth and New Zealand. By 2002 New Zealand was a member of, or observer on, 24 of the 49 ministerial councils and associated committees, which cover a wide field of policy.[90] Because decision-making about the Trans-Tasman Mutual Recognition Arrangement is given to COAG ministerial councils, the responsible New Zealand minister has voting rights where issues impact on the TTMRA; with observer status otherwise. Ministerial Councils usually meet annually or biannually – although there may be extraordinary meetings – and will often meet in conjunction with other related ministerial consultative bodies. Much business is carried out through correspondence. Meetings of officials – in some cases chief executives of relevant departments – support the councils at a senior level. Usually these officials meet before the ministerial conferences, although they may have separate meetings and meet more regularly. Supporting the ministerial meetings are secretariats, which are usually located in various Australian government agencies, at both federal and state level, although some are independent. These secretariats are often jointly funded by the various governments involved. In 1996 Australia and New Zealand agreed to develop a joint food standards system and agency, and Food Standards Australia and New Zealand now approves standards in both countries. CER and harmonisation, or coordination, have prompted increasing policy convergence; in many cases New Zealand, as the junior partner in COAG and CER, has adopted Australian models.

The closeness of New Zealand and Australian policy-makers, facilitated through such mechanisms as COAG, the various committees on harmonisation, and the exchange of officials, is possibly exceptional. Indeed, the information sharing goes well beyond formal links. Friendships and high levels of trust exist between policy-makers. Even policy papers at draft level are shared across jurisdictions.[91]

Relationships between political leaders have varied through time, but were warm between the New Zealand and Australian 'Progressives' of the 1890s, between Liberal prime ministers Richard Seddon and Alfred Deakin at the beginning of the 20th century (Chapter 5), the Labo(u)r parties of the 1930s, and wartime and postwar Labo(u)r governments. Party affiliation has not always assisted the closeness of the relationship. Conservative prime ministers Robert Muldoon (1975–84) and Malcolm Fraser (1975–83) were not seen to be close; nor were Labour's David Lange (1984–88) and Labor's Bob Hawke (1983–92). Conversely, the relationship was close between New Zealand Labour Prime Minister Helen Clark (1999–) and Liberal John Howard (1996–2007), who met annually in bilateral talks, as well as regularly through the Pacific Islands Forum, APEC meetings and Commonwealth Heads of Government Meetings. At times the closest – and most effective – relationships were between the Australian deputy prime minister and New Zealand's deputy or prime minister: between John McEwen and Jack Marshall in the 1960s, and Doug Anthony and Robert Muldoon in the late 1970s and early 1980s (Chapter 5). The two treasurers/ finance ministers also meet regularly, and historically have developed warm relationships. Australian and New Zealand policy elites often presented a united face to the world: from common positions on shipping to London, to similar views on the World Trade Organisation (WTO)/United Nations committees and trade liberalisation, to similar approaches to 'governance' and aid issues in the South Pacific, including the recent *Pacific Plan*.[92]

Institutional similarities, social networks and the interchange of people also assisted the most basic method of policy transfer between the two countries: copying. Copying, of course, is a useful cognitive shortcut, 'the simplest type of lesson drawing,'[93] particularly in times of constraint and urgency brought on by crisis – whether this crisis is real, perceived or created – as in the 1890s, the 1930s, and the 1980s and 1990s. Copying also legitimises; someone else has deemed it appropriate to introduce these policies. As the Australian press enthused about New Zealand's infant welfare scheme in 1919, the Plunket system was 'tested and proved.'[94] Australians and New Zealanders have had ready access to each other's laws and practices. That a neighbouring country with strong institutional and cultural similarities developed a law or practice bestows greater confidence that it will be relevant. Similar approaches are often followed in the English-speaking 'family of nations.'[95] The people who created the law or policy are also accessible. This simple policy transfer has been evident frequently from the 19th century, with copying of parts of the compulsory arbitration legislation in the 1890s, health reforms in the 1920s and 1930s, and public management reforms in the 1990s.

At the beginning of the 21st century copying remained a popular policy option. But the push for a single market changed the context. Rather than a useful cognitive shortcut adopted in times of alleged crisis for ideological or problem-solving reasons, copying was now in part an outcome of the increasing policy coordination and convergence that itself was partly an outcome of CER, but also of political will. Copying had become a form of 'coercive' policy transfer where the exigencies of economic integration drove convergence. In the late 19th century New Zealand provided much of what Kelly termed (incorrectly) the 'Australian settlement'. New Zealand was again an influential innovator in the 1930s and 1980s–90s. In the early 21st century New Zealand increasingly took a back seat in policy innovation, where 'harmonisation' and 'mutual recognition' obliged it to adopt the policies, particularly commercial ones, of its richer and more powerful neighbour.[96] There might increasingly be a new antipodean 'settlement', but it is more and more of Australia's making.

CHAPTER FIVE

Trading Places

Philippa Mein Smith

For New Zealand the cornerstone of relations with Australia is the economic relationship, which has grown closer since the implementation of the Australia New Zealand Closer Economic Relations Trade Agreement (CER), which came into force on 1 January 1983. The key principles of simplicity and comprehensiveness – everything was included unless specifically excluded – made CER a success, and encouraged integration of the Tasman economies to the point that a single economic market entered the political agenda at the beginning of the 21st century. Why, then, was it not until the 1980s that Australia and New Zealand reached a free trade agreement, given that New Zealand and South Australia aspired to such an agreement in 1895, and in 1901 New Zealand preferred the prospect of a reciprocal treaty to federation? Within a framework of global shifts across the 20th century, this chapter examines the people, institutions and beliefs that shaped the course of trade ties between New Zealand and Australia, in search of a deeper understanding of how and why the Tasman world resurfaced with globalisation.

Trade and doing business were dominant in trans-Tasman flows in the 19th century, though ties with Britain, the cataclysm and carnage of two world wars and the associated ideological and financial upheavals of the 20th century limited the scope of trade relations. More than in other spheres, trade made the Tasman world a southern realm of the British world until the Second World War. The usual story told in New Zealand history is that trade access to Britain plunged with her entry to the European Economic Community (EEC) in 1973, before Tasman economic relations could regain their 19th-century prominence. The Tasman economies diverged from the 1880s once the new technology of refrigeration allowed the export of frozen meat and dairy products. Consequently their rivalry for British market share grew, fostered by the economic dependency of settler capitalism.[1]

The goal of reciprocity
To unravel the puzzle of why the two neighbours took so long to achieve a free trade agreement, this chapter argues that it is necessary to look beyond differences

to consider long-run aspirations and continuities. We need to balance the shifts in trade flows induced by global forces with an awareness of local ambitions and hopes for a community of interest in trade, or a 'community of purpose'. The most serious gap in the history of trans-Tasman trade relations is the story of the long-run aspiration to 'reciprocity' by New Zealand in trade relations with Australia. The world economy thwarted this ambition until the Second World War through the dominance of trade ties with Britain, and quarantine decisions affected by the US. A major finding of this research is that the persistence of 'reciprocity' as the common-sense goal for New Zealand and Australia in the late 19th century and across the 20th century made a path towards CER. That persistence of belief about what was sensible, practical and of mutual benefit provided a path-dependent explanation for closer economic relations once world events allowed.

The history of the quest for reciprocity in trade began in 1870 when New Zealand passed the Colonial Reciprocity Act to gain the power to make reciprocal agreements with the Australian colonies, but this first attempt to create an Australasian trade bloc did not receive British approval.[2] Not for the last time would colonial ambitions be checked, with regional interests obliged to defer to the British national interest and the overarching imperial strategy of free trade. In 1895 the Liberal government in New Zealand tried again with the Customs Duties Reciprocity Act, which ratified a proposed agreement with South Australia. Although opposed by the Colonial Office, the statute received royal assent. Local developments proved the stumbling block: protectionist Victoria thwarted the initiative in light of the federal movement in the Australian colonies, which mooted an Australian common market. New Zealand Premier Richard Seddon tried to re-open negotiations in Adelaide in 1897 with his Liberal counterpart Charles Kingston, the South Australian premier. But Kingston deferred any deal because of the forthcoming federal convention, even though he favoured a treaty; his priority was to implement the idea of a new Australia.[3]

New Zealand's decision to stay out of the federation created in 1901 unsurprisingly soured the Australian perspective on reciprocity. Chapter 1 noted Sir John Hall's view of what the choice of a separate destiny meant for future relations with Australia: 'That does not prevent the existence of a community of interests between us.'[4] The New Zealand Federation Commission in 1901 thought the same. Seddon's Liberal government asked the commissioners to inquire, after the event, into whether New Zealand should become a state of Australia and, if the conclusion was that she should not, then 'to inquire and report as to the establishment of a reciprocal treaty'; if the 'latter course' was 'more desirable', the commissioners were to suggest the basis of such an agreement.[5] The commissioners recommended that if New Zealand favoured the (British) policy of free trade then she should stay a separate colony. Although the commission believed a reciprocal treaty would be mutually beneficial and likely to materialise in the future, it was 'not hopeful' of one 'at the present time'.[6] Effectively the new asymmetry of size and power between Australia and New Zealand trumped reciprocity because the Australian Constitution handed trade relations – tariff and customs issues – to the federal government.

'King Dick' Seddon aspired to grander things: no less than a 'British zollverein'. Introducing the Preferential and Reciprocal Trade Bill in 1903 he asked Parliament: 'Are you prepared to make a trade preference and a distinction between your own blood, your own kindred in the Empire, and alien nations?'[7] 'Reciprocity' complemented the idea of family (demonstrated in Chapter 3). Australian federation, however, threw up a fresh issue for New Zealand. The Commonwealth of Australia granted preference to Britain but not to the dominions, whereas New Zealand granted preference to both parties. Correspondingly, New Zealand *Year-books* distinguished between 'British countries' and 'foreign countries'. By this logic Australia was family, whereas the US was 'foreign'.[8] Consequently New Zealand goods entering Australia were subjected to 'general' and 'foreign' tariff rates, but Australian goods entering New Zealand were charged British or 'family' rates. The Australian protectionist policy accentuated these differences; New Zealand was not similarly protectionist until 1938.

Undeterred, Seddon sought 'closer touch with Australia' and advocated a reciprocal treaty on his final visit in 1906.[9] While in Melbourne he drafted a trade agreement with Alfred Deakin, the Australian Liberal Prime Minister, which aimed for a balance in trans-Tasman trade, and would have admitted fish, fruit and hay (fuel for horses) duty free, and imposed lower duties on some goods such as dairy products, timber and potatoes.[10] This proposal proved to be Seddon's last, and came to nothing because he died on the way home. Instead New Zealand sent a trade representative to Melbourne and opened a government agency in Sydney in 1906. Along with an agent in South Africa from 1904 – in the aftermath of the Boer War – these were New Zealand's only overseas posts outside the High Commissioner's office in London, until a trade commissioner was appointed to Canada and the United States in 1929.[11] Sydney rather than Melbourne became the principal Australian office from 1930 once the federal government set up home in the purpose-built bush capital of Canberra. Australia finally appointed an Australian trade representative to New Zealand, R. Nesbitt, in 1933.

New Zealand customs officials sought tariff reciprocity with Australia right up to the Second World War. By 1921 New Zealand manufacturers wanted Australian goods put on the 'foreign' tariff to persuade Australia to negotiate, and to limit competition.[12] The New Zealand government responded in December 1921 by withdrawing preferential tariff treatment from Australia. According to Keith Sinclair, New Zealand was unhappy with the Australian attitude to reciprocity, with the trans-Tasman trade imbalance, and with the effect of Australian competition on New Zealand industry, especially boot manufacturing. The Australian tariff of 1921 proved the 'final straw'.[13] The tariff – part of the Australian policy regime of 'Protection All Round' – prompted the first step toward reciprocity. This step was the Australia and New Zealand trade agreement of April 1922: the first such agreement between the two countries, by which each granted the other its British preferential tariff, except on certain goods (54 of 129 specified items). Appropriately for two British dominions, reciprocity was defined on a British basis, and led to lower duties on many items of food, clothing, floor rugs and agricultural implements. The exception was hops, put on a higher tariff because of lobbying from the Tasmanian hop industry. New Zealand secured the free entry of undressed timber to Australia, a development suggestive of the future, as we shall see.[14]

Restrictions between the wars

The problem of quarantine created a new stumbling block for trade between the wars. Sinclair focused on the squabbles over fruit and vegetables – which were disputes over quarantine – driven by his interest in nationalism and point-scoring.[15] More relevant to this book are the persistent efforts to cooperate made by New Zealand and the federal and state governments in Australia when faced with a menacing external environment. In this context, what were the quarantine rows about? First, in the wake of the First World War, Australia imposed restrictions on New Zealand potatoes in 1919 because of worries about powdery scab.[16] More famously, Australia placed a quarantine embargo on New Zealand apples and pears because of fire blight in 1924. That apple ban is still in place. At the time it was first imposed, the ban applied not just to New Zealand apples but also to apples from Canada and the US. Then in 1927 Australia raised the tariff on dairy products to protect dairy farmers. The 30 per cent tariff on his milk mixtures for bottle-fed babies motivated Sir Frederic Truby King to open a Karitane Products Society factory in Sydney; the factory failed in the 1930s and with it Truby King's plans to convert Australia to his feeding formulae.

New Zealand retaliated in 1932 by imposing a quarantine embargo on Australian fruit and vegetables because of fruit fly. Again the United States influenced this response because New Zealand wanted to export apples and pears to the US, and the US agreed to this trade provided New Zealand did not admit fruit or vegetables from any country where Mediterranean fruit fly was present (i.e. Australia). Through the 1930s the trans-Tasman spat settled into a tit-for-tat issue of apples versus oranges.

The path to resolve the dispute, however, was through potatoes. New Zealand Prime Minister Michael Joseph Savage was anxious to preserve the trade relationship but wanted to revise it in 1937. He announced he would compromise if the Australian Prime Minister, Joe Lyons, would go some way to meet him about the embargo on New Zealand potatoes. Lyons refused.

Ashley W. Smith, *New Zealand Shipping Gazette*, 13 July 2002.
DX-023-230, Alexander Turnbull Library, Wellington, courtesy of Ashley Smith

Australian interest groups sided with Savage: these groups ranged from New South Wales citrus growers who had exported mandarins to New Zealand for 50 years, to branches of the Australian Labor Party and the Communist Party, the unemployed, and women's guilds and housewives' associations keen to buy cheaper New Zealand potatoes. Savage was reported in the *Age* in January 1939 as saying that 'the position bordered on the stupid'. New Zealand was prepared to straighten out the whole thing.[17]

Potatoes are a symbol of the Tasman world's everyday 'no frills' quality: a counter to apples, which illustrate the rivalry in the relationship. The potato is yet another humble illustration of a common European culture possessed by the Tasman countries. In regional trade terms the potato tells a story of prolonged efforts at cooperation. It did not appear to be assisting cooperation when Australia reimposed the potato embargo in 1927, directed by the Director-General of Health, Dr J. H. L. Cumpston, who oversaw Australia's strict quarantine policy. This time, though, the Sydney Chamber of Commerce and the Housewives' Progressive Association were among the protesters against the embargo.[18] A conference of Australasian scientists in 1934 recommended that powdery scab be removed from the list of diseases justifying prohibition because of developments in biological knowledge, and that Australia resume imports of New Zealand potatoes. (Mycologist Dr G. H. Cunningham represented New Zealand at the conference.)[19] Unsurprisingly, the embargo took a long time to resolve. Representations by New South Wales premiers helped – with the exception of Labor Premier Jack Lang, who wanted New Zealand potatoes prohibited. After numerous prime ministerial exchanges through the 1920s and

1930s the ban on potatoes was eventually sorted by Prime Ministers Savage, Lyons and Robert Menzies when there was a more important issue at stake: war. The federal Cabinet approved the import of New Zealand potatoes in July 1940. The periodic embargoes did not end with the Second World War, but New Zealand exported potatoes to eastern Australia into the 1960s.[20]

A little digging in the archives also discloses that the disputes over fruit and vegetables were not merely national but inter-state. Each Australian state possessed the power to prohibit imports on quarantine grounds. Victoria, for example, did not just exclude New Zealand potatoes because of powdery scab: it banned Tasmanian potatoes in 1933 for the same reason. Tasmanian growers may have balked at New Zealand imports but shoppers had other ideas. Fishmongers insisted that Kiwi potatoes were an essential ingredient of Sydney fish and chips, and the president of the Federated Association of Australian Housewives wrote to the Prime Minister of New Zealand in 1939 to agitate for New Zealand potatoes.[21] A removal of the trans-Tasman embargo, however, had implications for inter-state embargoes.[22] This potential flow-on effect shows how the Tasman world operated beneath the level of the nation, between New Zealand and the eastern states, and how engagement with New Zealand obliged adjustments to the federal system in Australia.

The Tasman relationship was still seen as important between the wars, though in the more specific details New Zealand and Australia did not feel the same way. Joe Lyons explained to angry potato growers in 1933 that he was keen to 'restore some of the confidence in Australia that has been lost in the minds of the people of New Zealand': he wanted a 'better relationship between the two Dominions', and increased trans-Tasman trade.[23] So did Australian Senator Sir Walter Massy Greene, who visited Wellington in 1933 as part of a review of Australian trade in the wake of the imperial economic conference in Ottawa in 1932. Massy Greene thought Australians should be sympathetic to New Zealand difficulties, and emphasised that Australia's trade with New Zealand was 'so valuable' and could 'become so much more valuable' that Australia ought not to do anything that might jeopardise it. He opposed 'official antipathies, backed up by popular clamour', as a 'definite danger'.[24] For example, Australia shared New Zealand anxieties that Britain might impose a quota on butter from the dominions and import more European butter instead.

The agreements in Ottawa about preference for dominion products in British markets and vice versa obliged a revised trade agreement between New Zealand and Australia in 1933. Australian representatives at Ottawa made the case for a community of interest, stating that Australia had a 'community of interest with other Dominions' when submitting requests for British preference for certain goods.[25] This position reflected how trade relationships with Britain were still the most important. As with the trans-Tasman trade agreement in 1922, the revised agreement of 1933 derived its terms from those primary British relation-

NO SILVER LINING
Trevor Lloyd, c. 1933.
B-115-011, NZ Cartoon Archive, Alexander Turnbull Library, Wellington

ships. It was ushered through not by the prime ministers, who were responsible for those primary relationships, but by Massy Greene, head of the Australian trade delegation, and the New Zealand Finance and Customs Minister and former Prime Minister, J. G. (Gordon) Coates. The agreement fixed the anomaly whereby New Zealand goods entering Australia were subjected to higher rates than Australian goods entering New Zealand. But Australia was better able to take advantage of British preferential tariffs because of its stronger manufacturing sector. Manufacturing was also protected in Australia in a way it was not in New Zealand until the Labour reforms (import licensing) of December 1938, which were introduced to boost London funds and secure a home market for local secondary industry.[26]

War and postwar cooperation

The Second World War was the stimulus that propelled New Zealand and Australia together from the 1940s, despite their divergent responses to war in the Pacific. The demands of the postwar world shifted the superpower mantle from Britain to the United States and forged a new international order. Then as now, the role of individuals was important in building bilateral relations, and momentum grew when Australians looked sideways to New Zealand. A key player for the next generation was John McEwen, the future Australian Country Party leader. As Minister of External Affairs in August 1940, McEwen expressed the view: 'The interests of Australia and New Zealand are identical in many matters at present,' especially in Asia and the Pacific.[27] He sought machinery for trans-Tasman consultation, such as the high commissions that ensued in Wellington and Canberra in 1943. Once installed as New Zealand High Commissioner, Carl Berendsen duly reported to Wellington the words of Australian Labor Minister of External Affairs Dr H. V. Evatt: 'Australia and New Zealand simply must stick together especially in relation to Pacific postwar policy.'[28] Stick together they did, for example in according 'seventh-state status' to New Zealand in the allocation of Australian products critical to the war effort, such as steel and machinery; here 'was cross-Tasman cooperation in action on the ground, and really working'.[29]

Evatt followed up with the innovative Australian–New Zealand Agreement of January 1944 (the Canberra or Anzac Pact). This treaty is significant because Australia and New Zealand alone signed the agreement, and did not inform Britain until afterwards.[30] Nor did the neighbours consult other governments with Pacific interests, including the United States, because they had not been consulted themselves about the Cairo Declaration of December 1943 in which Churchill, Roosevelt and Chiang Kai-shek outlined their plans to carve up the Japanese empire. The agreement in Canberra may be read as a demand to participate in the armistice and to have a voice in South Pacific affairs as self-governing members of the British Commonwealth. Above all, Australia and New Zealand wanted their collective voice heard by their American ally, who had separated them into Southwest and South Pacific zones in the war against Japan, and emerged victorious as the dominant power in the Pacific. If there were to be a new order in the region, they did not want the US to set the terms in what they perceived as their realm, south of the equator.

At the conference where the prime ministers signed the pact in January 1944, New Zealand's Labour Prime Minister, Peter Fraser, spoke of the 'bonds of kinship and neighbourhood, of common interest and common ideals', and the 'spirit of Anzac' felt strongly in wartime. Australia's Prime Minister, John Curtin, mindful of the test of war, hoped the two would translate 'community of interest into practical conclusions under as many heads as possible'.[31] Remembered for its commitment to a 'regional zone of defence', the pact none-theless expressed economic aims to consult over the development of commerce and industry and 'in agreed cases' to pursue 'joint planning'.[32] Junior officials appointed to an Australia–New Zealand secretariat commenced informal daily contact through high commission channels in February 1944, while Miss J. R. McKenzie at the New Zealand High Commission was a key conduit through whom Australians sent postwar reconstruction material to Wellington.[33]

This joint planning on postwar reconstruction did happen, as far as external constraints and personal proclivities allowed. It began with a visit by Senator R. V. Keane, Australia's Minister of Trade and Customs, in June 1944 to strengthen the trade relationship.[34] In January 1945 economic discussions followed in Wellington among postwar luminaries B. C. Ashwin, New Zealand Treasury Secretary; L. C. (Leicester) Webb, New Zealand's Director of Stabilisation and later Professor of Political Science at the Australian National University (ANU); and J. G. Crawford, Research Director of Australia's Department of Post-War Reconstruction, who became Professor of Economics and Vice-Chancellor of the ANU.[35] Looking ahead, these were much like CER discussions, with similar-sized teams of officials. The two countries also set up subcommittees to study employment and the development of trans-Tasman trade. While the New Zealanders were more concerned about the impact of proposals for joint planning of industrial development on relationships with Britain, both negotiating teams agreed that they needed to act jointly to oppose agricultural protectionism by the US. Both were committed to full employment, which implied high consumption and therefore demand for imports.[36]

Motivated by the idea of coordinating postwar development, Ben Chifley, the Australian Labor Prime Minister, called on his New Zealand counterpart, Peter Fraser, in December 1947. The meeting was informal because Fraser was in hospital and was in his dressing-gown when he saw Chifley. Chifley himself was on holiday. In fact it was while travelling through the central North Island that he was struck by the plantations of exotic forests and the potential for Australia to obtain pulp and paper from New Zealand. On his way back to the aerodrome he asked Ashwin if New Zealand would be interested in a long-term project to supply Australia, and the Treasury Secretary advised that the New Zealand government was considering establishing a newsprint industry. Chifley also thought New Zealand might exchange timber for steel. He asked whether New Zealand intended establishing an aluminium smelter, thinking it might be sound economics for Australia to obtain water from New Zealand and manufacture in Australia.[37]

In February 1948 Bob Semple, Minister of Works, duly visited Australia to seek preference for New Zealand in the export of steel products, and advised Chifley of national plans to develop forestry to supply Australia with timber, pulp and newsprint. He told Chifley how New Zealand was developing the port of Tauranga, a timber town – Murupara, and a mill.[38] The Murupara project was a joint venture involving the government, big business – Fletchers – and a British multinational to earn export revenue from the radiata pine forests planted on the North Island's volcanic interior plateau. At the time the project was the largest industrial development ever undertaken in New Zealand, and it struggled financially until the 1960s.[39] That this ambitious project depended on Canberra's goodwill to succeed is strong evidence of a Tasman world in postwar development, at least in forestry. Without Australian cooperation New Zealand would not have built a forest products industry on such a scale, based on the joint venture of the suitably named Tasman Pulp and Paper Company. At the same time, the links with Australia had repercussions in New Zealand. They stoked power struggles among government departments about management of trade issues, as well as ideological disputes over public or private development of New Zealand's forestry industry. Chifley was keen on a proposal from Australian Newsprint Mills (ANM, a Murdoch company) that ANM and New Zealand Forest Products Ltd should combine in a joint trans-Tasman enterprise at another timber town, Tokoroa, to produce newsprint.[40] The outcome was that Tasman Pulp and Paper supplied Australian Newsprint Mills while

The first Holden car assembled in New Zealand, General Motors, Petone, Lower Hutt, April 1957.

F-177231-1/2, Morrie Hill Collection, Alexander Turnbull Library, Wellington

Forest Products developed to meet the needs of the New Zealand market.

Efforts to coordinate economic development continued apace. In December 1948 Dr H. C. Coombs, the new Governor of the Commonwealth Bank, visited New Zealand; in April 1949 Ashwin visited Australia.[41] All levels of government agreed that officials should meet regularly. Ashwin found that Australian Treasury officials were thinking on the same lines of long-term cooperation to rationalise industry rather than any immediate trade agreement.[42] Economic discussions in November 1949 in Wellington traversed broad issues of timber and paper pulp; steel; New Zealand import licensing, which gave preference to Britain; the General Agreement on Tariffs and Trade (Gatt); Britain's economic collaboration with Europe; and the dollar problem faced by members of the Sterling Area. New Zealand needed US dollars to import motor vehicles to satisfy the demand for American tractors and American-type cars. Both Australia and New Zealand hoped that development of the Australian motor industry might solve this problem, with Australia supplying the desired American-style cars.[43] Thus New Zealand began to import Australian Holden cars – and assemble them from 1957.

Towards a limited free trade area

The transition from Labo(u)r to conservative governments on both sides of the Tasman from the end of 1949 did not alter the tenor of trade relations. The

Prime Minister in New Zealand's new National government, S. G. Holland, also visited eastern Australia for six weeks in 1949 to investigate political and economic issues. Sid Holland had a personal interest: his brother was a jeweller in Adelaide, and a trip to Australia during the war convinced him that Australia and New Zealand should cooperate on postwar reconstruction.[44] The Liberal Prime Minister of Australia, R. G. Menzies, similarly visited New Zealand in August 1950 to establish personal contact and to exchange views on common problems. Menzies asserted that the big problem for Australia – second only to the Korean crisis – was the constraint imposed by trade in sterling on postwar development plans.[45] At the state luncheon for Menzies, Holland described the two leaders as 'close personal friends'. Peter Fraser added that Menzies 'has been our friend for a long time' (Fraser had met Menzies in London during the Manchurian crisis of the early 1930s). The conservative prime ministers invoked the spirit of the Canberra Pact and the interdependence of the 'British world'.[46]

Holland and Menzies, with John McEwen, the Australian Trade Minister, reached a trade understanding in Canberra in March 1956.[47] By this time the changed context in Australia, as well as internationally, obliged new terms. Australia had a new, more vigorous Department of Trade in 1956; a new minister, McEwen; and, like New Zealand, balance of payments problems.[48] The last of these conditions affected imports of Tasman Pulp and Paper Co. Ltd newsprint, which had been entering Australia on the basis of an informal ministerial understanding (the import concessions were on the quiet because they contravened Gatt). Henceforth McEwen drove the discussions. The leader of the Australian Country Party from 1958, McEwen was a former soldier-settler and dairy farmer who largely held together the Liberal–Country Party coalition under Menzies in the 1950s and 1960s. He was dubbed 'Black Jack' by Menzies, and the sobriquet aptly captured his often gloomy look and mood. A towering figure in stature and personality, McEwen was a formidable negotiator; he always knew what he wanted to achieve, yet could see the other side's point of view.[49] In his trans-Tasman talks McEwen emphasised that Australia's rapid industrial development made it practical to expect New Zealand to buy more equipment from Australia, saving dollars, while this purchasing deal would give Australia more overseas funds to pay for the exports (such as pulp and paper) that New Zealand sought. To avoid difficulties with Gatt, McEwen and Holland used the term trade 'arrangement' rather than 'agreement', under which New Zealand obtained additional import licences for two years, in return for buying more cars.[50] Later that year, in November 1956, McEwen renegotiated the Ottawa Agreement so that Australia could develop trade relations with Japan. The British started negotiating only after McEwen stated bluntly that the Australians 'would sooner have no treaty at all than one as unbalanced as the existing arrangements'.[51] Thanks, too, to McEwen's efforts, Australia signed an agreement with Japan in 1957, with the result that Japan emerged as Australia's major trading partner from the 1960s.

In New Zealand by 1958 the short-lived Labour government faced a severe balance of payments crisis, which prompted M. J. Moriarty, the Assistant Secretary of Industries and Commerce, to decide the time was right for a complete review of trans-Tasman trade. The Canberra Pact advocated closer ties but was 'prejudiced by Gatt'.[52] Moriarty favoured a free trade area to help prepare New Zealand for a changed world, should Britain succeed in its bid to join the EEC, in which case he thought Britain had little ground for objecting to a trans-Tasman agreement. New Zealand and Australian trade officials met in Wellington and set up two working parties to look at trans-Tasman trade and investment issues, but without result.[53]

At this point the major obstacles to – and the motive for – closer ties were international, revolving around the European common agricultural policy and Britain's moves to join the EEC, and Gatt's shortcomings from the dominions' perspective; issues pondered by Tasman trade officials in Canberra in May 1960. Characteristically they swapped papers to assist discussion.[54] In the five years 1955–59 only 4 per cent of New Zealand's exports went to Australia (New Zealand's fourth-biggest export market), but 17 per cent of New Zealand imports came from Australia, which made Australia New Zealand's second import market after Britain. Already by the late 1950s New Zealand had become Australia's biggest single market for manufactured goods, and was Australia's sixth market overall – parallel to its position 50 years later. In August 1960 'Black Jack' McEwen visited New Zealand for trade talks with Labour ministers. McEwen stressed that he would do what he could to expand New Zealand exports to Australia because 'there was much to be gained from binding the links between the two countries'. Australia was driven to manufacturing because of its development policy, which made the New Zealand market important. He also suggested a 'parallel approach' in negotiating with Britain.[55] As a result the ministers decided they should work together on common problems, and agreed to establish an Australia–New Zealand Consultative Committee on Trade to foster increased trade between the two countries and collaborate on overseas trade issues, especially Britain's entry to the EEC.[56]

New Zealand's National government had been in office only a few days in December 1960 when McEwen invited John Marshall, the Deputy Prime Minister and Minister of Overseas Trade, to the first ministerial meeting of the Australia–New Zealand Consultative Committee on Trade in February 1961. As a result, Marshall and McEwen became close personal friends.[57] The McEwen–Marshall partnership was strategically significant because Prime Minister Keith Holyoake valued Tasman ministerial exchanges as a means to help manage the changing structure of national development and international trade.[58] It had personal significance because 'McEwen had few very close friends'.[59] The friendship between McEwen and Marshall proved pivotal to achieving the New Zealand–Australia Free Trade Agreement (NAFTA) of 1965, and allowed them to drive the agreement through. Marshall 'soon discovered that [McEwen] said what he meant and meant what he said'.[60] Marshall recalled how the Australian Prime Minister, Menzies, who was not part of the discussions, was more interested in talking about cricket.

Both countries were preoccupied with the French veto on Britain's first bid to join the EEC in 1961, when General de Gaulle 'slammed the door in Britain's face'. Holyoake welcomed the respite; meanwhile in the Tasman world officials held trade talks in 1962.[61] By the time of the second ministerial meeting of the consultative committee in April 1963 the trend had become obvious that, though New Zealand exports to Australia were steady, at a mere 4 per cent of New Zealand's total exports, Australian imports were on the rise to over 20 per cent of New Zealand's imports because New Zealand was the main market for Australian manufactured goods including base metals, petroleum products and motor vehicles.[62] The Holyoake Cabinet decided that New Zealand would seek a free trade community for forest products.[63] Marshall's meeting with McEwen was 'forthright but friendly'. But the New Zealand proposal for free trade in forest products was unacceptable to Australia, just as the Australian counter-proposal for a wider free trade agreement was unacceptable to New Zealand. A joint standing committee was established to resolve the impasse, and to

New Zealand Prime Minister Keith Holyoake, Australian Deputy Prime Minister John McEwen, and New Zealand Deputy Prime Minister John (Jack) Marshall, February 1967.
AAQT 6401 A82716, Archives New Zealand, Wellington

submit proposals for free trade in forest products and other items 'suitable for inclusion in a free trade arrangement, either from the outset or subsequently'.[64] The joint standing committee of officials met intensively every four to six weeks in Canberra and Wellington for the next year, producing the first draft of an agreement that addressed the two basic principles of mutual growth and mutual advantage. McEwen and Marshall also met informally at conferences in London, Geneva and Asia.

In April 1964 – one year and six meetings later – the officials produced a 72-page report on the scope for a free trade area, including a draft agreement.[65] At this point Dr W. B. Sutch intervened. Sutch was Secretary of Industries and Commerce in New Zealand, an historian and an economic nationalist, known for his advocacy of protection and his nationalist histories. He demanded that the negotiations be postponed.[66] Others believed that the case for free trade in forest products had become compelling. New Zealand's High Commissioner urged the government to consider the arguments for a limited free trade area not simply in trans-Tasman terms 'but in the context of New Zealand's economic development during the next decade'.[67] All the relevant departmental heads apart from Sutch agreed.[68] The negotiations proceeded; but to achieve NAFTA the National government had to oust Sutch. By September 1964 he had gone. Thereafter Sutch published books that denounced New Zealand attitudes as still colonial in relation to Britain, and by the 1960s to Australia. He believed that the expansion of the Australian manufacturing industry would hurt New Zealand, which would be hollowed out. For Sutch, Australia was not family but 'foreign': he warned that overseas ownership and control of national enterprises was increasingly Australian and that NAFTA would encourage this process.[69]

With Sutch gone, Marshall suggested a compromise: a limited free trade area.[70] By 1965 that idea had urgency because Tasman Pulp and Paper's Murupara project was responsible for 50 per cent of New Zealand's exports of manufactured products and 45 per cent of total exports to Australia. In July 1965 officials 'hammered out' a final draft agreement before Marshall travelled to Canberra where, at a ministerial meeting in August, he concluded the treaty with McEwen. Marshall recalled that, supported by their officials, they settled outstanding issues by 'hard bargaining softened by a spirit of friendly frankness and a willingness on both sides to make concessions'.[71] McEwen's statement to the Australian House of Representatives on 17 August 1965 that the respective governments had confirmed the agreement displayed his singular directness. First he distinguished between a free trade area, where each country could maintain separate tariffs, and a customs union. He explained that the agreement covered 60 per cent of total trade between the two countries, that he considered this coverage met Gatt requirements for a free trade area to cover 'substantially all of the trade' between partners, and that the bulk of the items included – notably timber, pulp and paper – were already traded duty free. McEwen saw NAFTA as 'an historic landmark' in trade relations. Although immediate results would not be spectacular, he expected the agreement to have 'far-reaching long-term effects' on growth and development.[72] He was right. Already, in 1965, the aim was not only to develop the bilateral relationship but also – as business leaders reiterated 40 years later – to create a Tasman base for exporting to the world because the Tasman market was too small.

Association under NAFTA

NAFTA, signed on 31 August 1965 and in force from 1 January 1966, was not a free trade agreement; by incorporating the 1933 Australia–New Zealand trade agreement it preserved the British preferential system. On top of the old preferences the negotiators added 'Schedule A', a list of duty-free products. First came food items such as frozen vegetables, citrus fruit, dried fruit and wheat, which were part of the Tasman world's common culture of cooking and eating. The most important goods to New Zealand, however, were forest products; to Australia, manufactures. Schedule A reads as a reflection of modern life. The range of goods included asbestos, petroleum oils, zinc, iron and other oxides (including titanium), vitamins, antibiotics, paint, film, chemical products, travel goods, wood, pulp, paper and paperboard, books, newspapers and magazines, music, plans and drawings, fabrics, glassware, nails, gold, railway tracks, aluminium articles, articles of iron and steel, hand tools, coffee mills, mincers, gas turbine and jet engines, knives, forks and spoons, locks and padlocks, all sorts of plant and machinery, sewing machines, typewriters, taps, cocks and valves, electrical goods, lenses, tanks and armoured fighting vehicles, tractors, surveying equipment, drawing instruments, medical instruments, clocks, bombs, grenades, pianos and gym equipment, buttons, pencils and postage stamps.[73] But this range did not yet include cars, unlike the Canada–US auto pact of 1965; nor did it include whiteware for modern kitchens, which New Zealand wanted added to Schedule A from 1970.

Schedule A, viewed in perspective, reflected both the contemporary ambition for economic growth and development and the limits imposed by the reality that the Tasman economies were based on exporting primary products to other parts of the world, principally to Britain and (in Australia's case) to Japan. Only from the 1960s did the composition of Australia's exports change from pastoral products to minerals, including coal, as the dominant staple. The agreement was necessarily cautious and defensive because of the resistance to bilateral agreements mounted through Gatt by Britain and the US.[74] McEwen led the Gatt talks in London in October 1965, while Moriarty and Australian officials travelled to Geneva in November 1965 to assuage American concerns. Moriarty was as direct as McEwen: Australia and New Zealand as agricultural exporters were denied most of the advantages of Gatt membership because other countries used loopholes or 'open evasion' to escape their obligations; bilateral relations were much more effective for expanding trade.[75]

Economists generally agree that NAFTA made no difference to trade patterns or that its effect was 'slight'.[76] P. J. Lloyd, a New Zealander who migrated to Australia in 1969 and became Professor of Economics at the University of Melbourne, thought the agreement showed that 'trade in commodity groups produced on both sides of the Tasman could be freed without threatening the existence of the industry in one country'.[77] The agreement's significance proved to lie elsewhere. Politically and socially NAFTA was a turning point because of the bonds of association it engendered; it was a 'milestone' in trans-Tasman cooperation.[78] The agreement exerted an impact through the trans-Tasman networks established by the two governments, which obliged a parallel business response. NAFTA set the pattern whereby trade ministers met at least once a year, and officials twice, supplemented by special subcommittees and working parties, as well as phone calls and consultations between the high commissions and the bureaucracy. The private sector began to consult under the NAFTA umbrella, including the manufacturers, and firms came into closer contact. Growers set up a pea and bean panel in 1968, the governments a sawmilling products panel in 1971, and the dairy industries a joint committee on dairy products.[79] Australia and New Zealand also began to collaborate more internationally, for example in the Gatt Kennedy Round. The frequency of contacts – formal and informal – intensified.

By 1970 the two prime ministers, Keith Holyoake and John Gorton, could contemplate a 'Tasman Partnership' statement. Both were searching for a new language of national community, and that extended to a trans-Tasman community of interests. In the Tasman Partnership statement of 5 June 1970 the prime ministers invoked the 'community of purpose' that inspired the partners in all their dealings. According to their statement's rhetoric, they believed that the two countries had to 'nurture the full strength of this spirit' as they 'face[d] up to the challenges of a rapidly changing world' and collaborated in the 'wider search for peace and security' and to improve international relations. Gorton and Holyoake looked back to the voyages of Captain James Cook, prompted by the Cook bicentenary, with gestures to Gallipoli and the Second World War. Since Cook, the 'logic of history and the realities of political and economic geography' suggested that Australia and New Zealand should 'act in close concert'. To 'fulfil the vocation of nationhood' demanded no less.[80] Holyoake spent a week visiting the east coast of Australia. He also attended the inauguration ceremony for the New Zealand High Commission building in Canberra (opened in 1972), and paid a flying visit while in Victoria to the McEwens' farm at Stanhope.[81]

Although both countries were diversifying, Britain's return to Europe compelled a rethink of trade policies based on dominant staples. Australia, rich in mineral wealth, was concerned that New Zealand stay prosperous, while New Zealand had little alternative but to cultivate closer ties with Australia. In January 1973 the new Labo(u)r prime ministers, Gough Whitlam and Norman

Kirk, met in Wellington just as Britain joined the EEC and the Bretton Woods financial system came to an end. Whitlam and Kirk reaffirmed the principles of the Canberra Pact, as well as agreeing to consult on matters of joint interest, particularly in the South Pacific, and to meet informally at least once a year for an overall review of Tasman relations. Whitlam also suggested that permanent heads of the prime ministers' and foreign affairs departments meet every three or four months.[82] The rupture with Britain also obliged Australia and New Zealand to reconsider the British preferences embedded in NAFTA, so the Labo(u)r governments guaranteed tariff preferences in each other's markets until 1976, with a view to free trade in the longer term.[83]

Already the agreement had become bogged in detail. Ministers and officials found themselves trapped in nightmarish discussions about peas and beans and leather wallets, which proved a powerful learning experience: both positive – in terms of what to do better in the future; and negative – in terms of what to avoid. Seeking a focus on broader issues at ministerial meetings in 1975, Whitlam suggested that the agreement should 'perhaps be subjected to a new hard look on a "clean sheet of paper" basis'.[84] With CER this was precisely the approach taken.

The path to CER

Studies of the era presided over by Robert Muldoon, New Zealand's Prime Minister and Minister of Finance in the National government (1975–84), are problematic because the literature is highly politicised. Much is bedevilled by the neo-liberal agenda of Rogernomics. Routinely Muldoon is portrayed as an arch-regulator and king pin of a command economy who could not have been responsible for what is widely praised as the world's most successful and comprehensive free trade agreement. Conventional wisdom is that CER came into existence despite rather than because of Muldoon, who was not much interested.[85] Insider accounts claim that Muldoon went 'too slowly', confounding the efforts of innovators to deregulate.[86] Muldoon's memoirs equally need to be read with care. Yet archival sources back Muldoon, revealing him to be a consistent supporter of CER negotiations and a crucial participant in decision-making; they suggest that given the political realities, including election cycles, CER could not have happened any faster.[87] In *My Way* (1981) Muldoon described the exercise as 'a good example of cooperation', and predicted a closer relationship with 'our closest friends' and 'neighbours'. He believed that CER would increase trans-Tasman trade to the extent that a single economic market was 'logical' and 'inevitable'.[88]

CER was largely the result of a partnership between Muldoon and Doug Anthony, McEwen's protégé and successor as Deputy Prime Minister of Australia in a Liberal–National Country Party coalition (the Country Party changed its name to the National Country Party in 1975 and to the National Party of

New Zealand Prime Minister Robert Muldoon and Australian Prime Minister Malcolm Fraser, March 1980.
AAQT 6401 R8260, Archives New Zealand, Wellington

Australia in 1982). As Australia's Deputy Prime Minister and New Zealand's Prime Minister respectively, Anthony and Muldoon performed a double act just like their predecessors, McEwen and Marshall, and it was Muldoon and Anthony who signed the formal Heads of Agreement on 14 December 1982. Anthony later admitted that he got on well with Muldoon, whom he 'quite liked . . . in the end'.[89] Other trans-Tasman partnerships were also important to the development of CER, as between the New Zealand Deputy Prime Minister and Australian Liberal Prime Minister, Brian Talboys and Malcolm Fraser, during the late 1970s. These trans-Tasman pairings of respective prime ministers and their deputies were less newsworthy than the public image of the one-upmanship engaged in by the prime ministers, which Gerald Hensley aptly described as a 'cartoon contest between the lofty, rather ponderous Fraser and the stumpy, quick-witted Muldoon'.[90] But the lower-profile pairings were much more effective.

It was Brian Talboys who, as Minister of Foreign Affairs and Overseas Trade, prepared the ground for CER when he travelled to Australia for three weeks in March 1978 to demonstrate how he valued trans-Tasman relations rather than took them for granted. If the press focused on the monumental Colin McCahon word painting *Victory over Death 2*, which Talboys presented to the National Gallery of Australia, politicians were impressed that he made an extended visit. Talboys' achievement was the landmark Nareen Statement of March 1978, named after Fraser's rural property in Victoria, which became the policy statement for CER and declared that the two countries would collaborate on working for a larger and fairer world trade system. Journalist Colin James correctly predicted that the Nareen declaration would 'probably be seen by historians as a turning point.'[91] Related events were Talboys' speeches in 1977 and 1978 that 'the time had come for New Zealand to recognise that our relations with Australia are more important to us than our links with any other country in the world', which impressed Australian listeners.[92]

Following Nareen, New Zealand officials began informal discussions with their counterparts in Canberra. A number of trends motivated them: business attitudes were shifting with the restructuring of capital from industry to finance; manufacturers were shifting to export markets; and the Iranian Revolution intruded a shock to oil prices, the second since 1974. In April 1979 Anthony, as Australia's Minister for Trade and Resources, assumed the initiative. He recalled that he and his head of department, Jim Scully, were on their way home from the Gatt Tokyo Round en route to New Zealand for annual NAFTA talks. Steeled by the persistent failure to reduce European and American agricultural subsidies, he balked at the trivia that cluttered the agenda for the trade meeting in Wellington. The New Zealanders sought tariff reductions on wallets, taps and cocks, and frozen peas (Fred Turnovsky, a wallet manufacturer, constantly lobbied Muldoon). The Australians advanced a list of improved quotas into New Zealand. Anthony asked Scully why he was going to Wellington and relished the 'Yes Minister' response from Scully: 'Well, Minister, it's on the program.'[93] Anthony and Scully could not change the agenda of the talks so they floated the idea of CER. At the NAFTA ministerial meeting on 10 April Anthony expressed concern about New Zealand's economic problems, stating: 'Let's be frank – temperate agricultural producers are in for a rough time. We've got to hold hands.' Just as business leaders had got together, governments should 'ask where we go from here'.[94]

That idea needed Muldoon's backing and at a hastily arranged meeting with Anthony the next morning Muldoon surprised his officials by agreeing with Anthony in principle about the need for fresh thinking about closer economic relations. He said he would put the issue before Cabinet and directed the head of the Prime Minister's Department, Bernard Galvin, to put his advisory group of young talent to work 'straight away'.[95] Amidst the flurry of ensuing studies and trans-Tasman meetings, New Zealand officials met informally with John Stone, the Australian Treasury Secretary, to try to fathom what Anthony meant by his proposal. Stone advised the New Zealanders not to be too analytical and that both Fraser and Anthony were thinking in general terms.[96] Muldoon was definitely not moving slowly at this stage; he wanted concrete proposals to put to the Australians as soon as possible when his advisers thought that proposals would take at least a year to prepare properly. Any 'going slowly' resulted from a split in the bureaucracy between the cautious sector-by-sector approach favoured by Trade and Industry officials and the broad-brush approach of Dr Graham Scott in the Prime Minister's Department. Scott was an influential advocate of deregulation who presided over the Rogernomics reforms as Assistant Secretary to the New Zealand Treasury (from 1979) and as Treasury Secretary from November 1986. While the Department of Trade and Industry did not oppose trade liberalisation, its minister, Lance Adams-Schneider, resisted the more radical concept of a free trade area because of worries about whether New Zealand industries would survive.

Aware that the National government would have to sell CER to the electorate, officials carefully worded their advocacy of globalisation. Fourteen Australian and New Zealand permanent heads conferred at joint trans-Tasman meetings in Wellington in November 1979, and again in Canberra in February 1980.[97] Tim Groser, then Muldoon's foreign affairs adviser, summed up progress by mid-1980: the CER exercise had produced a 'huge volume of paperwork', its own language and 'some results too'.[98] Muldoon, Fraser and senior officials reached the core of the future CER agreement in March when the prime ministers issued a joint communiqué in which they agreed that it was 'timely for Australia and New Zealand to take the special relationship between them a step further'.[99] That step, and the agreement's hub, was gradual trade liberalisation, which demanded a restructuring of the New Zealand economy.

Applying the vocabulary of globalisation, the prime ministers endorsed the basic principles of the 'freest possible movement of goods between the two countries' and 'an outward-looking approach to trade', as well as the free movement of people and frequent consultation on issues of shared concern.[100] The objectives of CER extended not merely to trans-Tasman benefits but to building a stronger Tasman base from which to expand links with other countries. In contrast to NAFTA, CER addressed issues of access; in Groser's words, all goods were 'in' unless explicitly noted. Groser saw the exemptions list as the key. The Australian list could be short but would include all the items of most interest to New Zealand, such as cheese, whiteware and carpets. The main problem was the lack of a timetable, and the reason for this was political: the New Zealand and Australian elections were no longer synchronised, with an Australian election due late in 1980 and a New Zealand election in 1981.

Muldoon's caution at this stage is understandable. While he had settled the principles with Fraser and Anthony within a remarkably short timeframe, much work remained to be done on the details of a closer economic relationship, not least consulting interest groups such as manufacturers. Generally the New

UnCERtainty

Bill Paynter, 23 April 1982.

A-312-3-002, NZ Cartoon Archive, Alexander Turnbull Library, Wellington, courtesy of Bill Paynter

Zealand Manufacturers' Association and the Confederation of Australian Industry agreed that NAFTA no longer worked. They could support the concept of CER because major firms were increasingly manufacturing for export, and most of the increase in trans-Tasman trade was in this sector. The manufacturers' associations had met annually as a Tasman grouping since the 1960s, and at their meeting in September 1980 endorsed the idea of a closer relationship. They also established their own trans-Tasman working party. By December 1980 the Federated Farmers of New Zealand and the Australian National Farmers' Federation also supported CER.[101]

Trade negotiations are by definition slow, especially in primary produce, and by late 1980 the forces for CER had outpaced the officials' ability to achieve consensus on details. Momentum slowed because of three main unresolved issues, of which the first and foremost was access for New Zealand dairy products. Official talks had narrowed the gap between Australia and New Zealand, but for the gap to close, the governments had to show the necessary will and initiative. According to Hugh Templeton, who was New Zealand's Trade Minister from the end of 1981, Muldoon stalled because of the election, while the 1981 Springbok rugby tour of New Zealand angered Fraser; and the prime ministers agreed not to proceed with CER until 1982.[102] The archives disclose that from this point Anthony did the most work to resolve practical difficulties, while Muldoon deserves the most credit on the New Zealand side. In March 1981 Muldoon told the press he gave the chance of CER's success at 50:50. He wanted an agreement that he could sell, especially to the small New Zealand manufacturers who feared that they would go out of business. But he made clear to Anthony in May, as he had earlier to Fraser, that the New Zealand government 'did not share' New Zealand manufacturers' resistance.[103]

In April–May 1981 a delegation of five New Zealand politicians visited Australia where they met with Anthony and Fraser, after which Anthony returned to Wellington with officials in May to discuss the 'hard core' issues. As usual Anthony was 'forthright and positive' in his commitment to CER. He explained that he faced difficulties with the dairy industry and with persuading his Cabinet colleagues that New Zealand could not rapidly dismantle import licensing. Other factors were also affecting the 'atmosphere' around CER, namely the Springbok tour and Australia's introduction of passports for New Zealanders travelling across the Tasman.[104] It was significant for the eventual success of the agreement that Anthony and Muldoon were able to talk freely. In Wellington the two agreed that the outstanding issues were import licensing, wine, dairy products and, though they had 'come a long way', export incentives.[105] As one journalist observed of their May talks, 'Muldoon and Anthony cut through all the political friction over controversies like the Springbok tour and passports and moved with surprising speed through the comprehensive agenda that officials had drawn up'.[106] But Anthony warned that a date to end more than 40 years of import licensing had to be set or he would face more difficulty with his colleagues. A New Zealand mission to individual Australian states settled the issue of state government purchasing, about which Fraser let drop that 'anything the New Zealand Government could do to get the States off their "crazy" preferences system would be welcomed by the Commonwealth Government'.[107] By September, Fraser and Muldoon set March 1982 as the date for completing the agreement and 1 January 1983 for its implementation.

At this point Muldoon believed the Australians were stretching out the timetable for CER, and Fraser agreed that Australia was going slowly, one reason being the forthcoming New Zealand election. The hardest bargaining of all took place the year after the election, in 1982, when Anthony worked with Muldoon to resolve the impasse over when and how to end New Zealand import licensing and export incentives. Anthony warned that the Australians would not tolerate an end date for incentives beyond 1987, and in October put to Muldoon the tough, final, unresolved issues. He asked that export incentives be phased out not *from* but *in* 1985; import licensing had to be gone by 1988. He followed up with a critical meeting with Muldoon in Wellington on 28 October, where Muldoon agreed to the phasing out of export incentives: 50 per cent in 1985, 75 per cent in 1986, and totally in 1987. Discussion continued on import licensing.[108] Together Anthony and Muldoon achieved a breakthrough and sealed the CER agreement, signing the Heads of Agreement by video link on 14 December 1982.

Given the political realities, including election cycles, it is difficult to imagine how the two governments could have reached this landmark agreement more rapidly. Muldoon may not warrant the epithet of the 'architect' or 'builder' of CER, but he was the project manager. This is the role Gerald Hensley thought that Muldoon saw for himself: as a 'political manager'.[109] Muldoon was justified in believing that CER would ultimately be seen as one of his government's, and his, greatest achievements. In partnership with Anthony, he led in decision-making throughout the process, consistent with his belief in economic management on behalf of the people, and did not falter in his commitment to obtain a result. Muldoon consistently supported the negotiations that culminated in the free trade agreement that underwrites New Zealand's relations with Australia. His commitment was evident in what he did and in decision-making at critical moments rather than in what he said, particularly to the media. The only people Muldoon deliberately deceived were the press, and thereby the public at large. He did not deceive the Australian negotiators.

Circumstances in Australia rather than in New Zealand frequently dictated the pace of developments. They did so in 1982, when the Australian government needed time to allow consultation with interest groups, which had already occurred in New Zealand. Structurally the more complex, larger society ultimately determined the timing for the smaller partner, though local political realities contributed to the mix. Anthony and Muldoon performed a trans-Tasman double act. Through teamwork and good personal relations they achieved a remarkable deal that was timely and has endured. Muldoon deserves less credit than Anthony, who was the initiator and innovator at key moments. Yet each depended on the contribution of the other, and together they succeeded when the time was right.

Conclusion

From the archives a story emerges of the complex arrangements that preceded CER. To understand where New Zealand's cornerstone of relations with Australia came from requires shining a light on abiding aspirations and continuities. The enduring thread is the hope of achieving reciprocity in the relationship, and of creating a 'community of interests' or a 'community of purpose'. Such aims are based on common sense rather than on utopian ideals of creating an alternative modernity. Reciprocity was, and is, a commonsense goal, which lives on in the Trans-Tasman Mutual Recognition Arrangement, as we saw in Chapter 4, as well as in other policy areas, despite inequalities in power and scale. The archives reveal a persistence of belief that working together is of mutual benefit.

Reciprocity complements the idea of family as binding the Tasman world. History offers numerous examples of how engagement with New Zealand obliged Australia to contemplate adjustments to the federal system in order to

Bob Brockie, *National Business Review*, 1 November 1982.
DX-003-086, NZ Cartoon Archive, Alexander Turnbull Library, Wellington, courtesy of Bob Brockie

simplify relations among the states. Confronting the crisis of world war, Tasman prime ministers, to paraphrase Curtin, hastened to translate a community of interest into practical results. Their successors aspired to similar ideals. It has regularly seemed sensible for governments to plan for a Tasman basis from which to trade – and engage – with the world.

Circumstances, however, have to be in alignment to achieve success. NAFTA marked a turning point in the bonds of association in the 1960s. As the sun set on the British empire, Australia and New Zealand sought to foster postwar development by forging new connections with the emergent Pacific powers of the United States and Japan – and with each other. Trade with Britain dominated their export-led economies until Australia made the first turn to Japan in the changing environment of the 1950s. Under Trade Minister John McEwen, Australia struck a course between the British preferential system and the US-dominated system of postwar international economic order represented by Gatt. In the 'brave new world' of the 1960s Australia and New Zealand managed their own transformed circumstances in part by the creation of a limited free trade area.[110]

From there the pathway to CER, although shaped by external circumstances, depended on political leadership. CER was made possible by the hard work of officials as well as by strong political leadership and friendships on both sides of the Tasman, which led to creative partnerships such as between McEwen and Marshall, and Anthony and Muldoon. Their persistence and faith in reciprocity paid off.

CHAPTER SIX

Doing Business

Shaun Goldfinch

This chapter takes up one aspect of the Australia–New Zealand relationship to explore further: the shared business relationship. If government rhetoric is to be believed, the move to a single economic market may well be inexorable. Yet is there evidence of a 'trans-Tasman business world' that would facilitate such a market and make it more than simply a legislative artefact? Such a concept is highly amorphous, of course, and to test for the existence of a 'business world' we use a number of measures in this chapter.

First, we investigate whether there exists a shared 'business culture'. Its existence in itself would facilitate other aspects of business integration. Second, drawing on other chapters in this book, the degree of policy isomorphism is examined. This measure suggests the degree to which business practices and legal and other requirements are converging; as with cultural similarities, their convergence would further facilitate integration. Third, we investigate the existence of networks among business elites, including interlocking directorships and shared memberships of business and other associations. In tandem, we examine the existence of a trans-Tasman business elite: that is, is there a group of business executives who work on both sides of the Tasman? Anecdotal evidence suggests there is an abundance of successful business managers who are at home on either side, but is this impression confirmed by closer analysis? Finally, we examine the degree of cross-Tasman ownership of businesses.

To make these assessments we draw on interviews with business leaders and executives carried out in Auckland and Sydney, as well as published and primary material. Using a dataset developed by Nicholas Harrigan from the IBISWorld's 2000 Largest Enterprises in Australia, 7500 directors and executives of these corporations, *Who's Who in Australia* and *Who's Who in Australian Business*, and specialised software, we examine a number of social network links.[1] Through these investigations we find that there is indeed a trans-Tasman business world, and that such integration is likely to accelerate in the future.

The Bank of New South Wales building, Oamaru, c. 1885.
F-55305-1/2, Alexander Turnbull Library, Wellington

A trans-Tasman business culture

Is there a shared trans-Tasman business culture? Cultural differences (often linked to the term 'psychic difference') are often seen as a deterrent to foreign investment and other business engagement.[2] As a body of research shows, uncertainty about social and legal mores, levels of trust, tolerance and normalised corruption increases the risks – and stresses – of doing business. To rectify or reduce uncertainty requires the investment of resources, time and energy to understand and familiarise oneself with these differences. Even then, one may feel unease that deep-seated – and often unarticulated or unconscious – differences may never be fully understood. On the other hand, a shared culture, or cultural similarities, facilitates aspects of business integration. Over time, increasing business integration may itself reduce cultural differences, in a somewhat virtuous circle.[3]

There is considerable evidence of similarities in business culture between Australia and New Zealand. We can talk of three types of business culture: national culture, which applies to values and practices shared within national or state borders; organisational culture; and professional culture. To some extent these types overlap. To the outsider, Australians and New Zealanders are remarkably similar – albeit these nationalities are themselves contested – and various studies of culture confirm this likeness. In Hofstede's heavily cited studies

National Mutual Life Association of Australasia, on the corner of Customhouse Quay and Hunter Street, Wellington, n.d.
G-11638-1/2, Tyree Collection, Alexander Turnbull Library, Wellington

of business culture, Australia and New Zealand rank very closely. Hofstede based his original 1980 study on IBM surveys, which made it particularly useful for comparing business cultures.[4] The Globe Study of middle managers across 62 nations puts New Zealand and Australia in the 'Anglo cluster', which in this study includes the other usual suspects of Britain, the United States and Canada, plus South Africa and Ireland.[5] In the World Values Survey, New Zealand and Australia are again ranked very closely together in a group known as the Anglo or Anglo-American countries – Britain, Australia, the US, Canada and New Zealand. New Zealand often has a stronger focus on post-materialist values than Australia, but scores are very close on a number of other values.[6] Such studies are getting somewhat elderly, however (the New Zealand survey dates from 1998 and the Australian from 1995). There is also some dispute as to whether values change with time and age.[7] On measures of corruption – in this case by Transparency International – New Zealand and Australia are somewhat apart, with New Zealand ranked as least corrupt (along with Iceland and Norway) at an index score of 9.6, while Australia ranked ninth at 8.7. To sum up, on measures of culture – particularly ones based on surveys of actual business executives – New Zealand and Australia are extremely similar. Indeed, it is hard to find two countries that are more alike in cultural terms, which suggests that psychic distance between them is not great.

Although New Zealand and Australian cultures are strongly related on most measures, some Australians, and particularly some New Zealanders, may dispute the degree of cultural and value congruence; they are 'cousins' rather than 'brothers' in family terms. Certain shared myths and metaphors are as much part of the business culture as they are integral to the general culture of both countries. These myths include the defeat at Gallipoli commemorated by both nations; frontier societies; cultural myths often tied to a rural lifestyle, which in reality is enjoyed by a small minority of the total population; a shared popular culture, particularly in pop music and film (but not literature); and shared sporting ties and rivalry. However, what might be minor differences to outsiders can seem significant differences to businesses seeking to move across markets. Even between the Australian states there can be significant divergence.

From interviews of business leaders, two key perceived differences stand out. First, though some studies show that New Zealanders are less comfortable with uncertainty – which would imply a greater comfort with rule and regulations, there is a strongly held belief among New Zealand business executives and policy-makers that Australians are more bureaucratically inclined and rule bound than New Zealanders. Second, Australians are seen as more likely to be corrupt. As one New Zealand business executive noted:

> It's quite a bit more corrupt [in Australia] so there are ways of getting things done which are a little bit alien to us. You can talk to people in Sydney and they will show you basically that to get a consent through for your housing operation in time . . . you have to use the brown paper bag method – everyone will tell you that and maybe there is a certain amount of urban myth about it.
>
> In Auckland . . . you can talk to people 'til you're blue in the face and never find anyone who has ever thought it was worth bribing a council official to get their consent through.
>
> Maybe we're naïve and haven't tried it.

A Sydney-based New Zealand businessman noted similar problems:

> [I]f you focus on the similarities you start ignoring the differences, and you ignore the differences at your commercial peril. And we therefore think that NZ companies almost get lulled into a false sense of security by thinking that Australia will be the same as NZ.
>
> And it's not. It's a much more formal place to do business in. It's much more bureaucratic. They've got many more layers of government than we have. Companies tend to be more hierarch[ic]al . . . which makes it very important to be able to identify the decision makers when you are talking to companies and it may well be the people that you initially start talking to aren't.
>
> It's an incredibly networked market where things like old school ties count and lots of relationships that start at school go on into business. You look at the senior business echelon in Australia and it gets recycled from company to company, into the public service, out of the public service.

One business interviewee who similarly perceived Australia as having a more heavily regulated environment put the divergence down to cultural differences:

> You look up a law in New Zealand, and a law in Australia, [and] theirs literally will be kilos and kilos heavier in paper and it will tell you in great detail everything you shall and shan't do.
>
> Australians . . . are both more . . . anti-authoritarian and you . . . get that sort of larrikin rebel streak but at the same time they expect to be more heavily regulated . . . they sort of expect to be stepped on.
>
> They want more regulations; they're more prescriptive in the way they do things and that means that their outlook is a little bit more rigid and less flexible. Whereas New Zealanders I think are more, in my experience, self-motivating.

Even the differences between states can trouble New Zealand business investors, as a Sydney-based business leader observed:

> . . . from a NZ exporter viewpoint you need to be aware of those differences because they do influence how you do business.
>
> Victoria is more British. South Australia is more British as well. More traditional, more solid [in] financial decision making.
>
> . . . in contrast Sydney or New South Wales is a bit flashier . . . if people have got money, it tends to be more visible here.
>
> In contrast say to Queensland where with the beach, it's a much more laid back society. And business conditions there are probably more similar . . . to NZ.

Just as state differences may influence New Zealand attempts to establish business relations, tensions and rivalries also exist between different parts of Australia, particularly Melbourne and Sydney. In sum, if seen in terms of 'cultural distance', Australia and New Zealand are remarkably close. It may even be appropriate to talk of a 'trans-Tasman business culture'; although this closeness should not be overstated.

Institutional and policy convergence

Cultural similarity has been mirrored in a large degree of institutional isomorphism and policy convergence for over 150 years, as other chapters in this book examine. Institutional isomorphism is a key to reducing 'psychic distance'. 'Institution', as it is used in the literature known as 'new institutionalism', is a relatively slippery concept that may slide into culture. In March and Olsen's influential formulation, institutions are shared beliefs, norms, expectations and rules – written and unwritten, formal and informal – and, in their much quoted phrase, humans act and puzzle within certain 'logics of appropriateness' and certain constraints given by these institutions.[8] Formal institutions can have written constitutions and legislative structures; but even these may have attached to them certain shared understandings, and there may be a (known and accepted) departure from written rules in what is actually done. Castles writes of 'families of nations' that share similar institutional structures and some cultural similarities.[9] One 'family' is the 'Anglo-American' group of nations, of which Australia and New Zealand are members, and to which we have already referred. Within this group are the Westminster systems – excluding the US – but all members share a common law system. As with cultural similarity, institutional and policy convergence reduces the costs, uncertainties and risks of business relationships in other countries.

Institutional similarities between Australia and New Zealand are particularly apparent in business law and regulation. Victorian and wider Australian experiences influenced the growth of New Zealand pastoralism. Similarly, Victorian law provided the models for regulating New Zealand's goldfields, and its administrators were recruited to enforce them.[10] This borrowing continued throughout the two countries' mutual history, as noted in Chapter 4. The most fundamental realignment and policy convergence between Australia and New Zealand has occurred since the advent of CER on 1 January 1983 (Chapter 5). Harmonisation has often meant the adoption of Australian law (or law that is at least similar) by New Zealand, although not in all cases. This harmonisation, along with mutual recognition, has been carried out through such mechanisms as joint intergovernmental committees, cooperation between trans-Tasman governmental agencies and regular meetings of ministers. A single market remains the putative policy aim.[11] In sum, in terms of policy and institutional frameworks – particularly in business, consumer and commercial law and the free movement of labour – there are few countries that are closer, particularly outside the North American Free Trade Agreement and the European Union (EU).

Networks

Network ties – including social ties, business cooperation, shared memberships of associations and interlocking directorships – assist personal advancement, open up business opportunities, influence values and behaviour, and help to forge consensus on policy direction and political ideologies.[12] Social and other networks exist among trans-Tasman business elites, and among business and political, policy and other elites, and have done for some time.[13] A number of senior business leaders from both sides of the Tasman have involved themselves in policy 'entrepreneurship', including funding studies on diverse policy issues, initiating think tanks and building links between business and other elites.[14] Ideological similarity provides a linkage for trans-Tasman business, such as between Roger Kerr of the New Zealand Business Roundtable and leading financial businesspeople in Melbourne, Sydney and elsewhere.[15] An initial attempt to establish a Tasman university by one-time Deputy Governor of the

New Zealand Reserve Bank and former State Service Commissioner Roderick Deane, and the Australian economist and neo-liberal policy activist Michael Porter, along with several leading businesspeople, evolved in 1987 into the Tasman Institute. This influential think tank based in Melbourne has included leading New Zealand business members, some of whom sat on its board of directors, and was partly funded by New Zealand business organisations as well as leading Australian businesses. Other networks are significant, with common nationality forming a natural linkage. As a senior business executive noted, in New Zealand 'there's a sort of informal network of Australia CEOs who get together ... there's like 30 people and they're all pretty visibly Australian'.

A number of mechanisms exist expressly to facilitate Australasian business networks. The Trans-Tasman Business Circle (TTBC), for example, self-described as 'the major executive network between Australia and New Zealand', provides various services, meetings and contacts. The chief executive describes it as providing a 'home for executives who are either travelling to the other country [or] being relocated' and

> an opportunity to network and to profile what was happening between the two countries [with] an organisation for the top 50 companies in Australia and NZ to have profile, to have a forum where they can discuss what they're doing. They may be chief financial officers, chief information officers of major companies who ... have operations in NZ [and] therefore they are trans-Tasman companies.
>
> We do not speak on anyone's behalf [but] we provide the forum for people to lobby. But if the Prime Minister wants to speak or the Treasurer or the Reserve Bank Governors want to talk to the business community in the other country, then the Departments of Foreign Affairs use us as the forum. Now if somebody wants to sidle up to them or lobby them or make a pitch ...

There is some link between membership of the circle and interlocking Australia–New Zealand directorships. Of the top 200 Australian companies, 9 per cent are members of the TTBC, while 13 per cent of New Zealand's top corporations are members. There is some concentration of memberships among those with a trans-Tasman board of directors – as might possibly be expected. One-third of the 200 largest Australian corporations with a director on the TTBC also have a director with New Zealand 'nationality'. The consolidation is even greater for New Zealand corporations. Of the New Zealand corporations that are members of TTBC, over 50 per cent have a director with Australian 'nationality' (see Tables 6.1–6.4 at the end of the chapter).

Another significant network and consensus building mechanism is the Australia–New Zealand Leadership Forum, whose participants are linked through shared memberships and other connections to the TTBC and the Australia–New Zealand Business Council.[16] The forum's first New Zealand chair, Kerry McDonald, is a life member and former chair of the council. In response to debate about the future course of the Australia–New Zealand relationship, a number of business and other leaders in both countries looked to develop links further. In early 2004 Kerry McDonald, chair of the Bank of New Zealand, and Margaret Jackson, chair of Qantas, argued that the Australia–New Zealand relationship had 'plateaued' and lost momentum. These two were the key drivers of the subsequent leadership forums – the first in Wellington in 2004, the second in Melbourne in 2005 and the third in Auckland in 2006. The fourth, co-chaired by James Strong, chair of Insurance Australia Group and Woolworths Ltd, and John Allen, chief executive of New Zealand Post Group, was held in Sydney in 2007. Membership is by invitation.

Two-thirds of the Australian delegations to the forums were business or industry representatives, while around half the New Zealand delegations came from government departments, policy institutes, and academic and cultural areas. The New Zealand delegation to the 2005 forum was bolstered by the inclusion of a number of business 'big hitters' with a high trans-Tasman profile, including Roderick Deane, chairman of Telecom New Zealand, and John Palmer, chairman of Air New Zealand. Representation from both governments extended to the foreign ministers. The forums included briefing papers outlining issues for discussion, economic statistics, presentations, and specialist committees and working parties on particular issues, as well as opportunities for social networking. Between meetings, working committees were formed to develop issues further; between the 2004 and 2005 forums there were 23 such committees. Despite some attempts to broaden the discussion, business and economic issues took priority. The forum provided broad support for moves towards a single market and general harmonisation, albeit with some reservations by New Zealand representatives about sovereignty issues.[17]

There is some evidence that the leadership forums have facilitated or at least made apparent the policy consensus existing among policy elites, particularly business elites. Business members have given significant weight to the move to a single market, despite some initial resistance from New Zealand members. Border control reforms that resulted in common immigration queues for Australian and New Zealand passport holders in both countries (Chapter 3) represent a direct win for forum lobbying. Work continues on tax and research and development regimes, consumer and commercial law, intellectual property, and facilitating labour exchange. The working parties and other forum avenues continue to press for further integration and harmonisation.

A trans-Tasman business elite?

New Zealanders and the New Zealand media take note when New Zealand-born executives are appointed to senior jobs in the Australian business sector. Recent high-profile appointments include David Kirk as CEO of Fairfax, Ralph

Norris as CEO of the Commonwealth Bank, and Paul Costello to the Australian Superannuation Fund. The chief executive of the TTBC included them in a longer list of New Zealanders in top Australian positions:

> The heads of CBA Commonwealth Bank, Fairfax . . . Ralph Norris, David Kirk, Head of AGL the biggest gas company, Australian Gas Light Ltd. The Deputy CEO of IAG Insurance Australia Group. The CEO of Channel Nine, Nine Network Sam Chisholm. The head of Tab Corp in Melbourne, Matthew Slater. The head of HBOS the Halifax Bank of Scotland is Kiwi. Then you have [senior executives] in Telstra.
> Then you have quite a few chief financial officers of Westpac . . .

Given the importance of Australian businesses to New Zealand and the dominance of certain industries in New Zealand, Australian-born individuals likewise head companies and sit on boards in New Zealand, without, perhaps, similar fanfare. There is certainly a strong belief among business and policy elites that there is a trans-Tasman business elite of New Zealand and Australian executives who move easily across the Tasman. There is also a sense that there is an asymmetry in the Australia–New Zealand business relationship. As one financial executive working in an Australian business noted:

> [Y]ou could identify an elite, in a sense that there are business leaders [in New Zealand] who are Australians. And there [is] quite an identified group of New Zealanders who are running important businesses in Australia. I think one of the interesting things is that the Aussies that are [in New Zealand] are more visible. Partly because if you're a New Zealander and you want to succeed in Australia you generally play down your Kiwi identity. Kiwis who go over there, after they've been there four or five years many of them will take Australian citizenship. There's obviously some sort of pressure on them to conform to succeed over there – to be seen as an Australian.

Ironically, this asymmetry provides some benefits to New Zealand managers. The dominance of Australian firms provides an avenue by which New Zealanders can gain access to higher jobs in the Australian centre – Commonwealth Bank CEO Ralph Norris, for example, was a former CEO of ASB Bank, a subsidiary of the Commonwealth Bank. In interviews, business executives saw the smallness of New Zealand as an advantage in training managers, providing a complementary group of skills to more specialised Australian executives. As one noted:

> Australian executives will tend to be specialists in a particular area, so when you get to general management they will be very specialist in either one or two areas. Whereas New Zealanders, given the size of business, are used to having to deal with a whole range of issues.
> One of the difficulties of moving into general management is actually learning to deal with breadth and having to deal with many multiple functions. It's quite difficult [and] New Zealanders actually transition to that

quite well ... I think NZ executives are probably also better communicators with people at all levels of the business.

The Australians are more hardnosed and more financial [and] number orientated.

Does the belief that New Zealanders and Australians are over-represented in each other's businesses and the asymmetry of the Australia–New Zealand relationship stack up in terms of evidence? Indeed, there does seem to be a considerable number of trans-Tasman business executives with representation on boards of both New Zealand and Australian companies (Tables 6.1–6.4).[18] More than 10 per cent of the largest 200 publicly listed Australian corporations had at least one director of New Zealand origin (as measured by New Zealand birth, citizenship or education). Australian representation is considerably stronger in the other direction, with nearly 40 per cent of New Zealand listed firms having at least one Australian director on their boards. Australian and New Zealand firms also share directors. Around one in seven of the largest Australian corporations have a director who also sits on the board of a New Zealand corporation. More than half of the New Zealand corporations share directors with Australian corporations. Only 3 per cent of Australian companies have both a New Zealand director and a director who sits on a New Zealand board, whereas in New Zealand companies more than 30 per cent have Australians in both of these equivalent roles. This degree of integration is more strongly marked by state – New South Wales and Victoria are twice as likely as the rest of Australia to share at least one director with a New Zealand company. Anecdotal and qualitative evidence suggests New Zealanders and Australians are often highly represented at mid-management levels and, as such, are not captured by our measures; it is possible therefore that the measurement of interlocking directorships may understate the depth of the links between New Zealand and Australian business elites.

In sum, there is strong evidence for the existence of a trans-Tasman business elite, tied together through affiliation networks such as members of business associations and meetings, and through interlocking directorships. It is very likely that to some extent these links have facilitated a consensus on policy issues. There is also evidence for a significant degree of asymmetry in the Australia–New Zealand relationship. The majority of the New Zealand business community shows some form of social integration with the Australian business community, and many corporations are integrated with Australia along multiple dimensions. In contrast, the Australian business community has a much smaller but still significant group that has social and business ties to New Zealand. This asymmetry has significant policy implications which we discuss later in this chapter.

Business integration and investment
The asymmetry of the Australia–New Zealand business relationship is also apparent in the patterns of business investment. There is considerable Australian

Laurence Clark, 23 July 1992.
H-221-006, NZ Cartoon Archive, Alexander Turnbull Library, Wellington, courtesy of Laurence Clark

ownership of New Zealand companies: over 30 per cent of the largest New Zealand companies are 5 per cent or more Australian owned (Tables 6.1–6.4).[19] New Zealand ownership of Australian firms is low in contrast, with only 2.5 per cent of the largest 200 listed public Australian firms (a total of five) having New Zealand ownership of 5 per cent or more. New Zealand is the third most important destination for Australian foreign investment – accounting for 9 per cent of the total, a large percentage considering the small size of the New Zealand economy.[20] Australian private equity firms are important investors in New Zealand, with New Zealand accounting for a third of their total investments in 2005–06.

In some New Zealand industries Australian control is almost total. Australian presence in New Zealand banking, notable since the mid-19th century, increased to dominance by the late 20th century. The Bank of New Zealand, ironically established partly in response to foreign (that is mainly Australian) dominance of the banking market in 1861, was purchased by National Australia Bank Group in 1992. The Australian Commonwealth Bank purchased 75 per cent of ASB in 1989, with the remainder acquired in 2000. Further concentration into Australian hands occurred when ANZ acquired the Lloyds-owned National Bank in 2003. This purchase meant the top five banks were Australian controlled. By 2005, 98 per cent of financial assets were with foreign-owned banks, compared with 40 per cent in 1985, with the top five banks owning 90 per cent of all banking assets. St George Bank, the fifth largest in Australia, entered the New Zealand market in 2003 but withdrew in 2006. New Zealand continues to be the most important overseas market for Australian banks.

Retail, manufacturing and media and other industries were also targets for Australian investment for much of the 20th century. For example, by 1935 Australian Glass Manufacturers (AGM) had set up plants in all the Australian states and New Zealand (in Auckland in 1922), making it 'one of Australia's earliest manufacturing multinationals'.[21] For a short time AGM achieved a virtual monopoly in its core business of manufacturing glass containers, and maintained a long-term dominance in glass manufacturing in Australia and New Zealand.

BHP absorbed New Zealand Steel in 1989, and its Glenbrook steel mill is a leading employer and producer of steel in New Zealand, both for the domestic market and for export. Wattie's – an iconic New Zealand brand established in 1934 – was exporting food products to Australia by the mid-1950s, and expanded to dominate the New Zealand market. Acquired by Heinz in 1992, a 1997 merger saw it become part of Heinz-Wattie's Australasia. The Australian company John Fairfax Holdings publishes over 70 per cent of New Zealand's newspapers, magazines and sporting publications since purchasing Independent Newspapers

Glass Agee jars have long been popular for jam and preserves. AGM called their toughened glass 'Agee' for Australian Glass. The same firm set up Crown Crystal Glass in Christchurch in 1950.

Ltd (itself majority controlled by Murdoch's News Corp) in 2003 for $1.188 billion and continues to expand into New Zealand. Other media outlets – including radio and all but one major metropolitan New Zealand daily newspaper – are also Australian owned. In 2005 the Australian company Woolworths Ltd purchased what was Progressive Enterprises Ltd from its then owner, Foodland Associated Ltd (an Australian company based in Perth), and continues to operate it as a subsidiary. In 2006 this company controlled 45 per cent of the New Zealand grocery market. Recent purchases of well-known New Zealand companies and brands include Whitcoulls, Tegel (the leading poultry producer), Griffin's (the leading biscuit manufacturer) and Kathmandu (a leading outdoor equipment retail chain), as well as hotel and business properties.

The traffic is not entirely one way. In 1990 Fisher and Paykel set up a plant in Queensland, and enjoys a premium status in the Australian market, which takes 48 per cent of its total sales. In 2002 it won a series of Australian design awards. Fonterra Co-operative Group Ltd – New Zealand's largest company, formed in 2001 – expanded into the Australian dairy industry, acquiring leading Australian dairy brands such as Bega, and now controls over 20 per cent of Australia's milk production. Relocated to Australia in 2000, Lion Nathan controls around 42 per cent of the Australian beer market. New Zealand jewellery company Michael Hill International spread from New Zealand to open a shop in Brisbane in Australia in 1987 before expanding to 180 shops across New Zealand, Australia and Canada by 2006. In contrast, an attempt by The Warehouse to expand to Australia from its New Zealand base was widely regarded as a disaster and its 122 Australian stores and other assets were sold to an Australian equity firm in December 2005. One top 100 Australian company (Ansett) nearly bankrupted its New Zealand purchaser, Air New Zealand, and led to Air New Zealand's renationalisation.

Although not always removing risks, particularly when stupidity is involved, cultural and other similarities may reduce the high risks entailed in mergers and acquisitions. Additionally for Australian investors,

> the smallness of the New Zealand market means it . . . is easier to capture market leaders . . . than in Australia [with] typically only two or three leading players.
> The 'number eight wire'[22] philosophy of management teams is another factor, with New Zealand bosses generally considered to be flexible, innovative and pragmatic.
> An injection of cash and enthusiasm can reap decent awards.[23]

The New Zealand market provides extra revenue for Australian firms without greatly increasing overheads, and has few barriers for expansion. For New Zealand niche manufacturers, Australia provides access to a larger market as well as greater scope for research and development.[24] A move in either direction can facilitate economies of scale, as well as opening up avenues for learning from subsidiaries and new businesses – although the recognition of superior business practices in cross-Tasman subsidiaries has not always translated to changes in behaviour.

In some cases New Zealand can act as a test market for Australian products. Australian states can serve the same function for New Zealand companies. One business leader noted that the advantages of expanding to Australia for New Zealand companies are

> scale, scale, scale, [a] big market [that is] often perhaps misinterpreted as being one market. Many NZ companies who have come here haven't recognised that

there are probably four or five regional markets within this vast continent and that what works in Brisbane doesn't work . . . in Melbourne or Sydney or vice versa. We don't see that as much between Auckland and Wellington.

Conversely, the advantages of moving into the New Zealand market for Australia companies are

besides the market or the relative size of the market – *proximity*. So, for many Australian companies NZ is the size of the Queensland market – *not insignificant*. Certainly the closest offshore market. It's recognised as a very good test market. It's recognised for very good managers and innovation and entrepreneurship and we only have to hear that from Australian CEOs who come back from running NZ companies raving about NZ inventiveness.

In a number of studies Australian and New Zealand businesses have noted problems preventing further integration.[25] Although Australian companies report few difficulties, New Zealand companies have noted the higher legal, bureaucratic, insurance and other start-up costs in Australia compared with New Zealand. Some interviewees remarked on cultural differences, higher levels of unionisation, and in some cases active steps to shut out potential New Zealand firms. As one business executive noted:

. . . businesses come up [against] . . . informal networks. I've had businesses here that have set up and the customer that they're trying to target will ring their competitor and say we don't want these Kiwis to come in here and we'll gang up against them sort of thing. Little bit of solidarity, because it's an outsider coming in.

Towards a single economic market?

In a speech in Sydney in March 2005 the New Zealand Minister of Finance, Michael Cullen, urged closer economic integration on two levels: first, the creation of a 'common citizenship for business' to develop a 'single domestic economy' between the two nations; second, the linking of the economic strengths of both countries to trade as 'Australasia Inc' in the global economy.[26] In February 2006 support for a single market was reaffirmed by both countries, and this economic and business integration continues apace at the time of writing. This chapter has demonstrated the large degree of integration of Australian and New Zealand business across a number of measures: a somewhat shared business culture; institutional and policy convergence; shared memberships of business associations and other business networks, particularly interlocking directorships; and ownership and foreign direct investment. In a number of cases, directorships and memberships of business associations are strongly intertwined and are likely to have fostered the development of a cross-Tasman business consensus on a number of issues. In a related vein we have also pointed to the existence of a highly interlinked trans-Tasman business elite. The strength of the links gives considerable traction to the concept of a Tasman business world. One noteworthy feature of this business world is the considerable asymmetry in the relationship. What implications does further integration have for business in both countries?

A number of Australian businesspeople strongly support a single trans-Tasman market, or single economic market as it is often termed, which would include one competition regime, a single regulatory framework in commerce and banking, a merged stock exchange and, according to some business leaders, a common currency – if that currency is the Australian dollar.[27] As one senior Australian business leader in Sydney noted in an interview, having separate economies made no sense to him, and both countries needed to create'critical mass' for mutual advantage when dealing with the outside world. Many New Zealand businesses agree with the thrust for a single market but are more conscious of the potential loss of sovereignty and often support greater harmonisation and mutual recognition of regulatory systems rather than a single system.[28]

Where there are qualifications to this general support for increasing integration, the reservations also come largely from the New Zealand side. One example comes from the banking sector. The dominance of the New Zealand market by Australian banks has led to calls for a single regulating agency for the financial sector, and discussion on this possibility continues. The Trans-Tasman Council on Banking Supervision was formed in February 2005 to enhance cooperation and further harmonise and/or mutually recognise the different regulatory regimes. Senior Australian ministers have been explicit in linking broader integration and a single banking regulator to a single economic market. Australian business elites remarked in interviews that they bear New Zealand particular goodwill, as one might a 'little brother', and that they have New Zealand's best interests at heart. New Zealand regulators have shown less enthusiasm, however, and 14 'senior participants in the New Zealand banking system' interviewed by the New Zealand Treasury and Reserve Bank agreed with their assessment.[29] Even senior New Zealand executives working in Australian banks have expressed reservations. As one noted in an interview:

> [I]n the case of bank regulation, the Australian view is well, look, all the banks in NZ are basically Australian, mostly. And we've got an Australian regulator for Australian banks, then why don't you just trust us on that one. That sounds plausible but then you think okay, if you sign up to that, we could never then regulate bank behaviour. And the Australian regulator which is answerable to Australian parliament and Australian people is regulating our bank system, sure. So if the bank was to fail, nobody is sitting there worrying about the effect on New Zealanders.
>
> So sovereignty, I think, is important and sovereignty can be an emotional word but what it means to me is, you know, who's looking after NZ?

Another banking executive made a similar point:

I don't believe you can have one regulator. Common regulation would make sense. But that's differentiated as to whether it's Australian regulation or it is common regulation.

... the Australian argument is oh, but we're all in favour of harmonisation, which is a great idea for us both, so we'll harmonise everything – it's just that the first issue is bank regulation. We'll get to the other stuff later on. Well hang on, sorry what about apples – that's been going since 1918 [sic] – you won't allow our apples, and why don't we deal ... with that first.

So I think we've got to be more assertive about our ... sovereign rights. But we've got to get our own house in order so that we're seen to be a more attractive model to compare Australia to.

Another move towards integration stumbled and fell when a merger of the Australian and New Zealand stock exchanges failed to eventuate. The matter was dismissed in 2002 ostensibly because of concerns over sovereignty and related issues.[30] This dismissal came despite extended debate on the matter and some support from governmental circles and New Zealand businesses, including 70 per cent of New Zealand fund managers.[31] It is something that rankles still with some Australian elites, with an Australian stock exchange leader claiming in an interview that the failure of the merger would facilitate the hollowing out of New Zealand as firms moved to where 'the liquidity was' (Sydney). This argument, ironically, was also often made by opponents of the merger.[32]

There is some concern among business leaders in New Zealand that harmonisation often means 'Australianisation'. Indeed, the concern that a common market – particularly one unaccompanied by a political union – may not work in New Zealand's interests is voiced not only by academics such as Catley,[33] but by some New Zealand business executives. As one business executive noted:

Harmonisation with Australia is a very a good thing as long as it's actually on our terms.

The downside . . . is that the Australian environment is [more] government and regulatory environment plays such a larger part. I think one of the risks we [run] in NZ is we've imported a lot of Australian regulators. We're harmonising more regulation, more compliance. I don't think that's a good thing; that's unproductive for our economy.

Harmonisation is a great word but harmonisation with a larger neighbour is normally a takeover.

Related to these concerns are the 'hollowing out' of New Zealand, as companies and executive talent relocate to Australia, or as New Zealand companies are absorbed into larger Australian or other organisations. According to one business executive interviewed, Australian businesses

will apply a policy that works for their whole business but may not work in NZ. When they want to build a call centre, they will say okay, in NZ . . . wage rates are much lower, you know the staff I can recruit for the same dollars might be better educated or whatever it is. But across my whole business . . . my constituency really is in Australia, and the New South Wales government or South Australian government is going to pay me some subsidy so I'll start the call centre in Australia.

Those sorts of opportunities tend to hollow out local operations. The most extreme example was probably ANZ before the merger with National Bank. All their computer processing was done in Australia really, and most of the decision-making was in Australia, and really NZ is just becoming more and more of just a sort of a shop front.

And that's fine except that . . . there's less job opportunities for New Zealanders.

On the other hand, just as New Zealand faces the problem of businesses relocating to Australia, being acquired by Australian interests, and a 'brain drain' of senior executives to better-paid jobs, Australia finds itself facing a similar situation in relation to larger markets in Europe and the United States.[34] For example, recently Australian firm James Hardie relocated to the Netherlands, while well-recognised Australian brands recently acquired by non-Australian companies include Arnotts biscuits, Cottees Foods and, of all things, Kraft Vegemite, acquired by US company Phillip Morris but then reportedly banned in the US.[35] New Zealand may just be a step further down the international food chain in this process.

Table 6.1 **Integration of Australian firms with New Zealand**

	Total number of firms	Firms with one director of NZ 'nationality'		Firms with a director with a directorship of an NZ company		Members of the Trans-Tasman Business Circle		Firms with at least 5% of shares NZ owned	
		Number of firms	%	Number of firms	%	Number of firms	%	Number of firms	%
Australian top 200 public companies	200	26	13.0	27	13.5	18	9.0	5	2.5
All Australian private-sector firms in top 2000	1574	89	5.7	67	4.3	83	5.3	25	1.6

Table 6.2 **Integration of New Zealand firms with Australia**

	Total number of firms	Firms with one director of Australian 'nationality'		Firms with a director with a directorship of an Australian company		Members of the Trans-Tasman Business Circle		Firms with at least 5% of shares Australian owned	
		Number of firms	%	Number of firms	%	Number of firms	%	Number of firms	%
Largest NZ public companies	53	21	39.6	29	54.7	7	13.2	16	30.2

Table 6.3 Trans-Tasman integration of Australia's top 200 publicly listed companies

	Number of firms	Firms with a director of NZ 'nationality'	Firms with a director with a directorship of an NZ company	Firms that are members of the Trans-Tasman Business Circle
Firms with a director of NZ 'nationality'	26	–	–	–
Firms with a director with a directorship of an NZ company	27	6	–	–
Firms that are members of the Trans-Tasman Business Circle	18	6	7	–
Firms with at least 5% of shares NZ owned	5	1	1	1
Top 200 Australian publicly listed firms	200	26	27	18

Table 6.4 **Trans-Tasman integration of New Zealand's 53 largest publicly listed companies**

	Number of firms	Firms with a director of Australian 'nationality'	Firms with a director with a directorship of an Australian company	Firms that are members of the Trans-Tasman Business Circle
Firms with a director of Australian 'nationality'	21	–	–	–
Firms with a director with a directorship of an Australian company	29	18	–	–
Firms that are members of the Trans-Tasman Business Circle	7	4	5	–
Firms with at least 5% of shares Australian owned	16	12	13	2
New Zealand's 25 largest publicly listed firms	53	21	29	7

CHAPTER SEVEN
Learning Together

Peter Hempenstall

Under the *Pax Britannica* the New Zealand and Australian colonies shared a common learning environment in the 19th century. Young, crude but maturing societies of convict and free immigrants, they learnt to shape their very different landscapes and agricultural terrains in an ecological experiment that is still running, and that has had far from benign effects. Science and colonial governments were allied from the middle of the century with the foundation of universities, and the knowledge shared across the Tasman through the Australasian Association for the Advancement of Science (AAAS), established in 1888.[1] Hand in hand with 'improvement' of the lands went the creation of social communities that would deliberately and systematically avoid the poverty and hierarchical class structures of the old world. Both New Zealand and Australia would be social laboratories founded on the prospects brought by gold, coal, rich grasslands, and the policies of colonial progressives allied to representatives of the working class. These experiments, for which the French observer Albert Métin coined the phrase 'socialism without doctrines', were not carried out in isolation from or hostility to the old world. They proceeded within the imperial framework of the British empire, connected through the Union Jack and their common Victorian heritage.[2] Britain supplied the migrants, the capital and the Royal Navy to drive and protect the young economies. The irony was that each country proceeded to carve out a separate national story to explain its history during the 20th century.

Both antipodean histories contained some common elements: precocious political rights and freedoms, the closing of the land frontiers, the blooding of Anzacs in war, technological innovation and sporting prowess to fill the world with wonder. But each also proclaimed a special character for itself. Australia's case was built on its 'white Australia' policy, later succeeded by a workable multiculturalism, a relaxed beach culture that bronzed Anzac men (and some women) exemplified, and an assertion of middle power status in the Asia–Pacific world. New Zealand had the Treaty of Waitangi, which allegedly ensured race relations with its powerful indigenous people, the Maori, that were better than those achieved in Australia. New Zealand's island Pacific credentials would be strengthened in the later 20th century by an influx of other Polynesians to make it the most developed Polynesian society in the world. A passionate anti-nuclear stance and an image as a clean, green arcadia rounded out an identity as a small country of compact provincial strengths, its people rugged mountaineers, self-effacing, modest and adaptable. Again, this was a masculine identity. But a different gender dynamic was at work than in Australia because New Zealand's pioneer mythology allowed room for mother figures and aunts to become women leaders. By the end of the 20th century New Zealanders did not think it odd to have women running the country.[3]

Educational links

Amid such nation-building, Rollo Arnold's 'Perennial Interchange' of people and ideas went on undisturbed.[4] Arnold lists a roll-call of managerial, professional and entrepreneurial people who criss-crossed the Tasman: bankers, businessmen, miners, axemen, shearers, clergy and journalists. He gave limited attention to school teachers. But education is one of the areas where the consistent movement of ideas, institutions and people has been most dynamic.

Education is an area ignored in Paul Kelly's tendentious claim about an 'Australian Settlement', which was in fact a Tasman-wide ensemble of themes. The 'chain of education for Everyman', as the visiting American historian Robin Winks called it in 1954,[5] was of roughly equivalent quality and length in both countries. Designed to deliver literacy and basic numeracy for all, the chain linked primary to secondary and post-secondary educational institutions. An expanding democracy provided equal opportunity to working-class and lower middle-class families, and sought to inculcate 'attitudes appropriate to democratic citizenship'.[6] The pioneering ethos remained strong in state schools and emphasised manual skills, commercial and technical courses for boys, while girls were trained in home science for domestic pursuits. The more elite, private schools, modelled on the English public schools – that imperial inspiration again, set themselves to the moral task of producing predominantly boys for leadership in a Christian environment within the empire.[7]

A deep-seated and British-based 'moral curriculum' lay at the heart of school education across New Zealand and Australia. Less a coherent philosophy than a series of well-worn practices, it strove for habits of industry, obedience and respect for authority through strict routines and unswerving discipline; discipline through corporal punishment was a universal 'good' in the eyes of young settler societies fearful of racial degeneration. Homework, lots of it, was a standard exercise as a model for life. Military training plus team sports provided the rest of the moral compass by which young people were expected to orient themselves. Girls received a diluted version of these lessons of life, designed to fit them as mothers and loyal homemakers.[8]

Textbooks contained stories of British pluck and exemplary deaths, as well as the moral exhortations that underpinned the moral curriculum. In the 19th century both New Zealand and Australia used textbooks published in Britain, most notably the 'Irish' books originally published by the National Commissioners of Education in Ireland and used in at least a dozen other countries besides Britain.[9] In New Zealand, as in the Australian states, British textbooks gradually gave way to local works tailored to the local syllabus. The New Zealand publisher Whitcombe and Tombs dominated the Kiwi textbook market in the first half of the 20th century and had a close relationship with the Department of Education. Whitcombe and Tombs' first successful series appeared in the 1890s, and its strongest selling point was how closely the books followed the New Zealand syllabus. The New Zealand publisher's histories, geographies and arithmetic books quickly displaced British publications. In 1912 it included Australian as well as New Zealand material in a new series of Pacific Readers. These referred to the need for local material for 'Australasian children'; the third reader, for example, included items on the dingo and on Edward Eyre as well as on swamphens and hongi.[10]

Whitcombe and Tombs' trans-Tasman contacts gave it a wider pool of potential authors on whom to draw. Professor J. W. Gregory of the University of Melbourne wrote the Imperial Geographies and the Southern Cross Geographical Readers that appeared at the end of the 19th century. The Public School Historical Readers, designed for New Zealand schools, were very much a joint effort: William Gillies of Australia wrote two of the four books and James Hight, Professor of History at Canterbury College, wrote the others. Early in the 20th century there was considerable discussion of the need for a health book for New Zealand schools, and it was originally hoped that James Pope, author of *Health for the Maori*, would oblige, but he retired in poor health. Then it was reported that Charles Chilton of Canterbury College would write it. When the *Southern Cross Health Reader* finally appeared, circa 1905, it was the work of Dr J. S. C. Elkington, the Medical Officer of Health in Tasmania, and illustrated by Norman Lindsay of *Magic Pudding* fame.

On the other side of the Tasman at least one Australian series used material recycled from an earlier New Zealand series. The Vivid History Readers, specially written to meet the requirements of the social studies course in Victorian elementary schools, include passages from *Our Nation's Story*, histories for the revised 1928 New Zealand primary school syllabus. Such borrowing made sense when both countries' texts dealt largely with the expansion of England and elements of British history. Whitcombe's Story Books also brought the Tasman cousins together in simple saddle-stapled, card-covered, modestly priced books. Some 12 million copies of around 450 titles in various editions were printed between 1905 and 1962. Originally designed as supplementary readers, they were sold in bookshops and a range of other outlets across the Tasman world, including general stores in small towns, and they were popular stocking fillers at Christmas time. The series included a large number of condensed versions of novels such as *Ivanhoe*, *The Black Arrow* and *Lorna Doone*, as well as stories by Australian and New Zealand authors, folk and fairytales, Maori and Aboriginal legends.[11]

The trans-Tasman school systems did not, of course, run simply on books and a common values system. There was in the early 20th century plenty of looking at each other's ideas, copying the best of them or using the case of the other country as an argument against a policy decision. Otago's Senior Inspector of Schools went to Australia in 1902 and reported back on the New Zealand local board system's superiority compared with the centralised state systems of New South Wales, Victoria and South Australia.[12] The Victorian Director of Education, Frank Tate, travelled the other way in 1904 and wrote admiringly of New Zealanders' enthusiasm for education, the secondary school system and its local administration by school committees, though he believed Victoria was ahead in teacher training facilities and technical instruction.[13] Tate was back in New Zealand as a member of a commission on New Zealand universities in the 1920s and he was also invited to report on secondary education.[14] George Hogben, Inspector-General of New Zealand schools 1899–1915, made a number of visits to Australia, where heads of state education departments took the opportunity to meet him in conference; he was also a member of the AAAS. In 1921 the New Zealand Education Department followed Victoria's example in establishing the *New Zealand Education Gazette*, which contained official notices, job vacancies and articles on education at home and abroad. Postwar inspectors of schools held trans-Tasman conferences.

Australia – in particular Victoria – figured in debates on the control of education in New Zealand both as an example of the benefits to be gained from centralised control and as a grim warning against it. New Zealand gave considerable autonomy to elected regional boards that controlled primary and district high schools; these boards were abolished only with the 'Tomorrow's Schools' reforms of the late 1980s. Under Hogben the boards' powers were considerably reduced but they defended themselves consistently as having the local knowledge and fostering local interest in and support for schools. Hogben found it necessary to assure the 1912 Cohen Commission on administration that 'I am very strongly against central administration. I do not believe in the Australian system.'[15]

The 'Australian system', however, appealed to those concerned to limit educational expenditure in the straitened 1920s and 1930s. Cumming attributes the centralising urges of James Parr, Minister of Education 1920–26, to 'the distant influence of Frank Tate' and to Parr's estimate of 'what could be done under a benevolent despotism'.[16] The Director of Education in the 1920s, T. B. Strong, also proposed complete centralisation of control and the abolition

Australian and New Zealand Association of Institutes of Inspectors of Schools, Delegates to the Biennial Conference at Christchurch, August 1952.
AAQT 6401 A27864, Archives New Zealand, Wellington

of local education authorities, on the argument that administration costs per pupil were lower in New South Wales, Victoria and Queensland than in New Zealand. A parliamentary commission on educational reorganisation in 1930 strongly opposed him. The writer who drafted the commission report was educational historian A. G. Butchers, himself a trans-Tasman migrant. Born in Victoria, schooled in Geelong, with a degree from the University of Melbourne, Butchers taught in secondary schools in Australia and went to New Zealand in 1918 as principal of John McGlashan College in Dunedin. He became headmaster of the New Zealand Correspondence School in 1935. His 1930 history of education contains many comparisons of the trans-Tasman systems, including statistics on expenditure on administration per pupil for New Zealand, New South Wales and Victoria, and a sober assessment of the costs to the education system were Catholic schools to abandon their own system.[17]

Religious links

Mention of Catholic schools is a reminder of how often religion, its extensive infrastructure of churches, schools and hospitals, and its congregations of people and their ministers are undervalued or omitted in the national stories of New Zealand and Australia. Religion is foundational to the national history of each country. The central state and community institutions in both countries were impregnated with Christian values or their derivatives. Religious connections demonstrate better than most themes under investigation the integrated, transnational nature of the Tasman world, a world that also extended intimately into societies in its Pacific and Asian neighbourhoods.

Throughout the 20th century, Anglicanism in the antipodes struggled to define itself away from the Church of England and to delineate the outer limits of its identity and reach. Nonetheless, the traffic in ministers and teachers across the Tasman, especially from east to west, was regular and sustained: Sydney provided bishops for Nelson until the 1960s.[18] The Scottish Presbyterian links to Otago are well known to the point of cliché. But Australia was more important than Scotland as a recruiting ground for ministers by the beginning of the 20th century. Churches sought outstanding preachers from across the Tasman for leading pulpits in New Zealand, often guided in these appointments by laypeople who had knowledge of local talent through family, friends or business contacts on the other side. Many ordinary 'calls' were also made the same way. Prentis counted 199 individual ministers between 1840 and 1977 who served on both sides of the Tasman; 40 per cent of them made three or more cross-Tasman moves.[19]

New Zealand evangelical Presbyterians were also prominent in opposing liberal tendencies within the Australian church.[20] Presbyterian teachers were an important part of the roll-call. The Scottish educational system with its democratic, merit-based reputation was a strong influence in both countries. According to Prentis, an Australasian common market operated among church and private schools.[21]

The Catholic school system, set up in response to secular education legislation in both countries from the 1870s, provides perhaps the most coherent and widespread example of a common frontier of exchange across the Tasman. Though the Australian and New Zealand Catholic churches had evolved separate identities by the end of the 19th century, commonalities continued to tie them together, from the problem of creating Catholic educational systems and the threat posed to clerical manpower by conscription during the First World War, to negotiations with the state over funding for their schools and the common problem of declining vocations and shrinking finances.[22] Christian Brothers, Marists, Sisters of St Joseph, the Sisters of Mercy, Jesuits and Redemptorists worked in tandem across the Tasman, in the cities and rural areas.

Some groups travelled across the Tasman to work literally side by side with their Australian or New Zealand counterparts. The Sisters of St Joseph arrived in Wanganui from New South Wales in 1880, a breakaway group – 'black Joeys' – from the original 'brown' Sisters of St Joseph founded by Mary McKillop. With a much lower profile than in Australia, where McKillop was absorbed into the pantheon of self-sacrificing, frontier heroes,[23] the black Joeys toiled with a common trans-Tasman commitment to Catholic education and the preservation of the faith. By the 1970s they were organised in a new federation with their 'black' sisters in Australian congregations: Perthville, Lochinvar, Goulburn and Tasmania, and tentatively exploring their common roots with McKillop's 'brown Joeys'.[24]

McKillop's New Zealand parallel was Mother Suzanne Aubert, who founded the Daughters of Our Lady of Compassion. Like McKillop, she became a heroic figure suited to the story of a pioneering community showing its concern for the poor. Both are 'saints for modern times' for the Catholic Church.[25] Both represent particular virtues of new world societies: egalitarianism, independence, improvisation and acceptable female exceptionalism. Aubert's French origins and intimate work with Maori lend her an exoticism that expresses the nuanced differences in New Zealand's sense of its pioneering history compared with Australia's. But these women and their followers – and the many more like them from other orders – embody a Tasman Catholic world of teaching, nursing, care for the poor and personal piety that was recognisable in every nook and cranny. In Australia alone, by the Second World War, 8470 sisters in 914 convent schools taught 165,915 pupils.[26]

Among men and boys, the equivalent congregation was the Christian Brothers. Founded in Ireland by Edmund Rice to educate the poor, the Christian Brothers were an integral feature of the heavy migrant flow between Australia and New Zealand during the 19th century. First the French Marists established Catholic communities and then, in an increasingly disputatious relationship, Irish priests and bishops responded to the influx of Irish into the West Coast and Otago goldfields from the 1860s. The Brothers were distinctive carriers of the Cullenite 'devotional revolution', practising a high level of formal ritual and devotions as celibate males, sworn to poverty and obedience, and dedicated to building a sustainable education system.[27] The first four Christian Brothers arrived in Dunedin in 1876 from Melbourne. By 1950 the diaspora amounted to 72 communities conducting 93 schools in Australia and New Zealand, 49 of which provided a full primary and secondary curriculum. New South Wales and Victoria contained the highest proportion of these schools, and Queensland had the largest number of country schools. But all the states possessed Brothers' schools, while New Zealand had day schools in Dunedin and Auckland and a boarding and primary school in Oamaru. Later foundations occurred in Christchurch, Rotorua and West Auckland.[28] The number of pupils attending these schools was 22,000, taught by more than 600 Brothers. The number of Brothers who served in New Zealand between 1876 and 1959 was 148, of whom 47 were New Zealand born. In the decade to 1970 another 40 men were trained on the east coast of Australia for service across the Tasman.[29]

The curriculum at Brothers' schools was a heightened, Catholic version of that 'moral curriculum' that underlay both nations' education systems. The Christian Brothers strove to inspire virtue and manly ideals, both religious and civic, using along the way the physical disciplining taken for granted in all quarters. *Our Studies*, the Brothers' magazine that disseminated educational and religious models for teachers, expounded upon 'character training' in 1934:

> Boys must be taught that a motive of action based on personal ease and convenience is almost invariably cheap and unworthy. As soon as they understand that the secret of character is to know when to deny themselves they will recognise that striving to exercise self-control and self-denial is the best of educators. Doing the noble, unselfish thing brings a reward which more than compensates for self-sacrifice.[30]

Sport was an instrument in forming the whole man, and military training was an adjunct to the disciplines of school life: 'Quickness of mental reaction, smartness of person and good bodily figure and pose, correction of physical defects, team spirit, esprit de corps' were but some of the benefits to flow from school cadet corps, according to *Our Studies*.[31] St Kevin's College in Oamaru proudly boasted a visit by the Minister of Defence, Hon. Mr Cobb, and a prominent general of the armed forces in 1933 to inspect the latest crop of disciplined Kiwis.

Our Studies was for the whole of the Tasman world. Sixty-nine New Zealand-related articles or illustrations appeared between 1929 and 1993, at least one a year, and every issue made passing reference to the life of schools on both sides of the Tasman. The readership included Papua New Guinea, where Australian and New Zealand Brothers worked side by side both before and after its independence in 1975.

While Australia and New Zealand constituted a common field of endeavour, Australian numbers and influence predominated. New Zealand, though, contributed a weight of leadership above its numbers. Two of the 20th century's most influential Provincials of the Congregation in Australia were Kiwis – Michael Benignus Hanrahan and Christopher Claver Marlow, both from Otago. A third Otago man, Br David Gabriel Purton, founded *Our Studies* and was its editor from 1929 to his death in 1948. Purton's migration history is instructive of the geographical range and level of influence that the trans-Tasman culture of the Christian Brothers encompassed. Born in 1884, Purton came to Sydney at the age of 14 to join the Brothers, having lost his mother and father before he was 12. After reception he was sent to Albany, Western Australia, as a religious under vows at 15, taking with him a windmill and a cow. When he left Western Australia for South Australia in 1920 he carried the reputation of being the 'father of secondary education in Western Australia'.[32] In Adelaide he taught in schools while studying for his MA in philosophy, which he took with first-class honours and the University Medal. Appointed temporary Professor of Psychology and Logic, Purton taught at the university and was invited to join the permanent staff. During his time in South Australia he presided over the first years of the boarding school at Rostrevor. He was also headmaster of St Kevin's Melbourne, Nudgee College in Brisbane, St Patrick's Goulburn and his great love, St Patrick's College Ballarat, where he died in 1948, much revered as an innovative educator, a magnetic teacher and 'moulder of character', and a classical scholar who praised Aristotle and Aquinas in philosophy, Homer, Virgil and Cicero in classical literature, and Belloc and Chesterton in history and criticism.[33]

Such stories are part of the Tasman region's 'religious settlement' that saw the Australian and New Zealand religious educational systems march together in lockstep with the rhythms of changes in secular education. Three years after the Christian Brothers began teaching in Melbourne in 1871, legislation established a free, secular and compulsory system of education in Victoria. The equivalent Queensland Act was passed in 1875, the year of the foundation of Gregory Terrace Brothers' school in Brisbane. The Brothers opened their first school in New Zealand in 1876, the year before the government introduced free, compulsory and secular primary schooling and withdrew state aid from religious schools. In South Australia state aid was withdrawn the year before the first Brothers school was opened in Adelaide. They opened their first Sydney school in Balmain the year after Henry Parkes' Education Act of 1880. Western Australia was the last mainland colony to withdraw state aid from denominational schools, which it did in 1895, the year after the foundation of the Christian Brothers' College in Perth.[34] The Brothers were in an advance position to build an alternative system for Catholics in both countries. They also found it particularly difficult to win state aid back after the strains put upon all religious education systems by rapid population growth in the 1950s.

In both countries, conservative national governments granted state aid to religious schools in the early 1960s – in this policy Australian Prime Minister Robert Menzies clearly influenced New Zealand Prime Minister Keith Holyoake – and the amounts of aid steadily increased during the decade. Conversely, the Australian Labor government followed its New Zealand cousin in 1972 in establishing an Australian Schools Commission to dispense state aid to prevent the Catholic parochial schooling system from collapsing. New Zealand's integration of religious schools into the state system of funding proceeded further than Australia's and achieved a balance between opposing interests that the Australian system still manifestly lacks. Nonetheless, as Sweetman demonstrates, the campaign that led to state funding of religious schools was circular, with ideas, personnel and tactics exchanged across the Tasman.[35]

The Christian Brothers have exemplified that circular movement right through their history. In 1907, already 30 years in New Zealand, the Brothers decided to withdraw from Dunedin because of the lack of vocations, unsatisfactory finances and the isolation of the community. Only the reassurance of the Bishop of Dunedin to keep the Marist Brothers out, and a visit from the

Australian Provincial who agreed to find an extra £100 a year, enabled the Brothers to pay their way and stay.[36] It was the struggle over men – getting them and keeping them – that tied the countries closely together during the 20th century. New foundations in Oamaru and Auckland in the 1920s needed transfers of men from across the Tasman to get them off the ground. In the 1950s the New South Wales Provincial sent a Visitor to make regular inspections of New Zealand communities, to compare developments with those in Australia and to identify Brothers-in-training who had leadership potential.[37] In 1959, after the New Zealand Catholic Bishops had regularly expressed their unhappiness at the number of young Kiwi men disappearing across the Tasman for training and never returning, the Brothers established the four New Zealand houses as a Vice-Province and returned Claver Marlow, after 50 years' teaching in Australia, to his home country to be its first Provincial. Mount St Mary Province, centred in Sydney, promised to subsidise the new entity by £30,000 over five years and help to set up a juniorate to prepare schoolboys for the vocation.[38]

The Brothers in New Zealand remained debt-ridden. Marlow and his successors were also forced to make regular requests of Mount St Mary Province to transfer men across the Tasman. Relations were sometimes testy in these exchanges, with Australia reluctant to surrender men and Marlow having to remind his colleagues how many men New Zealand had given to the cause over the years. Occasionally the Tasman journey was a way of saving the vocation of men having doubts or suffering incurable homesickness. From the mid-1960s both sides felt the haemorrhaging of men from the novitiates; worse still, many men were leaving after they had been put through university degree educations. In a desperate letter to the New South Wales Provincial in January 1965 the New Zealand Consultor, Brother Hanley, remarked, 'Any man who can stand up is pressed into a job these days', and Marlow added ruefully that New Zealand men did not seem to have the staying qualities of New Zealand horses.[39]

Despite such difficulties New Zealand was made a full province in 1966, in the hope that this new status would stimulate development in the shaky isles. It did not. Rationalisation continued apace as the pressures for integration into the state funding system mounted in the 1970s and 1980s. Finances remained tight, in some cases impossible. The cross-Tasman relationship of the Christian Brothers, with its inbuilt tensions, remained one of tight interdependence, though New Zealand had to work the harder and was worse off in men and finances because of its size.[40]

Of the Protestant denominations, the Seventh Day Adventists, with the largest Protestant church school system worldwide, conducted the most extensive trans-Tasman network of schools and colleges. Three elements of Adventist history tied New Zealand and Australia together throughout the 20th century.

The first was the common presence of Ellen White, the American prophetess of the millennial coming and the importance of a holistic lifestyle, whose writings brought 19th-century Adventist teachings together into a coherent whole. White spent nine years in the Tasman world, mostly in Australia but some of it in New Zealand, and wrote extensively on education and the formative experiences Adventist students should enjoy. White had an equal interest in the physical, mental, moral and spiritual education of learners, preferably to be conducted in rural settings, and with a strong emphasis on health education and training for living.[41] As a response, the Adventist community school at Cooranbong, New South Wales, was established in 1897, and grew into Avondale College. Longburn, near Palmerston North in the North Island of New Zealand, became the junior/intermediate school designed to shepherd Adventist young people towards missionary and life education at Cooranbong.

Cooranbong/Avondale became the 'pattern school' for Adventism, with trans-Tasman, indeed transnational implications for the development of its educational programmes. Tensions occurred between Australian Adventists and their 'junior partners' in New Zealand, but the two sides of the Tasman grew together during the middle years of the 20th century, stimulated in 1938 and 1948 by large Australasian conventions to encourage unity and purpose among teachers.[42] Avondale remained the senior partner. A Kiwi principal, Ernest Gordon McDowell, who had a working knowledge of educational systems in Australia, New Zealand, the Pacific Islands and North America, presided over its great period of infrastructural growth from the late 1950s.[43]

Curriculum is the second strand that connects Australia and New Zealand. Much of the 20th-century history of Adventist education revolves around the search for a uniform and unified curriculum, based on Adventist beliefs, while negotiating a place for its institutions and graduates in the secular societies of the Tasman world. Avondale was designed to be different:

> …located in a country setting, removed from city influences; courses were not based on any programme known to be in Australia; methods of evaluation and progress were to be individualised; teaching was Bible-based; teachers lived in the same quarters as students in an endeavour to give a strong character mould; and industrial training was established as an important feature of the programme.[44]

Educational, physical and moral development were bound together. Cooranbong/Avondale inspired the development of more than 20 primary schools based on the same principles, from Perth to Wellington and from Hobart to Brisbane. Intermediate schools were started in Western Australia in 1907 and at Pukekura in the Waikato in 1908, after New Zealand Adventists had already sent more than a dozen students to the United States for training and others to both Cooranbong and Victoria. In 1918 Longburn became the bridge to Avondale for Adventist Kiwi secondary students.

An early attempt to merge Adventist education with state examination requirements was made in New South Wales in 1916 and 1917 but a period of tension followed as evangelical non-educationists influenced curriculum development. Only from the late 1940s was Avondale enabled to expand beyond a narrow religious education into secular training and a full repertoire of tertiary studies, while retaining a distinctive Adventist tone.[45] However, the campaign for a unified curriculum across the whole of the Tasman world ultimately failed. Not all Adventist parents were workers for the church, ready to go wherever the mission called them. They had to make compromises with secular, state systems of education in the places they lived and worked rather than support a church school. The state systems themselves differed one from another, with varying approaches to the content of children's education; the New Zealand system was different again. Such differences and rivalries made a common Adventist curriculum impossible to achieve.

The third thread that joined the two countries and their region was evangelical leadership. That becomes clearer in considering Adventist missionary activities beyond the Tasman world. Between 1914 and 1918 the local Adventist church appointed 136 new workers, most from Avondale College, Sydney, Western Australia and New Zealand. Many trained for foreign mission fields – Solomon Islands, the New Hebrides, Polynesia, Burma, India and the Philippines – but a new evangelical wave also gripped Australia and New Zealand in the years after the First World War, inspired partly by portents of the end times, such as the earthquake that destroyed Napier in 1931 and the Vatican's treaty with Italian Fascism that seemed to echo the message of the Book of Revelations. Kiwi evangelists played a prominent role. Roy A. Anderson commenced his career in the 1920s in the North Island of New Zealand but was quickly called to Australia to lead large city crusades in Brisbane. James W. Kent captured large audiences in Christchurch and in deeply Presbyterian Dunedin before becoming the leading evangelist for the South New South Wales Conference.[46] The Seventh Day Adventists were not afraid to operate in the heartland of other Protestant denominations.

On the outer wing of the Protestant churches, in the Pentecostalist movement, such traffic of charismatic preachers was so regular and intimate that Hutchinson argues for a 'joint religious consciousness' underpinning the Tasman world that was natural enough to remain unremarked.[47] Pentecostalists are the largest and fastest-growing movement in both countries. Local origins were with the Assemblies of God in the 1920s, but the strongest growth in Australia occurred between the 1960s and 1990s – from 16,572 to just under 1 per cent of the total population, at 174,720. Kiwi Pentecostalists numbered 69,182 in 1996, almost 2 per cent of the population; in Papua New Guinea they were 7 per cent.[48]

The names of New Zealanders are prominent among those running the Australian churches: Peter Morrow, David and Ray Jackson, Phil Pringle, and

Frank Houston of the Christian Life Centre.[49] Australians and New Zealanders criss-crossed the Tasman to preach and offer support. Hutchinson treats both countries as a 'unitary field of religious endeavour', with New Zealand and Australia becoming 'exchangeable terms for Australian Pentecostal consciousness very early in its history'.[50] Hutchinson even claims the Maori prophet Tahupotiki Wiremu Ratana as a model for the growth of global Pentecostalism reflected in the communities, leaders and literature of the Tasman world. The influences come from both Britain and the US but Queensland and New Zealand in particular feature in the growth of insurgent Christianity and the assertion of charismatic leadership.

Christianity and its educational values and institutions constituted a common currency in a single Tasman market, even if those values were constantly in tension among the various denominations and were either contested or unacknowledged by secular society. The guise under which religion usually enters into national histories – a divisive sectarianism – does not sufficiently acknowledge the solidarities, trans-Tasman and imperial, that bound the religious cultures of New Zealand and Australia, even when they looked to different centres: Canterbury, Geneva, Rome or Dublin.[51] Mission networks, clergy transfers, universities and colleges, common publications and international denominational structures were all sites for this cultural traffic and provided recognisable pathways for people to move within communities of faith.[52]

If there were ever to be a 'settlement' between the states of Australia and New Zealand and their social groupings then it must recognise the profundity of the religio-cultural landscape of both countries, together and apart. Religious groups have engaged with all the great themes of New Zealand and Australian history, including the relationship of settler societies to the new land, the struggles with indigenous peoples, the impact of world wars and economic depression, and the changes in social structure and group power.[53] Most of the flow within the Tasman world favoured Australia. New Zealand always had to do more work to make its impact felt; that is the reality for a small, remote neighbour. But New Zealand institutions, resources and personnel have had a multiplier effect within these communities of faith, spreading the risk and creating a critical mass that supported denser institutions and powerful leaders for generations of New Zealanders and Australians.

Professional associations

The variety of learning environments that Australia and New Zealand shared extended well beyond schools, secular and religious. Many professions incorporated both countries in their training reach while they were still colonies, and continued to do so throughout the 20th century, retaining the original notion of 'Australasia' in their official titles. Others, like the Royal Australasian College of Physicians (RACP), started life in the 1930s as an association, with New Zealand associate members. By 1938, with the *Medical Journal of Australia* pouring scorn on the official title 'The Association of Physicians of Australasia (including New Zealand)', because 'everyone who knows anything at all about geography knows that Australasia includes New Zealand', the association became a college under royal patronage. For the next 50 years it attended to common examinations and the setting of credentials for physicians of internal medicine on both sides of the Tasman. A Wellington headquarters was set up in 1962 (when the New Zealand committee was still known as 'the Dominion committee') and the college, together with the similarly named Royal Australasian College of Surgeons (RACS), became the adviser to governments on both sides of the Tasman regarding changes to specialist training. These 'Australasian' colleges have been conspicuously successful, unlike the organisations for general practitioners, in building bridges for the Tasman world, even extending their brief to Malaysia and Singapore.[54] Today all physicians and surgeons in the region work under either the RACP or the RACS. As with most Tasman organisations, the weight lies heavily on the Australian side, though Australian physicians travel to New Zealand for short-term fellowships. Medical specialists are one group among many such cross-Tasman organisations in science, law and business; thousands of linkages bear the 'Australasian' title and continue to flourish, though the degree of trans-Tasman integration is extraordinarily variable.[55]

Academic migrants and messengers

Education remains the area where a close-knit community encompasses both countries. An unknown but sizeable number of teachers have crossed the 'ditch' both ways during the 19th and 20th centuries. Australia's 'national' literary figure, Henry Lawson, though not a teacher when he crossed over, spent a brief unhappy period at a small school in the South Island.[56] But the most regular traffic of all has been that of university academics – scientists, humanists, policy-makers and administrators. We know comparatively little about this flow, except through personal stories and memoirs and the occasional university history, or by combing dictionaries of biography. Yet a trans-Tasman migratory tradition operated through the 20th century, not ceasing with Australian federation nor functioning merely as a stepping-stone to careers outside the Tasman world. Though part of traditional educational flows within the British empire and Commonwealth, the individuals who undertook these journeys display an array of attitudes to the British heritage of the Tasman world: some hostile to what they found in the old world, some loving England as a revelation and never returning south, and some, like Keith Hancock, the Australian historian who became a professor at Oxford and a Fellow of All Souls, finding it possible to love two soils.[57]

Hancock is a useful individual around whom to examine the trans-Tasman nature of academics' migration. He was one of the advisers chosen by the Australian government to help build the new research schools of the postwar foundation, the Australian National University (ANU), at the heart of the Commonwealth in Canberra. The vision of its founders was to help solve the postwar problems of the wider region, including the Pacific and South-East Asia, with researchers and thinkers connecting Australia to the world. Hancock was joined by eminent Australians in Britain – medical scientist Howard Florey and physicist Mark Oliphant – and Raymond Firth, Professor of Anthropology at the University of London. Hancock chose Firth as the next best option to an Australian because he was a New Zealander with a similar background to the others, to advise Canberra on a Pacific studies research school.[58] The inaugural Vice-Chancellor, who sported the robes of a University of New Zealand DSc, was also a Kiwi: Sir Douglas Copland, born near Timaru, educated at Canterbury University College and a pioneer professional economist who had moved to Australia to become a professor at the University of Melbourne. By 1946 he was Australia's Minister to China.[59]

Other New Zealanders took up positions of power and influence at the ANU in its growing postwar years. J. W. Davidson was recommended by Firth and Hancock as the world's first Professor of Pacific History and went on to a career as constitutional adviser to Pacific Island states emerging into independence. Hancock brokered an offer to W. D. Borrie, from Otago, of a Research Fellowship that led to his establishing the world's first Department of Demography at the ANU in 1952; Borrie was later director of the Research School of Social Sciences as well as chair of Australia's national population inquiry, and had close links to the United Nations and American universities.[60] Gerard Ward travelled the usual Tasman networks from Auckland to London to become foundation Professor of Geography at the newly established University of Papua New Guinea in 1967, then to a professor in the ANU's Research School of Pacific Studies. He, too, rose to become a director of one of the research schools.

Ward's journey is emblematic of many such migrations by trans-Tasman intellectuals. Born and raised in Taupo, Ward's entry into university education was via a teacher's bursary, then a masters degree and an unexpected vacancy in Auckland University's Geography Department. Ward considers himself part of the 'lucky generation' of 1950s academic aspirants: he never once applied for a position other than when he was asked to, and could chance his arm on untenured positions in a growing market. The universities were just beginning to expand throughout the Commonwealth and opportunities were plentiful. New Zealand had enjoyed a higher proportion of its population at university than Australia since the 1930s;[61] and by the 1950s its geography departments were turning out more postgraduates than Australian universities were, though research and publication were increasingly difficult to resource.[62] Ward, like others, was able to take advantage of the demand overseas. The route through a British university was natural, though Ward was one of those antipodeans slightly disappointed by what he found in Britain and more drawn to the Pacific and mid-west cities of the US as closer to the new world society of his upbringing in their economic shape, community structures and architecture; Kiwi postgraduates were already heading to the US for further study before Australians began on that path.[63] Living and working in Australia was more congenial than his experience in England, a feeling of being 'naturalised', but Ward never lost his Kiwi identification with the mountains, native trees, Maori spaces and volcanic soil around Lake Taupo.[64] He remains a trans-Tasman citizen, with two passports, conscious that his identity is now less sharp than it was, embedded with his family in two landscapes.

New Zealanders like Ward created a bridge for other Kiwis, helping to bring other good prospects across the Tasman. Copland had invited Borrie to come to the ANU, as well as Siegfried Nadel, the Austrian anthropologist whom ANU wanted; Nadel promptly recruited Derek Freeman, a New Zealand anthropologist who had worked in Western Samoa and Borneo, studied under Firth in London and was lecturing at Otago University. Copland also sought out Leicester Webb in Wellington. Webb was a senior government administrator, Director of Stabilisation and Marketing in New Zealand during the Second World War, and Copland talked to his masters to tempt him across the Tasman. Webb had lectured in political science at Canterbury University College and was well published; he went to Canberra as Reader in Political Science and became a noted public figure.[65] J. W. Davidson also deliberately sought New Zealand prospects for his Pacific history department, Colin Newbury, Ken Gillion and Alan Ward among them; Newbury was ANU's first PhD in Pacific history.[66]

ANU academics occasionally spoke of a 'Kiwi mafia', but their visibility was high because New Zealand was a neighbourly source of good-quality academics for a community of interests that expanded favourably in the postwar years. Richard Barwick, a scientist born in Christchurch with experience in Antarctica, was one of several recruits around 1960. He saw the Kiwi ability to improvise in outdoor field research as an advantage and believed an unofficial network of trust operated among Kiwis strewn throughout ANU.[67] New Zealanders were also prominent in the surrounds of academic life. Dale Trendall, a classicist, came via academic chairs in Sydney to be the first master of University House, the social heart of the early university. Bill Packard ventured from Canterbury to be the first warden of Bruce Hall.[68] Other New Zealanders with careers of distinction at the ANU were Jack Golson, Ralph Bulmer and Atholl Anderson in archaeology and prehistory, and Anthony Reid in Southeast Asian history. Don Ramson was Dean of Arts and Max Neutze director of the Research School of Social Sciences.

Kiwis were also sliding into prominence in other Australian universities – E. J. Tapp as Professor of History at the University of New England, and W. R. Geddes, Professor of Anthropology at Sydney. A. P. Elkin, the anthropologist who had most influence on Australia's mid-century Aboriginal policies, though born in Australia, spent his formative years in Auckland and looked to the blending of settler and indigenous cultures he discerned in New Zealand. The geographers' diaspora was particularly marked – Murray McCaskill to the new Flinders University, Stuart Duncan to Monash by way of Manchester, Murray Wilson to Monash then Wollongong, Ross Dick to Queensland, and Ken Robinson to Newcastle.

In the Tasman world the flow of people was disproportionately towards Australia. But in the world of academia several high-profile moves went in the opposite direction. Philosopher John Passmore from Sydney went to Otago as professor in 1949, as a follower of John Anderson. He stayed five years before returning to the ANU, unhappy at the egalitarian tertiary education system in which everything was duplicated in four colleges around the country, at extra cost for New Zealand's size and with poor results for the majority of students.[69] John Eccles, the brilliant neurophysiologist and later Nobel prizewinner, was tempted to Otago University in 1944 and came under the influence of the philosopher Karl Popper at Canterbury University College in Christchurch while he was there teaching before returning to Europe. Eccles, too, was poached by the ANU in the mid-1950s, from what was seen effectively as a unified recruiting ground for the universities.[70]

Another Australian to travel back and forth across the Tasman was R. S. Parker, educated in the Economics Faculty of Sydney University. He went first to Canberra University College as administrative officer, then across to Wellington as a lecturer in political science at the university. He also worked for the Public Service Commission in Wellington during the war. In 1946 he returned to lecture and research in Canberra, but went back to Wellington as Professor of Political Science and Public Administration in 1949. He made major contributions to senior public service training and the establishment of an Administrative Staff College before setting sail once again for Canberra and the ANU. Parker made one more attempt to cross back over the Tasman, conceding that New Zealand 'is the one place that seems like home to me', but New Zealand said no.[71] Parker was an early trans-Tasman policy adviser who in practical ways and through his writing helped improve the public services of New Zealand, Australia and Papua New Guinea.

J. B. Condliffe was Melbourne born and moved to New Zealand in 1904 at the age of 13. He became the first Professor of Economics at Canterbury in 1921, went on to the Institute of Pacific Relations in Hawaii, then spent the rest of his life as Professor of Economics at the University of California and a member of the Stanford Research Institute. Other Australians stayed across the Tasman: O. W. Parnaby in history and Ralph Piddington in anthropology at Auckland, H. Winston Rhodes in English at Canterbury, and F. L. W. Wood in history at Victoria University in Wellington. Wood is perhaps the most illustrious, though often forgotten connection between the separated lands of the Tasman world.[72] 'Freddie' Wood (1903–89) was the son of George Arnold Wood, Sydney University's first Professor of History. He was educated in Sydney and at Oxford. Though he inherited his father's non-conformism and took an active part in the British general strike of 1926, Wood won the Chair of History over Wellington's own J. C. Beaglehole, whose leftist leanings cost him the job.

Wood wrote a number of big books in both Australia and New Zealand: *A Concise History of Australia*; *New Zealand in the World*; *Understanding New Zealand* (*This New Zealand* in the New Zealand edition); and the magisterial *The New Zealand People at War* in the Official History of New Zealand in the War series. His *Concise History* sold 40,000 copies over the years. His keynote addresses on New Zealand foreign policy at Australian and New Zealand Association for the Advancement of Science (ANZAAS) congresses and on public radio were printed and reprinted year after year. Like his father, Wood was a man of public affairs, with influence among diplomats and public servants, asked by the press and radio to comment on national and international issues. Though he did not identify himself as a New Zealander until 1960, Wood had taken part in the construction of a New Zealand national story since the 1940s. His *New Zealand in the World* was the beginning of a critique of New Zealand's stance of subordination to Britain, echoing international affairs specialists around Ernest Scott, the Professor of History in Melbourne who had begun to move away from a British-oriented foreign policy stance towards one more engaged with and educated about the Asian 'Near North'.[73] He maintained a frank and independent set of views through the postwar period. His *The New Zealand People at War* crafted the story of a developing sense of nationhood that had little use for a continuing colonial dependence on Britain. By the 1960s, though increasingly sceptical of US guarantees in the Security Treaty between Australia, New Zealand and the US (Anzus), Wood was still sure that friendship with the US was critical, as it was with 'our hard headed cousins' across the Tasman, with whom, though they did not recognise it, a closer association would be advantageous.[74]

Wood, like R. S. Parker and Leicester Webb, was integral to a Wellington-based public intellectual tradition that influenced policy by training public servants. Like them he remained fundamentally a citizen of the Tasman world, supporting the major historical journal from Australia and keeping ties to Australian historians in the postwar years through the ANZAAS congresses. He was also an important mentor to a lineage of historians who had influence across the Tasman world and its Pacific neighbourhood. One of these, J. W. Davidson, developed a Pacific history department in Canberra that educated a generation of graduates for the ever-widening circle of regional universities and island government institutions that constituted the periphery of the old Australasia. Another, A. D. Ward, after a distinguished career as a participant historian in the area of land conflicts between indigenous people and settler communities in Australia, Papua New Guinea and other Pacific Islands, became an influential figure in New Zealand's Waitangi Tribunal as its overseeing historian. All three have quietly broadened the nationalist history traditions of both countries and helped to bridge the chasm between them.[75]

Conclusion

Such cultural messengers show how the nationalist projections of New Zealand and Australia have masked an interactive history and a longstanding trans-Tasman dialogue in frameworks for learning, both secular and religious. The traffic of institutions, people and ideas has been regular and sustained, if uneven and heavily in Australia's favour. School, church, academic and scientific links are perhaps the most easily demonstrated among learning environments. Less easy to isolate but pervasive nonetheless is the trans-Tasman world of shared culture. Miles Fairburn argues there is nothing 'exceptionalist' about New Zealand's history and institutions. Its language, its political and educational ideas and its 20th-century, commercialised popular culture apparent in radio, magazines and cinema are overwhelmingly derivative of Australia, Britain and North America. New Zealand's uniqueness lies perhaps paradoxically in its unusual dominance by others' cultures, especially its 'unconscious yet powerful' neighbour Australia.[76] Leaving aside the obvious rejoinder that this same position can be argued for any number of societies, the point underlines the interconnectedness of the Tasman countries in a common cultural alliance.

But how much regular learning from each other has gone on? New Zealand and Australia have been described as sharing 'an affectionate and competitive cultural solidarity'.[77] The competitiveness is certainly regular, the solidarity fluctuating. The Australia–New Zealand Foundation established in 1979 to strengthen relations by encouraging study and discussion of common issues was disestablished barely two decades later.[78] Though literary relations were sustained regularly through the *Bulletin* in the early 20th century, mutual ignorance of each other's literature and art, beyond a few internationally recognised figures, was a constant complaint at the end of the century.[79] Trans-Tasman dialogue by thinkers and policy-makers, business elites and media observers was taken up in serious ways at the dawn of the 21st century, in academic conferences and the government-sponsored leadership forums, but it is not yet clear that such venues have become learning environments that will deepen the relationship. Like the volcanoes that dot the New Zealand landscape, the Tasman world is always there in the background, smoking quietly away, with irregular eruptions of activity and noise to remind people it exists.

CHAPTER EIGHT
Playing Together

Rosemary Baird and Peter Hempenstall

The form of popular culture whose antipodean expression has remained most hidden in both national stories is, ironically, the most high-profile activity between the two countries: sport. In the grand national narratives any sign of a common Tasman history in general, let alone in sport, is studiously ignored. Sport was rarely given a place in earlier histories but in recent years has gained space as a key outgrowth of colonial and subsequently national communities. Sport is now recognised as the engine of masculinity, harnessed to the disciplinary rituals, intense competition, and cadet militarism generated by boys' schools.[1] The middle-class private schools of the Tasman world shared this 'moral curriculum' in particular, as we pointed out in Chapter 7. This common basis generated an early community of interest and both countries gained international credibility in sport by first playing together as 'Australasia'.

In tennis, the New Zealand Lawn Tennis Association in 1904 proposed joint teams to increase the likelihood that a British team would tour the Tasman world, and in order to field the best players in the international Davis Cup tournament. The partnership of Norman Brookes of Melbourne and Anthony Wilding of Christchurch, who were good friends, won the Wimbledon doubles final for 'Australasia' in 1907, as well as the Davis Cup. Much like the America's Cup in the late 20th century, the Davis Cup stirred up media frenzy and parochialism when carried home in triumph. Wilding and Brookes defeated the Americans to win the cup in 1908 in Melbourne, and again in Sydney in 1909.

New Zealand joined forces with the Australians to win international supremacy in cycling and athletics as well.[2] The first 'Australasian' track and field championships were held in Melbourne in 1892, and the Amateur Athletic Union of Australasia was created with the idea of sending a joint team to London. New Zealand and Australia competed as 'Australasia' at the Olympics in London in 1908 and in Stockholm in 1912. But the war stirred desires for a distinctive identity; New Zealand attended its first Olympics as a separate nation at Antwerp in 1920. Davis Cup tennis was the last example of an 'Australasian' sporting venture, a joint team competing for the cup until 1923.

Beyond these early links, New Zealand and Australia have shared four dominating codes of sport for the whole of the 20th century: rugby league, rugby union, cricket and netball. When their tales of origin and glory are told, they are subsumed into national New Zealand and Australian narratives, or retailed as self-contained epics. Seeing them as stories that bridge the Tasman and encompass one population brings into focus a history that recognises a common past. Our approach synthesises national sporting literature for these four codes on both sides of the Tasman into a trans-Tasman account of sport-making in New Zealand and Australia.

Rugby league

A major factor contributing to the establishment of rugby league in the Tasman world was the players' dissatisfaction with the amateurism of rugby union, the main football code in New South Wales and Queensland. Victoria had already developed its own style of Gaelic-derived football, Australian Rules. The 1905 All Black tour of Britain was extremely successful and made a profit of over £7000 for the New Zealand Rugby Football Union (NZRFU). However, because of the strict amateurism of the game, players did not receive any of the money. The tour convinced local rugby players that, although there was significant money in rugby union, they personally would be debarred from a share of the profits while they were amateurs.[3] Other causes of discontent common to both nations, though felt more strongly in Australia, were the lack of reimbursement for lost wages, injury leave from work, and doctors' bills. To many, the very rules of rugby union stifled enjoyment for players and spectators.[4]

In New Zealand, Albert Baskerville, a 23-year-old postal worker and rugby player, heard tales from the returning All Blacks about a breakaway group from the English northern counties who set up a Northern Union in opposition to the Rugby Football Union. Baskerville was inspired to organise a New Zealand rugby team that would tour and play the Northern Union clubs. Participants would pay their own costs but share equally in any profits. General player dissatisfaction with the amateur system was so high that players were willing to take the risk of NZRFU disqualification from rugby for life while at the same time investing a significant amount of money in this new opportunity. Of the 200 top players in New Zealand, 160 applied for the team; the final team chosen contained nine former All Blacks and 14 provincial representatives.[5] Fortunately most players made a profit from their investment, which guaranteed them financial security.

The creation of a professional rugby league team was not purely a domestic affair: key New Zealanders encouraged rugby players in Sydney to break away from rugby union. George Smith, when in Australia on his way home from the All Blacks 1905 tour in which he had played, had talked enthusiastically about the new Northern Union rules he had heard of in England. In 1907 he telegraphed Peter Moir, a leading Australian player, to see if Australians would like to put together a team to play the professionals.[6] Their response was immediate and a group of rugby players met surreptitiously at Victor Trumper's sports store to discuss the possibility of forming a professional rugby league in Sydney. On 8 August 1907 the discontented players decided to form the New South Wales Rugby League, and a local businessman and cricket umpire, James J. Giltinan, offered to provide the £500 guarantee required by New Zealand's team.[7]

These professional All Blacks visited Sydney on their way to tour England in 1907. They were pejoratively dubbed the All Golds by the Australian press, a title that soon lost its negative connotations. An important development was the addition of Dally Messenger, a popular Australian rugby union player.[8] Messenger made the All Golds an 'Australasian' team, and his achievements in Britain gave Australians their own early rugby league hero. The All Golds visited Sydney again in 1908 on their return from England. The New Zealanders had developed an almost reformist zeal for the new code, and over a two-week period they coached the Australians intensively in Northern Union rules.[9] The All Blues (New South Wales) played three matches against the All Golds and won two. Their success gave the new game credibility with the Sydney public and began the rhythm of Tasman world contests: New Zealand might innovate but Australia quickly dominated.

Until the early 1920s Tasman links remained tight. In 1908 a Maori team played league in Australia. Their visit was a spectacular success and drew large crowds. In 1911 and 1921 combined Tasman teams toured Britain. New Zealand sent teams to Australia in 1909, 1911, 1912, 1913, 1919 and 1921. New South Wales teams toured New Zealand in 1912, 1913 and 1922, while an Australian team visited in 1919, an interchange that especially benefited New Zealand, where rugby league was slow to become established.[10] After the 1920s Australian and New Zealand experiences of rugby league diverged. In Australia – or more precisely Sydney – rugby league became increasingly popular and well organised, whereas rugby league in New Zealand struggled to overcome rugby union's dominance over the national imagination.

Australian rugby league began in a more organised manner than in New Zealand. Entire clubs, rather than just individuals as in New Zealand, switched to the code. By the time the All Golds returned to Australia, eight district clubs had been set up and the Australian club competition had started. By 1911 rugby league matches were attracting huge audiences in Sydney, and increasingly in Brisbane, at the expense of rugby union.

Circumstances weighed more heavily against the growth of rugby league in New Zealand, where rugby union was deeply entrenched. The success of the 1905 All Blacks fed into the young dominion's thirst for a uniqueness that helped build a sense of national identity.[11] New Zealand also lacked the large clusters of working-class people who generally formed the basis of league players and supporters in Sydney and northern England. The game existed at interprovincial and national but not club level, with teams developing as individual players joined up.[12] Progress was best in Auckland, the largest and most cosmopolitan city, which from 1910 had an uninterrupted club championship. Yet rugby league remained amateur in New Zealand, struggling behind rugby union.

Little changed until the 1980s. The Winfield Cup had become Australia's premier rugby league competition, courtesy of growing commercial sponsorship, and by the 1980s had acquired a group of followers in New Zealand who listened to the games on the radio, went to pubs that screened matches, and travelled to Sydney for finals. The expansion of the competition, growing numbers of New Zealanders who lived in or travelled to Australia, and the move of the Kiwis' coach, Graeme Lowe, to train Manly, were all reasons for the growing popularity of Australian rugby league in New Zealand. By 1990 New Zealand television gave major coverage to the Winfield Cup. National rugby union players, such as Matthew Ridge, switched to playing league in Australia. In 1994 the Winfield Cup involved 40 New Zealanders, and many more had played in the past 15 years.[13] This interest led Auckland rugby league to seek entry for a local team to the Winfield Cup for this purpose, and in 1994 the Auckland Warriors came into being.

The era of professionalism brought Australian and New Zealand rugby league closer together and pitted the Tasman world against Europe. The successful 1982 and 1986 Kangaroo tours of Europe revealed that the Australians were far ahead in their game. They employed organisational novelties like tackle counts and match statistics; the players were psychologically motivated, and had clear game plans. The Kiwis' historic winning campaign in the 2005 Gillette Tri-nations had similar hallmarks. Their success was attributed to 'coaching, psychological and emotional masterstrokes'; a team psychologist used weekly themes for games such as 'burn the boat', 'bully the bully' (Australia) and 'slay the dragon' to build up the players.[14]

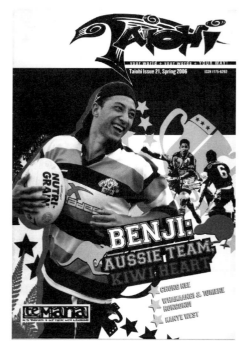

Benji Marshall, who made his NRL debut with the Wests Tigers at age 18.

Te Mana: Taiohi, issue 21, Ministry of Education, Wellington, 2006

165

There were still differences in the two rugby league cultures, mirroring the contradictory impulses and structural variations that mark the Tasman world. The working-class origins and continued loyalties of Sydney clubs often had more in common with their northern England counterparts than with Kiwi clubs, at least in the first half of the 20th century.[15] In New Zealand rugby league never gained the widespread working-class support it enjoyed in Australia and England. New Zealand's first rugby league players were largely middle class. The 1907 All Golds included 13 white-collar workers (compared with six white-collar workers in the 1905 All Blacks). The All Golds' tour was not the result of working-class defiance. Rather, it was an entrepreneurial trip requiring significant investment, which aimed to provide travel, adventure and financial benefits for its participants.[16] The attempts to implement rugby league in New Zealand also lacked the driving force of working-class dissatisfaction. Class issues of snobbery were never as strong in New Zealand rugby union as they were in Australia and Britain. In New Zealand rugby union was generally socially inclusive and competitive, but rugby league did quickly become known as a 'working-class' sport; it prospered in working-class Auckland, the inner-city suburbs of Christchurch, and mining towns on the West Coast. However, rugby union remained a more popular option for working-class men than rugby league.[17]

Ever since the acrimonious split of the Northern Union from the Rugby Football Union in England, league has always had a difficult relationship with rugby union. The English, New Zealand and Australian rugby unions all tried together to stifle the development of league.[18] The animosity between the two codes was compounded by rugby league's predilection for poaching union players. The basis of rugby league's success in Sydney was its 1911 coup in bribing 13 Wallabies to change codes. On a Wallabies tour to Britain in 1947 professional Northern Union clubs purloined three key players, the first defectors out of a total of 57 Wallabies who were to switch codes from 1945 to 1995. The poker machines of New South Wales clubs provided the money that Australian clubs needed to entice amateur rugby union players to change to league. In five years from 1969 to 1974, 11 Wallabies players defected to league. These departures contributed to the poor performances of the Wallabies in the late 1960s and early 1970s.[19] Although Australia was the most extreme case, code swapping also occurred in New Zealand and England. A major reason for the professionalisation of rugby union in the 1990s was union officials' fears that the proposed worldwide Super League competition would attract all the top union players to league. As a result, the Super 12 and annual Tri-nations series between New Zealand, Australia and South Africa were established (see next section).

On both sides of the Tasman, league has had strong international links that have helped it to globalise. Despite, or perhaps because of league's limited regional bases, international transfer of players has been common. Even before the All Golds' tour, Northern Union teams recruited New Zealand players. George

'As the only Aussie amongst a fine sporting bunch of Kiwis I'd like to say how much
I've appreciated all the condescending advice you've given me.'

Nevile Lodge, 31 August 1964.

B-133-287, NZ Cartoon Archive, Alexander Turnbull Library, Wellington, courtesy of Debby Edwards

Stevenson, an Otago representative, joined Warrington Club in the 1890s, and
Wellington representative Alf Ramsden was playing for Hunslet when the All
Golds arrived in England.[20] The first import to an Australian team was in 1922,
when Huatahi Turoa Brown Paki, the captain of the Maori team, played for the
St George club.[21] In spite of bans on transfers, every time restrictions were lifted
or threatened, British clubs in particular would race to snatch up players from the
antipodes. As teams in the Winfield Cup grew wealthier, many Australian clubs
targeted Britons and New Zealanders. By 1979 the New Zealand Rugby League
realised the benefit of this trend and granted transfers on the condition that the
players be allowed to play for the national team. As a result, both Australian and
English teams imported many New Zealand players.[22]

The Tasman world has also been influential in expanding the code to new
overseas converts. The All Golds enthusiastically taught the new Sydney league
teams about Northern Union rules. The Northern Union itself was so determined to expand that it sent a team to Australia and New Zealand in 1910,

entirely prepared to lose money on the tour.[23] Rugby league was introduced to Papua New Guinea in 1949 and soon became the national game. Western Samoa, Tonga and the Cook Islands were also encouraged to take up league. Australia has made periodic attempts to popularise league in the US, but only the three original nations, England, Australia and New Zealand, play at a competitive international level.

Rugby union

Rugby union was started in Australia and New Zealand by English immigrants in the mid-19th century. In Australia the game was played in Sydney and Queensland. In New Zealand it was widespread, and especially strong in the four main urban centres. Boys' schools in both nations, initially private schools but later also public schools, adopted rugby as the quintessential character-building sport, part of the empire's inheritance. By the end of the 19th century provincial clubs and national unions existed in both countries. However, rugby union's popularity in Australia dwindled after the successful rugby league competition grew in Sydney as outlined above; rugby union became the preserve of the upper middle class. During the two world wars many Australian rugby union competitions were discontinued, to the great detriment of the code. By contrast, rugby union in New Zealand was played at all levels of society, in both rural and urban settings, and continued throughout the war, both at home and in the armed forces. The Kiwis (the service team of 1945) toured Britain to great acclaim.[24] While rugby in Australia remained amateur for most of the 20th century, New Zealand rugby, amateur in name, trained, organised and rewarded its national team in a semi-professional manner.

New Zealand rugby, aware of its strength relative to Australia, consciously attempted to aid the Australian code throughout the 20th century. From the early 1880s New Zealand sent teams to Sydney. The international games attracted large crowds and gave Australian rugby the profits it needed to survive.[25] In 1914 New Zealand and Australia, as part of a plan to win back Sydney from league to union, planned annual tours with each other, but the war intervened.[26] In the 1920s New Zealand, aware of the uphill battle in rebuilding the game in New South Wales, toured Australia frequently.[27] Indeed, New Zealand saw the rugby union tours to league territory in Australia as missionary work. The *New Zealand Herald* editorial of 1947 asked rhetorically, 'If rugby is the national religion of New Zealanders who can blame them if they regard an Australian tour as the perfect opportunity to show the light to the multitudinous heathen?'[28] New Zealand reprised its benefactor role in 1973 when Australian rugby was again in crisis. By that time the Australian national team had earned the nickname the 'Woeful Wallabies' and crowd numbers were decreasing. Colin Meads and Wilson Whineray crossed the Tasman for a special conference to address the problem. Using their insights an action plan was developed to reach the Australian community via touring schoolboy sides. New Zealand also helped revive rugby in Queensland during the 1970s by sending regular tours there.

Occasionally, especially at an international level, Australian and New Zealand rugby unions have worked together. On the 1905 Originals' tour of Britain there are reports of New Zealand and Australian supporters welcoming the All Blacks and doing the haka together at games.[29] In 1909 the NZRFU refused to make reforms in the game, arguing that it would be wrong to adopt alterations before the Australian unions of New South Wales and Queensland had considered them.[30] In 1920 several proposals to speed up rugby and make it more skilful were developed by New Zealand and Australian officials to present to the English Rugby Football Union.[31] The New Zealand and Australian rugby unions worked together at International Rugby Board (IRB) meetings to push for an international rugby competition, and in 1984 gained their objective of jointly hosting the inaugural World Cup in 1987. Australia and New Zealand also worked together to create a professional rugby franchise system in 1995.

Frequent exchange of rugby players and officials between New Zealand and Australia during the 20th century is further evidence of a common Tasman approach to the code. Admittedly such exchanges have been a result of immigration rather than intentional player purchasing and, following the trend of immigration between the two nations discussed in Chapter 3, most of the traffic has been from New Zealand to Australia. However, a Tasman approach has ensued.

There has been no systematic study of the numbers involved in trans-Tasman player movement, though the range of individual stories suggests they are considerable. In the 1936 Wallaby team, one member had played for Auckland, and another was the son of a New Zealand international who had moved with his family to Australia.[32] In 1951 Keith Gudsel, a New Zealander studying at Sydney University, played for the Wallabies; the IRB had just passed a 'two cap' rule that allowed each union to choose any player to represent it regardless of whether they had played for another union. It was a timely rule, given that by the mid-20th century there were an estimated 60,000 New Zealanders in Sydney. Typically, they made their presence felt in the rugby world. T. P. Pauling, an Australian selector in 1951, was the son of a New Zealand representative player. Harold Masters, an All Black in 1922, coached Sydney University. Former Wallaby captain Des Connor played for the All Blacks in the early 1960s, and then in 1968 returned to Australia to coach the Wallabies. The 1972 Wallaby captain, Greg Davis, emigrated to Australia after he failed to get into the All Blacks.[33] There are few researched examples of such movement in the other direction but it is noteworthy that as of 2001, 14 of the total number of All Blacks were born in Australia.[34]

Rugby Nomads, a book detailing New Zealand's recent rugby exports, highlights the continuing informal nature of this player migration. Although there are many examples of New Zealand players gaining professional club contracts in England, France and Japan, the three profiled New Zealanders who moved to Australia did so for personal reasons. Jeremy Paul moved to Australia with his family when he was starting high school, and later became a Wallaby. Grant Holmes, who played top-level provincial rugby in New Zealand, retired to Queensland, joined a golden oldies team and became the patron of Hervey Bay Rugby Football Club 1989–99. Paul Koteka, who played two tests for the All Blacks in the late 1970s, received a proposal in 1984 to play as an amateur for Nedlands rugby club in Perth. He accepted because Australia offered him better job opportunities.[35]

Some of the steady stream of New Zealanders migrating to Australia often play, coach and support Australian club rugby. However, many Kiwis living in Australia remain loyal to the All Blacks. At trans-Tasman test matches held in Sydney, New Zealand support has occasionally been so strong that the All Blacks have benefited from an atmosphere akin to a home game. The links between Australian and New Zealand rugby are thus complex, accommodating seemingly contradictory loyalties.

These complexities have only increased as rugby union has become fully professional in a global market. In 1995 the creation of the Super League competition by media magnate Rupert Murdoch, in opposition to Kerry Packer's National Rugby League (NRL) competition, started a bidding war for league players. Both New Zealand and Australian rugby unions realised they were in grave danger of losing their best players to league. At a secret meeting in the Australian Rugby Union (ARU) headquarters both nations formally decided to abandon amateurism. From this point a 'rugby war' started, with two competing groups seeking to create an international professional rugby competition. One side was represented by the New Zealand, Australian and South African rugby unions, who at the World Cup in 1995 created the SANZAR body that worked with Murdoch's News Corp to sign up its players to a new Super 12 contest and Tri-nations series. Meanwhile a group of Australian businessmen and rugby enthusiasts working with Packer tried to create a World Rugby Council (WRC), in which England and France would also play.[36]

Ultimately Murdoch and SANZAR prevailed, signing a $550 million deal over 10 years. The resulting Super 12 competition was a great success and has recently added two more teams. The renamed Super 14 administration works with the national rugby unions and attempts to regulate players' club distribution to avoid the creation of super clubs, as found in the English premier soccer league. Overall, Australian and New Zealand teams have tended to do better, partly because the South African teams have found it difficult to adjust to long and frequent flights.[37]

Commentators see the impact of professionalism on Australian rugby union as almost entirely positive. By 2002 more men and women played union than league in Australia, and the country had as many players as New Zealand.[38] In a reversal of past patterns, Australian rugby union now buys up Australian league stars. By contrast, although New Zealand has reaped the same financial benefits from professional rugby as Australia, some argue that professionalism is ruining the traditional game. Joseph Romanos claims that since rugby was professionalised it has become a commodity. Secondary school rugby is supposedly dying out, soccer is overtaking rugby in popularity, and the Super 12 (14) wears players out so they perform less well in international tests.[39] New Zealanders tend to be more pessimistic about the professionalisation of rugby than Australians, a typical reflex of the sibling relationship of these Tasman nations. The fear is common that the Wallabies will become better than the All Blacks, with the hard rural men of New Zealand rugby replaced by soft professionals.[40] More pragmatic views reject this populist nostalgia: given the social, economic, demographic and technological changes in society, rugby had to go professional to survive.

One of the signal effects of the professionalisation of rugby has been the enhanced opportunities for a range of ethnic groups who have been important to the code but traditionally relegated to the margins of the Anglo-Celtic mainstream. In New Zealand, Maori have illustrated the contradictions inherent in the Tasman world's attitude to rugby. For many decades they were expendable for tours to apartheid South Africa, or tokenised, always in the name of the 'good of the game'.[41] The paradox is that Maori stayed loyal to rugby union over league; indeed, the NZRFU created opportunities for Maori in union to prevent them defecting. Since the 19th century they have also been included in national teams. Maori rugby teams toured Australia regularly from 1910 to 1958 and were very popular there.[42] Maori could also use rugby to their own ends. Rugby success was a key reason for recognition of Ngati Ruahine as an iwi in its own right in the 1950s.[43] The haka, while not always done correctly, is performed before every All Blacks test and has become an integral part of the team's identity. When Buck Shelford, a proud Maori, was captain of the All Blacks during the 1980s, the haka became much more serious and impressive.[44] In recent years a phenomenon referred to as 'the browning of rugby' has occurred as Maori and Pacific Islanders make up an increasingly large proportion of players in both New Zealand and Australia. They have been integral to rugby culture in a way that demonstrates the links of the Tasman world to the wider region.

Aboriginal players in Australia have not been as well treated. They only started to play rugby at representative level late in the 20th century. The middle-class nature of rugby and its promotion in the private-school system in Australia worked against their involvement, though there was resistance to exploitation of indigenous culture. Rugby officials attempted to make the 1908–09 Wallabies perform an Aboriginal war cry before their matches in England. However, the players rejected the practice as false and a wretched parody of a dispossessed people.[45] In later years some Aboriginal players, such as the Ella brothers and

Andrew Walker, have become well known, indeed emblematic of a certain 'Australian' flair for playing the game. But rugby league remains the rugby code with the highest level of Aboriginal participation.[46] Australian Rules attracts even more Aboriginal players across the country.

The phrase 'imaginary grandstand' refers to the idea that nations perform in front of an invented audience of international spectators.[47] Accordingly, some nations are more important to defeat and impress than others. Despite frequent rugby interaction with Australia, for most of the 20th century New Zealand's significant foes were the British Lions and the South African Springboks. New Zealand and Australian national teams competed for the first time in Sydney in 1903 but the game was overshadowed by the famous 1905 All Blacks tour of Britain. For most of the 20th century winning a test series in South Africa was the holy grail of New Zealand rugby. As sociologists Camilla Obel and Terry Austrin argue, though tours to and from Australia were far more frequent than with the Springboks, they were less capable of securing the link between the game and the imagined nation.[48] New Zealand rugby officials tended to treat the Wallabies as it suited them, the very manner in which Australia tended to treat New Zealand when it came to other sports. In 1904 the NZRFU refused an offer from New South Wales to field an 'Australasian' rugby team against

75th jubilee rugby test between New Zealand and Australia, August 1967.
AAQT 6401 R4126, Archives New Zealand, Wellington

a touring British side because it would demean New Zealand rugby to play alongside Australia. New Zealand rugby authorities gave touring Wallabies teams punishing travel schedules and free Bluff oysters to make them ill before test matches.[49] In 1938 the NZRFU refused to tour Australia because the rules then used in Australia were slightly different from international rules. After five days Australia capitulated and agreed to play the way New Zealand wanted.[50] More than once the Wallabies had to play inferior New Zealand teams, as the All Blacks were touring South Africa or England. In 1972, after an extremely one-sided series, the NZRFU even threatened to discontinue trans-Tasman tests.[51]

Then in 1981 the riotous and divisive South African rugby tour of New Zealand destroyed the special relationship between the All Blacks and the Springboks, and New Zealand turned to a newly resurgent Australia to fill the gap. The Bledisloe Cup competition came to symbolise the new competitiveness between the two nations. In 1931 Lord Bledisloe, New Zealand's Governor-General, had donated the cup for trans-Tasman tests. For many years the public largely ignored the competition; it was the newfound prowess of the Wallabies and the televising of rugby that increased its importance. In 1979 Australia won two out of three Bledisloe Cup matches. Thousands of New Zealanders watched the Wallabies pick up the trophy and run around the Sydney Cricket Ground, brandishing it before the crowd. From that moment the Bledisloe Cup assumed a deeper significance for New Zealanders.[52]

After the resurgence of Australian rugby, confident paternalism was replaced by heated rivalry. New Zealand stopped dismissing the Wallabies and instead attacked them. During the 1986 Australian tour of New Zealand there were persistent anti-Australian jokes on New Zealand talkback radio. The loathing directed at the Wallabies was intense and unremitting.[53] Advertisers marketed a brand of New Zealand potato chip as 'thick as an Aussie forward', and anti-Wallabies anecdotes became common. In a 1999 test match the NZRFU joined in with popular attacks on the Wallabies through its plans for a 'Blackout Night' to promote the new All Black uniform. Organisers asked the crowd to wear all black clothing. Once the Wallabies had been introduced on the ground before the match began, the lights were turned out. When they were switched back on again the All Blacks were on the field. The normally laconic crowd sang the national anthem stridently and booed the Wallabies. The intimidation tactics worked; the Wallabies had a nightmare game. In response the Australian team organised a 'Gold Rush' night for an Australian test.[54]

Australian rugby for much of the 20th century displayed a singular and unusual deference towards this most Kiwi of sports. Rugby aficionados always acknowledged the All Blacks' superiority and treated them with respect. During the 1920s, All Black–Springbok tests were given more coverage in the Australian sports newspaper, the *Referee*, than All Black–Wallaby games. Amicable relationships prevailed between the two national teams up to the 1950s. In

Brisbane in 1929 the All Blacks were welcomed onto the rugby field to the accompaniment of 'For they are jolly good fellows'.[55] This sporting comradeship faded after a 1968 series that was violent and spiteful on both sides, returning the trans-Tasman relationship to the tradition of sibling rivalry.

In the 1980s, with Australia's rugby resurgence, the Wallabies focused on overcoming their psychological disadvantage against the All Blacks. Two World Cup triumphs and a continuing competitiveness in both Tri-nations and Bledisloe Cup matches have enabled Australian rugby to lose its sense of inferiority, though it still respects the All Blacks' historical achievements. The irony is that, in this one area where New Zealand has consistently dominated Australia, since the 1980s Australia has become the most important nation in New Zealand's imaginary rugby grandstand: yet more evidence of the growth of a Tasman world meaningful to both sides.

Cricket

Cricket is the game that the two antipodean nations play less frequently together than they do the three other major sports. Yet cricket springs from the same English passion for the game and was taken up vigorously from the earliest days of new settlement in both countries. The first account of cricket played in New Zealand is from Charles Darwin during the *Beagle*'s stopover in the Bay of Islands in 1835.[56] According to Greg Ryan, cricket in New Zealand has traditionally highlighted the limitations, insecurities and realities of being a small nation. Cricket was strongest in the four main cities and dominated by Anglo middle-class interests.[57] For much of the 19th and 20th centuries the game was of poor quality, the reasons being the lack of large cities, a small population, insufficient financial support and unsuitable grounds.[58] The interwar years were a period of domestic growth but continued international failure for New Zealand cricket.[59] New Zealand did not achieve a test victory until 1956, which was against the West Indies, and did not beat Australia until 1974 and England until 1978.[60] New Zealand only became competitive in international cricket during the late 1970s and 1980s, but after a brief flurry among the frontrunners internationally, the Black Caps – as they were called from 1998 – in the early 21st century began to decline again.

New Zealand more than its Tasman cousins has always leaned towards identification with the English, and has correspondingly identified less with Australians.[61] New Zealand cricket was much closer to the official English cricket establishment, the Marylebone Cricket Club (MCC), than the Australian Cricket Board (ACB). New Zealand papers provided more commentary on English county cricket than on the Australian state Sheffield Shield games, and provincial cricket associations preferred to bypass Australian coaches in favour of more expensive English coaches. The New Zealand press gave extensive coverage to the 1932–33 'Bodyline' controversy during an English tour of Australia.[62] Despite not having witnessed any of the games, journalists assumed a firmly pro-English stance: they accused the Australian press of sensationalism in order to inflame anti-English sentiment, and attacked Australia and its sporting traditions. Letters to the editor claimed that England won because they were the better team and that the Australian protests were an example of how mob spirit was threatening to destroy the game.[63]

For most of the 20th century the English were New Zealand's main international competition. There has been relatively little documented trans-Tasman migration of Kiwi players. Clarrie Grimmet, a New Zealander rejected by his nation's cricket selectors, moved to Australia aged 17, became one of Australia's best-known spin bowlers and played for Australia between 1924 and 1936. Jeff Crowe, captain of the Black Caps in the late 1980s and early 1990s, formerly played for Australia. Richard Hadlee is the only New Zealander who has played for an Australian club. But in the late 20th century New Zealand's best players, such as Glenn Turner, Geoff Howarth, John Wright and Richard Hadlee, played professional English county cricket rather than join Sheffield Shield teams.[64]

Australian cricket, on the other hand, had more wide-ranging national significance; cricket was the first team sport established in Australia, was played as early as 1803, and was first organised into club and inter-regional competitions in the 1830s. Though Australian settlers played cricket as a sign of normalcy, nostalgia and linkage to England, by the end of the 19th century cricket had come to dramatise the relationship between the Australian colonists and England.[65] Bill Mandle (an expatriate Kiwi) argued that cricket was a vehicle for emerging Australian nationalism well in advance of federation, and this idea is generally accepted, though early Australian cricket was often deferential and pro-imperial.[66] The game became hugely popular during the 1930s and 1940s but its dominance lessened in the 1950s. Officials at the time believed cricket was in trouble and made rule changes to speed up the game, though in reality there had been no serious loss of public support.[67] From the 1970s, with the advent of television and professionalism, Australian cricket rose to new heights. It became enshrined as the national game, a position that has yet to be challenged.

Part of cricket's nationalistic appeal is the belief that Australian cricket is unique in style and in the traditions associated with it. Richard Cashman argues that Australian players and officials have always had a more pragmatic and commercial view of cricket than England; that the game has always been more egalitarian in the antipodes, which prevented private schools dominating; and that Australian crowds have developed to an art form the rude yet humorous banter yelled at players.[68] Certainly in comparison with New Zealand, Australia has a distinctive style of play. New Zealand, like England, uses a combination of attacking batting and attacking bowling, and thus selects batsmen who can bowl. Australia, because of its harder pitches that favour batsmen, uses defensive bowling. In Australia, bowlers are 25 per cent more important than batsmen, and specialists rather than all-rounders are likely to be selected.[69]

Legends abound in Australian cricket too: its greatest hero is Donald Bradman, swashbuckling batsman of the 1930s and 1940s. The Bradman legend is particularly powerful as it includes aspects of the Australian bush mythology, the alleged fount of national virtues. In the 1930s he became the object of hero-worship. Crowd numbers increased hugely when he played. On retirement he became an establishment figure in Australian cricket administration. A Bradman museum was opened in his hometown in 1989.[70] Indeed, Bradman is no longer a hero just for the cricketing community; he is an iconic figure for Australia, and was represented as exemplary for the entire nation by John Howard during his term of government.

Australian cricket also has a symbol as meaningful as New Zealand's All Black jersey: the baggy green cap. Cashman investigates the symbolic evolution of the baggy green cap in his *Sport in the National Imagination*. Its origin lies in the 19th century when players wore distinctive caps to differentiate themselves from their opponents. Australian caps became uniquely baggier in the 1920s. Despite challenges to its shape throughout the 20th century from other hat styles, the cap rose in value and significance from the 1970s. Steve Waugh, Australian captain in the 1990s, augmented the status of the cap, always wearing his original cap during opening sessions of test matches. Waugh used it to motivate his team and link them to Australian cricket heroes of the past.

The widespread consensus among cricket writers on both sides of the Tasman is that the Australian Board of Control for International Cricket neglected New Zealand cricket during the first half of the 20th century. As J. P. Carr puts it, '[T]he decline in the trans-Tasman relationship during the latter 1920s and 1930s ... caused long-term irreparable damage to the New Zealand game.'[71] New Zealand had to wait until 1946 for its first one-off test against Australia, and until 1973–74 for its first three-test series when other countries in the Commonwealth were treated better. Part of the reason for Australia's neglect was its long and valued connection with English cricket; Australia and England played test cricket from 1851 onwards. In 1882 Australia won its first test victory over England on English soil, and so began the compelling myth of the 'ashes of English cricket', interred in a small urn. It took some years for the Ashes tradition to develop, and there is much mystery as to what is actually contained in the urn (there are four differing versions).[72] The notorious 'Bodyline' tour of 1932–33 reinforced the importance of Anglo-Australian cricket. England has been, and still is in many ways, Australia's most important cricketing rival.

In contrast, successive generations of Australian officials were quick to identify weaknesses in New Zealand cricket, and were slow to assist.[73] After the Australian tour of New Zealand in 1927–28 the relationship between the two nations broke down. Relations between the ACB and New Zealand Cricketing Council (NZCC) reached an all-time low in 1930. The ACB stated that, while willing to assist New Zealand cricket by sending young Australian players on development tours after the Sheffield Shield competition was over, it would not send more experienced players as this would unfairly deprive Australian clubs. For much of the 20th century, most Australian cricket teams sent to New Zealand were second elevens, made up of novices or retirees.

This official Australian neglect continued throughout the 1930s when Australia obstructed other national teams from including New Zealand in their Australian itineraries. This stance is ironic, given popular support for trans-Tasman cricket among Australian players and public. The captain of a New South Wales team that toured New Zealand in 1924 emphasised that his team 'was out to do what they could for the game in New Zealand', while his tour manager stated that he would do all in his power to see that both English and Australian teams played in New Zealand in the future.[74] After a cancelled 1933 tour to New Zealand, the Australian press appeared to be on the side of New Zealand. The Sydney *Daily Telegraph* wrote that 'the helping of a weaker cricketing country should also be considered', and the *Australian Daily* claimed that the ACB had 'shown a deplorable lack of vision, a total disregard of its duties to the game in the sister dominion and rank parsimony in its attitude to the players.'[75]

There were logical reasons for the Australian administration's lack of interest, no less so today as the Australian cricketers sweep all before them. In fact a reasonable amount of trans-Tasman cricket has been played. Before 1973 there were 26 tours that crossed the Tasman. In spite of playing inferior second eleven Australian teams, New Zealand usually lost abysmally. Moreover, New Zealand tours were usually unprofitable. Even into the 1960s New Zealand tours regularly lost money.[76] By contrast, English cricket tours and Ashes contests in Australia were extremely lucrative. No wonder the ACB preferred tours against teams who would play high-quality cricket, attract big crowds and pull in the money.

Since the 1970s the links between Australian and New Zealand cricket have become closer. As New Zealand's cricket improved, it became a worthy international opponent; New Zealand played its first official test against Australia in 1973 and defeated Australia in a test in March 1974.[77] New Zealand cricket also became more confident in its attitude to the Australian Cricket Board. In the late 1970s the NZCC put pressure on the ACB to come to terms with World Series Cricket. In 1992 the running of the Cricket World Cup was awarded jointly to Australia and New Zealand. In spite of some weak New Zealand teams since the 1990s, the cricketing relationship between the two nations has now become stable, thanks to a more broad-minded and cooperative administration in Australia.[78] During the last decade of the 20th century a growing interchange began between state, provincial, university and secondary school teams, as well as a number of private tours. New Zealand cricketers and administrators gained much over this period from emulating Australian professionalism and dedication.

One particular incident perhaps did more than anything to charge the atmosphere of trans-Tasman cricket and ironically usher in this new cooperation.

That was the infamous underarm bowling incident of 1981, which occurred in the third final of the World Series Cup in Melbourne. The Australian captain, Greg Chappell, told his brother Trevor Chappell to bowl underarm on the last ball of the game to avoid giving New Zealand's Brian McKechnie any chance of hitting a six and winning the series. The public and political response to this unsporting act was intense. New Zealand's Prime Minister, Robert Muldoon, accused the Australians of cowardice and concluded that it was appropriate they were wearing yellow. The Australian Prime Minister, Malcolm Fraser, and Sir Donald Bradman also condemned it. Trans-Tasman competitiveness, previously mild in cricket, became frenzied. The controversy led to a sell-out Australian tour of New Zealand in 1982, fuelled by a palpable sense of New Zealand grievance and vengeance.

The underarm incident was a reflection of the sibling rivalry that had always underlain the Tasman relationship: the older brother unthinkingly dudding the younger; the younger throwing his bat away in disgust, determined to have his revenge. Part of the irony is that the brothers now get on better than ever, which seems almost to be a formula for what happens in the Tasman family after a crisis.[79]

Netball

Netball is at the other end of the spectrum of Tasman sport from cricket: played everywhere, indoor or outdoor, on every weekend across the two countries, and passionately contested between New Zealand and Australian women players of superlative athletic ability. The game was founded in 1891 in Massachusetts, as a spinoff from the new game of basketball for men. Women's basketball spread to England, and then out to other nations of the British empire. In North America it evolved into a game akin to modern-day men's basketball. In England, however, women's basketball was further modified to suit contemporary ideas of femininity. Called 'women's basketball' until the 1970s, the game is now known as netball.[80]

The first documented netball games in the Tasman world were played in 1897 in Victoria. The game was pioneered by English school teachers and supported by the Young Women's Christian Association (YWCA). Netball became established in the states of Victoria, New South Wales and Queensland by the 1920s, and developed slightly later in Tasmania and South Australia. Matches between state representative teams started from 1924; by 1926 there were formal inter-state competitions. The All Australian Women's Basket Ball Association (AAWBBA) was formed in 1927, and held its first national tournament in 1928. There were attempts to standardise netball rules in the 1930s but these were only partially successful; different states used different rules until the 1960s.

Netball in New Zealand is traditionally thought to have been introduced in 1906 by the Rev. J. C. Jamieson from the game he had seen played in Australia.

However, there is evidence that Wanganui Girls' College had four netball teams in 1899.[81] Organised national administration of netball began slightly earlier in New Zealand than Australia. Netball was initially played in girls' schools but became so popular that ex-pupils formed their own leagues. The New Zealand Basket Ball Association (NZBBA) was formed in 1924.

Netball has done well across New Zealand and Australia because it was unfazed by the traditional lack of resources for women's sport. Netball uses limited resources effectively; its courts are small, easy to maintain and can double as tennis courts. The game caters for a large number of players and does not impinge on male sporting arenas. Also, the relatively mild winters in New Zealand and Australia allow netball to be played outside, putting the Tasman world at an advantage over Britain.[82]

The first official link between Australian and New Zealand netball began at the inaugural NZBBA annual general meeting, which passed a motion to invite a Sydney team over to visit in 1926.[83] The tour was the first in a series and, during the 1930s and 1940s, the main agenda, on the Australian side in particular, was rule standardisation. Both countries, in the absence of international netball rules, played markedly different versions of the game, Australia employing seven-member teams compared with New Zealand's nine.

After a hiatus during the great depression a New Zealand team planned to cross the Tasman in 1936 but the tour was cancelled due to a polio outbreak in Australia. In the meantime Mrs Hull, president of the AAWBBA, visited New Zealand in 1937 with a commission to investigate New Zealand netball and invite a New Zealand team to the 1938 Australian inter-state competition. The AAWBBA hoped her visit would lead New Zealanders to adopt the seven-a-side game and start a regular interchange of visits.[84] The main aim of the 1938 tour was to iron out rule differences between Australia and New Zealand. In 1948 Australia again attempted to make New Zealand conform to Australian netball rules. An Australian team toured New Zealand and played two matches against every provincial team it met: one with seven-a-side rules and the other with nine-a-side rules. At the end of the tour an 'Australasian' rules conference was held in an effort to achieve uniformity but New Zealand was not prepared to adopt the Australian code.[85]

During the first half of the 20th century New Zealand behaved towards its Australian netball cousins rather like the Australian cricketing authorities behaved towards New Zealand cricket. The NZBBA showed a remarkable obstinacy about adopting Australian netball rules. On receiving the 1938 invitation to play in Australia, the NZBBA belatedly accepted on condition that Australia watch demonstrations of the nine-a-side game and that a compromise set of rules be formulated.[86] After the war the NZBBA still refused to adopt the seven-a-side game, which cost it international competition with Australia. In 1954 a proposed tour of Australia was cancelled over this issue.[87]

Pragmatism and pride explain New Zealand's reluctance to switch to Australian netball rules. A lack of resources was a key concern: if they changed to seven-a-side, there would be more teams and insufficient courts to accommodate them. In Greymouth, for example, during the 1950s, the main street was blocked off on Saturday afternoons and converted into three courts.[88] Moreover, international competition was not the main aim of the NZBBA, and the cost of touring, especially before air travel was commonplace, was prohibitive. Another part of New Zealand netball's reluctance to acquiesce to Australia's demands was the common theme in all trans-Tasman sports: national rivalry and a determination not to be bossed around by its larger neighbour.

Despite the local bickering, the Tasman world of netball came together on the international scene. In 1960 the first International Conference of Basketball in Ceylon altered the rules. New Zealand and Australia resisted as they were in the middle of a three-test series played under a draft set of seven-a-side rules that New Zealand had agreed to when it became a founding member of the world federation of Women's Basketball and Netball Association in 1957. The Tasman cousins did not want their games to be disrupted by further change.[89]

Netball is unlike the other trans-Tasman sports in that New Zealand and Australia have always considered each other their greatest rival. Partly this perception exists because of historic links and frequent tours but also because Australia and New Zealand have dominated international competition in this sport from its inception. At the first World Netball Championships in 1963 New Zealand and Australia were the joint favourites, and Australia won the final. From the moment they came second, New Zealand started planning the 1967 campaign and felt vindicated when they won the Netball World Cup.[90] In World Championships, Australia and New Zealand keep count of their previous losses to each other and focus on evening the score with their traditional rivals, as when New Zealand's loss by one goal to Australia in the 1999 competition spurred their win against Australia in the 2003 World Championships. This netballing rivalry is openly admitted by both nations on their official netball websites.

Little has been done to compare gender relations in the women's world of netball, which is itself a comment on the trans-Tasman similarities and connections. However, there are a few indications that New Zealand netball has suffered less from sexism and gender stereotyping than the Australian game. New Zealand media have traditionally given more attention to netball than Australian media. A second difference is symbolic. When the Australian netball Super League competition turned professional in 1997, all the teams were given bird names: Adelaide Falcons, Adelaide Ravens, Melbourne Kestrels, Melbourne Phoenix, Perth Orioles, Queensland Firebirds, Sydney Eagles and Sydney Swifts. Although these names were supposed to suggest feminine grace and strength, they also (perhaps unconsciously) carried the connotation of 'birds', the unflattering slang term for girls and women.[91] By contrast, the teams in New Zealand's professional league

were originally named the Otago
Rebels, Southern Sting, Canterbury Flames, Auckland Dia-
monds, Northern Force and
Waikato Wildcats: names that
are more overtly aggressive and
'Amazonian'[92]

Two other differences
between New Zealand and
Australia highlight the subtle
variations that exist within
the Tasman world. One is the
history of ethnic participation.
In Australia, women of British
origin have dominated netball.
A profile of netball players in
Australia composed from a
1995–98 population survey
shows that the average netball
player is female, aged 18–24,
Australian born, of Anglo-
Saxon descent, unmarried
and employed full time. The

Australia v New Zealand at Wellington, June 1969.
AAQT 6401 A90612, Archives New Zealand, Wellington

reasons for this trend are sparsely documented but Taylor suggests that non-
Anglo-Celtic immigrants' daughters come from cultures where sport is not
important to women, or are driven to excel in academia rather than sport. Only a
few Aboriginal women have played netball. Currently, Australia is attempting to
encourage more indigenous and rural women to play the game.[93]

By contrast, Maori participation in netball has a long history in New
Zealand. The captain of the first national team in 1938, Meg Matangi, was
Maori. Teams of Maori women entered local competitions in many parts of New
Zealand from the outset. Maori urbanisation and improved transport since the
Second World War led to greater prominence for Maori players. Indeed, in the
1950s the NZBBA set up a subcommittee to examine ways that Maori could be
made more welcome in netball, investigating rugby league's success in including
Maori players.[94] Polynesian immigrants also took to netball readily and began
to be selected for the national team in the 1970s. Netball, like the rugby codes,
was popular with Maori and Pacific Islanders because it was cheap to play and
team-based: attractive qualities for people who were likely to be low on the socio-
economic scale, and have strong family- and church-based cultures.[95]

The final difference lies in the sport's exposure to popular media. Australian
netball has suffered from a lack of coverage, with little change until the 1990s.

The turning point came in 1991 when Australia beat New Zealand in the final of the World Netball Championships in front of a crowd of 12,000 in Sydney. After this event the ABC began to cover the netball super league. Even with increased publicity, netball still receives less media attention in Australia than in New Zealand. From the earliest days the NZBBA was aware of the need for media coverage. From the 1920s to the 1960s it paid newspapers to run coverage and advertisements about netball tournaments, while for the 1978 World Championships in Trinidad and Tobago New Zealand sent a radio reporter to cover the games. In the 1983 World Championships, New Zealand's three games were televised live. The advent of a New Zealand premier league in 1985 resulted in fervent public interest. In 1983 some 125,750 Kiwis watched netball on television. By 1985 netball's viewing audience had almost trebled to 377,000.[96]

No other exclusively female sport during the 20th century in the western world was as dominant as netball across New Zealand and Australia. This powerful status hints at a unique trans-Tasman sporting culture in which large numbers of women participate. The inaugural trans-Tasman competition, the ANZ Championship in 2008, confirms that a Tasman culture exists in netball. Teams adopted new names for the new competition; the Flames, for instance, became the Tactix. With all its restrictions, netball was an experience of emancipation from male authority and empowered ethnic population groups to model their athletic and social skills on a trans-Tasman, then world stage.

Conclusion

What are the trends and patterns across these four sporting rivalries between New Zealand and Australia? Many informal links existed throughout the 20th century because of the countries' geographical proximity, cultural similarities, parallel sporting opportunities and frequent intermigration. Migration, for reasons apart from sport, or with family at a young age, has led to an exchange of talent that is a key dynamic in the Tasman world, and heavily in Australia's favour. Such sporting exchanges occur not only at representative level but also in coaching and in amateur sport. Often state or provincial teams will travel across the Tasman for pre-tournament training and development. Youth representative teams do likewise. In addition, school teams follow a well-trodden path as they criss-cross the Tasman to play and learn from one another.

At key moments in sport where important decisions have to be made, New Zealand and Australia have also often worked together on international boards and committees to bring about rule changes, promote world cup bids and professionalise rugby and rugby league. The changes resulting from professionalism of sports in the last 20–30 years (the growth of televised sport, commercial branding, sponsorship and importing of players) have affected all four sports markedly in both nations, often simultaneously. Though such changes are part of a larger global trend, many of the first acts of professionalisation occurred in and through the Tasman world, for instance, Kerry Packer and World Series Cricket, and the rebel rugby and super league wars. New Zealand and Australia have been intimately tied together through playing together.

None of these links has eliminated trans-Tasman rivalry, which has increased in all sports in the last three decades, and indeed in some cases become more antagonistic. The reasons are manifold: the Tasman cousins have generally become closer in ability, making games more competitive, with higher stakes in the professional era; the loss of other traditional opponents like South Africa earlier in the century had also sharpened trans-Tasman contests. The commercialisation of sport has led to more frequent interaction, both at a domestic level (Warriors in the NRL; Rugby Super 14; ANZ Championship netball) and internationally (the rugby Tri-nations series). Former Crusaders coach and All Black Robbie Deans embodied this trend with his appointment to mentor the Wallabies in 2008. Trans-Tasman matches have become a brand, symbolised most publicly in Bledisloe Cup clashes and netball series. Finally, netball and rugby union have gained higher profiles in Australia, while rugby league has done the same in New Zealand. As larger numbers of the population watch, the matches become more of a national concern. Citizens of one country living in the other heighten the fervour of these encounters.

Sport is of immense importance to each nation's identity, whatever the cross-Tasman links. In the national stories cricket is king in Australia, while rugby union has that status in New Zealand; each story is surrounded by unique national symbols of baggy green caps or All Black jerseys. These symbols highlight important differences that still exist. Maori have generally been more involved in New Zealand national sports than Aboriginal people have been in Australian sport. Other countries outside the region have also figured more prominently than trans-Tasman rivalry in some sporting codes, such as cricket and rugby union. Playing together does not mean doing everything together, even in a remade Tasman world.

CHAPTER NINE

Defending the Realm

Stuart Mcmillan

The Anzac tradition has already been referred to in Chapter 1 as the emotional cornerstone of the trans-Tasman relationship. As that and other chapters have demonstrated, it is by no means the only remarkable aspect of the Tasman world. Nevertheless it has been important in defining how Australia and New Zealand have seen one another in the past and how others have seen them. Whatever historical links exist, a core function of any government continues to be, in the quaint but accurate phraseology of traditional terms, the defence of the realm. This issue has haunted both countries, sometimes consciously, sometimes subconsciously, throughout their histories, sometimes entwining them, sometimes sending them in different directions.

It would be an exaggeration to say that the Anzac experience still dominates the military relationship. All the same it is never quite forgotten. Modern armed forces are often concerned with the technicalities of such cooperative measures as interoperability.

Cooperation in defence[1] matters is often a pragmatic affair, a division of duties, a simple if necessarily precise arrangement. It is based on the shared national interests of the participants. A total defence and security relationship between countries is altogether more complex. Perceptions assume huge importance, based on the global and regional interests of the two countries, how they perceive themselves, how they perceive one another, and how they assess threats both to themselves and others.

Perceptions

The history of the defence and security relationship between New Zealand and Australia is not without some forthright perceptions of each other. A vigorous assessment comes from the memoirs of Paul Keating with reference to his period as Prime Minister of Australia (1991–96):

> The resources New Zealand committed to defence continued to shrink and,
> as a result, its defence capabilities were declining. It was spending less than

half as much as Australia on defence as a percentage of GDP (1.1 per cent compared with 2.4 per cent). We were dangerously approaching the point at which the two forces would not be able to operate together effectively.

Largely at New Zealand's behest, our defence forces were talking about something called Closer Defence Relations (CDR), which was intended to mirror Closer Economic Relations. The agenda for CDR included more integrated defence planning, force structure planning, and logistical and training support. I was sceptical. I worried that New Zealand would see this as a way of getting defence on the cheap. And I did not want any situation to arise where we might leave gaps in our own defence capabilities to be filled by New Zealand.[2]

Hugh White, an eminent Australian strategic studies thinker, put it this way after New Zealand decided to scrap the strike wing of the Royal New Zealand Air Force in 2000:

At last, it's official. Australia and New Zealand are going separate ways on strategic policy. Australia is committed to long-term increases in defence spending so that it can retain its place among the significant air and naval powers of Asia. New Zealand has decided to cut its air and naval forces to the point at which they will virtually disappear.[3]

He concluded:

Australians can stop worrying about New Zealand getting a free ride. The fact is that most New Zealanders do not even want to be on our bus.[4]

Helen Clark, Prime Minister of New Zealand, robustly denied the charge of freeloading when she replied to a question on the topic at the Trans-Tasman Business Circle in Sydney in 2004. She outlined the various countries and conflicts to which New Zealand had contributed troops, and finished with:

So as I said at the outset, Neville, while I try to stay good humoured about such questions because the assumption always is that New Zealand is some kind of bludger which doesn't spend . . . I can tell you that our record is second to none.[5]

White argued further that acknowledging the differences would make it easier to deal with each other, a view similar to the one Keating advances:

Australia needs to give New Zealand as much objective attention as our other foreign interests. If China defines its relationship with Hong Kong as 'one country, two systems', ours with New Zealand is 'one system, two countries'. So, contrary to the usual rules, I'm all in favour of playing down the family metaphors and thinking about New Zealand as a foreign country. This is not because I don't understand the closeness of the history or the ties, or their importance, but because I think we will understand each other better and get more out of the relationship if we try to look as objectively as we can at our individual interests.[6]

Keating's strong opinion and White's equally pronounced, if slightly kindlier view reflect attitudes created by one event during the mid-1980s, and some important differences in outlook between Australia and New Zealand.

The nuclear ships debate

The refusal of New Zealand in February 1985 to accept a visit by an American warship on the ground that it might be nuclear armed marked a watershed in the defence and security relationship between New Zealand and Australia. Differences had existed previously but they had been muted. After that refusal the differences became consolidated and the attitudes were articulated more often and were more sharply defined.

The events over the denial of port access to the USS *Buchanan* have been documented in many places and will not be repeated here.[7] New Zealand's denial of port access was an event of great moment to Australia. New Zealand, as a member of the security treaty between Australia, New Zealand and the United States of America (Anzus alliance), was seen as putting at risk a treaty that Australia regarded as of fundamental importance to its own security. At least as important to the politicians was that the action of the New Zealand government also had the potential to influence Australian attitudes to the visits of American warships. The Australian Labor Party was in power and the left of that party applauded the New Zealand move. The government was alarmed not because it thought there was greater danger to Australia because US ships were not getting access to New Zealand ports, but because of the domestic political implications. Now it was faced with the tasks of not only preserving the relationship with the US but also managing a push within its own party ranks to take the same stance as New Zealand's.

The left of the Labor Party used the New Zealand action as the basis of a challenge to Bob Hawke, the Australian Prime Minister. Realising this challenge was under way, the New Zealand government dispatched Mike Moore, its forceful Trade Minister, who ranked third in the government, to try to pacify the left of the Labor Party and to assure its members that Bob Hawke's prime ministership was helpful to the New Zealand government.

Although for various reasons the temper of Australia was more attuned to defence issues, there was enough similarity in the attitudes of the two populations for Australia to grasp where New Zealand was heading. The Australian government with the then Foreign Minister, Bill Hayden, leading the way responded with a deliberate and persuasive campaign to head off like-minded attitudes taking hold in Australia. There was a certain irony in Hayden's position because he had earlier embraced similar views to those taken in New Zealand, an attitude that cost him dearly in his aspirations to lead the Labor Party.

Eric Heath, *Dominion*, 28 August 1985.
H-459-004, NZ Cartoon Archive, Alexander Turnbull Library, Wellington, courtesy of Eric Heath

For its part, the New Zealand government was concerned about any undermining of Hawke. The Moore mission was a fraternal gesture to a fellow Labor leader and an acknowledgement that a Labour government in New Zealand could not afford to undermine the position of a Labor Prime Minister in Australia.

Although the immediate party political crisis was addressed, a diplomatic crisis remained. In the past New Zealand had acknowledged that Australia was the most important country to New Zealand. Yet in denying port access to the USS *Buchanan* New Zealand was, in Australia's view, harming Australia's basic security interests by damaging the Anzus alliance. At the political level this neglect is easiest to explain. Alongside a gung-ho attitude within the New Zealand government were the all-absorbing dynamics of the anti-nuclear movement in New Zealand and within the New Zealand Labour Party. There was no doubt in the government's mind that the public backed the nuclear-free policies being pursued, and this domestic environment overwhelmed external considerations (though the government kept a wary eye on any trade implications).

At the level of the New Zealand Ministry of Foreign Affairs, one incident had a profound effect. Ministry officials asked for a meeting with their Australian counterparts at which they could speak their minds freely and in confidence. This meeting took place, but afterwards New Zealand officials found that what they had said in Canberra was immediately made known to United States officials. This breach of trust inhibited further free discussion. The position for New Zealand officials was also complicated by suspicions, from within sections of the Labour Party and within the Labour government, that officials might try to undermine the anti-nuclear policy.[8]

All of these events altered the dynamics of the defence and security relationship. Not only were dealings between New Zealand and Australia affected but also the former triangular relationship of New Zealand, Australia and the US. The effective removal of New Zealand from the Anzus Council precipitated Australia into a one-to-one situation with the US. Previously, despite their differences in size, the US had tended to treat New Zealand and Australia on a par (sometimes to the chagrin of Australia). Previously, too, New Zealand's often more sanguine approach to regional affairs had been influential. Any modifying effect that New Zealand had had on Anzus attitudes was lost after the rupture. Australia attained a status that it had not had previously with the US and to which it had often aspired.

After the break between New Zealand and the United States, Australia considered taking some action to punish New Zealand, but in the end took the view that there had been a dispute between its two alliance partners and that, for its part, it would maintain good relations with both. It was, for all intents and purposes, a continuation of the Tasman world, though with some differences. One of the unintended and almost certainly unforeseen consequences was that New Zealand became more dependent on Australia. This change was particularly evident in regard to intelligence flows and defence exercises. While within the treaty, New Zealand had been a recipient of raw US intelligence; after the break the US severely restricted its intelligence flows to New Zealand. Australia made available intelligence reports to New Zealand but 'sanitised' them to avoid giving certain intelligence sourced from the US. Similarly, while New Zealand was an active member of the Anzus treaty, there had been tripartite exercises annually with such names as Triad and Kangaroo. After the break US defence forces would not take part in exercises with New Zealand, so Australia conducted its usual annual exercises with the US, then conducted separate exercises with New Zealand. Chapter 1 discussed how New Zealand's reliance on Australian training increased significantly after the conflict over Anzus. Both the processing of intelligence and the separate defence exercises increased defence expenditure somewhat for Australia – a cause of minor irritation to the Australian defence establishment.

These actions were undoubtedly generous to New Zealand. Although any recipient of intelligence does not have to accept or believe any specific part of the information received, being in touch with the framework through which certain events and developments are being viewed by others is a critical part of being able to function in the modern world. Similarly, the experience of exercising with the military forces of another country is important, especially for a small country with a small defence force.

The dynamics among New Zealand, the US and Australia also changed in Washington. Australian ambassadors to Washington were under instructions to see that their hosts held the line on New Zealand. The Australian Embassy made recommendations to Washington to the effect that the rules of membership had to be the same for all parties to the Anzus treaty. Thus, even if the New Zealand government had found a way of repairing its relationship with the US, Australian representations ensured that progress would be difficult or even impossible to make.[9] Such an Australian policy would be entirely consistent with the Australian government's concerns about how the New Zealand anti-nuclear policy might affect the Australian population, as noted above. It could also be argued that with New Zealand removed, Australia was determined to consolidate its own special relationship with the US. In a curious twist of history the US, which had unintentionally prompted New Zealand and Australia to come together in the 1944 Canberra Pact to ensure a voice in the postwar policy in the Pacific – much to the irritation of the US – became in 1985 the force that drove them apart.

These changes gave rise to a series of Australian perceptions about New Zealand that developed into significant factors in the relationship. One of the most persistent was that New Zealand was not contributing a fair share to its defence, that New Zealand was 'freeloading' on Australia. A second perception was that New Zealand was becoming isolationist in outlook, and a third was that New Zealand was reshaping its defence forces not for combat, but for peacekeeping. These fears were deepened by a fall in the level of defence spending by the New Zealand government,[10] by its decision not to go ahead with the leasing of a number of F16 aircraft, by its later decision to disband the strike wing of its air force, and by its decision not to buy a third frigate constructed under the Anzac programme.[11] Australia had originally hoped that New Zealand would take four of the 12 frigates planned, and that they would have relevance for the defence of Australia. The abandonment of the strike wing of the air force had particular salience for Australia because the Skyhawks were stationed in Australia and constantly used during training with the Royal Australian Air Force.

One of the sharpest comments at the time on New Zealand's position came from Paul Dibb, a former Deputy Secretary of Defence in Australia and also a former head of the Strategic and Defence Studies Centre at the Australian National University, who told an Australian parliamentary inquiry that New Zealand was a strategic liability to Australia. By that he meant that in a serious military action New Zealand would depend on Australia for air cover and possibly for logistics. It is interesting that Dibb later modified his views after a boost in defence spending by the Clark Labour government in New Zealand. He concluded that New Zealand's defence forces were more logically aligned with its strategic circumstances.[12]

Differences between Australia and New Zealand

One puzzle about the differences in the postwar years is why is it that New Zealand and Australian strategists, often with the same or similar academic backgrounds, working in defence or foreign affairs departments or in academic institutions, come to different conclusions about the region? The answer lies in a combination of geographical, historical, political and military circumstances. The geographical positions of the two countries and the strategic implications arising from these positions might appear similar, but on deeper investigation they differ considerably. The islands of the Pacific, which make up the northern reaches of a country otherwise surrounded by a huge ocean, could not mount a serious threat to New Zealand. Its 1991 defence paper said simply: 'We have the world's largest moat.'[13] By contrast, Australia is much closer to the island and landmasses of Asia, and fears of mass Asian migration, though they have been common to both countries, have shaped Australia's history more profoundly and consistently than New Zealand's.[14]

Historical influences on the Australian outlook include the Japanese attacks on Darwin during the Second World War, the submarine incursions down its eastern coast and the invasion of Papua New Guinea. New Zealand suffered similar fears of an invasion from Japan during the war but was not actually attacked. Apart from some brief periods of uncertainty, New Zealanders developed a strong sense of being secure in their remoteness and a general sense that they lived in a benign environment.

Defence and security have played out differently in the Tasman world among politicians, public and pressure groups. The greater consciousness in Australia of security and defence affairs has led to the occasional 'khaki election' phenomenon and a readiness to enhance the status of the military so that a prime minister may wrap himself in the Australian flag. By contrast, the young ages and the backgrounds of a group of politicians who came into power in New Zealand in 1984 were influential.[15] Since 1985 political parties in New Zealand have come to recognise the sensitivity of the anti-nuclear stand and the legislation preserving it. For instance, before the 1990 election the National Party said that it would not revoke the anti-nuclear legislation. It feared that it would lose the election if it did not take this stance. The cost for it was continued exclusion from the Anzus alliance. Although this outcome sat uncomfortably with the National Party, another period in opposition would have been even more uncomfortable. Later, in the period leading up to the 2005 election, Don Brash, leader of the National Party, flirted with the idea of abandoning the anti-nuclear legislation but deemed it prudent in the end to drop the idea. Finally a number of pressure groups helped bring about the anti-nuclear ban in New Zealand; although such groups existed in Australia they did not attain the same strength of influence.

The two major Australian political groupings, the Liberal–National Party coalition and the Australian Labor Party, accept that the Anzus alliance is fundamental to the defence of Australia, though the position has a number of nuances. The coalition veers towards cultivating 'great and powerful friends' and a preoccupation with power. There are at least two strands within the Labor Party: the left veers towards idealism and universalism; the centre/right faction favours international law and places great emphasis on regionalism. Nevertheless, the Labor Party still places great importance on the American connection, though whether this position is due to its own conviction or the fear that the Australian public would not countenance an abandonment of reliance on the United States is not altogether clear.[16]

New Zealand's behaviour during the Falklands War, including the offer of the frigate *Canterbury* to relieve a British warship in the Indian Ocean, might seem an exception to a generally unwarlike disposition. This involvement arose, however, from a personal initiative of Prime Minister Robert Muldoon rather than any war fever. Muldoon asked his Cabinet colleagues for their opinion.[17] The New Zealand Ministry of Foreign Affairs presented a paper to the Prime Minister, which in essence stated that no New Zealand interests were involved and that New Zealand should stand clear of the dispute. Muldoon, however, spurned the advice of the ministry in a particularly forthright manner and determined that New Zealand would offer the frigate to free up a British warship. Muldoon also expelled the Argentinean Ambassador to New Zealand, which went a step further than any other government, including that of Britain. This contribution to the Falklands War was based on an appeal to British sentiment and may have subsequently helped to bring about British support for an imminent trade negotiation with the European Community. In making these gestures Muldoon judged the reaction of the British public and the British Prime Minister correctly, however irrelevant the Ministry of Foreign Affairs might have assessed the Falklands War to be to the security and defence of New Zealand.[18] Differing trade patterns influenced the warship gesture, which marked a divergence between New Zealand and Australia.

Domestic debates on security and defence matters are influential in preserving differences between New Zealand and Australia. Australia has a strong tradition of strategic thinkers in various research institutes. Denis Healey, a former British Secretary of State for Defence and later Chancellor, observed this area of strength many years ago:

> Even more impressive were the Australian academic exports on defence. From the middle fifties Australia has contributed far more to international understanding of defence problems than any country of similar size. The reputation of people like Hedley Bull, Coral Bell, and Larry Martin has

been high for two decades and there is now a new generation of comparable stature, such as Des Ball and Andrew Mack.[19] The climate of the Antipodes seems conducive to producing good defence intellectuals and Air Marshals, as well as great sopranos.[20]

It is also difficult to overestimate the influence of some of the strategic thinkers, many of whom write frequently and ably in Australian newspapers as well as respond to requests for comment from news media. Some Australian journalists are also very well informed and their contributions to the debate are significant. The commentators help provide a framework for the discussion of security and defence matters. The intellectual debates about defence in Australia are often about the defence of the Australian continent on the one hand or, on the other, about Australia's involvement in conflicts far from its shores in association with other countries. This continuous bubbling of the defence debate is sustained by good funding of the defence and security think-tanks in Australia. Without a doubt Australia has attained critical mass in its defence and strategic research.

New Zealand is not, of course, without its own able strategic thinkers. Nevertheless, research in strategic studies is not funded at anything like the level that it is in Australia. Take, for instance, the Centre for Strategic Studies at Victoria University of Wellington. Its director, Peter Cozens, has an executive assistant and one part-time researcher. A number of research associates, mostly with considerable diplomatic experience, contribute to the centre's work voluntarily. Cozens, a former naval commander, provides media comment and publishes papers on regional affairs, but the financial support for the centre is very limited, and the centre's main responsibility lies in being the New Zealand base for the Council on Security Co-operation in Asia-Pacific (CSCAP). The centre is heavily involved in track 2 diplomacy, the non-official networking conducted mainly by academics throughout Asia and the Pacific, including the United States and Canada.

The sheer differences in size, military might and wealth are highly pertinent to the way each country sees the world and its role within it. In world terms Australia is a middle power economically, strategically and occasionally in sport. New Zealand is a small power. The prolonged booms in housing, the sharemarket and minerals brought about a major increase in wealth and, with it, a major boost in self-confidence in Australia. Such an outlook affects, inter alia, attitudes to international organisations. One of the classical characteristics of small powers is their heavy reliance on international law and on international organisations. In New Zealand's case this reliance is shown in the weight it gives to the United Nations. By contrast, although Australia is a strong supporter of the UN, it is rather more sceptical about that organisation's performance.

In military prowess Australia has a capacity to take major action on its own if need be. Again, this potential contrasts with New Zealand's. The 1991 New Zealand defence policy paper comments: 'Successive governments have concluded that New Zealand cannot be defended solely by our own efforts.'[21] New Zealand could not act alone in a major conflict. Its military is designed to be a niche force, acting in concert with other forces. Australia aims to have forces of its own with a sufficient capability to defend Australia from any credible attack.[22]

For those who have listened to debates within New Zealand and Australia, it is evident that in New Zealand the discourse moves towards 'security'– often defined rather widely, for example human security – while the more prominent theme in Australia is 'defence', meaning military defence. Although Australia's defence posture and middle power status seem strong by New Zealand standards, Australia compares itself with the countries to its north. This comparison puts a different perspective on Australia's size and prowess. New Zealand neither has nor aspires to similar military power; nor could it afford to have it.

Often the two countries see their world and regional roles in different ways. In 1999, for instance, John Howard was given a headline that suggested he saw Australia as the United States' deputy sheriff in the region. President George Bush later used the word 'sheriff' to convey the idea that the US and Australia were equals. Howard eventually disowned the term, putting it down to Texan talk, but it took a long time and some sharp reactions from Asian countries before he did so. No New Zealand politician would ever allow New Zealand's role to be portrayed in that manner. Although a New Zealand foreign minister was not above asking the US for recognition of the role New Zealand played in the region, the possibility of depicting this role as that of a deputy sheriff would be totally rejected by any New Zealand political party.[23]

Puzzles

While this summary of differences between Australia and New Zealand illuminates attitudes to be found within the countries, it does not entirely explain why the approaches differ. Nor does it solve the question of why security experts in the two countries often make assessments that do not appear to correspond. A philosophical difference throws light on the seeming paradox. Strategic thinkers on both sides of the Tasman would make that same assessment about the influence of the geographical location. They are also likely to reach similar conclusions within the usual parameters of strategic assessment: arms purchases by neighbouring countries, capabilities of various countries to project power, the declared intentions of governments and so on. But it is possible to take the same sets of facts and come to different conclusions about the dangers of the region by viewing those facts through a pessimistic lens, a realist perspective, or optimistically. Looking through the lens of realism (or at least not optimism) is part of the proper discourse of strategy. It is not surprising that the country with the luxury of being further removed from possible points of conflict takes the more optimistic view. It can also be argued that, because of its location, Australia cannot afford to take a highly optimistic view and to get its assessments wrong.

The tendency towards a somewhat optimistic view of the world has led New Zealand to believe that intra-state conflict is a more likely form of instability in the future than inter-state conflict, whether regionally or globally. It is, of course, a matter of judgement whether that will continue to be the case. Various arguments can be raised against a benign view of the region. It might be, as in the view above, attributed to some New Zealand defence thinkers, that no regional country has the intention or capacity to threaten Australia, or it might be that Australia is not threatened because it has a formidable deterrent defence force of its own. Hugh White, for instance, wanted to ensure that Australia had a bigger navy than any country between India and China.[24] Proving or disproving that deterrence has occurred in the past has a difficulty that is probably surpassed only by proving or disproving that it will work in the future.

Another puzzle is why New Zealand has spurned the notion of the two countries being a single strategic entity. The notion has a long history. Peter Fraser wrote to Winston Churchill in 1942 about the arrangements being made for American command in the Pacific and New Zealand's regret that Australia and New Zealand were going to be in separate subcommands. He stated that New Zealand was opposed to any such carving up of the Pacific and, in particular, 'we are opposed to any degree of separation from Australia. Australia and New Zealand are inevitably one strategical whole ...'[25] New Zealand lies on Australia's eastern flank and is therefore important to Australia strategically. New Zealand's attitude was summed up in the 1991 *Defence of New Zealand* paper thus:

> The natural protection of geography has led both countries to recognise that the security of either would be at risk if the other were threatened. It has always been assumed that in such circumstances both nations would act in concert. [26]

This concept has been expressed in various other ways, for example: 'Our two nations are for all practical purposes a single strategic entity,' said a defence ministers' communiqué.[27]

The Labour-led government in New Zealand said, however, that it no longer acknowledged that the two countries formed a single strategic entity, causing Allan Hawke, as Australian High Commissioner to New Zealand, to comment: 'New Zealand's strategic perceptions and outlook differ from Australia's in significant ways. For example, New Zealand no longer regards itself and Australia as a Single Strategic Entity'.[28] The time of dropping the phrase was 2000. It did not appear in the communiqué issued after the talks between Prime Minister Howard and Prime Minister Clark, and has not appeared in official New Zealand documents since.

What caused the New Zealand government to spurn the phrase? Those who used it found that their readers or listeners interpreted it to mean that New Zealand and Australia had to pursue the same foreign policy. Yet in its essence the phrase does not imply that; nor is it a statement that the strategic circumstances of the two countries are identical. The Labour-led government in New Zealand, which wanted to be seen as putting forward an independent foreign policy, considered nevertheless that use of the phrase confounded the issue. From a domestic political point of view it is necessary for the New Zealand government to be seen not as automatically following the position of Australia but as free to choose its own way. Sometimes this stance lapses into a form of nationalism that Denis McLean identified and treated so thoroughly in his book.[29]

Whatever the form of words used (or avoidance of a phrase) it would be unthinkable for the New Zealand government not to go to Australia's assistance if Australia came under attack. It is also necessary, for the sake of good relations with Australia, to make that point from time to time. This bottom line creates some interesting dilemmas within the relationship. New Zealand cannot configure its defence force for the defence of the Australian continent because doing so would raise domestic political objections, not because of a lack of willingness for the country to go to Australia's defence if the need arises but because of the seeming loss of sovereignty. At the same time New Zealand needs to leave no doubt in Australian minds that New Zealand would immediately rise to Australia's defence. This position was given formal expression in a major government paper on the direction for defence policy. The second priority for the Defence Force, after the defence of New Zealand, was

[a] strong strategic relationship with Australia in support of common interests for a secure and peaceful region.[30]

In support of common interests

Security and defence relations between Australia and New Zealand did not remain static despite the differences over Anzus and the ban on nuclear-armed or -powered ships visiting New Zealand ports. The development of Closer Defence Relations – noted above as a twin to Closer Economic Relations – was concluded in 1991. Two of its main purposes were to coordinate purchases of defence equipment and to ensure that there would be compatibility between the defence forces of the two countries. It was conceived by General Peter Gration, Chief of the Defence Force in Australia, and Gerald Hensley, Secretary of Defence in New Zealand, over a long dinner at the Canberra residence of Ted Woodfield, the New Zealand High Commissioner to Australia. It has generally functioned well but not without hiccoughs. One such hiccough occurred when New Zealand and Australia decided to make a joint purchase of Seasprite helicopters from the United States. After the decision had been taken, the Royal Australian Navy decided that it wanted the helicopter to be fitted with advanced electronics in the cockpit. Hensley had a principle that he would not buy technology in the process of development but only technology that had a proven functioning record. There was a sharp row between New Zealand and Australia over this matter. In the end Australia opted for the advanced cockpit technology and New Zealand for the other model. One result was that New Zealand had a functioning helicopter in service, and the Australian model could not fly at night and had several other severe limitations. Australia has since decided it will buy no more Seasprites.

That aside, the Closer Defence Relations Agreement remains in force and is a factor in purchasing decisions taken by the two countries. A substantial factor in repairing relations between New Zealand and Australia was the series of interventions the two made in the Pacific island region from 1997.[31]

In late 1997 New Zealand hosted a number of the factions that had been pursuing a civil war on the island of Bougainville, part of Papua New Guinea. It was not the first attempt to seek peace on the island but it was the first successful attempt. The conflict had been continuing for about nine years and estimates of the numbers killed ranged from 10,000 upwards. The decision to host the talks was taken by the then New Zealand Foreign Minister, Don McKinnon. Foreign Affairs officials, particularly John Hayes, played a large role in both the planning and the execution of those talks. The move had significant implications for New Zealand–Australian relations. Australian interests were directly involved. A copper mine, which was one of the causes of the conflict, was owned by an Australian company, Bougainville Copper Limited, in which the majority shareholder was Rio Tinto Limited, a major Australian mining consortium. Papua New Guinea was a major recipient of Australian aid and a former Australian colony and trusteeship territory. Australia's historical links with Papua New Guinea were therefore strong. Moreover, a secure Papua New Guinea was considered to be important for the northern flank of Australia, while the western Pacific was traditionally regarded as within its sphere of interest.

Nevertheless, Australia accepted the New Zealand initiative, if a little warily, understanding that New Zealand could act without Australia's historical and commercial baggage. New Zealand made a deliberate point of involving Australia in aspects of the talks. Although the talks were facilitated by New Zealand, a senior Australian official was present at the talks venue, and at the leaders' talks at the end the Australian Foreign Minister, Alexander Downer, was present, as was the Australian High Commissioner to New Zealand, Geoff Miller. Throughout it was New Zealand that conducted the negotiations, but it pursued a policy of keeping Australia up to date as the talks progressed.

As a result of the accord reached at Burnham, troops from New Zealand, Australia, Fiji and Vanuatu went to Bougainville and served under the leadership of a highly experienced New Zealand military officer, Brigadier Roger Mortlock. The peacekeeping forces were not armed. In time the leadership was replaced by Australia, then by the United Nations Observer Mission on Bougainville. New Zealand eventually bowed out of any leadership role because the money ran out.

Australia then took the lead in conducting talks, which ended in the Bougainville Peace Agreement, signed in August 2001.

Although Australia remained cautious, New Zealand conducted the talks well and took no action Australia considered inimical to its own interests. The Bougainville intervention, because it did not entail great numbers of people and because the troops were unarmed, did not significantly ease the concerns Australia was harbouring after the Anzus break-up. It was important, however, because it was the first intervention of its kind in the Pacific Islands.[32]

The 1999 intervention in East Timor was on an altogether different scale. East Timor had conducted a referendum whose outcome was that it chose independence instead of continuing under Indonesian sovereignty. Anti-independence militia, enraged by the vote and with the tacit support of the Indonesian military, were killing people in East Timor and wreaking devastation. So the intervention was into a chaotic situation. It was also dangerous because there was uncertainty about how Indonesia would react to foreign forces landing in East Timor. Although an assurance had been given by the Indonesian government that it would accept foreign troops, nothing could be guaranteed about the behaviour of the Indonesian military, which might have acted independently from the wishes or instructions of Jakarta. Thus the potential was there for a major conflict. The prospect of conflict with Indonesia was one of the nightmares that had haunted Australian consciousness. (In fact the Indonesian government honoured the assurance it had given and the Indonesian military, if it did intervene, did so by proxy.)

Once the decision to intervene was taken, Australia was faced with a major problem: a shortage of light infantry. There was huge relief among Australian military planners after New Zealand offered a battalion and promised to have it ready in a short time. New Zealand also sent the frigate *Te Kaha*, the supply ship *Endeavour*, two Hercules aircraft and a helicopter squadron. By that action New Zealand did much to change the perception of itself that had taken hold in Australia.

The intervention also reflected other aspects of the relationship. New Zealand relied on air cover to be provided, if needed, by Australia. It also relied on Australia for some logistics. Australia had sought to involve the United States in the action, but the US remained on the sidelines, though it supplied intelligence information for the operation. Two Indonesian submarines put to sea during the intervention, for what reason it has not been disclosed publicly.

The intervention threw light on one intimate side of the relationship between New Zealand and Australian armed forces. The Australian commander, General Peter Cosgrove, decided he needed a headquarters at Dili and wanted Martyn Dunne, a New Zealander who had been sent to Australia to liaise with the Australian Defence Force, to command the headquarters. The then Colonel Dunne was appointed acting brigadier after an approach to the New Zealand

Defence Force by General Cosgrove. Brigadier Dunne had attended the Australian College of Defence and Strategic Studies, now known as the Australian Defence College. He had also been a New Zealand exchange officer at the Officer Cadet School, Portsea, before it became Duntroon, and had attended the Australian Army Command and Staff College, Queenscliffe. He personally knew all the senior Australian officers involved in the planning for the intervention. It was all a reflection of the tradition of New Zealand sending some of its leading soldiers across the Tasman for study and training. In a tangible gesture that reflected the closeness of the defence relationship, the stripes that marked his promotion were at first Australian, because New Zealand stripes were not immediately available.[33] For New Zealand the military commitment was its largest since the Second World War.

The deployment of troops cannot be separated from the events that preceded it. The decision to intervene with international backing came during a meeting in Auckland of the Asia Pacific Economic Co-operation (APEC) forum attended by a number of world figures, including the then president of the United States, Bill Clinton, though it was never part of the formal agenda. East Timor was moving to crisis point just as participants in the APEC meeting were gathering in Auckland. With almost all the key players there – foreign ministers, heads of government and economic ministers – it was obvious that East Timor would be a major point of discussion. The awkwardness was that APEC was not designed or mandated to discuss security issues. Indonesia and maybe other Association of Southeast Asian Nations (ASEAN) countries would have objected to its inscription on the agenda. It never appeared as such and was dealt with in sideline meetings.

The subject was also raised and discussed at the leaders' meeting, albeit unofficially. Ramos Horta, then leader of Fretilin, did a great deal of lobbying. Two meetings of officials were held. There was ongoing contact with all the relevant foreign ministries and the United Nations. It was one of those issues in which Australia and New Zealand worked extremely closely together, each being able to play a useful role, each bringing a set of strengths to the table and together making for a strong combination. From the start it was clear that Australia would lead any intervention force. Discussions continued with Australia during the APEC meeting on New Zealand's contribution to a United Nations peacekeeping force.

The next major regional commitment of New Zealand and Australian troops was to Solomon Islands on 24 July 2003. In March of that year a United States–led force had invaded Iraq – an invasion in which Australia participated and New Zealand did not (though New Zealand and Australia had participated militarily in the 2001 action in Afghanistan, which was sanctioned by the United Nations). It is worth considering those differences over Iraq because of the light they throw on different attitudes in New Zealand and Australia. The then

Australian Prime Minister, John Howard, who was in the United States at the time of the terrorist attacks there on 11 September 2001, invoked the Anzus pact when he returned to Australia. He later committed Australian troops to Iraq, mirroring publicly some of the concerns about weapons of mass destruction expressed by President Bush. He went on to argue that if weapons of mass destruction fell into the hands of terrorists then this would constitute a threat to Australia.[34]

New Zealand refused to commit any troops because the action did not have the backing of the United Nations. Concern was also expressed within New Zealand about the effect that the invasion of Iraq would have on the standing of the United Nations. There was general dislike and suspicion of the readiness of the United States to take military action unilaterally. Reflecting a small nation's reliance on international law and the United Nations, the refusal to take part in the invasion of Iraq may be considered a defining moment.[35] Australian policy, on the other hand, was driven not by an anti-United Nations but a pro-United States attitude, and a conviction that its involvement was the cost to be borne for the United States alliance commitment to the defence of Australia.

The Iraq invasion loomed large at the time of the Solomons crisis. An agreement that New Zealand would send troops to accompany the Australian force was reached in a meeting between Alexander Downer, the Australian Foreign Minister, and Phil Goff, the New Zealand Foreign Minister. There was, however, a delay between that meeting and approval given by the New Zealand Cabinet – a delay that undid a great deal of the gain that had been made by the New Zealand commitment to the East Timor intervention. So what caused the delay? Although a Cabinet paper had been circulated previously on the problems in the Solomons and the probable need for intervention, Goff still needed to persuade his Cabinet colleagues that an intervention was justified. He had to argue forcefully.[36] Apparently, the suspicions engendered by the Iraq action, the determination not to jump or to be seen to jump to do the bidding of Australia, a scepticism about identifying Afghanistan-type 'failed states' in the Pacific and the unwillingness to be seen as part of any action that could be described as fulfilling the duties of an American 'deputy sheriff' all played a part in the Cabinet's examination of the issue. It was, nevertheless, regrettable that the commitment entered into by Goff was delayed by the Cabinet. It revived an Australian uncertainty about New Zealand that seemed to have been laid to rest after East Timor.

Although both New Zealand and Australia expressed concern about stability, governance and the possibility of criminal activity in Solomon Islands, rhetoric about a failing state was more pronounced in Australia. Australian enthusiasm for intervention, which hitherto had not been noticeable, was boosted by a publication of the Australian Strategic Policy Institute, which had the main title of *Our Failing Neighbour*.[37] Probably some of that emphasis was intended for American consumption, to help identify the action in the Solomons with what had become known as the war on terror. The point is suggested sharply in the following passage:

> Without an effective government upholding the rule of law and controlling its borders, Solomon Islands risks becoming – and has to some extent already become – a petri dish in which transnational and non-state security threats can develop and breed.[38]

The Solomons, with its Guadalcanal association, was not unknown to the United States. One academic provides another interesting aspect to the Solomons intervention, in arguing that 'it provided Australia with a solid reason to rebuff US requests for a more sustained presence in Iraq.'[39]

Another minor difference of opinion arose over the number of troops. Australia planned to put in close to 2000 and New Zealand, thinking that unnecessarily large, tempered its contribution accordingly. This divergence is a reflection both of style and tactics in peacekeeping. Australia favours the use of overwhelming force in an effort to avoid casualties. New Zealand, even if it favoured such an approach, does not have the resources to conduct its military actions in such a way. Similar differences appeared in the manner in which patrols were conducted in Timor-Leste, especially after the renewed intervention of 2006. Australian soldiers patrolled in fours wearing body armour; New Zealand soldiers took a shared-risk attitude, not wearing body armour, often unarmed and in the blue caps of the United Nations, and mixing individually with Timorese. (One of the advantages of the more casual New Zealand practice was that there was probably better ground intelligence and New Zealanders had a reasonable grasp of what was going on in their area.)

These differences in style struck Rosemary Baird, whose thesis supervisors have made available a summary of her work,[40] which reads:

> During the Truce Monitoring Group operations in Bougainville, Australia would have preferred a more gradual and cautious approach, preparing the ground firmly and sending in large numbers of armed personnel. However, New Zealand went in early and quickly, unarmed and with fewer resources. This was successful and gained the New Zealanders' trust with local villagers. Antiquated equipment, on the other hand, frequent breakdowns, and lack of back-up resources soured the relationship with Australian officials at times in Bougainville and threatened success at some points. The belief that the New Zealanders conformed better than the Australians to the 'Pacific way' also influenced New Zealand troop behaviour. The reasons allegedly lay in the history of cultural interaction with Pacific Islanders; the significant number of Maori in the New Zealand Defence Force; the adoption of Maori protocol into the NZDF; and the use of Maori cultural ceremony and language in encounters with locals.

But, as Baird demonstrates, it is possible to overplay the notion of New Zealand's cultural sensitivity. Australian officials learned lessons from Bougainville that they were able to implement successfully in both East Timor and Solomon Islands. Australian forces were well informed about Melanesian culture from their own colonising history, while New Zealanders were found to be naïve in their assumptions, and just as capable of unfounded stereotypes about the islands as others.

In fact a revived Anzac relationship permeated the regional peacekeeping missions in Bougainville, East Timor and the Solomons. Australian and New Zealand forces enjoyed increasing interoperability thanks to participation in joint planning, reciprocal contributions of equipment, and the tradition of training New Zealand officers in Australia. The result was mutual friendship and close cooperation. The 'Anzac spirit' was an integral part of peacekeeping by the Tasman partners.[41] Subtle feelings of shared mateship predominated in the field. Anzac days celebrated in the islands and East Timor were particularly emotional experiences for both sides, reinforced by Pacific Islander sharing of wartime memories. A certain competitiveness in the daily round of business and in sports was the other side of the Anzac coin. This was important, particularly for New Zealanders in differentiating themselves from Australians.

Reflections on a Tasman future

The defence and security relationship between New Zealand and Australia is, of course, only one aspect of the total relationship but it is a critical one. As observed at the beginning of this chapter, the defence of the state is a fundamental function of any government. The two countries are important to each other strategically. Furthermore, security concerns are given considerable weight in Australia and Australia's relationships are often seen through a defence and security lens. The Anzac tradition reinforces the relationship though continuing military cooperation sustains it.

The two countries have been involved in a series of interventions in the Pacific since 1997 and the need for such actions has not come to an end. The interventions, which have mostly been by invitation, arouse sensitivities both in the countries in which they take place and in the region as a whole. For these reasons, probably neither Australia nor New Zealand would like to act without the other.

The continuing security and defence relationship between New Zealand and Australia will reflect the interplay of regional and international involvements. Regional military interventions in which New Zealand cooperates with Australia may not be matched by similar cooperation in international actions. The record to date shows that although New Zealand forces take part in a number of international actions, these actions have been initiated or at least sanctioned by the United Nations. New Zealand was not prepared, as Australia was, to join the 'coalition of the willing' to invade Iraq, an action to which the United Nations had not given its approval. A government in New Zealand under National leadership might bring about a different approach but it would be a reasonable, though not certain, assumption that New Zealand will stick to missions approved by the United Nations. The Australian Labor government elected on 24 November 2007 committed itself to withdrawing the combat troops from Iraq. Whether this decision indicates a new determination not to be drawn readily into actions by 'coalitions of the willing' without the blessing of the United Nations remains to be seen.

Various factors might draw the two countries closer or underline their separateness. One possible development that would draw them closer would be a growth in criticism in Australia of the costs of the American alliance. Many Australians protested against the country's commitment of troops to invade Iraq, arguing that if participating in such actions is the price for the alliance, then that price is too high. Nevertheless, even if the two countries come closer in their outlooks through such a development, Australian reluctance to accept the effectiveness of the United Nations is likely to persist in a manner that is not reflected in New Zealand.

The dual role Australia sees for itself will be reflected in its weaponry. Taking part in international actions such as the invasion of Iraq will lead Australia to continue to purchase high-technology weaponry, including the means for network-centric warfare, an advanced form of information technology that among other features enables commanders to see in real time what is happening on a battlefield. Such a capability is of no use in the type of operations undertaken in the Pacific islands. The acquisition of such weaponry would also arguably leave New Zealand far behind and reinforce divergences between Australia and New Zealand. It can be argued, too, that the shaping of the New Zealand Defence Force has become highly focused, earning commendation from Australian strategic thinkers who had previously been concerned about New Zealand's direction. The decision to abandon the strike wing of the air force to make more money available for other parts of the military was made easier by the work of Derek Quigley, a former National Cabinet minister and later co-founder of the ACT New Zealand Party, who was chair of the Foreign Affairs, Defence and Trade Select Committee during the 1997–99 parliament. This committee produced the *Inquiry into Defence Beyond 2000* report, which became the blueprint for the Clark government's subsequent changes to New Zealand defence policy.[42]

World events may affect, though not hurt, the Australia–New Zealand relationship. Non-state actors are major players in much of the world's present conflicts, but while their role seems likely to continue, there is no guarantee that it will do so. Australia's defence and security posture is more fitted to deal with state-to-state conflict than is New Zealand's. State-to-state conflict has traditionally been signalled and if such a tragic event occurred New Zealand might need to rethink its highly focused military posture. But overall that possibility should not alter the relationship. New Zealand and Australia have the same or very similar perspectives on such issues as terrorism, people-smuggling, trans-national crime and money laundering, and cooperate extensively in combating these. Putting aside differences of policy, the military forces of the two countries work remarkably well together – cooperation that is partly born out of the active programmes of planning together, exercising together, training together and ensuring as much interoperability as possible. There is as much cooperation and knowledge-sharing in security as in other communities of interest discussed in this book.

It is sometimes argued that while Australia has a Prime Minister of Anglo-Celtic origin the relationship with New Zealand will be maintained, but once someone with a background of European continental culture from among Australia's diverse migrants becomes Australia's leader then the Anzac tradition will not figure in his or her thinking. There are two reasons for doubting that. One is that people with a migrant background tend to identify strongly with the traditions of their new country, and the Anzac tradition is strong in Australia. Another is that political leaders do not come to power without an understanding of the values and traditions of their country. There is also what may be called a generational risk – the coming to power in Australia of a younger age group not stirred by the shared traditions of the Anzac experience.

Might New Zealand take an action that would harm the relationship? One move that would do some damage would be a formal withdrawal from the Anzus treaty. Australia continues to define its relationship with New Zealand partly through that treaty:

> Defence relations between Australia and New Zealand are close and longstanding. Formal expressions of our security partnership are found in the 1944 Canberra Pact and 1951 ANZUS Treaty. The ANZUS Treaty remains in effect between Australia and New Zealand, notwithstanding the United States' suspension of its ANZUS security obligations to New Zealand in August 1986 in response to New Zealand's anti-nuclear policy.[43]

Occasionally withdrawal from Anzus is suggested in New Zealand, the argument being that it is more or less defunct after the United States suspended its security obligations. To withdraw from the treaty would seem to tidy up a piece of history. Yet because Australia still regards the treaty as a significant bond between New Zealand and Australia, a withdrawal by New Zealand would have the potential to damage relations.

Theoretically, although unlikely at the moment, another possibility is that a political leader will come to power in New Zealand who either seeks isolationism or identifies the country solely with its Pacific island links. Because of geography,

New Zealand will continue to have strategic relevance for Australia, but such a development would probably make New Zealand seem effectively irrelevant to Australia as a regional partner.

In the early part of this chapter, three Australian perceptions that took hold after the Anzus split were discussed: the view that New Zealand was spending insufficiently on defence; the suspicion that New Zealand was drifting into isolationism; and the concern lest New Zealand was configuring and training its defence forces for peacekeeping rather than conflict. The question in 2008 is whether developments since 1985 and the cooperation in regional interventions have left these perceptions intact.

To begin with, the New Zealand government has embarked on a $3.5 billion programme of arms acquisitions called the Defence Sustainability Initiative. It might not raise the percentage of GDP spent on defence but it is still substantial expenditure and will vastly enhance New Zealand's helicopter and logistics capability, significantly increasing the military weight New Zealand can contribute to any engagement.

Secondly, the isolationism charge was not well founded. New Zealand did not hesitate over committing troops to Afghanistan – hardly the action of a country favouring isolationism. Moreover, the government did commit troops to Iraq after the United Nations supported the idea of reconstruction efforts. Nor does the country's willingness to engage in military activities in Timor-Leste and the Pacific islands suggest any form of isolationism.

The concern about New Zealand configuring its defence forces for peace-keeping, not conflict, is a complex one. Support can be found for the view that the training and skills required for peacekeeping are the same as those required for conflict.[44] This is not a universally held view. It can be argued that a double dose of training needs to be given: that there will be a point at which, the threat of conflict having disappeared, soldiers may need to take off their helmets and wear berets to maintain order. The post-conflict situation is gaining more attention in policy and academic studies. Indeed there is a good argument to say that a major reason for the failure of the coalition forces in the post-conflict period in Iraq was a lack of training for situations other than combat.[45]

What is the relevance of this peacekeeping for relations between Australia and New Zealand? There is little doubt that both Australia and New Zealand will be involved for years, possibly decades, in peacekeeping in the region. The dilemmas of peacekeeping include policing and institution-building after a conflict ceases. Both countries are considering ways in which these tasks can be done, including through seconding police and civilians. Australia has a separate problem: it might eventually have to choose between the low-tech needs of soldiers in the islands and the high-tech possibilities of such means as network-centric warfare.

Perceptions of one country by another are often not easily altered. Never-theless, in the first decade of the 21st century the Australian views that once prevailed in relation to New Zealand's defence and security seem less likely to damage the defence and security relationship between New Zealand and Australia than they did in the later part of the 1980s and over most of the 1990s. The Anzac tradition was always remarkable. The continuing relationship stands a chance of being not less remarkable, but different from what it was during the major crises of the 20th century.

CHAPTER TEN

Australasia Dreaming

Peter Hempenstall and Philippa Mein Smith

In uncovering a history of multiple ties between New Zealand and Australia this book itself contributes to the remaking of the Tasman world. We began this study with the idea of moving beyond the stereotypes that dominate public accounts of trans-Tasman relations. Our goal of recovering a hidden history urged us to remap systems and traffic within the region that encompasses Australia and New Zealand, and to get beyond the trans-Tasman to the global. It demanded a new storyline that sits in addition to and between Australian and New Zealand histories; a storyline that, rather than comparing the two countries' stories, shows how those histories have interrelated with others.[1] How the two histories have connected and interacted with each other, in the southern ocean, through time and especially since the federation of Australia in 1901, is the concern of this book. Our findings represent a case study of what historians call transnational history.[2] Regionally, they amount to what we see as a remaking of the Tasman world.

We began by repudiating the term 'Australasia' as unsuited to the different perceptions each Tasman country has of the other. There is a problem of meaning to overcome because dictionaries give different definitions on each side of the Tasman. *The Concise Australian National Dictionary* defines Australasia as 'the Australian continent and neighbouring islands', which implies that the idea equates to Australia's region and is therefore centred on the Australian mainland. *The New Zealand Oxford Dictionary* distinguishes between Australian usage and New Zealand usage. It notes that whereas the Australian definition refers to 'Australia, New Zealand, New Guinea and the neighbouring islands of the Pacific', the New Zealand understanding is that Australasia is shorthand for New Zealand and Australia.[3]

The notion of Australasia is different again for outsiders peering into the region from the United States of America or Europe. Maps show that this difference of perspective has existed at least since the 19th century. Historically, defining the region has varied (not to mention Australia's region or New Zealand's region) depending on whether the onlooker's perspective was from Britain, continental Europe, the United States or China. In Chapter 1 we showed how maps record changes in the way Europeans imposed frames of meaning, and how Australasia flexed through time, shrinking from the British possessions south of Asia to the seven colonies of Australasia (Australia and New Zealand) by the 1860s. Although federation carved up Australasia, Chapter 7 showed how a variety of organisations – scientific, scholarly and professional – continue to employ the term as a way of representing joint interests across the Tasman world. An aircraft charter business called Australasian Jet flew one of us from Darwin into Seven Spirit Bay on the Cobourg Peninsula in Arnhem Land, at the top of the Top End in the Northern Territory of Australia, during a break from this project. Australasian Jet's manager in Darwin was Maori, and the eco-lodge's managers in Garig Gunak Barlu National Park were New Zealanders with experience of Papua New Guinea. This and many similar experiences suggest that Australasia refers to a complex of histories south of Indonesia. Is one frontier for Australasia therefore the Arafura Sea?

New Zealanders still fret that Australasia aligns them too closely with a hegemonic continental nation, Australia: to many of them it is a word that acknowledges the larger partner but renders the smaller country invisible. Australians are similarly vexed at the word's failure to capture their country's multicultural quality as it grew up in the 20th century. Asians themselves think the term is too 'imperialising' by largely European neighbours.[4] There is a history to be created for the space between Asia and Antarctica that, as J. G. A. Pocock expresses it, is 'the history of small communities in an ocean of planetary size', and one that looks back along the lines that their varying cultures have travelled.[5] That history is what we have attempted to create in writing *Remaking the Tasman World*. We have cut across the national stories of both New Zealand and Australia that have functioned as the charters of their separate identities, to reveal a Tasman world that operated throughout the 20th century, at first haltingly, then in an increasing rush from the 1960s.

One way of addressing the diverse misgivings about the term Australasia is to hyphenate the word and thereby remove the asymmetry implied by a concept that, for some New Zealanders, suggests a takeover by omitting any reference to 'NZ'. Denis McLean argues it is logical for the neighbours to develop an 'Austral-Asian' worldview, but observes ruefully that this change in outlook is unlikely to happen because of the hurdle posed by national sentiment.[6] Would a hyphen and a capital letter, as he suggests, be sufficient to rebalance the word? This book's two principal authors cannot be subjective on this question because both of us are dual citizens – a New Zealander who added Australian citizenship to her identities and an Australian who became a Kiwi – while the third author did his PhD in Australia. A psychoanalytic approach to the past would ask what has the past done to us?[7] One answer is that our collective experience living on both sides of the Tasman motivated us to undertake this project. As trans-Tasman travellers and citizens we set out to ask trans-Tasman questions about a history of multiple ties between New Zealand and Australia.

In the course of these searches we rediscovered the Tasman world, a concept that better summarises what this book is about: a working region, defined by a history of traffic linking the countries. The Tasman world is built on histories of political and bureaucratic cooperation, and occasional conflict, and on a host of popular cultural expressions from music to media to sport. It is enmeshed in the dialogue about strategic foreign and defence policy in the region, and in the concrete evidence of working together on a string of frontiers, from the Second World War to the present. The everyday history of the Tasman world is manifested in increasing ties of commerce and trade, migration and growing kinship. Its less visible, but nonetheless real signs lie in the continuing flow of ideas, personnel and institutions in education and government. Living together, working together and playing together, however, do not mean doing everything together.

There are striking differences between the two countries, beginning with size, climate and environment, which may grow more significant in an era of climate change. Australia has all the soft, moulded and stretched topography of an ancient continent reaching from the tropics to the sub-Antarctic. New Zealand is an archipelago, a world of two large islands with central spines of alps and volcanic plateaus, valleys and rivers that sustain a wealth of small, enclosed provincial communities. According to advertising gurus, both peoples love the land, though Australians are in awe of the land as a force to be tamed, while Kiwis treat theirs as a playground.[8] Lively, self-organising provincial communities are strong in New Zealand, whereas Australian historian Geoffrey Bolton believes that the Hume Highway connecting Sydney to Melbourne dominates too much of Australia's history, which is structured largely around the country's southeastern corner.[9]

Also differing between countries is the relationship of their indigenous peoples to the varied landscapes, and the sequence and outcomes of their encounters with the white settler societies. One of the stereotypes in New Zealand national history for a long time was the story of better race relations between Pakeha settlers and Maori compared with white Australian settlers' confrontations with Aboriginal people. Both indigenous societies suffered depopulation, deprivation and land loss. Yet a treaty and partnership in New Zealand, however flawed, gave Maori greater political potential from an early date compared with Aboriginal people subject to colonial settler states in Australia that maintained policies of control long after federation.

The identities crafted as separate national histories were intimately affected by these records of encounter. Australians have struggled to come to terms with their inheritance of settler–indigenous relations – segregated Aboriginal communities, high infant mortality, low life expectancy, accusations of 'stolen generations', squalor and neglect. This history has not stopped their fashioning an image as a society defined largely by masculine ideals and loyalty to mates, amiability and a love of sport. New Zealanders revel in their island and mountain paradise, confident they are superior in their attitudes to women, endlessly inventive on a small platform of resources, equally easy-going, and enthusiastic about sport. Again, according to the advertisers, 'team is everything to the Kiwis, who do not like individual sportsmen or women overshadowing the national team'. Australians, on the other hand, idolise the individual sporting hero.[10]

Nationalism is a powerful force, and yet we hope – adding our historians' voices to policy perspectives – this new Tasman history has demonstrated the absurdity of nationalist rhetoric.[11] During the 20th century citizens of this world south of Asia lost their common history that had been in their heads as collective memories were rewritten around nationalist narratives. The common past was there, and can be retrieved and rewritten as a shared history, as laid out in the pages of this book. British history bequeathed a common culture from Balclutha to Broome, Perth to Gisborne, and Darwin to Dunedin, across very different environments. British history made Australia and New Zealand extended family and neighbours. With increased migration and travel, family ties are strengthening, not weakening, while they are extending connections to other histories. Ties are between kith as well as kin: kith means 'one's friends, fellow-countrymen, or neighbours', says the OED.[12] So we might take our cue from Shakespeare's Mark Antony at Julius Caesar's funeral and make more effort to lend each other our ears and to speak what we do know.

Since 2005 single queues for holders of Australian and New Zealand passports at airports in New Zealand, Melbourne, Sydney and Brisbane have signposted to travellers that there is a Tasman world. Pivoted on the trans-Tasman travel arrangement(s) and the Trans-Tasman Mutual Recognition Arrangement (TTMRA), the notion of a Tasman world as a going concern could pose a fresh start as a community facing the 21st century. Cultural exchanges are deeply embedded in existing circuits in banking, commerce, sport, religion, education and a host of other activities and institutions to the extent they have consolidated what social theorists call 'transnational social fields' between New Zealand and Australia.[13] The Tasman partners have organised the space between them as a common world.[14] The trans-Tasman tradition of training public servants, for instance, continues in the Australia New Zealand School of Government (ANZSOG), and of forest research in Scion.

New Zealand and Australia have shared ideas over time, to the extent that as colonies and later settler states they shared state experiments. The height of that sharing occurred at the very moment Australasia was split by the formation of the Commonwealth of Australia. The key institution of compulsory arbitration was a shared experiment. Health and social policy innovations regularly circulated across the Tasman. As Chapter 4 argued, the Tasman world's historical ties, cultural and institutional similarities, the Westminster system and social and organisational links provided a field for sharing policy innovations, lessons, successes and failures. New Zealand offers a cognitive shortcut for Australia, just as the various Australian jurisdictions provide examples for New Zealand. The closeness of policy-makers and policy-making is possibly exceptional to the Tasman world.

One example is New Zealand's involvement in the Council of Australian Governments (COAG). Official ties have their origin in the 19th century, and intensified from the 1960s, aided by technological advances in travel and communications and by closer dealings under the New Zealand–Australia Free Trade Agreement (NAFTA). Historical ties are strong in areas where New Zealand today is a full COAG Ministerial Council member with voting rights, as in education, consumer affairs, health, tourism, transport, sport and culture. Conversely, historical ties are weak where New Zealand is not a member, as in indigenous issues, immigration and minerals. Most recently, in 2006, New Zealand officials joined the Commonwealth, States and Territory Advisory Council on Innovation and the Australian National Science Forum to share ideas on research and innovation.[15]

A classic instance of close ties in health that grew from COAG is the joint food standards system and agency established in 1996, now Food Standards Australia and New Zealand. Equivalent to a state, New Zealand has one vote among 10 on this joint institution, along with the six Australian states, two territories and the federal government. Joint food standards are common sense when three-quarters of the food items on supermarket shelves are Australasian. The TTMRA, in force since 1998, developed from an earlier federal agreement between the Australian government and state and territory governments. By stretching to New Zealand the TTMRA became more far-reaching than any other regime for mutual recognition. New Zealand has full membership and voting rights on ministerial councils about any decision involving the TTMRA. As consumers we belong to a Tasman world because consumer issues sit inside the arrangement. Those familiar with the Tasman world's 'plumbing' also advise the use of mutual recognition rather than uniform law. In civil proceedings, where the two treat each other as any other country, knowledge of the Australian federal system helped to provide a model of trans-Tasman enforcement of judgements and service of proceedings. Close analysis showed the Australian model worked.[16]

There are occasional policy failures, however, which provide lessons. In 2007 an innovative joint institution in the form of a Therapeutic Products Authority did not receive enough political support in New Zealand to proceed. Yet a joint trans-Tasman agency to regulate therapeutic products would have abolished asymmetry by according New Zealand a status superior to that in the food standards model, as a nation state equal to Australia. A dispute over the regulation of complementary medicines scuttled the proposal. New Zealand nationalism assumed a medical guise in the form of the bicultural narrative which, in this case, asserted the uniqueness of local, especially indigenous, alternative medicine. This was not the issue which the Therapeutic Products Authority was designed to address. A joint agency would have safeguarded public health and safety by regulating therapeutic products and given New Zealand the ability to regulate complementary medicines, a capability lacked by the existing agency, Medsafe.

From this experience both countries learnt the advantages of having templates that outline a range of ways institutional cooperation might develop, and of preparing for attacks deploying nationalist rhetoric. A splendid paper ensued by the Australian government's Department of Finance and Administration and the Ministry of Economic Development in New Zealand, 'Arrangements for Facilitating Trans-Tasman Government Institutional Co-operation'.[17] Copying, as we have shown, remains a popular policy alternative, though in an asymmetric relationship the transfer is often from the larger to the smaller partner.

A central finding in Chapter 5 was the persistent aspiration to reciprocity with Australia by New Zealand in trade relations, and the enduring wish to create a 'community of interests' or a 'community of purpose'. The language of interests and purpose speaks of a shared dose of philosophical common sense. To understand where CER came from it was necessary to reconstruct trans-Tasman trade history from archival sources because national histories have not addressed this strand of ideas and experience. The belief endured from the 1870s at least that reciprocity would be of mutual benefit, and subsequently CER has created an 'Australasian market'.[18] CER has also developed efficiency and competitiveness on both sides of the Tasman, as in the dairy industry, so that Australia and New Zealand can compete in the world market together.[19] The TTMRA is a key exemplar of reciprocity.

The aspiration for a single economic market goes substantially beyond CER. There are a variety of aims, strategies and mechanisms that will move New Zealand and Australia further along the path of convergence in trade and business. The increasing integration of the two economies makes common rules even more a matter of common sense. Senior ministers and officials cooperated in aligning competition law, accounting standards and banking regulation. CER history shows that much depends on the personal relationships between prime ministers on each side of the Tasman and their deputies, who served as treasurers and trade ministers. Much depends on the quality of political leadership. Trading, tourism and investment links with individual Australian states will perhaps be the strongest force drawing New Zealand into closer economic ties. The extent to which the wider region of the Pacific islands could be incorporated into a single market, though, is fraught with political questions whose answers cannot be predicted.[20]

A full economic union raises questions of sovereignty. These questions will continue to block a common currency.[21] Nationalistic suspicions of Australian dominance of the New Zealand economy surface whenever closer ties are suggested, as the Australia–New Zealand Leadership Forums have demonstrated. Broader national interests are not always aligned with business interests, and we need to be clear what national interests look like. Australian big banks already own most of the New Zealand banking sector, and there continue to be concerns about a hollowing out of the economy and local talent if the process of convergence involves lighter regulation that allows Australian banks to escape New Zealand Reserve Bank control. A past spending spree by Australian business that took Australia's total investment from NZ$32.4 billion in 2000 to NZ$51.3 billion four years later generated newspaper descriptions of 'the buy-up of New Zealand Inc.' and 'the Australianisation of business life', with the Minister of Finance and the Governor of the Reserve Bank expressing alarm.[22] Evidence in Chapter 6 showed there is a trans-Tasman business elite tied by affiliation networks and interlocking directorships, which is asymmetric as well, with the Australian business community in New Zealand smaller and more visible than New Zealand business leaders – many of whom are CFOs and CIOs – in Australia. The issue on the Australian side of the Tasman has been a degree of indifference to the yearnings of New Zealand business for more integration, except on Australian terms. The more integration, the more care is necessary. The future may look like the past: New Zealand may work the harder, to attract attention from Australian policy-makers and to secure prosperity in a single market structure, without too many strings attached.

The growth of the Tasman world into Asia is an area of practical growth that bids fair to regenerate 'Australasia' as a meaningful target. The message of the leadership forums from 2004 to 2006 was not to submerge the Tasman partners in a struggle over the minutiae of freeing up commerce between them, but to build a single economic market as a regional unit that will make the Tasman world competitive in expanding Asia–Pacific markets. The alternative is to be left in the backwash of an accelerating global economy. Here New Zealand may be the leading edge of an Australasian initiative as it sealed a free trade agreement with China in April 2008. Whichever prognostication about China's growth potential proves correct in the end, China represents the behemoth of the 21st century for the Tasman partners. Eight of her provinces contain more people than the whole of Europe, each estimated to have an economy the size of France or Germany by 2040. Her emerging middle classes are increasingly flowing overseas as tourists. Despite controls and censorship, an information explosion is occurring through the internet. China is changing the environment in which New Zealand and Australia operate. They are entangled with her as part of the changing strategic architecture of the Asia–Pacific region. Knowing more about China and adapting swiftly to her growth are imperatives the Tasman partners face, even as they grow their investments in that country, moving labour forces offshore and developing their international education industries.

India is also part of the Asian horizon for this new Australasia. Her population will likely exceed China's in 50 years, though with a less even pattern of growth. One billion consumers is the market for an Australasian business world primed for the 21st century. As wealth transfers to Middle East financial markets during the next decades the new Australasia will have to deal with this shift in global business as well.

In addition, the 10 Association of Southeast Asian Nations (ASEAN) members, together with Australia and New Zealand, moved closer towards the goal of signing a regional ASEAN–Australia–New Zealand free trade agreement by December 2008. This trade deal will strengthen the Tasman world's engagement with the ASEAN countries and links with the Asia–Pacific region.

The security complications as China in particular stakes a claim for geopolitical pre-eminence in the region may require both New Zealand and Australia to make hard choices. India and Japan compound them; indeed, Japan's relationship with China represents a potential flashpoint in the background. Whose side does one take, if that is required of countries with important trading links to Japan and a security alliance with the United States? The choices will be harder for Australia than New Zealand.[23]

Meanwhile, the area that will require the expanded attention of both countries as they wrestle with these issues is the area that connects the Tasman world to these Asian giants: the near Pacific, especially the chain of Melanesian islands overlooked by Papua New Guinea. In 2007 New Zealand's Labour Trade Minister, Phil Goff, advocated a Pacific regional economy as a subset of the new Australasian integrated economy – a Pacific CER or even a free trade area of 35 million people.[24] Such an economy is a long way away and if it were to be established it would be necessary to solve the question of increasing labour mobility from the islands to the Tasman partners, both as aid to the islands and as an adjunct to the ageing labour forces of the Tasman world. Australia has in recent years formulated a bleaker outlook than New Zealand about the region's population growth, lack of industry, and health hazards. Both Tasman partners, however, have cooperated in dealing with security crises in Bougainville and Solomon Islands, as discussed in Chapter 9. A regional partnership that extends beyond peacekeeping requires an oceanic perspective that knows better the islands' people and environments.

Anzac links are precious, and with time the Anzac tradition is growing more, not less important as younger people look back to the previous generations who fought to defend the world as they knew it. The Anzac tradition is unlikely to lose its power in the future, though it will change with time. Since Anzac weekend 2008, a First World War New Zealand digger who wears the ceremonial lemon squeezer hat stands in silent reflection on one side of Sydney's Anzac bridge, facing his mate, the Australian digger who has stood there since 2000.

Chapter 9 reflected on how defence of the realm entwined as much as it sent the pair in different directions. One area of divergence has been over relations with the United States. New Zealand's refusal of port access to the USS *Buchanan* in 1985 was a turning point that changed the dynamic of the defence and security relationships between the Tasman partners and the United States, and with each other. Each already had differently configured historical relationships with the United States, Britain's heir as the world's superpower. We may attribute different philosophical outlooks – realistic and optimistic – in Australia and New Zealand to physical remoteness, geopolitics, New Zealand arcadianism, and divergent historical experience. One view is that a 'new realism, recognising difference' marked the Tasman relationship early in the 21st century.[25] A community of interests in securing a peaceful Pacific does not behove the two countries to adopt the same foreign policy.[26] Stuart McMillan suggests that criticisms of the costs of the American alliance might draw Australia and New Zealand closer together. He also counsels New Zealanders not to withdraw formally from the Anzus alliance because to do so would irrevocably damage the Tasman world. It would also repress the history recovered in this book.

The future holds both practical, material possibilities and a wider vision that suggests we may have a common future in a *new* Australasia. An oceanic, archipelagic perspective is essential even to see the practical possibilities, let alone to dream of a new hemispheric history that provides a platform for a shared future.[27] Such a historically informed future would reach out to the Pacific region. Fittingly, the Australia 2020 Summit held in April 2008 did that by suggesting a 'partnerships for development' initiative and deeper engagement through 'confederation or free association between Australia and the Pacific, beginning with micro-states'.[28] Such ideas developed from the Pacific islands Forum, which endorsed the *Pacific Plan* in 2005. Australia and New Zealand were strong advocates of the plan, which grew out of awareness that the challenges facing Pacific island countries required regional cooperation.[29] This process may strengthen ties with Europe through a trilateral relationship with the European Union (EU) in the Pacific to address issues of development, security, and environmental and climate change. Only this time Australasia would include the Tasman segment missing from Australian and New Zealand consciousness because it possesses a French history, as opposed to a British history: the settler society of New Caledonia, which connects the region to Europe through the EU.

New Zealanders like to think their archipelagic environment and extensive Islander populations give them a sympathetic perspective on the Pacific islands to the north. The government allows the importing of Islander labour to work the vineyards and orchards, and in horticulture, while the Australia 2020 Summit recommended a labour mobility programme. Climate change and rising sea levels may well force the introduction of other small island populations as their homes vanish. One commentator has spoken of the 'Pacific-ation' of New Zealand, with over a fifth of the population in 2006 made up of Maori and Pacific Islanders, who make up nearly a third of people under 25 years of age. Such proportions have implications for economic performance and the nature of New Zealand's social cohesion in the 21st century. Productivity growth depends in particular upon lifting levels of education, training and prosperity in these ethnic descent groups. Their input has created a vibrant Pasifika art, literature and music in New Zealand, modifying the values and institutions with which they interact. So will the growing proportion of Asian new settlers, who were already 10 per cent of the population in the 2006 census.[30] Added to this subtle social change is the 'indigenisation of the ex-British' as generations born in New Zealand express a home-grown Kiwi identity.[31] Nonetheless, their British history remains important for Australians and New Zealanders to understand themselves and their worlds.

Australia's demographic challenges are subtly different. The Australian government's focus is on greater participation of a more mixed, multicultural population in the workforce, providing for flexible options, especially as the population ages sharply in this century and the taxation base correspondingly shrinks.[32] Immigration policy will need to consider the steady immigration of New Zealand residents. Since movement between the countries is more like internal than international migration, Graeme Hugo recommends a cooperative scenario of sharing research and experience, joint activities and some harmonisation of policies.[33]

The mobility of Kiwis is likely to continue in the context of high international mobility. More than half of New Zealand's population exchange is with Australia.[34] The rate at which New Zealanders cross the Tasman is unlikely to change unless travel costs soar, the trans-Tasman real earnings gap closes, or there is an unforeseen cataclysmic event. One of the quirkier effects of increased Kiwi mobility will be an increased browning of the Tasman world's games of rugby union and rugby league. One knowledgeable commentator is confident that the population playing National Rugby League will be almost 50 per cent Polynesian by 2012. 'The strength of New Zealand league is in Australia now, not New Zealand' could be a warning cry for the whole of the Tasman relationship.[35]

That brings us to a wider vision for a resurrected Australasia, whether in pursuit of greater prosperity, knowledge and understanding, or collaborating in the interests of our common humanity, and to avoid conflict. Our research suggests that a deliberate getting together will not happen across the board but only in areas where there is already a long history of interactions. The way ideas and policies have transferred across the Tasman has been conditioned historically by the density of institutional and cultural factors. That will continue and the flow will likely be more from Australia to New Zealand than the other way round. Global forces, meanwhile, will in all likelihood pull people towards higher incomes in Australia for some time yet, just as they draw Australians overseas. New Zealand characteristically has lighter structures and fewer resources. Integration generally makes people more aware of each other, and for Australia that is so towards the north and west but often not so towards its island neighbours in the South Pacific.[36] Australia ignores the Land of the Long White Cloud unless there is self-interest involved, or a crisis beckons that threatens Australia's national interest. What would it take to bring New Zealand, and the Tasman world, into focus?

A number of people, if not many, before us have speculated knowledgeably about Tasman futures. In 1968 Geoffrey Sawyer, Professor of Law at the Australian National University, outlined the constitutional problems if New Zealand became a seventh state under section 121 of the Australian Constitution. He pointed out that many of these problems would be avoided if New Zealand became a territory under section 122, which would give New Zealand more 'powers of local self-government' than the states possess, and wider tax powers. The catch is that New Zealand would then be subjected to the will of the federal parliament – an unpalatable prospect.[37] A more attractive idea is of a nimble New Zealand stepping between the status of a seventh state and a sovereign nation, depending on the issue. This versatile role is the one British history and its subset, Tasman history, reveal that New Zealand has played, and continues to play. Brian Galligan, Professor of Political Science at the University of Melbourne, encouraged such thinking as appropriate for the 21st century when he posited a hybrid 'asymmetric pluralist association' built on existing arrangements.[38]

The Australia 2020 Summit's call for a 'modern Australian federation' therefore invites curiosity.[39] The summit's rural session too 'almost abolished the states' by demanding national harmonisation of state-based transport and agricultural rules.[40] The top idea for the economy's future was 'an independent body to carry out a "clean sheet of paper" review of the roles and responsibilities of federal, state and local governments in areas of major economic activity'.[41] This chorus to reform or even abolish the federal system suggests that the next opportune moment – the best since 1900 – for when New Zealand might contemplate some type of political union with Australia would be if and when Australia abolished the federation and finally formed one economy. After all, only in the 1960s were barriers inter-state reduced and the standard-gauge rail link completed between Melbourne and Sydney.[42] Whether serendipity allows the necessary conjuncture of circumstance for the federal idea to bridge the Tasman remains to be seen. If the Australian government does contemplate a treaty with the indigenous people and New Zealand likewise ponders a written constitution, the neighbours are bound at the least to be drawn towards sharing cognitive shortcuts with each other.

It is also too early to say what new sense of identity or identities the people of this new congeries might evolve. It would depend partly on relations among the increasingly varied ethnic migrant communities and two very different indigenous groups – Maori and Australian Aboriginal people – who have unfinished business with the settler societies in the two countries. A new layer of identity would also depend on a sense of common culture that is more than just the traffic between them. As Peter Beilharz observes about how art historian Bernard Smith's work helps us to think about culture and identity:

> . . . cultures are mobile . . . even within the context of asymmetrical power relations; culture works as assemblage. Culture is relational, as is identity; neither is usefully viewed as essential, emanating from spirit, place, land, language or race.[43]

Maori put turangawaewae (a place to stand) at the centre of their identity. Is it too much to hope that the new Australasians will shape an identity built on their joint place to stand in the southern ocean, with all their provincial niches and provincialisms asserted against other worlds? For that to happen a community of sentiment as well as interests would need to develop, which would call for a shift in attitudes in both countries, and a writing of poetry. If Australians and New Zealanders looked sideways across the 'ditch' as well as in every other direction they might help to bring out the creative best in one another.

Our map of this Australasia would have concentric circles, making up an inner and more remote Australasia.[44] Inner Australasia would encompass much of the east coast of Australia and the whole of the New Zealand archipelago, an already working region according to our arguments in this book. Economically, New Zealand has behaved like a 'peripheral' Australian state since the 1990s.[45] Rediscovery of the Tasman world, however, reorients the picture, and places New Zealand within inner Australasia, along with Queensland. Consistent with the historical maps recovered for this book, Australasia would have elastic boundaries.[46] As the 21st century becomes the Asian century the closest or furthest boundary (depending on the perspective) would stretch into south and east Asia; it already does for such regional centres as Western Australia. On its eastern edge it might encompass the islands of the near Pacific. One Pacific scholar already refers to 'Anglo-Austronesia', and this mode of thinking, if not language, would overcome the current 'ghettoisation' of the Pacific as an alien place for Tasman citizens.[47]

Contemplating this new Australasia suggests we might do well to deconstruct 'Asia', especially if it is to form the last two syllables of 'Australasia'.[48] The Australia 2020 Summit effectively called for an 'Asian' Australia in declaring that the future lies with Japan, China and India, in addition to the US. This direction is what trade statistics foreshadow, although Britain still sat in fourth and fifth place as a trading partner for both Australia and New Zealand respectively in 2007. A notion of an Asian future requires more discrimination of terms. What does Asia mean, let alone Asia–Pacific? The term is indeterminate; it overlooks states and histories, and how these interrelate, both within Asia and south of Indonesia.

Such a grouping of peoples in the southern hemisphere would look outwards to the world very differently from the classic antipodean sensibility that the northern hemisphere has traditionally imposed upon it. There would be many different antipodes for the cultural groupings and regional niches represented in this new Australasia. The Britain that fostered white settlement would be only one among them.[49] The point is that the autonomous communities that fashioned the Tasman world – a cultural archipelago reaching back to Britain and, increasingly, other countries of migrants – belong together and have been together in their asymmetric but intimate relationship for the whole of the 20th century, albeit in different degrees, at different times, on multiple levels.

Historians are not soothsayers; we are trained to look back. So we offer a backward-looking perspective on speculative obstacles that stand in the way of permitting a remade Tasman world to meld and metamorphose into a new and more interconnected Australasia. The two world wars – what one scholar calls the 'war of the world'[50] – present abundant examples of the sorts of crises that could boost or sever trans-Tasman traffic. Ethnic conflict and economic volatility are still with us in the 21st century, and worsening. The Great War dealt a blow to globalisation by loosening the grip of empires that provided political support for free trade. The decline of the American empire is changing the balance with other empires in Europe and with a resurgent 'Asia' that is demonstrating the resilience of 'Eurasia' (another word to deconstruct) over the long run.[51] A variety of forces and 'wild card' occurrences could speed up or slow down the processes and forms of association that make up the Tasman world.

Ecological crises, such as the hyper-critical drying up of settled parts of Australia, would cause major, disruptive change. A failure of a major bank on both sides of the Tasman would unsettle close economic relations. Nothing short of an economic catastrophe in New Zealand is likely to lead her to take up the place still allotted in the preamble to the Constitution of Australia as a seventh state, presuming Australians would assent. Another wild card would be a significant continuing crisis in federal–state relations in Australia. A move to republicanism on the part of one without the other would change the tone of the Tasman relationship. An avian influenza virus emerging once again out of Asia might unleash more havoc than did the influenza epidemic of 1918–19, which raised quarantine barriers between Australia and New Zealand (and saved Australian lives as a result). An outbreak of mad cow disease, inducing paralysis in the dairy industry, is another awful scenario. On the other hand, a major terrorist attack on Sydney or Melbourne might well strangle the flow of people from New Zealand to Australia, and grand plans for a common border (notwithstanding different visa and migrant policies) would disappear. A regional national disaster in the Pacific or serious conflict in the Asia–Pacific region could spark refugee inflows to both countries, with consequences for the economic climate, as would a deepening energy crisis worldwide. A global swing away from free trade driven by the World Trade Organisation would deeply affect the Tasman world, and a swing away from free trade may yet accelerate with world food shortages.

We began this book by introducing the concepts of Australasia and the Tasman world. Mindful that people find differences more interesting and fun than similarities, we placed a study of trans-Tasman jokes, cartoons and differences soon after, in Chapter 2. The purpose of this book, however, is to take seriously the history of New Zealand's most important and extensive relationship – with Australia. We initially proposed that the deficits in knowledge about trans-Tasman relations over the 'long' 20th century impoverished both countries' histories and diminished the quality of public commentary. By retrieving a common past and reordering it as a shared history we have written a book that contributes to the remaking of the Tasman world and that, we hope, provides pointers to a global future.

NOTES

Chapter One

1. J. G. A. Pocock, 'British History: a plea for a new subject', reprinted in J. G. A. Pocock, *The Discovery of Islands*, Cambridge, 2005, ch. 2, p. 43.
2. W. K. Hancock, *Australia*, London, 1930; Alan D. Gilbert, K. S. Inglis and S. G. Foster (gen. eds), *Australians: A historical library*, 10 vols, Sydney, 1987.
3. John A. Moses (ed.), *Historical Disciplines and Culture in Australasia: An assessment*, Brisbane, 1979; see Bill Gammage, 'Truth and Tradition in Australia, New Zealand and Papua New Guinea', p. 46.
4. G. Osborne and W. F. Mandle (eds), *New History: Studying Australia today*, Sydney, 1982.
5. Paul Kelly, *The End of Certainty: The story of the 1980s*, Sydney, 1992, p. 1.
6. John Rickard, *Australia: A cultural history*, 2nd edn, New York, 1996 (1st pub. 1988), ch. 6.
7. Geoffrey Brennan and Francis G. Castles (eds), *Australia Reshaped: 200 years of institutional transformation*, Cambridge & Melbourne, 2002; Erik Olssen, *Building the New World: Work, politics and society in Caversham 1880s–1920s*, Auckland, 1995; James Holt, *Compulsory Arbitration in New Zealand: The first forty years*, Auckland, 1986.
8. Francis G. Castles, *The Working Class and Welfare: Reflections on the political development of the welfare state in Australia and New Zealand, 1890–1980*, Wellington & Sydney, 1985; Francis G. Castles, *Australian Public Policy and Economic Vulnerability: A comparative and historical perspective*, Sydney, 1988.
9. ACSANZ 2002, Converging Futures? Canada and Australia in a new millennium, Canberra, 12–15 September 2002.
10. Philippa Mein Smith, 'New Zealand Federation Commissioners in Australia: One past, two historiographies', *Australian Historical Studies*, Vol. 34, No. 122, October 2003, pp. 305–25. See also James Belich, *Paradise Reforged: A history of the New Zealanders from the 1880s to the year 2000*, Auckland, 2001.
11. Keith Sinclair (ed.), *Tasman Relations: New Zealand and Australia, 1788–1988*, Auckland, 1987, and his 'Why are Race Relations in New Zealand Better Than in South Africa, South Australia or South Dakota?', *New Zealand Journal of History*, Vol. 5, No. 2, October 1971, pp. 121–27.
12. Editorial Introduction, *New Zealand Journal of History*, Vol. 34, No. 1, April 2000.
13. Belich, *Paradise Reforged*, pp. 46–52.

14. E. J. Tapp, 'New Zealand: The seventh state of Australia?', *Australian Quarterly*, Vol. 34, December 1962, pp. 74–81, and his 'Australian and New Zealand Relations', *Australian Outlook*, Vol. 5, 1951, pp. 165–74, 231–35; Rollo Arnold, 'Some Australasian Aspects of New Zealand Life, 1890–1913', *New Zealand Journal of History*, Vol. 4, No. 1, April 1970, pp. 54–76; Keith Sinclair, 'The Past and Future of Australia–New Zealand Relations', *Australian Outlook*, Vol. 22, 1968, pp. 29–38.

15. Nicolas Haines (ed.), *The Tasman: Frontier and freeway?*, Proceedings of the Second Conference on 'Australia's World', Canberra, 1972; Alan Burnett and Robin Burnett, *The Australia and New Zealand Nexus*, Canberra, 1978. Kiwi economists P. J. Lloyd, based at the University of Melbourne, and F. W. (Sir Frank) Holmes, of Victoria University of Wellington, played an important role on each side of the Tasman from the 1960s.

16. Ralph Hayburn (ed.), *Foreign Policy School 1978: Australia and New Zealand relations*, Dunedin, 1978; Bob Catley (ed.), *NZ–Australia Relations: Moving together or drifting Apart?*, Papers from the 36th Otago Foreign Policy School, Wellington, 2002; also Bob Catley, *Waltzing with Matilda: Should New Zealand join Australia?*, Wellington, 2001.

17. Ian F. Grant, *The Other Side of the Ditch: A cartoon century in the New Zealand–Australia relationship*, Wellington, 2001; Bruce Brown (ed.), *New Zealand and Australia – Where are we going?* NZ Institute of International Affairs seminar, Wellington, 2001; Arthur Grimes, Lydia Wevers and Ginny Sullivan (eds), *States of Mind: Australia and New Zealand 1901–2001*, Wellington, 2002.

18. K. R. Howe, *Race Relations Australia and New Zealand: A comparative survey 1770s–1970s*, Wellington & Sydney, 1977; Simon P. Ville, *The Rural Entrepreneurs: A history of the stock and station agent industry in Australia and New Zealand*, New York & Melbourne, 2000. Other examples include H. R. Jackson, *Churches and People in Australia and New Zealand 1860–1930*, Wellington, 1987; Shaun Brawley, *The White Peril: Foreign relations and Asian immigration to Australasia and North America 1919–78*, Sydney, 1995.

19. Bain Attwood and Fiona Magowan (eds), *Telling Stories: Indigenous history and memory in Australia and New Zealand*, Wellington, 2001; Klaus Neumann, Nicholas Thomas and Hilary Ericksen (eds), *Quicksands: Foundational histories in Australia and Aotearoa New Zealand*, Sydney, 1999. Tara Brabazon, *Tracking the Jack: A retracing of the Antipodes*, Sydney, 2000, is a cultural studies text that sees Australia and New Zealand as a combined antipodean space yet does not treat them accordingly. The biggest absence is the trans-Tasman relationship, which Brabazon agrees is 'astonishingly under-defined', p. 161.

20. Eric Fry (ed.), *Common Cause: Essays in Australian and New Zealand labour history*, Wellington, 1986; Melanie Nolan, 'The High Tide of a Labour Market System: The Australasian male breadwinner model', *Labour & Industry*, Vol. 13, No. 3, April 2003, pp. 73–92; James Bennett, 'Rats and Revolutionaries': *The Labour movement in Australia and New Zealand 1890–1940*, Dunedin, 2004; Raelene Frances and Melanie Nolan, 'Gender and Labour in "a Manzone Country" and "A Man's Country": National, transnational, international and comparative labour history', *Labour History*, Vol. 95, November 2008.

21. J. A. Dowie, 'Studies in New Zealand Investment 1871–1900', PhD thesis, ANU, 1965; John Singleton and Paul L. Robertson, *Economic Relations between Britain and Australasia 1945–1970*, Houndmills, Basingstoke, 2002; Gary Hawke, 'Australian and New Zealand Economic Development from about 1890 to 1940', in Sinclair (ed.), *Tasman Relations*, ch. 6; Angus Young, 'Two Countries, One Currency? Evolution in trans-Tasman trade and monetary relations', MCA thesis, Victoria University of Wellington, 2002.

22. Marian Simms, 'Australia and New Zealand: Separate states but path-dependent', *Round Table*, Vol. 95, No. 387, October 2006, pp. 679–92; Francis Castles, Rolf Gerritsen and Jack Vowles (eds), *The Great Experiment: Labour parties and public policy transformation in Australia and New Zealand*, Auckland, 1996. In the follow-up special issue of the *Australian Journal of Political Science*, Vol. 41, No. 2, June 2006, scholars were put in pairs to undertake a comparative analysis. Shaun Goldfinch contrasts the New Zealand 'crash through' approach to reform with the Australian experience of 'bargained consensus' in the 1980s and 1990s in his *Remaking New Zealand and Australian Economic Policy*, Wellington, 2000.

23. Brian Galligan and Richard Mulgan, 'Asymmetric Political Association: The Australasian experiment', in Robert Agranoff (ed.), *Accommodating Diversity: Asymmetry in federal states*, Baden-Baden, 1999, pp. 57–72.

24. Denis McLean, *The Prickly Pair: Making nationalism in Australia and New Zealand*, Dunedin, 2003.

25. Colin James, 'Three-step with Matilda: Trans–Tasman relations', in Roderic Alley (ed.), *New Zealand in World Affairs IV: 1990–2005*, Wellington, 2007, p. 46, and his 'Foreign and Family: The Australian Connection – sensible sovereignty or niggling nationalism?', in Brian Lynch (ed.), *New Zealand and the World: The major foreign policy issues, 2005–2010*, Wellington, 2006, p. 36.

26. C. Hartley Grattan, *The Southwest Pacific since 1900: A modern history: Australia, New Zealand, the Islands, Antarctica*, The University of Michigan History of the Modern World, Ann Arbor, 1963.

27. Donald Denoon and Philippa Mein Smith, with Marivic Wyndham, *A History of Australia, New Zealand and the Pacific*, The Blackwell History of the World, Oxford, 2000.

28. Donald Denoon, 'Re-Membering Australasia: A repressed memory', *Australian Historical Studies*, Vol. 34, No. 122, October 2003, pp. 290–304.

29. Charles de Brosses, *Histoire des Navigations aux Terres Australes*, Paris, 1756; Engl. trans. by J. Callander (without acknowledgment), Edinburgh, 1766–68. Callander's translation of the 'first [division] in the Indian Ocean, south of Asia' is quoted in Edward E. Morris, *Austral English: A dictionary of Australasian words phrases and usages*, London, 1898, p. 9.

30. John M. R. Young (ed.), *Australia's Pacific Frontier*, Melbourne, 1967; cf. Jim McAloon, 'New Zealand on the Pacific Frontier: Environment, economy and culture', *History Compass*, Vol. 4, No. 1, 2006, pp. 36–42. See works by Robert McNab, e.g. *Murihiku and the Southern Islands*, Christchurch, 1996 (1st pub. 1907); and E. J. Tapp, *Early New Zealand: A dependency of New South Wales, 1788–1841*, Melbourne, 1959.

31. T. A. Coghlan, *A Statistical Account of the Seven Colonies of Australasia, 1901–1902*, Sydney, 1902.
32. Courtesy of Bill Willmott. California was called Jin Shan, Gold Mountain.
33. Morris, *Austral English*, p. 9.
34. E.g. compare Joan Hughes (ed.), *The Concise Australian National Dictionary*, Melbourne, 1992, p. 15, and Tony Deverson and Graeme Kennedy (eds), *The New Zealand Oxford Dictionary*, Melbourne, 2005, p. 68.
35. Belich, *Paradise Reforged*, pp. 46–7, 52, 440.
36. Interestingly the most intriguing critiques of Captain Cook are from Aboriginal Australians – Cook and stories about him became the metaphor for a history of dispossession and cruelty by white modern society. See the film *Too Many Captain Cooks* by P. McDonald and P. F. Wainburranga, Canberra, 1988.
37. Sir John Hall, *Official Record of the Proceedings and Debates of the Australasian Federation Conference*, Melbourne, 1890, p. 175, Australian Federation Full Text Database.
38. E.g. at the Imperial Economic Conference, Ottawa, 1932: Australians had a 'community of interest with other Dominions'. National Archives of Australia [NAA], Canberra, Microfilm, Lyons government, CRS A6006, 1934/12/31.
39. Calculated from I. H. Nicholson, *Shipping Arrivals and Departures Sydney, 1826–1840*, Roebuck Series, Roebuck Society Publication No. 23, Canberra, 1964 (reprinted 1981), courtesy of Peter Tremewan.
40. Jim McAloon, *No Idle Rich: The wealthy in Canterbury and Otago 1840–1914*, Dunedin, 2002.
41. Nicholas Brown, 'Born Modern: Antipodean variations on a theme', *Historical Journal*, Vol. 48, No. 4, 2005, pp. 1139–54.
42. Christopher Pugsley, *Gallipoli: The New Zealand story*, Auckland, 1984, p. 79; Christopher Pugsley, *Anzac: The New Zealanders at Gallipoli*, Auckland, 1995, p. 21.
43. Brabazon, *Tracking the Jack*, p. 24.
44. Ian McGibbon (ed.), *The Oxford Companion to New Zealand Military History*, Auckland, 2000, p. 29.
45. Pocock, *Discovery of Islands*, p. 18.
46. Don Watson, *Recollections of a Bleeding Heart*, Sydney, 2002, pp. 180–81, 383–85.
47. Mary Boyd, 'Australian–New Zealand Relations', in W. S. Livingstone and W. R. Louis (eds), *Australia, New Zealand and the Pacific Islands since the First World War*, Canberra, 1979, pp. 53–54; also Robin Kay (ed.), *The Australian–New Zealand Agreement 1944*, Wellington, 1972, Introduction and pp. 146–47.
48. David Lange, *Nuclear Free: The New Zealand way*, Auckland, 1990, p. 11.
49. McGibbon (ed.), *Oxford Companion to New Zealand Military History*, p. 49.
50. Adapted from Geoffrey Blainey, *The Tyranny of Distance: How distance shaped Australia's history*, revised edn, Sydney, 2001 (1st pub. 1966).
51. P. J. Cain and A. G. Hopkins, *British Imperialism: Crisis and deconstruction, 1914–1990*, London & New York, 1993, p. 254. This section owes a debt to an earlier draft of chapter 6 by S. Goldfinch.
52. Erik Olssen, 'Lands of Sheep and Gold: The Australian dimension to the New Zealand past, 1840–1900' and Hawke, 'Australian and New Zealand Economic

Development', in Sinclair (ed.), *Tasman Relations*, chs 2 & 6; McAloon, *No Idle Rich*; Ville, *Rural Entrepreneurs*.
53. Ville, ibid.
54. D. Merrett, 'Australian Firms Abroad before 1970: Why so few, why those, and why there?' *Business History*, Vol. 44, No. 2, April 2002, pp. 65–87.
55. Philippa Mein Smith, 'Did Muldoon Really "Go Too Slowly" with CER?', *New Zealand Journal of History*, Vol. 41, No. 2, October 2007, pp. 161–79.
56. '2007 CER Ministerial Forum', 31 July 2007: www.beehive.govt.nz/release/2007+cer+ministerial+forum (16 June 2008).
57. Miles Fairburn, 'Is There a Good Case for New Zealand Exceptionalism?', *Thesis Eleven*, No. 92, February 2008, pp. 29–49.
58. Paul Hamer, *Maori in Australia: Nga Maori i te Ao Moemoea*, Wellington, 2007.
59. Peter Beilharz, 'Cultural Traffic across the Tasman', note promoting the joint TASA/SAANZ Sociology conference, Auckland, December 2007.
60. Rory O'Malley, 'The Eclipse of Mateship: The "wide comb dispute" 1979–85', *Labour History*, No. 90, May 2006, pp. 155–76.
61. McLean, *Prickly Pair*, p. 22.
62. Denoon, 'Re-Membering Australasia'.
63. Kevin Grant, Philippa Levine and Frank Trentmann (eds), *Beyond Sovereignty: Britain, Empire and transnationalism, c. 1880–1950*, Houndmills, Basingstoke, 2007, p. 6.
64. C. A. Bayly, *The Birth of the Modern World 1780–1914*, The Blackwell History of the World, Oxford, 2004.

Chapter Two
1. 'Loathe Thy Neighbour: Our relationship with Oz', *Sunday Star Times*, 3 August 2003, p. A4. See also 'Loathe Thy Neighbour', *Weekend Australian Magazine*, 26–27 July 2003, pp. 12–13.
2. Ian F. Grant, *The Other Side of the Ditch: A cartoon century in the New Zealand–Australia relationship*, Wellington 2001, p. 7.
3. Phrase adapted from Simon Schama, *Landscape and Memory*, London, 1995, p. 5.
4. Charles W. Dilke, *Problems of Greater Britain*, 2nd edn, London, 1890, pp. 156–7.
5. William Pember Reeves, *The Long White Cloud: Ao tea roa*, 2nd edn, London, 1899, p. 5.
6. Geoffrey Blainey, 'Two Countries: the same but very different', in Keith Sinclair (ed.), *Tasman Relations: New Zealand and Australia, 1788–1988*, Auckland 1987, p. 318.
7. Geoffrey Blainey, *The Tyranny of Distance: How distance shaped Australia's history*, preface to revised edn, 1985 (1st pub. 1966). On ideas transfer, see Chapters 4 and 7 in this volume.
8. David Walker, *Anxious Nation: Australia and the rise of Asia 1850–1939*, Brisbane, 1999, p. 1.
9. Walker, *Anxious Nation*, p. 5.
10. Donald Denoon and Philippa Mein Smith, with Marivic Wyndham, *A History of Australia, New Zealand and the Pacific*, The Blackwell History of the World, Oxford, 2000, p. 211; Manying Ip, *Dragons on the Long White Cloud: The making of*

Chinese New Zealanders, Auckland, 1996, p. 13.

11. Walker, *Anxious Nation*; Warwick Anderson, *The Cultivation of Whiteness: Science, health and racial destiny in Australia*, Melbourne, 2002.

12. Peter Beilharz, *Imagining the Antipodes: Culture, theory and the visual in the work of Bernard Smith*, Melbourne, 1997, p. 32.

13. Bernard Smith (with Terry Smith), *Australian Painting 1788–1990*, 3rd edn, Melbourne, 1991, pp. 68, 82.

14. For an overview of art in New Zealand, see Hamish Keith, *The Big Picture: A history of New Zealand art from 1642*, Auckland, 2007, especially pp. 102–04 on van der Velden.

15. Libby Robin and Tom Griffiths, 'Environmental History in Australasia', *Environment and History*, Vol. 10, No. 4, 2004, p. 439.

16. Tom Brooking, Robin Hodge and Vaughan Wood, 'The Grasslands Revolution Reconsidered', in Eric Pawson and Tom Brooking (eds), *Environmental Histories of New Zealand*, South Melbourne & Auckland, 2002, pp. 169–70.

17. Geoffrey Blainey, *The Rush that Never Ended: A history of Australian mining*, Melbourne, 1963.

18. David King, 'Costello fuels tax spat', *Press*, 20 May 2006, p. A1.

19. Benedict Anderson, *Imagined Communities: Reflections on the origin and spread of nationalism*, revised edn, London & New York, 1991.

20. Murray McCaskill, 'The Tasman Connection: Aspects of Australian–New Zealand relations', *Australian Geographical Studies*, Vol. 20, April 1982, p. 5.

21. Mambo, 'In Reg's Own Words' : www.mwk16.com/perfectstrangers/GRUV/mambo/mbohome.htm (21 February 2008).

22. Tim Flannery, *The Future Eaters: An ecological history of the Australasian lands and people*, Sydney, 1994.

23. K. S. Inglis, *Sacred Places: War memorials in the Australian landscape*, Melbourne, 1998, p. 23.

24. Te Maire Tau, email to P. Mein Smith, 5 March 2008.

25. E.g. Denoon and Mein Smith, *A History of Australia, New Zealand and the Pacific*, pp. 58–61; Roland Robinson, 'Captain Cook' (related to Percy Mumbulla), in Valerie Chapman and Peter Read (eds), *Terrible Hard Biscuits: A reader in Aboriginal history*, Sydney, 1996, introduction.

26. K. R. Howe, *Race Relations Australia and New Zealand: A comparative survey 1770s–1970s*, Wellington & Sydney, 1977.

27. C. D. Rowley, *The Destruction of Aboriginal Society*, Canberra, 1970, p. 15.

28. Inglis, *Sacred Places*, p. 84.

29. Lydia Wevers, 'Books: Are New Zealand and Australia part of the same literary community?', in Bruce Brown (ed.), *New Zealand and Australia: Where are we going?*, Wellington, 2001, p. 80.

30. W. Pember Reeves, 'Attitude of New Zealand', *Empire Review*, February 1901, pp. 111–15.

31. Stella M. Allan, 'New Zealand and Federation', *United Australia*, October 1900, p. 10.

32. Keith Sinclair, *A Destiny Apart: New Zealand's search for national identity*, Wellington, 1986, and 'Why New Zealanders are not Australians: New Zealand

and the Australian federal movement, 1881–1901', in Keith Sinclair (ed.), *Tasman Relations: New Zealand and Australia, 1788–1988*, Auckland, 1987, ch. 5.

33. John Hirst, *The Sentimental Nation: The making of the Australian Commonwealth*, Melbourne, 2000, pp. 4–5.

34. Ibid., pp. 15, 26.

35. Right Hon. E. Barton, Sydney, Royal Commission on Federation, Evidence, *AJHR*, 1901, A-4, p. 479.

36. Allan, 'New Zealand and Federation', p. 10.

37. John McCullough, Christchurch, Royal Commission on Federation, Evidence, *AJHR*, 1901, A-4, p. 223.

38. Capt. Russell, *Record of the Proceedings and Debates of the Australasian Federation Conference*, Melbourne, 1890, p. 125, Australian Federation Full Text Database: http://setis.library.usyd.edu.au/oztexts/fed.html (22 July 2005).

39. Capt. Russell, *Official Report of the National Australasian Convention Debates*, Sydney, 1891, p. 66, Australian Federation Full Text Database.

40. Frederick Revans Chapman, barrister and solicitor, Dunedin, Royal Commission on Federation, Evidence, *AJHR*, 1901, A-4, p. 37.

41. Allan, 'New Zealand and Federation', p. 11.

42. The words are those of W. M. Hughes, cited in Denoon and Mein Smith, *A History of Australia, New Zealand and the Pacific*, p. 210.

43. Russell questioning Hon. F. W. Holder, Premier of South Australia and new member of Federal House of Representatives, Adelaide, *AJHR*, 1901, A-4, p. 619.

44. McCullough, Royal Commission on Federation, Evidence, *AJHR*, 1901, A-4, p. 223.

45. *Report of the Royal Commission on Federation*, *AJHR*, 1901, A-4, p. xxiv. On the myth of natural abundance, see Miles Fairburn, *The Ideal Society and Its Enemies*, Auckland, 1989.

46. Russell questioning Chapman, Royal Commission on Federation, Evidence, *AJHR*, 1901, A-4, p. 39.

47. E.g. Irven W. Raymond, stock and station agent, Invercargill, Royal Commission on Federation, Evidence, *AJHR*, 1901, A-4, p. 25.

48. Reeves, 'Attitude of New Zealand', p. 112.

49. William Curzon-Siggers, Dunedin, Royal Commission on Federation, Evidence, *AJHR*, 1901, A-4, p. 109.

50. This separate approach is lamented by Inglis, *Sacred Places*.

51. Allan Hawke, 'The Anzacs', unpub. seminar paper, University of Canterbury, 21 April 2005, p. 4.

52. W. David McIntyre, 'Australia, New Zealand, and the Pacific Islands', in Judith M. Brown and Wm. Roger Louis (eds), *The Oxford History of the British Empire*, Vol. 4, Oxford & New York, 1999, ch. 29.

53. On the 'hard man' stereotype, see Jock Phillips, *A Man's Country?*, Auckland, 1987, chs 3 & 4, esp. p. 212.

54. On the British heroic myth, see Jenny Macleod, *Reconsidering Gallipoli*, Manchester, 2004.

55. Denoon and Mein Smith, *A History of Australia, New Zealand and the Pacific*, pp. 271–72.

56. W. G. Malone, 'A Man's Life: The Gallipoli diary of William George Malone, 10/1039', in Jock Phillips, Nicholas Boyack and E. P. Malone (eds), *The Great Adventure: New Zealand soldiers describe the First World War*, Wellington, 1988, p. 25.

57. Ibid., p. 31.

58. Ibid., p. 44.

59. C. E. W. Bean, *The Official History of Australia in the War of 1914–1918*, Vol. 1, *The Story of Anzac: From the outbreak of war to the end of the first phase of the Gallipoli campaign, May 4, 1915*, Brisbane, 1981, (1st pub. 1921), p. 129.

60. On the gentleman stereotype, see Phillips, *A Man's Country?*; on the larrikin, Russel Ward, *The Australian Legend*, Melbourne, 1958.

61. As depicted by Ward, *The Australian Legend*.

62. W. David McIntyre, 'From Dual Dependency to Nuclear Free', in Geoffrey W. Rice (ed.), *The Oxford History of New Zealand*, 2nd edn, Auckland, 1992, ch. 20.

63. Hiroyuki Umetsu, 'The Birth of Anzus: America's attempt to create a defense linkage between Northeast Asia and the Southwest Pacific', *International Relations of the Asia–Pacific*, Vol. 4, No. 1, February 2004, pp. 171–96.

64. F. L. W. Wood, 'Foreign Policy 1945–1951', in NZIIA, *New Zealand in World Affairs*, Vol. 1, Wellington, 1977, pp. 111–12.

65. M. A. McKinnon, 'From Anzus to SEATO', in NZIIA, *New Zealand in World Affairs*, Vol. 1, p. 124.

66. Denis McLean, *The Prickly Pair: making Nationalism in Australia and New Zealand*, Dunedin, 2003, pp. 263–4.

67. John Clarke, 'Some Tips on Getting it Together', *The Bulletin*, 12 April 1988, p. 51.

68. *Report of the National Australasian Convention Debates*, 1891, p. 67.

69. 'The Bulletin Interview, David Lange/Politician, "A mistress, never a wife"', *Bulletin*, 12 April 1988, p. 63.

70. Arthur Grimes and Frank Holmes with Roger Bowden, *An Anzac Dollar? Currency union and business development*, Wellington, 2000; Angus Young, 'Two Countries, One Currency?', MCA thesis, Victoria University of Wellington, 2002.

71. 'Momentum Builds for Anzac Dollar', *Press*, 15 April 2000.

72. Helen Leach, personal communication, 8 December 2006.

Chapter Three

1. New Zealand information courtesy of Helen Leach, personal communication, 8 December 2006. For an Australian history of the Anzac biscuit see Sian Supski, 'Anzac Biscuits – A Culinary Memorial', *Journal of Australian Studies*, No. 87, 2006, pp. 51–59.

2. Leach, pers. comm.; also Jennifer Hillier, 'The Pavlova and the "Fate of Nations"', in Arthur Grimes et al (eds), *States of Mind: Australia and New Zealand 1901–2001*, Wellington, 2001, pp. 345–63.

3. Rollo Arnold, 'Some Australasian Aspects of New Zealand Life', p. 54; Rollo Arnold, 'The Australasian Peoples and their World, 1888–1915', in Keith Sinclair (ed.), *Tasman Relations: New Zealand and Australia 1788–1988*, Auckland, 1987, ch. 3; Rollo Arnold, 'Family or Strangers? Trans-Tasman migrants, 1870–1920, in *Australia–New Zealand: Aspects of a relationship*, proceedings of the Stout Research

Centre 8th annual conference, 8 September 1991. Arnold completed his MA thesis in history at the University of Melbourne: Rollo Arnold, 'New Zealand in Australasia 1890–1914', MA (Hons) thesis, University of Melbourne, 1952.

4. Ruth Park, *A Fence Around the Cuckoo*, Ringwood, Vic, 1993, p. 269; also Ruth Park, *Fishing in the Styx*, Ringwood, Vic, 1994.

5. W. D. Borrie, 'The Peopling of Australasia, 1788–1988', in Sinclair (ed.), *Tasman Relations*, p. 206.

6. Details from New Zealand Dictionary of Biography: www.dnzb.govt.nz (16 June 2008); Australian Dictionary of Biography: www.adb.online.anu.edu.au (16 June 2008).

7. Statistic courtesy of Kris Inwood, University of Guelph.

8. *Canterbury College Review*, No. 29, May 1908, No. 32, May 1909; St Michael's School magazine and newspaper clippings courtesy of Mrs Wene McMillin, pers. comm., 4 March 1994. On educational links see Chapter 7 in this volume.

9. 'Queensland Harry is a Legendary Figure', *Christchurch Star*, 28 July 1951.

10. John Foley, *Queensland Harry*, Waimate, 2005.

11. Borrie, 'Peopling of Australasia', pp. 205–06, 209; Murray McCaskill, 'The Tasman Connection: Aspects of Australian–New Zealand relations', *Australian Geographical Studies*, Vol. 20, No. 1, April 1982, p. 13.

12. 'Reg Mombassa', in Jan Morgan, *Speaking for Themselves: Ex-pats have their say*, Auckland, 2008 p. 33.

13. 'Artist Profiles: Reg Mombassa': www.mambo.com.au/artists (September 2003); www.regmombassa.com (February 2008).

14. McCaskill, 'The Tasman Connection', p. 12.

15. Gordon A. Carmichael (ed.), *Trans-Tasman Migration: Trends, causes and consequences*, Canberra, 1993, p. 6; Jacques Poot and Lynda Sanderson, 'Changes in Social Security Eligibility and the International Mobility of New Zealand Citizens in Australia', PSC Discussion Papers, No. 65, June 2007, p. 2.

16. Jacques Poot, 'Twenty Years of Econometric Research on Trans-Tasman Migration', MOTU seminar paper, Wellington, 8 November 2007.

17. Data courtesy of Jacques Poot, Population Studies Centre, University of Waikato.

18. Graeme Hugo, 'New Zealanders in Australia in 2001', *New Zealand Population Review*, Vol. 30, Nos 1 & 2, 2004, p. 61.

19. Ibid., p. 75.

20. Richard Bedford and Elsie Ho, 'Migration from Australia to New Zealand: Who are these trans-Tasman migrants?', paper, 2005, p. 2, courtesy of Richard Bedford.

21. Ibid., p. 3.

22. Hugo, 'New Zealanders in Australia in 2001', pp. 72–75.

23. Alan Burnett and Robin Burnett, *The Australia and New Zealand Nexus*, Canberra, 1978, pp. 19–20; also Nancy McMillan, 'Pressures for Change to the Trans-Tasman Travel Arrangements', MA thesis, University of Canterbury, 1989, pp. 102–04, 107.

24. Matthew Connelly, 'Seeing Beyond the State: The population control movement and the problem of sovereignty', *Past and Present*, No. 193, November 2006, pp. 197–233; Jeremy Martens, 'A Transnational History of Immigration Restriction:

Natal and New South Wales, 1896–97', *Journal of Imperial and Commonwealth History*, Vol. 34, No. 3, September 2006, pp. 323–44; Marilyn Lake and Henry Reynolds, *Drawing the Global Colour Line*, Melbourne, 2008 (after article by Martens).

25. Burnett and Burnett, *Australia and New Zealand Nexus*, p. 23.

26. Prime Minister's Visit to Australia, transcript of question session at the National Press Club, Canberra, 20 June 1972, and text of joint communiqué by the PMs of Australia and NZ, 22 January 1973, Archives NZ, ABHS 18069 W5402 Box 119 BRU 64/1/6 Pt 1.

27. McMillan, 'Pressures for Change', pp. 150–51, 158–59. For a general summary of trans-Tasman migration policy, see Carmichael (ed.), *Trans-Tasman Migration*, pp. 5–8.

28. Carmichael, *Trans-Tasman Migration*, p. 8.

29. Hugo, 'New Zealanders in Australia in 2001', p. 64.

30. Poot and Sanderson, 'Changes in Social Security Eligibility', pp. 3–4.

31. For a useful summary, see John Wood, 'The Movement of People', in Bruce Brown (ed.), *New Zealand and Australia: Where are we going?*, pp. 81–86.

32. Hugo, 'New Zealanders in Australia in 2001', p. 85.

33. Martyn Dunne, 'New Zealand Customs and the Border', and Philippa Mein Smith, 'Trans-Tasman Ties: An historian's response', in Brian Lynch (ed.), *New Zealand and the World: The major foreign policy issues, 2005–2010*, Wellington, 2006, pp. 98, 41.

34. Department of Transport and Regional Services, Australia's trade and investment relations under ANZCER, Joint Standing Committee on Foreign Affairs, Defence and Trade, Trade Sub-committee, submission No. 5, Canberra, April 2006.

35. Miles Fairburn, 'Is There a Good Case for New Zealand Exceptionalism?', in Tony Ballantyne and Brian Moloughney (eds), *Disputed Histories*, Dunedin, 2006, p. 156; and abbreviated version republished in *Thesis Eleven*, No. 92, 2008, p. 37.

36. On trans-Tasman transport, see Burnett and Burnett, *Australia and New Zealand Nexus*, ch. 5.

37. Archives NZ, Visits – Qantas jet inaugural, 1964–66, TO 1 40/100/10; Visits – Air NZ inaugural Sydney–Christchurch, 1965–66, TO 1 40/100/11.

38. Australian Tourist Commission, *Annual Report 1967–68*, p. 14.

39. Exhibitions – Sydney, 1925–58, TO 1 28/4.

40. Visits – Australian Dairy Farmers Pt 1, 1929–36, TO 1 40/13 Pt 1; Visits – Australian Farmers Parties – General, 1936–52, 1953–59, TO 1 40/13 Pts 2 & 3.

41. McCaskill, 'The Tasman Connection', pp. 14, 16.

42. Hugo, 'New Zealanders in Australia in 2001', pp. 79, 81–82.

43. Paul Hamer, *Maori in Australia: Nga Maori i te Ao Moemoea*, Wellington, 2007; R. Bedford, R. Didham, E. Ho and G. Hugo, 'Maori Internal and International Migration at the Turn of the Century: An Australasian perspective', *New Zealand Population Review*, Vol. 30, Nos 1 & 2, 2004, pp. 131–41.

44. Hamer, ibid., p. 164.

45. Interviews, Sydney, August 2003.

46. Australian Dictionary of Biography: www.adb.online.anu.edu.au

47. Kerry Taylor, 'The Lost World of "ANZAC" Communism: The relationship

between the Communist Parties of Australia and New Zealand in the 1920s', in *Australia–New Zealand: Aspects of a relationship*, proceedings of the Stout Research Centre 8th annual conference, 8 September 1991.

48. James Bennett, 'Rats and Revolutionaries': The labour movement in Australia and New Zealand 1890–1940, Dunedin, 2004, pp. 156–57, 13–14.
49. Rory O'Malley, 'The Eclipse of Mateship: The "wide-comb dispute" 1979–85', *Labour History*, No. 90. May 2006, p. 165.
50. Shelley Harford, 'A Trans-Tasman Community: Organisational links between the ACTU and NZFOL/NZCTU, 1970–1990', MA thesis, University of Canterbury, 2006.
51. John Dix, *Stranded in Paradise: New Zealand rock'n'roll 1955–1988*, Auckland, 1988, p. 330.
52. Mahora Peters with James George, *Showband! Mahora and the Maori Volcanics*, Wellington, 2005, ch. 3.
53. 'Howard Morrison': www.sergent.com.au/howardmorrison.html (16 June 2008).
54. Alan Turley, 'The Incredible Tex Morton', *New Zealand Memories*, August/September 2002, p. 12.
55. Fairburn, 'Is There a Good Case for New Zealand Exceptionalism?'.
56. Jim Davidson, 'Dominion Culture', *Meanjin*, Vol. 63, No. 3, 2004, pp. 75–83.
57. Fairburn, 'Is There a Good Case for New Zealand Exceptionalism?'.
58. See J. Cookson and G. Dunstall (eds), *Southern Capital: Christchurch: Towards a city biography 1850–2000*, Christchurch, 2000, pp. 250–51.
59. Rollo Arnold, 'The Dynamics and Quality of Trans-Tasman Migration 1885–1910', *Australian Economic History Review*, Vol. 26, No. 1, March 1986, pp. 1–20.
60. The phrase and argument belong to Veronica Kelly, 'A Complementary Economy? National markets and international product in early Australian theatre managements', *NTQ*, Vol. 21, No. 1, February 2005, pp. 77–95.
61. Pop music details are from Dix, *Stranded in Paradise*, pp. 45–49, 51–55, 128–41; and from an Honours research paper by Rosemary Baird at University of Canterbury, 2006 drawing on music histories by Mike Chunn and G. Spittle.
62. See for example, on the Melbourne Club, J. O'Hara, *A Mug's Game: A history of gaming and betting in Australia*, Sydney, 1988, p. 32, and the Wellington Club, David Grant, *On a Roll: A history of gambling and lotteries in New Zealand*, Wellington, 1994, p. 24. The following section also draws on a database created by a summer studentship project for the NZAC Research Centre by Julia Macdonald, 'Gambling as a Major Trans-Tasman Enterprise', 2004–05.
63. Grant, ibid., p. 21; O'Hara, ibid., p. 71.
64. O'Hara, ibid., p. 145.
65. Grant, *On a Roll*, pp. 104–05, 201.
66. O'Hara, *A Mug's Game*, p. 78; Grant, ibid., p. 168.
67. Grant, ibid., p. 199.
68. Ibid., pp. 54, 96–98; O'Hara, *A Mug's Game*, p. 99.
69. Wendy Selby, 'Social Evil or Social Good? Lotteries and state regulation in Australia and the United States', in Jan McMillen (ed.), *Gambling Cultures: Studies in history and interpretation*, London, 1996, p. 66; Grant, *On a Roll*, p. 214.

70. M. Tolich, 'Against the Odds: The TAB and the sunset of the horse racing industry', in Bruce Curtis (ed.), *Gambling in New Zealand*, Palmerston North, 2002, pp. 197–98.

71. Grant, *On a Roll*, p. 289.

72. O'Hara, *A Mug's Game*, pp. 200–01.

73. Grant, *On a Roll*, p. 296.

74. John Costello and Pat Finnegan, *Tapestry of Turf: The history of New Zealand racing, 1840–1987*, Auckland, 1988, p. 209.

75. Auckland Racing Club History, courtesy of Angela Findlay.

76. Costello and Finnegan, *Tapestry of Turf*, p. 106.

77. O'Hara, *A Mug's Game*, pp. 145–48; Ron Bisman, *A Salute to Trotting: A history of harness racing in New Zealand*, Auckland, 1983, p. 25.

78. Inter Dominion Championship official website via the Australian Harness Racing Council's official website, 'Brief History': www.harness.org.au/inter/history.htm (16 June 2008).

79. Costello and Finnegan, *Tapestry of Turf*, pp. 479, 524; S. Brassel, *A Portrait of Racing: Horseracing in Australia and New Zealand since 1970*, Brookvale, 1990, p. 251; G. Hutchinson, *They're Racing: The complete story of New Zealand and Australian racing*, Melbourne, 1999, p. 263.

Chapter Four

1. Alan Ward, 'Exporting the British Constitution: Responsible government in New Zealand, Canada, Australia and Ireland', *Journal of Commonwealth and Comparative Studies*, Vol. 25, 1987, pp. 3–25. US models also influenced the Australian Commonwealth's constitution. The US is of course a former British possession.

2. D. Dolowitz and D. Marsh, 'Learning from Abroad: The role of policy transfer in contemporary policy-making', *Governance*, Vol. 13, 2000, pp. 5–24.

3. Phrase adopted from J. G. A. Pocock, *The Discovery of Islands*, Cambridge, 2005, p. 191.

4. Graeme Powell, 'A Diarist in the Cabinet: Lord Derby and the Australian colonies 1882–85', *Australian Journal of Politics and History*, Vol. 51, No. 4, 2005, pp. 481–95.

5. Maurice Ollivier, *The Colonial and Imperial Conferences from 1887 to 1937*, Ottawa, 1954; Margaret Glass, *Charles Cameron Kingston: Federation father*, Melbourne, 1997.

6. Graeme Dunstall, *A Policeman's Paradise? Policing a stable society, 1918–1945: The history of policing in New Zealand*, Vol. 4, Palmerston North, 1999, pp. 436–37. C.f. the Australasian Association for the Advancement of Science established in 1888 (ANZAAS from the 1930s).

7. James Smithies, 'The Trans-Tasman Cable, the Australasian Bridgehead and Imperial History', *History Compass*, Vol. 6, April 2008: www.blackwell-compass.com (4 April 2008).

8. S. J. Potter, 'Communication and integration: The British and dominions press and the British world, c. 1876–1914', *Journal of Imperial and Commonwealth History*, Vol. 31, 2003, pp. 190–206.

9. Paul Kelly, *The End of Certainty: The story of the 1980s*, Sydney, 1992, p. 1.

10. Daniel T. Rodgers, *Atlantic Crossings: Social politics in a progressive age*, Cambridge, Mass. & London, 1998, p. 55.

11. P. J. Coleman, 'New Zealand Liberalism and the Origins of the American Welfare State', *Journal of American History*, Vol. 69, No. 2, 1982, pp. 372–91; Albert Métin, *Le Socialisme sans Doctrines*, 2nd edn, Paris, 1910; James E. Le Rossignol and William Downie Stewart, *State Socialism in New Zealand*, New York, 1910; Pat Moloney, 'State Socialism and Willliam Pember Reeves: A reassessment', in Pat Moloney and Kerry Taylor (eds), *On the Left: Essays on socialism in New Zealand*, Dunedin, 2002.

12. Stuart Macintyre, *A Colonial Liberalism: The lost world of three Victorian visionaries*, Oxford & Melbourne, 1991; Marian Simms, 'Waltzing Matilda: Gender and Australian political institutions', in G. Brennan and F. G. Castles (eds), *Australia Reshaped: 200 years of institutional transformation*, Cambridge & Melbourne, 2002.

13. Sidney Webb, 'Impressions of New Zealand', *The Echo*, 7 October 1898, in William Pember Reeves, Scrapbooks of Newspaper Clippings, qMS-1683-1685, Vol. 2, ATL, Wellington.

14. Webb quoted in Keith Sinclair, *William Pember Reeves: New Zealand Fabian*, Oxford, 1965, p. 210.

15. Francis G. Castles, *Australian Public Policy and Economic Vulnerability*, Sydney, 1988.

16. Philippa Mein Smith, *A Concise History of New Zealand*, Cambridge, New York & Melbourne, 2005, ch. 5.

17. Miles Fairburn, *The Ideal Society and Its Enemies*, Auckland, 1989.

18. John Braithwaite, 'Globalization and Australian Institutions', in Brennan and Castles (eds), *Australia Reshaped*.

19. R. P. Davis, 'New Zealand Liberalism and Tasmanian Labor, 1891–1916', *Labour History*, Vol. 21, November 1971, pp. 24–35.

20. Henry Demarest Lloyd, *Newest England: Notes of a democratic traveller in New Zealand, with some Australian comparisons*, New York, 1900, p. 233; Lloyd, *A Country Without Strikes: A visit to the compulsory Arbitration Court of New Zealand*, New York, 1900, p. 177.

21. Francis G. Castles, *The Working Class and Welfare*, Sydney, 1985. On arbitration acts, see S. Macintyre and R. Mitchell (eds), *Foundations of Arbitration: The origins and effects of state compulsory arbitration 1890–1914*, Melbourne, 1989.

22. Shaun Goldfinch and Philippa Mein Smith, 'Compulsory Arbitration and the Australasian Model of State Development: Policy transfer, learning and innovation', *Journal of Policy History*, Vol. 18, No. 4, 2006, pp. 419–45.

23. Royal Commission on Strikes, *Report of the Royal Commission on Strikes (New South Wales)*, Sydney 1891; C. C. Kingston, 'Memorandum re Conciliation Bill', October 1892, PRG 1039/2, State Library of South Australia; NZ Industrial Conciliation and Arbitration Act 1894, preamble; Sinclair, *William Pember Reeves*, p. 152.

24. William Pember Reeves, *State Experiments in Australia and New Zealand*, 2 vols, London, 1902; 'Reminiscences', Reeves, William Pember 1857–1932, MS-Papers-0129-32, ATL, Wellington.

25. Naomi Segal, 'Compulsory Arbitration and the Western Australian Gold-mining

Industry: A re-examination of the inception of compulsory arbitration in Western Australia', *International Review of Social History*, Vol. 47, 2002, pp. 59–100.

26. Alfred P. Backhouse, *Report of Royal Commission of Inquiry into the Working of Compulsory Conciliation and Arbitration Laws*, Sydney, 1901.

27. Philippa Mein Smith and Linda Moore, 'Statisticians making settler states and economies in Australasia, 1870–1930', in M. Lyons (ed.), *History in Global Perspective: Proceedings of the 20th International Congress of Historical Sciences, Sydney 2005*, Sydney, 2006.

28. J. C. Hammack, 'Report to the Statistical Society on the Proceedings of the Fourth Session of the International Statistical Congress, held in London, July, 1960', p. 14; J. McArthur et al., 'Remarks on the Irregularity of the Statistical Phenomena Observable in the Australian Colonies since the Gold Discovery of 1851 . . .', *Journal of the Statistical Society of London*, Vol. 24, No. 2, 1861, p. 198.

29. H. H. Hayter, *Notes of a Tour in New Zealand*, Melbourne, 1874; Archives NZ, Colonial Secretary, 1873–1874, IA 1 1874/342, Hayter to Julius Vogel, 10 November 1873.

30. Hayter to Premier of Victoria, 'Introductory Letter', 1 May 1875, in *Report of the Conference of Government Statists held in Tasmania, January 1875*, p. 5; Archives NZ, Registrar-General New Zealand, 1874, BDM 1 RG1874/414.

31. Colin Forster and Cameron Hazelhurst, 'Australian Statisticians and the Development of Official Statistics', *Yearbook Australia*, Vol. 71, 1988, pp. 24–26.

32. Conference of Statists, 'Census of Australasia, 1891 (Report of)', in *Conference of Statists*, Hobart, 1890.

33. Graeme Davison, 'Australia: The first suburban nation?', *Journal of Urban History*, Vol. 22, No. 1, November 1995, pp. 40–74.

34. Robert Freestone, 'An Imperial Aspect: The Australasian town planning tour of 1914–15', *Australian Journal of Politics and History*, Vol. 44, No. 2, 1998, pp. 159–76; Caroline Miller, 'The Origins of Town Planning in New Zealand 1900–1926: A divergent path?', *Planning Perspectives*, Vol. 17, 2002, pp. 209–25.

35. Miller, ibid.

36. Philippa Mein Smith, *Mothers and King Baby: Infant survival and welfare in an imperial world: Australia 1880–1950*, Basingstoke & London, 1997, chs 4 and 5.

37. Ibid.; Linda Bryder, *A Voice for Mothers: The Plunket Society and infant welfare, 1907–2000*, Auckland, 2003.

38. E.g. Truby King's counterparts, Dr Helen Mayo of South Australia, and Dr E. Sydney Morris of New South Wales: Mein Smith, ibid., pp. 107, 129.

39. Bryder, *A Voice for Mothers*, p. 254. The government removed funding for Plunketline in 2006.

40. Archives NZ, J. F. Copplestone to Director, Division of Public Health, Wellington, 22 July 1965, H1 139/87.

41. D. T. Studlar, 'The Political Dynamics of Tobacco Control in Australia and New Zealand: Explaining policy problems, instruments, and patterns of adoption', *Australian Journal of Political Science*, Vol. 40, 2005, pp. 255–74.

42. Tony Abbott, Speech Notes for Consilium: The trouble with reform, Coolum, 2005; c.f. Robin Gauld, *Revolving Doors: New Zealand's health reforms*, Wellington,

2001, which Abbott cites at length.

43. Jeremy Finn, 'New Zealand lawyers and "overseas" precedent 1874–1973: Lessons from the Otago District Law Society Library', *Otago Law Review*, Vol. 11, No. 2, 2006, p. 15.

44. Kosmas Tsokhas, 'The Matson Line: Australian shipping policy and imperial relations 1935–1939', *Australian Journal of Politics and History*, Vol. 40, No. 3, 1994, pp. 364-78.

45. James Bennett, 'Social Security, the "Money Power" and the Great Depression: The international dimension to Australian and New Zealand Labour in office', *Australian Journal of Politics and History*, Vol. 43, No. 3, 1997, pp. 312–30.

46. D. G. Bolitho, 'Some Financial and Medico-political Aspects of the New Zealand Medical Profession's Reaction to the Introduction of Social Security', *New Zealand Journal of History*, Vol. 18, No. 1, 1984, pp. 34–49; Elizabeth Hanson, *The Politics of Social Security: The 1938 Act and some later developments*, Auckland, 1980.

47. See G. R. Hawke, *Between Government and Banks: A history of the Reserve Bank of New Zealand*, Wellington, 1973.

48. Richard Davis, 'New Zealand Labour Government and the ALP 1939–40: An image of independence', *Electronic Journal of Australian and New Zealand History*, October 1996.

49. R. P. Davis, '"A real and quite unique affinity"': New Zealand and Tasmanian Labor, 1934–1949', *Labour History*, No. 40, May 1981, p. 68.

50. Davis, 'New Zealand Labour Government and the ALP'.

51. Ralph Pervan, 'Policy Formulation and Implementation: The W.A. Branch of the A.L.P. in the 'thirties', *Labour History*, No. 20, May 1971, p. 30.

52. Wendy Selby, 'Motherhood in Labor's Queensland 1915–1957', PhD thesis, Griffith University, 1992.

53. John Kenneth Galbraith, *The World Economy Since the Wars: A personal view*, London, 1995; Jim McAloon, 'Unsettling Recolonisation: Labourism, Keynesianism and Australasia from the 1890s to the 1950s', *Thesis Eleven*, No. 92, February 2008, pp. 50–68.

54. Walter Nash, *New Zealand Financial Statement: 1946*, Wellington, 1946.

55. W. J. Waters, 'Australian Labor's Full Employment Objective, 1942–45', *Australian Journal of Politics and History*, Vol. 16, No. 1, 1970, pp. 48–64; Greg Whitwell, 'The Power of Economic Ideas? Economics policies in post-war Australia', in Stephen Bell and Brian Head (eds), *State, Economy and Public Policy in Australia*, Melbourne, 1994.

56. John Singleton, 'Introduction', *Australian Economic History Review*, Vol. 41, No. 3, 2001, pp. 233–40.

57. Gary Whitcher, History summer scholarship project, University of Canterbury, 2007.

58. Shaun Goldfinch and Daniel Malpass, 'The Polish Shipyard: Myth, economic history and economic reform in New Zealand', *Australian Journal of Politics and History*, Vol. 53, No. 1, 2007, pp. 118–37; Colin White, *Mastering Risk: environments, markets and politics in Australian economic history*, Melbourne, 1992.

59. P. Robertson and J. Singleton, 'The Old Commonwealth and Britain's First

Application to Join the EEC, 1961–63', *Australian Economic History Review*, Vol. 40, No. 2, 2000, pp. 153–77.

60. Singleton, 'Introduction'.

61. Goldfinch and Malpass, 'The Polish Shipyard'.

62. Denis McLean, *The Prickly Pair: Making nationalism in Australia and New Zealand*, Dunedin, 2003.

63. C.f. John D. Gould, *The Muldoon Years: An essay on New Zealand's recent economic growth*, Auckland, 1985; Russell Mathews and Bhajan Grewel, *The Public Sector in Jeopardy: Australian fiscal liberalism from Whitlam to Keating*, Melbourne, 1997.

64. Ann Capling and Brian Galligan, *Beyond the Protective State*, Cambridge and Melbourne, 1992.

65. Robert Muldoon, *New Zealand Financial Statement: 1979*, Wellington, 1979.

66. Goldfinch and Malpass, 'The Polish Shipyard'.

67. Lewis Evans, Arthur Grimes, Bryce Wilkinson and David Teece, 'Economic reform in New Zealand 1984–95: The pursuit of efficiency', *Journal of Economic Literature*, Vol. 34, 1996, pp. 1856–1902. Shaun Goldfinch, *Remaking New Zealand and Australian Economic Policy: Ideas, institutions, and policy communities*, Wellington & Washington DC, 2000. OECD, *OECD Economic Surveys 1995–1996: New Zealand*, Paris, 1996.

68. Goldfinch, *Remaking New Zealand and Australian Economic Policy*.

69. Shaun Goldfinch, 'The Old Boys' Network? Social ties and policy consensus amongst Australian and New Zealand economic policy elites', *Policy, Organisation and Society*, Vol. 21, No. 2, 2002, pp. 1–25.

70. Goldfinch, *Remaking New Zealand and Australian Economic Policy*.

71. Davis, 'New Zealand Labour Government and the ALP'.

72. Both countries shared similar levels of economic performance until the mid-1980s on a number of measures, but New Zealand's performance dropped well below OECD and Australian averages of GDP per capita after 1984 when it had sat at 100 per cent of the OECD average. This divergence was particularly marked during 1987–92, which is one of the worst periods of economic performance in New Zealand's history. See also Tim Hazledine and John Quiggin, 'No more free beer tomorrow? Economic policy and outcomes in Australia and New Zealand since 1984', *Australian Journal of Political Science*, Vol. 41, No. 2, 2006, pp. 145–59.

73. Interview, Maurice Newman, Sydney, October 2004.

74. The act also requires disclosure of the fiscal consequences of economic policy decisions, which includes publishing three-year forecasts every half year, and four to six weeks prior to a general election. Forecasts include the usual financial statements, as well as a statement of fiscal risks and contingent liabilities, which describe and (if possible) quantify the fiscal risks associated with the forecasts. The Minister of Finance and the Secretary to the Treasury sign statements of responsibility declaring that all policy decisions have been included in accordance with the act, and that the Treasury has used its best professional judgment in preparing the fiscal impacts of the policy decisions. C.f. John Wanna, Joanne Kelly and John Forster, *Managing Public Expenditure in Australia*, St Leonards, NSW, 2000. The Fiscal Responsibility Act was incorporated into the Public Finance Act

in 2004 through the Public Finance (State Sector Management) Bill.

75. Joint Committee of Public Accounts, Parliament of the Commonwealth of Australia, *Financial Reporting for the Commonwealth: Towards greater transparency and accountability*, Canberra, 1995.
76. National Commission of Audit, *Report to the Commonwealth Government*, Canberra, 1996.
77. OECD, *OECD Best Practices for Budget Transparency*, Paris, 2001.
78. International Monetary Fund, *Manual on Fiscal Transparency*, Washington DC, 2001.
79. Simon Crean, MP (Hotham, ALP, Opposition), Second reading, A New Tax System (Goods and Services Tax) Bill 1998, in *House Hansard*, Canberra, 1998.
80. Colin Campbell, 'Juggling Inputs, Outputs and Outcomes in the Search for Policy Competence: Recent experience in Australia', *Governance*, Vol. 14, 2001, pp. 253–82.
81. Shaun Goldfinch, 'Economic reform in New Zealand: Radical liberalisation in a small economy', *Otemon Bulletin of Australian Studies*, Vol. 30, 2004, pp. 75–98.
82. Michael Ferguson, 'Workplace Relations Amendment (Work Choices) Bill 2005', Second reading, in *House Hansard*, Canberra, 2005; Tanya Plibersek, 'Workplace Relations Amendment (Work Choices) Bill 2005', in *House Hansard*, Canberra, 2005.
83. Goldfinch and Malpass, 'The Polish Shipyard'.
84. Shaun Goldfinch, 'Evaluating Public Sector Reform in New Zealand: Have the benefits been oversold?', *Asian Journal of Public Administration*, Vol. 20, 1998, pp. 203–32.
85. David Osborne and Ted Gaebler, *Reinventing Government: How the entrepreneurial spirit is transforming the public sector*, Reading, Mass., 1992.
86. Vanessa Roberts, 'The Origin of Victoria's Public Sector Reforms: Policy transfer from New Zealand?', MA thesis, University of Canterbury, 2005.
87. Campbell, 'Juggling Inputs, Outputs and Outcomes in the Search for Policy Competence'.
88. Goldfinch and Mein Smith, 'Compulsory Arbitration and the Australasian Model of State Development'; Roberts, 'The Origin of Victoria's Public Sector Reforms'; Shelley Harford, 'A Trans-Tasman Community: Organisational links between the ACTU and NZFOL/NZCTU, 1970–1990', MA thesis, University of Canterbury, 2006, epilogue.
89. G. Palmer, 'New Zealand and Australia: Beyond CER', *New Zealand International Review*, Vol. 15, No. 4, 1990, pp. 2–7.
90. New Zealand was and continues to be a member of the following councils: Administration of Justice; Attorneys-General; Consumer Affairs; Crime Prevention; Cultural Ministers; Education, Employment and Youth Affairs; Environmental Protection and Heritage; Food Regulation; Health; Housing; Local Government and Planning; Natural Resource Management; Primary Industries; Sport and Recreation; The Status of Women; Tourism; Transport. It is an observer on: Aboriginal and Torres Strait Islander Affairs; Drug Strategy; Energy; Immigration; Minerals and Petroleum Resources; Procurement and Construction;

Small Business; Workplace Relations. See Council of Australian Governments, *Commonwealth–State Ministerial Councils: A compendium*, July 2006. In 2006 New Zealand joined the Commonwealth, States and Territory Advisory Council on Innovation, and the Australian National Science Forum.

91. Interview, Secretary to the Treasury, Australia, November 2004.
92. Shaun Goldfinch, 'Australia, New Zealand and the Pacific Island Nations: Interweaved histories, shared futures', *Otemon Bulletin of Australian Studies*, Vol. 31, 2005, pp. 29–45.
93. R. Rose, 'What is Lesson Drawing?', *Journal of Public Policy*, Vol. 11, 1991, pp. 3–30.
94. Mein Smith, *Mothers and King Baby*, p. 112.
95. F. G. Castles (ed.), *Families of Nations: Patterns of public policy in western democracies*, Dartmouth, 1993.
96. E.g. Gordon Walker, 'The CER Agreement and Trans-Tasman Securities Regulation: Part 1', *Journal of International Banking Law*, issue 10, 2004, pp. 390–97, and 'Part 2', *Journal of International Banking Law*, issue 11, 2004, pp. 440–46.

Chapter Five

1. James Belich, *Paradise Reforged: A history of the New Zealanders from the 1880s to the year 2000*, Auckland, 2001; Gary Hawke, 'Australian and New Zealand economic development from about 1890 to 1940', in Keith Sinclair (ed.), *Tasman Relations: New Zealand and Australia, 1788–1988*, Auckland, 1987, ch. 6.
2. *New Zealand Official Year-book 1951–52*, Census and Statistics Department, Wellington, 1952, p. 275.
3. Seddon to Premier Adelaide SA, 19 February 1897, and Kingston to Seddon, 22 February 1897, ATL, Seddon family: MS-Papers-1619-020. Margaret Glass, *Charles Cameron Kingston: Federation father*, Melbourne, 1997, p. 133.
4. Sir John Hall, *Official Record of the Proceedings and Debates of the Australasian Federation Conference*, Melbourne, 1890, p. 175.
5. *Report of the Federation Commission*, AJHR, 1901, A-4, p. vi.
6. Ibid., p. xxii.
7. Preferential and Reciprocal Trade Bill, speech by R. J. Seddon, 18 November 1903, *NZPD*, 18 November 1903, p. 715.
8. E.g. *New Zealand Official Year-book 1938*, Wellington, 1937, pp. 61, 253.
9. 'New Zealand Interests: Mr Seddon seeks closer touch with Australia', *Age*, 30 May 1906, ATL, Seddon family: MS-Papers-1619-020.
10. Rt Hon. A. Deakin and Rt Hon. R. J. Seddon, Agreement, unsigned document, Melbourne, June 1906, and Reciprocal Trade Agreement between the Commonwealth of Australia and the Colony of New Zealand, Seddon family: MS-Papers-1619-020.
11. Colin Murray, 'The New Zealand Trade Commissioner Service', 1961, courtesy of Paul Cotton.
12. Memorandum for Cabinet re Customs Agreement with Australia, n. d. [1922], Archives NZ, EA 1 58/4/2/1 Pt 1A.
13. Keith Sinclair, 'Fruit Fly, Fireblight and Powdery Scab: Australia–New Zealand

trade relations, 1919–39', *Journal of Imperial and Commonwealth History*, Vol. 1, No. 1, October 1972, p. 30.

14. Commercial Relations, Pacific Conference Papers, January 1944, EA 1 58/4/2/1 Pt 1A; *NZ Official Year-book 1938*, p. 275.
15. Sinclair, 'Fruit Fly, Fireblight and Powdery Scab'; Sinclair, 'The Great Anzac Plant War', in Sinclair (ed.), *Tasman Relations*, ch. 7.
16. NAA, Department of Commerce, Potatoes New Zealand Part 1, A458 Q500/14 Part 1.
17. News clipping, *Age*, 17 January 1939, Younger, Hawkesbury Citrus Growers' Assn to Lawson, MHR, 2 January 1939, Bankstown Unemployed & Relief Workers Council, Sydney, to PM, 14 February 1939, ARU Women's Auxiliary, Bathurst, 15 February 1939, and other submissions in NAA, Department of Commerce, Potatoes – New Zealand Part 4, A461/9 G325/1/10 Part 4; Macdermott, NSW Chamber of Fruit and Vegetable Industries to Lyons, 13 July 1938, Housewives' Assn of NSW to Lyons, 23 August 1938, Department of Health, Potatoes from New Zealand (Powdery Scab) Section 4, A1928/1 820/3 Section 4. Cablegram Savage to Lyons, 23 November 1937, Trade: Commercial Relations between Australia and New Zealand, A981/4 TRAD96. Since the Labour government had imposed import controls in April 1938, New Zealand had imported 115,000 cases of Australian oranges and 10,000 cases of mandarins, cable Lyons to Savage, 2 September 1938, Department of Commerce, Potatoes – New Zealand Part 3, A461/9 G325/1/10 Part 3. Lyons was a Labor turncoat.
18. Cumpston to Australian Prime Minister's Department, 20 January 1927, Cumpston to Coates, 14 March 1927, submissions, 1929, NAA, Potatoes New Zealand Part 1, 1920-1931, A458 Q500/14.
19. Cumpston to Minister, 23 January 1935, Department of Health, Potatoes from New Zealand (Powdery Scab) Section 4, A1928/1 820/3.
20. Archives NZ, Fruit and Vegetables – Potatoes – Trade with Australia – Export and Import, 1938–1961, IC 1 12/76/1 Pt 1.
21. Unreferenced newsclipping [Jan. 1935?] re deputation from Fishmongers' Association to Commonwealth Minister of Health, NAA, A601 878/10/3; Eleanor Glencross, President of Federated Association of Australian Housewives to PM of NZ, 16 October 1939, Archives NZ, IC 1 12/76/1 Pt 1.
22. Cablegram Acting PM NZ (Coates) 29 August 1933, A601 878/10/2.
23. Lyons to deputation of potato growers, Canberra, 5 May 1933, Department of Commerce, Potatoes New Zealand Part 2, A461/9 G325/1/10 Part 2.
24. W. Massy Greene, memo to PM, 22 April 1933 (emphasis in original), NZ negotiations in Canberra, 1933–35, NAA, Microfilm, Lyons government, 1934/12/31, CRS A6006.
25. Imperial Economic Conference – Ottawa, second meeting of subcommittee, Canberra 22–25 February 1932, Microfilm, Lyons government, 1934/12/31, CRS A6006.
26. Commercial Relations, Pacific Conference Papers, January 1944, EA 1 58/4/2/1 pt 1A.
27. McEwen, paper for Cabinet, 13 August 1940, NAA, Department of Commerce,

New Zealand: Australian Trade Commissioner in New Zealand, 1935–1945, A1667 277/B/5A.
28. Berendsen to PM, Wellington, 1 April 1943, Archives NZ, EA 1 203/4/1 Pt 1.
29. However, R. H. Wade reflected that he had to maintain a balance between that 'generous cooperation and a certain amount of one-up-man-ship that was then, and I think probably still is, characteristic of the trans-Tasman relationship.' R. H. Wade, 'Recollections of Australia/New Zealand Relations in the 1940s', handwritten ms, November 1995, courtesy of Paul Cotton.
30. 'Introduction', in Robin Kay (ed.), *The Australia–New Zealand Agreement 1944*, Wellington, 1972, pp. xxi–xxx.
31. Ibid., pp. 112, 107, 110.
32. Ibid., pp. 142, 144, 147.
33. Archives NZ, Australia–NZ Affairs Secretariat, 1944-47, EA 1 58/4/3 Pt 1.
34. NAA, New Zealand–Australia. Foreign Policy – Ministerial visits to New Zealand – Minister for Trade and Customs, 1944/630/5/1/12/2, A989/1.
35. Australian–New Zealand Economic Discussions, Wellington, January 1945, EA 1 58/4/2/1 Pt 1A. On Webb see Chapter 7 in this volume.
36. Australian–New Zealand Economic Discussions, Wellington, January 1945, Summary of Proceedings, EA 1 58/4/9.
37. Ashwin to Fraser, 20 January 1948, Mr & Mrs Chifley, 1947–48, EA 1 59/3/303 Pt 1; also memo, conversations between the PM and Mr Chifley 30 December 1947 and Secretary to Treasury to PM 20 January 1948, EA 58/4/2/2 Pt 1.
38. Semple to Chifley 25 February 1948, EA 58/4/2/2/ Pt 1.
39. Morris Guest and John Singleton, 'The Murupara Project and Industrial Development in New Zealand 1945–65', *Australian Economic History Review*, Vol. 39, No. 1, March 1999, pp. 52–71; John Singleton and Paul L. Robertson, *Economic Relations between Britain and Australasia 1945–1970*, Houndmills, Basingstoke, 2002, pp. 80–83.
40. Semple to PM, 24 March 1948 and S. L. Kessell Australian Newsprint Mills to Chifley, 10 January 1948, Archives NZ, F 1 W3129 339 de 80.004. The Minister of Forestry, C. F. Skinner, who favoured the government-sponsored Murupara scheme, was 'fully aware of Mr Ashwin's antagonism' to state development of the industry and thought the Department of Industries and Commerce should head Australia–New Zealand trade discussions. W. C. Ward to Director of Forestry, 2 June 1948, F 1 W3129 339 de 80.004.
41. Economic Cooperation between Aust and NZ 1948–1949, 18 January 1950, EA 1 58/4/2/2 Pt 1. Coombs became Governor of the Commonwealth Bank in January 1949.
42. Ashwin to Min. of Finance, 29 April 1949, memo Secretary to Treasury to Nash, 26 April 1949, EA 1 58/4/2/2 Pt 1.
43. Notes of Aust–NZ Economic Discussions 3–4 November 1949, Wellington, EA 1 58/4/2/2 Pt 1.
44. Visits of S. G. Holland to Australia, 1943–49, EA 1 59/2/13 Pt 1.
45. PM of Australia, Mr Menzies, 1950–54, EA 1 59/3/455 Pt 1.
46. Addresses at State Luncheon in honour of R. G. Menzies, 22 August 1950, EA 1

59/3/455 Pt 1.

47. Trade Discussions: PM's draft, March 1956, Press Statement: Increased Australia–NZ Trade, ATL, Holland, Sidney George: MS-Papers-1624-079/1.
48. Note for PM, PM's Office, Wellington, 10 January 1956, Holland, Sidney George: MS-Papers 1624-078/5; J. A. Malcolm, Senior Trade Commissioner to P. B. Marshall, Secretary Industries and Commerce, 16 January 1956, MS-Papers-1624-079/2.
49. Peter Golding, *Black Jack McEwen: Political gladiator*, Melbourne, 1996, pp. 13, 24.
50. Documents supplied for Holland to table in the House, and Cabinet Office Circular CO (56) 14, 28 March 1956, MS-Papers-1624-079/2.
51. Golding, Black Jack McEwen, p. 176.
52. M. J. Moriarty to Min. Industries and Commerce, 24 April 1958, Archives NZ, AG 40 1960/24a.
53. Trade Discussions Australia–NZ, Wellington July 1958, IC 22/20 44A.
54. Notes on discussions with Australian officials, Canberra 10 May 1960, AG 40 1960/24a.
55. Australia–NZ Trade Discussions at 10am, 1 August 1960, AG 40 1960/24a.
56. Meetings between the Australian Minister for Trade and New Zealand Ministers, Wellington, 1–2 August 1960, and Press Statement, 2 August 1960, AG 40 1960/24a.
57. John Marshall, *Memoirs Volume Two: 1960 to 1988*, Auckland, 1989, pp. 19–21.
58. Min. External Affairs, Wellington to High Commissioner, Canberra, 18 January 1961, AG 40 1961/23c.
59. Golding, *Black Jack McEwen*, p. 26.
60. Marshall, *Memoirs Volume Two*, p. 20; on cricket, pp. 22–23.
61. Ian Bowen, 'De Gaulle's Europe and Australia', CEDA, Growth, No. 4, May 1963, p. 5; Australia–NZ Trade Talks, 17–19 January 1962, Archives NZ, C Box 93 22.22/8 Pt 20.
62. New Zealand's trade with Australia, Officials Meeting 18–20 March 1963, IC W2458 record 125.
63. Cabinet Committee Decision on NZ Approach to Talks with Australia, 12 March 1963, IC W2458 record 125.
64. Minister of Overseas Trade [Marshall] to Cabinet, Trade Negotiations with Australia, AG 40 1963/64B Pt 7; Marshall, Memoirs Volume Two, p. 26.
65. Australia/NZ Joint Standing Committee, Report of Study of Scope for a Free Trade Area, Canberra 16 April 1964, AG 40 1964/106A Pt 8. See also Marshall, ibid., p. 27.
66. Sutch to Officials Committee on Economic and Financial Policy, 8 May 1964, AG 40 1964/106B Pt 9.
67. Economic Cooperation between Australia and New Zealand: Free trade proposal, 26 May 1964, pp. 1–2, 21, ABHS 18069 W5402 Box 119 BRU 64/1/6 Pt 1.
68. Secretary, External Affairs to Prime Minister, 31 July 1964, AG 40 1964/106B Pt 9.
69. W. B. Sutch, Colony or Nation? Economic crises in New Zealand from the 1860s to the 1960s, Sydney, 1966, pp. 167–70, 179–81.
70. Cabinet Economic Committee meeting, 3 November 1964, AG 40 1964/106B Pt 9.

71. Marshall, *Memoirs Volume Two*, p. 27; ATL, Marshall, John Ross (Sir): MS-Papers-1403-139/4.
72. New Zealand–Australia Free Trade Agreement, Statement by McEwen in the House of Representatives 17 August 1965, Australian Documents 24 August 1965, ABHS 18069 W5402 Box 119 BRU 64/1/6 Pt 1. See also 12.3 New Zealand–Australia Free Trade Agreement, in J. G. Crawford (ed.), *Australian Trade Policy 1942–1966: A documentary history*, Canberra, 1968, pp. 419–22.
73. NAFTA text, IC W1842/1958 107/4/1/1. On NAFTA see also AJHR, 1965, A-19.
74. Note by Legal Division, External Affairs, NAFTA: Action by the Gatt, 2 February 1966, AG 40 1966/121B Pt 11.
75. Meeting with Blumenthal, November 1965, IC W1842/1958 107/4/1/1.
76. Ian McLean, 'Trans-Tasman Relations: Decline and rise', in Richard Pomfret (ed.), *Australia's Trade Policies*, Melbourne, 1995, pp. 179–80; P. J. Lloyd, 'Australia–New Zealand Trade Relations: NAFTA to CER', in Sinclair (ed.), *Tasman Relations*, p. 151.
77. Lloyd, ibid., p. 154.
78. Singleton and Robertson, *Economic Relations between Britain and Australasia 1945–1970*, p. 203.
79. Alan Burnett and Robin Burnett, *The Australia and New Zealand Nexus*, Canberra, 1978, pp. 10–11; Nicholas Haines (ed.), *The Tasman: Frontier and freeway?*, Canberra, 1972, pp. 3, 14.
80. The Tasman Partnership, 5 June 1970, ABHS 18069 W5402 Box 119 BRU 64/1/6 Pt 1.
81. Holyoake, official visit to Australia, 4–11 June 1970, PM 11.
82. Telegram EA Wellington to Canberra and all Diplomatic Posts re Whitlam Visit, 23 January 1973, ABHS 18069 W5402 Box 119 BRU 64/1/6 Pt 1.
83. J. F. Cairns to W. W. Freer, Min. of Trade and Industry, Wellington, 11 September 1974, IC Box 5 422A; Telegram Canberra to Wellington, 27 March 1975, AG 40 1975/21B Pt 26.
84. Walding meeting with Crean, Canberra, 20 February 1975, Telegram Canberra to Wellington, 7 August 1975, AG 40 1975/21B Pt 26.
85. Belich, *Paradise Reforged*, p. 400 (quoting Gustafson, *His Way*, p. 273) and p. 455.
86. Hugh Templeton, *All Honourable Men: Inside the Muldoon Cabinet 1975–1984*, Auckland, 1995, p. 128.
87. This argument is elaborated in more detail in Philippa Mein Smith, 'Did Muldoon Really "go too slowly" with CER?', *New Zealand Journal of History*, Vol. 41, No. 2, 2007, pp. 161–79.
88. R. D. Muldoon, *My Way*, Wellington, 1981, pp. 106, 107, 105, 81; and his *The New Zealand Economy: A personal view*, Auckland, 1985, p. 160.
89. Doug Anthony, '20 Years of Trans-Tasman CER: Where to now?', speech at CER 20th anniversary luncheon, Sydney, 28 August 2003.
90. Gerald Hensley, *Final Approaches: A memoir*, Auckland, 2006, p.242. Foreshadowing these key friendships, Talboys had suggested a joint committee on dairy products at a ministerial meeting in the early 1970s, an idea taken up by Anthony; MFA memo, PM's Visit to Australia, June 1972, ABHS 18069 W5402

Box 119 BRU 64/1/6 Pt 1.

91. Colin James, *A New Path: The Tasman connection*, Wellington, 1982, p. 43.

92. B. E. Talboys, 'Australia and New Zealand: A ministerial view', in Ralph Hayburn (ed.), *Foreign Policy School 1978: Australia and New Zealand relations*, Dunedin, 1978, p. 10; B. E. Talboys, *New Zealand Foreign Affairs Review*, Vol. 27, No. 3, July–September 1977, p. 28.

93. Doug Anthony, '20 Years of Trans-Tasman CER: Where to Now?'. Muldoon recounted his version of this episode in *The New Zealand Economy*, p. 54.

94. Pamela Andre, Stephen Payton and John Mills (eds), *The Negotiation of the Australia New Zealand Closer Economic Relations Trade Agreement 1983*, Canberra & Wellington, 2003, doc. 15, attachment 11 April 1979, p. 34.

95. Ibid., doc. 3, pp. 5–7; Anthony interview with Ian Grant, *New Zealand Management*, May 2003, p. 30. On the advisory group, see Hensley, *Final Approaches*, p. 226.

96. Andre et al., ibid., doc. 18, p. 38. On Stone's New Zealand links, see M. McKinnon, Treasury, Auckland, 2003, p. 299.

97. The seven-strong Australian delegation comprised Jim Scully of Trade and Resources; Sir Geoffrey Yeend, head of the Prime Minister's Department; N. Currie, Secretary of Industry and Commerce; P. Henderson, Secretary of Foreign Affairs; D. Moore, First Assistant Secretary of the Treasury; J. Cahill, First Assistant Secretary, Business and Consumer Affairs; and G. Miller, Director of the Bureau of Agricultural Economics. The New Zealanders comprised N. Lough, Secretary of the Treasury; Bernard Galvin, head of the Prime Minister's Department; J. W. H. Clark, Secretary of Trade and Industry; Frank Corner, Foreign Affairs; M. L. Cameron, Director-General of Agriculture; P. J. McKone, Acting Comptroller of Customs; and R. W. R. White, Governor of the Reserve Bank.

98. Andre et al., *Negotiation*, doc. 122, p. 361.

99. Ibid., doc. 93, p. 285. See also *New Zealand Foreign Affairs Review*, Vol. 30, No. 1, January–March 1980, p. 15.

100. Ibid., doc. 93, p. 286; *New Zealand Foreign Affairs Review*, ibid., p. 16.

101. Alan Bollard and Darcy McCormack assisted by Mark Scanlan, *Closer Economic Relations: A view from both sides of the Tasman*, Wellington & Melbourne, 1985, p. 68; Andre et al., *Negotiation*, doc. 103, pp. 313–14, doc. 113, pp. 340–41.

102. Templeton, *All Honourable Men*, pp. 135, 138, 177.

103. 'Tasman Talks Off Until May', *NZ Herald*, 18 March 1981; Andre et al., *Negotiation*, doc. 170, p. 490.

104. Andre et al., ibid., docs 152 and 153, p. 451; doc. 167, pp. 485–86.

105. Ibid., doc. 170, p. 518.

106. Ian Templeton, 'Anthony Cements Move for Closer Economic Ties', *Bulletin*, 26 May 1981, p. 96.

107. Andre et al., *Negotiation*, doc. 229, pp. 618-19.

108. Ibid., doc. 209, pp. 582–84; doc. 219, p. 599.

109. Hensley, *Final Approaches*, p. 230.

110. John McEwen, *Australia's Overseas Economic Relationships*, Sixteenth Roy Milne Memorial Lecture, Brisbane, 1965.

Chapter Six

1. Some of this software was developed as part of Nicholas Harrigan's PhD study. See Nicholas Harrigan, 'Political Power and Political Divisions within Australian and New Zealand Business', paper presented to the Politics and Interlocking Directorates Conference, University of Barcelona, 28–29 September 2006.
2. J. Johanson and F. Wiedersheim-Paul, 'The Internationalization Process of a Firm: Four Swedish case studies', *Journal of Management Studies*, Vol. 12, 1975, pp. 305–22; A. Cuervo-Cazurra, 'Who Cares About Corruption?', *Journal of International Business Studies*, Vol. 37, 2006, pp. 807–22.
3. For Hofstede, culture is that 'collective programming of mind which distinguishes one national group or category of people from another ... [thus] ... the interactive aggregate of common characteristics that influence a human group's response to its environment'; cf. G. Hofstede and G. J. Hofstede, *Cultures and Organizations: Software of the mind*, New York, 2005.
4. On Hofstede's masculinity index, Australia ranks 19th and New Zealand 21st – although Australia at 61 is closer to the US (at 62) than New Zealand at 58 (1991). Measures of masculinity include assertiveness, materialism/material success, self-centredness, power, strength, and individual achievements. On the 'power distance', which measures aspects of equality, Australia and New Zealand are further apart, at 36 (13th to last) and 22 (fourth to last) respectively, although both are at the more egalitarian end. Both rank highly on the individualism measure at 90 for Australia (the second highest) and 79 for New Zealand (fifth). The uncertainty avoidance index which measures tolerance for uncertainty and ambiguity puts Australia at 51 and New Zealand at 49 – with Norway in between at 50 – positioning both countries in the lower middle (i.e. they are more comfortable with uncertainty). The long-term orientation index measures Australia at 31 and New Zealand at 29, with Germany between them on 30.
5. Neal Ashkanasy, Edwin Trevor-Roberts and Louise Earnshaw, 'The Anglo Cluster: Legacy of the British Empire', *Journal of World Business*, Vol. 37, 2002, pp. 28–39. The Globe Study measures additional factors to Hofstede's studies: in this case, assertiveness; uncertainty avoidance; future orientation; power distance; institutional collectivism; humane orientation; performance orientation; family collectivism; and gender egalitarianism.
6. World Values Survey, 2006: www.worldvaluessurvey.org (17 June 2008). This survey measures such features as perceptions of life, environment, work, family, politics and society, religion and national identity.
7. B. Tranter and M. Western, 'Postmaterial Values and Age: The case of Australia', *Australian Journal of Political Science*, Vol. 38, 2003, pp. 239–57.
8. J. G. March and J. P. Olsen, 'Institutional Perspectives on Political Institutions', *Governance*, Vol. 9, 1996, pp. 247–64.
9. F. G. Castles (ed.), *Families of Nations: Patterns of public policy in western democracies*, Dartmouth, 1993.
10. Erik Olssen, 'Lands of Sheep and Gold: The Australian dimension to the New Zealand past 1840–1900', in Keith Sinclair (ed.), *Tasman Relations: New Zealand and Australia 1788–1988*, Auckland, 1987, ch. 2.

11. John Howard, 'Transcript of the Prime Minister the Hon. John Howard PM Joint Press Conference with the Prime Minister of New Zealand, Helen Clark, Parliament House, Canberra', 8 February 2006: www.pm.gov.au/news/interviews/ Interview1767.html
12. Shaun Goldfinch, 'The Old Boys' Network? Social ties and policy consensus amongst Australian and New Zealand policy elites', *Policy, Organisation and Society*, Vol. 21, No. 2, 2002, pp. 1–25.
13. Ibid.; Jim McAloon, *No Idle Rich: The wealthy in Canterbury and Otago 1840–1914*, Dunedin, 2002; M. Brayshay, M. Cleary and J. Selwood, 'Interlocking Directorships and Trans-national Linkages within the British Empire, 1900-1930', *Area*, Vol. 37, No. 2, 2005, pp. 209–22.
14. Shaun Goldfinch, *Remaking New Zealand and Australian Economic Policy*, Wellington, 2000; Goldfinch, 'The Old Boys' Network?'; Jane Kelsey, *Economic Fundamentalism*, London, 1995.
15. Interview, Maurice Newman, Sydney, October 2004.
16. The Australia–New Zealand Business Council was established in 1978, with separate arms in both countries. Its objectives are
    + promoting industrial and commercial relations between Australia and New Zealand,
    + supporting and encouraging trade and investment between the two countries,
    + arranging regular consultation between business enterprises in the two countries, and
    + maintaining liaison with the two governments to promote these objectives and to provide the governments with information on the state of trade relations between Australia and New Zealand.

    The council commissioned and published reports pushing for further integration, organised meetings between business and politicians, and made regular submissions on government policy on these issues. In 2003 it commissioned a report by the New Zealand Institute of Economic Research looking at the benefits of a single market between Australia and New Zealand, arguing that the benefits outweighed the costs. The council also actively supported the establishment of a 'Trans-Tasman Advisory Council' which took shape in the form of the Leadership Forums. However, it has not produced a newsletter since 2004.
17. Peter Hempenstall, 'The Australia New Zealand Leadership Forums': www.nzac. canterbury.ac.nz/docs/leadershipforums
18. At least 1.5 per cent of executives (executives who serve on the board of the corporation, generally the CEO and chief financial officer and sometimes a few other executives) of the top 200 publicly listed Australian companies are of New Zealand origin. At least 5 per cent of the executives of the Top New Zealand companies are of Australian origin. This proportion is likely considerably understated, given the limits to our data.
19. Five per cent is thought of as a significant shareholding. Most countries have legislation forcing owners with more than 3–5 per cent to declare themselves, as 5 per cent is considered the threshold at which owners can have significant influence over management of the company. Seven of the top 20 and 44 of the top 100 NZ

companies in 2002 were more than 50 per cent overseas controlled. In 2006 foreign ownership of shares fell to 41.4 per cent from 44.3 per cent in March 2005. Of the top 100 Australian companies, 31 per cent had a majority foreign ownership in 2002, a proportion that has remained largely constant. Department of Foreign Affairs and Trade, *The Big End of Town and Australia's Trading Interests*, Canberra, 2002.

20. Australian Bureau of Statistics (ABS), 'International Investment Position, Australia: Supplementary country statistics (cat. No 5352.0)': www.abs.gov. au/AUSSTATS/abs

21. H. Fountain, 'Technology Acquisition, Firm Capability and Sustainable Competitive Advantage: A case study of Australian Glass Manufacturers Ltd, 1915–39', *Business History*, Vol. 42, No. 3, 2000, p. 92.

22. 'Number eight wire' is a metaphor for enterprise and ingenuity based on the idea that a New Zealander can build anything out of a piece of number eight wire.

23. K. Perry, 'Building to a crescendo', *Dominion Post*, 17 March 2007, p. 7.

24. ACIL Tasman, 'New Zealand–Australia Economic Interdependence', prepared for Ministry of Economic Development, 4 May 2004.

25. Ibid.

26. Michael Cullen, Address to NZ Gala Day Dinner, Sydney Foundation Hall, Museum of Contemporary Art, 10 March 2005.

27. F. O'Sullivan, 'Qantas Chair Gets Behind Single Australasian Market', *NZ Herald*, 10 May 2004; Margaret Jackson, 'It's Time for the Tasman Economic Area (TEA)', Address to Trans-Tasman Business Council, 12 May 2004.

28. Allan Hawke, 'From CER to One Market', Speech to CPA Australia New Zealand Branch, Wellington 30 June 2004; New Zealand Treasury, 'Progress on the Single Economic Market', Discussion Paper for Australia–New Zealand Leadership Forum, 2005.

29. Reserve Bank of New Zealand, Review of the Regulation and Performance of New Zealand's Major Financial Institutions: www.rbnz.govt.nz/finstab/banking/supervision/1498932.html (6 November 2006).

30. NZPA, 'Govt Advisers Back Stock Exchange Merger Plan', 17 December 2000 (accessed Factiva); Daniel Hoare, 'Kiwi Link-up a No-Go – ASX', *Australian*, 24 September 2002, p. 20.

31. 'Concern Over Stock Exchange Merger', *Money Management*, 30 March 2000, p. 10.

32. By 2007 the New Zealand Stock Exchange was looking to compete with the ASX 'crossing market'. These are off-market transfers of large parcels of shares, often outside normal hours and at agreed prices.

33. Bob Catley, *Waltzing with Matilda: Should New Zealand join Australia*, Wellington, 2001.

34. DFAT, *The Big End of Town*.

35. www.nzherald.co.nz/section/1/story.cfm?c_id=1&ObjectID=10407273 www.nzherald.co.nz/section/1/story.cfm?c_id=1&ObjectID=10407273

Chapter Seven

1. Libby Robin and Tom Griffiths, 'Environmental History in Australasia', *Environmental History*, Vol.10, No. 4, 2004, p. 448. This later became ANZAAS,

the major vehicle for cross-Tasman transmission of conference knowledge in the sciences and humanities until the late 1980s. See Roy MacLeod (ed.), *The Commonwealth of Science: ANZAAS and the scientific enterprise in Australasia, 1888–1988*, Melbourne, 1988.

2. Tara Brabazon, *Tracking the Jack: A retracing of the Antipodes*, Sydney, 2000, p. 3.
3. Philippa Mein Smith, *A Concise History of New Zealand*, Cambridge, New York and Melbourne, 2005, pp. 239–40.
4. Rollo Arnold, 'The Dynamics and Quality of Trans-Tasman Migration 1885–1910', *Australian Economic History Review*, Vol. 26, No. 1, March 1986, pp. 1–20.
5. Robin Winks, *These New Zealanders*, Christchurch, 1954, p. 126.
6. Alan Barcan, *A History of Australian Education*, Melbourne, 1980, p. 203.
7. John Thompson, 'British Roots, Australian Fruits', *Meanjin*, Vol. 63, No. 3, 2004, p. 88.
8. Colin McGeorge, 'The Moral Curriculum: Forming the Kiwi character', in Gary McCulloch (ed.), *The School Curriculum in New Zealand: History, theory, policy and practice*, Palmerston North, 1992, pp. 40–43, 47–52. See also J. A. Mangan (ed.), *The Imperial Curriculum: Racial images and education in the British colonial experience*, London, 1993.
9. The section on textbooks draws on Colin McGeorge's 'Notes on Some Australia–New Zealand Links in Education' (2005), prepared for this chapter. I am grateful for Colin's erudition as a historian of education.
10. Whitcombe and Tombs also produced works specifically tailored to schools in Victoria, e.g. William Gillies' *Simple Studies in English History* and Walter Murdoch's *The Struggle for Freedom*.
11. McGeorge, 'Notes', p. 14; see also Ian McLaren, *Whitcombe's Story Books: A trans-Tasman survey*, Parkville, 1984.
12. Peter Goyen, *A Report to the Otago Education Board on State Education in Three Australian States and New Zealand*, Dunedin, 1902.
13. A. G. Butchers, *Education in New Zealand*, Dunedin, 1930, pp. 152–53.
14. *Report of Royal Commission on University Education in New Zealand*, Wellington, 1925; Frank Tate, *Investigation into Certain Aspects of Post-primary Education in New Zealand*, Wellington, 1926.
15. Quoted in L. C. Webb, *The Control of Education in New Zealand*, Wellington, 1937, p. 63.
16. Ian Cumming, *Glorious Enterprise: History of the Auckland Education Board 1857–1957*, Christchurch, 1959, p. 517.
17. Butchers, *Education in New Zealand*. On the Catholic system, pp. 438–45. For the parliamentary report see *New Zealand Parliament, House of Representatives: Recess Education Committee*, Wellington, 1930.
18. Ian Breward, *A History of the Churches in Australasia*, Oxford, 2001, p. 306.
19. Malcolm Prentis, 'Minister and Dominie: An Australasian Scottish world?', New Zealand Historical Association Conference, Dunedin, 30 November 2003, p. 3.
20. Mark Hutchinson, '". . . Goes without Saying": Themes for trans-Tasman religious research', *Australasian Pentecostalist Studies*, No. 5–6, March–October 2001, p. 57.
21. Prentis, 'Minister and Dominie', p. 11.
22. Rory Sweetman, 'Outposts of a Spiritual Empire: Catholicism in nineteenth

century Australia and New Zealand', in *Australia–New Zealand: Aspects of a relationship*, proceedings of the Stout Research Centre 8th annual conference, Wellington, 1991.

23. Katie Pickles, 'Colonial Sainthood in Australasia', *National Identities*, Vol. 7, No. 4, December 2005, p. 400.

24. Diane Strevens, *In Step with Time: A history of the Sisters of St Joseph of Nazareth, Wanganui, New Zealand*, Auckland, 2001.

25. K. Pickles, 'Colonial Sainthood', p. 399.

26. Barcan, *History of Australian Education*, p. 285. See also p. 319 for statistics. In New Zealand 742 nuns of a variety of orders were teaching in Catholic schools by 1930; Butchers, *Education in New Zealand*, p. 440.

27. H. Laracy, 'The Catholic Church in New Zealand: A historical perspective', in H. Bergin and S. Smith (eds), *He Kupu Whakawairua: Spirituality in Aotearoa New Zealand: Catholic voices*, Auckland, 2002, p. 15.

28. 'An Historical Survey', *Our Studies*, Vol. 22, No. 1, May 1950; and Vol. 22, No. 2, October 1950.

29. Miscellaneous, File 2, Christian Brothers Archives, Balmain, Sydney (CB).

30. 'Character Training', *Our Studies*, Vol. 6, No. 2, p. 36.

31. 'New Zealand Notes', *Our Studies*, Vol. 5, No. 2, pp. 44–46. There is a strong need for studies of Christian variations on the theme of masculinity in Brothers' schools in both countries: see Anne O'Brien, 'Masculinism and the Church in Australian History', *Australian Historical Studies*, Vol. 25, No. 100, April 1993, pp. 437–57; also Martin Crotty, *Making the Australian Male: Middle class masculinity 1870–1920*, Melbourne, 2001.

32. *Our Studies*, Vol. 20, No. 2, October 1948, p. 3.

33. J. A. McGlade, 'Australia's Debt to New Zealand', *Christian Brothers Studies*, Vol. 50, No. 2, 1977, pp. 1–5.

34. 'An Historical Survey', *Our Studies*, Vol. 22, No. 2, October 1950, pp. 41–42.

35. Rory Sweetman, '*A Fair and Just Solution'? A History of the Integration of Private Schools in New Zealand*, Palmerston North, 2002, pp. 215–18.

36. Book of Foundations, p. 192, Item 310, CB.

37. Ibid.; St Joseph's Province Correspondence 1954–57, 1959–62, Item 03462, CB.

38. Book of Foundations, p. 420, CB.

39. Hanley to Marlow 10 January 1965; Marlow to Garvey 18 August 1965, Item 03463, CB.

40. In 2005 the New Zealand province was reintegrated into an expanded Oceania Province, combining the Tasman world with the Brothers' outreach to Asia and the Pacific, as a 21st-century response to the need for a fresh mission.

41. W. G. Litster, 'Factors Influencing the Development of the Curriculum in Seventh Day Adventist Schools in Australia and New Zealand 1892–1977', PhD thesis, University of Newcastle, 1982, p. 10; Trevor Lloyd, 'Church Schools', in Noel Clapham (ed.), *Seventh Day Adventists in the South Pacific 1885–1985*, Warburton, Victoria, 1986, p. 168; G. Litster, 'The SDA School System in New Zealand', in Peter Ballis (ed.), *In and Out of the World: Seventh Day Adventists in New Zealand*, Palmerston North, 1985, p. 110.

42. Litster, 'Factors', pp. 237–39, 248.
43. Milton Hook, *Avondale: Experiment on the Dora*, Cooranbong, 1998, pp. 247–50.
44. Litster, 'Factors', p. 66.
45. Ibid., pp. 2–25, incl. statistics 1977, p. 24.
46. Ross Goldstone, 'Opportunism in Evangelism 1919–1939', in A. J. Ferch (ed.), *Journey of Hope: Seventh Day Adventist History in the South Pacific 1919–1950*, Wahroonga, 1991, pp. 94–96.
47. Hutchinson, ' ". . . Goes without Saying" ', p. 53.
48. Breward, *History of the Churches*, pp. 392–93. See also J. Stenhouse and Brett Knowles (eds), *The Future of Christianity: Historical, sociological, political and theological perspectives*, Adelaide, 2004, ch. 3.
49. See Michael Reid, 'But by my Spirit: A history of the charismatic renewal in Christchurch 1960–1985', PhD thesis, University of Canterbury, 2003; also Brett Knowles, *The History of a New Zealand Pentecostal Movement: the New Life churches of New Zealand from 1946 to 1979*, Lewiston, 2000.
50. Hutchinson, ' ". . . Goes without Saying" ', pp. 55, 56.
51. See A. K. Davidson, 'Christianity and National Identity', in Stenhouse and Knowles (eds), *Future of Christianity*, pp. 28–29.
52. Compare Hutchinson, ' ". . . Goes without Saying" ', p. 60.
53. See S. Emilsen and W. W. Emilsen (eds), *Mapping the Landscape: Essays in Australian and New Zealand Christianity*, New York, 2000, p. 260; A. K. Davidson and P. Lineham, *Transplanted Christianity*, Palmerston North, 1997.
54. Ronald Winton, *Why the Pomegranate? A history of the Royal Australasian College of Physicians*, Sydney, 1988, pp. 3–90 passim.
55. Claire Dann documents a vast range of such organisations in her study 'A Continuing Community of Interests: A database of Australasian organizations 1880–2003', Social Science Research Centre Summer Project, University of Canterbury, 2003. Copy held at NZ Australia Research Centre, School of History, University of Canterbury.
56. W. H. Pearson, *Henry Lawson among Maoris*, Wellington, 1968.
57. S. G. Foster and Margaret Varghese, *The Making of the Australian National University*, St Leonards, 1996, p. 24; see also James McNeish, *Dance of the Peacocks: New Zealanders in exile in the time of Hitler and Mao Tse-Tung*, Auckland, 2003.
58. Foster and Varghese, ibid., p. 26.
59. Marjorie Harper, 'Copland, Sir Douglas Berry 1894–1917', Australian Dictionary of Biography: www.adb.online.anu.edu.au (16 June 2008).
60. J. Rowland, G. W. Jones and D. Broers-Freeman, *The Founding of Australian Demography: A tribute to W. D. Borrie*, Canberra, 1993.
61. Butchers, *Education in New Zealand*, p. 415.
62. Grant Young, ' "The War of Intellectual Independence"? New Zealand historians and their history, 1945–1972', MA thesis, University of Auckland, 1998, pp. 15–21, 49.
63. Interview R. G. Ward, Canberra 28 November 2002; see also M. McArthur, 'Luck and the Unexpected Vacancy', *Research School of Pacific and Asian Studies (RSPAS) Quarterly Bulletin*, Vol. 2, No. 4, December 2001, pp. 12–14.

64. R. Gerard Ward, 'Taupo Country, New Zealand: On place, naming and identity', in Brij Lal (ed.), *Pacific Places, Pacific Histories*, Honolulu, 2004, pp. 95–118.
65. Correspondence Webb to Copland 1949, File 9.2.1.6, Webb Papers, ANU Archives, Canberra; John Warhurst, 'Webb, Leicester Chisholm 1905–1962', *Australian Dictionary of Biography*: www.adb.online.anu.edu.au (16 June 2008)
66. Interview W. N. Gunson, Canberra, 27 September 2002 (Gunson, a longstanding member of the department, had family ties on both sides of the ditch).
67. Interview R. Barwick, Canberra, 8 July 2003. Until 1952 the ANU's Physiology Department was actually run from New Zealand: M. Freeman, 'Australian Universities at War', in Roy Macleod (ed.), *Science and the Pacific War: Science and survival in the Pacific 1939–45*, Dordrecht, 2000, p. 132.
68. See Foster and Varghese, *The Making of the Australian National University*, p. 10; interview R. G. Ward, 28 November 2002.
69. Aitken to Passmore, 31 March 1954 and Partridge to Passmore 22 October 1953; undated newspaper clipping *Otago Daily Times* (by Passmore), Passmore Papers, Series 1, Box 7, Folder 52, National Library of Australia (NLA).
70. Foster and Varghese, *The Making of the Australian National University*, pp. 57, 92.
71. Parker to Ellis, 23 August 1954, Parker papers, Series 1, Box 9, File 73, NLA. See Boxes 1, 8, 9 for correspondence on Parker's career. See also G. R. Curnow and R. L. Wettenhall (eds), *Understanding Public Administration: Essays in honour of R. S. Parker & R. N. Spann*, Sydney, 1981. The continuing tradition of trans-Tasman training of public servants can be seen today in the Australia New Zealand School of Government (ANZSOG), a consortium of universities on both sides of the Tasman using their combined resources for senior level postgraduate training.
72. For a detailed examination of Wood's contribution to trans-Tasman history see Hempenstall's 'Overcoming separate histories: Historians as 'ideas traders' in a trans-Tasman world', *History Australia*, Vol. 4, No. 1, June 2007, pp. 4.1–4.16.
73. Stuart Macintyre, *A History for a Nation: Ernest Scott and the making of Australian history*, Carlton, 1994, pp. 134–37.
74. F. L. W. Wood, *New Zealand and the Big Powers: Can a small nation have a mind of its own?* Sir Sidney Holland Memorial Lecture, Wellington, 1967, p. 16.
75. For a more detailed treatment of Davidson and Ward see Hempenstall, 'Overcoming Separate Histories'. Another of Wood's protégés was the historian and philosopher Peter Munz. See James N. Bade (ed.), *Out of the Shadow of War: The German connection with New Zealand in the 20th century*, Melbourne, 1998; Peter Munz (ed.), *The Feel of Truth*, Wellington, 1969. The roll-call, particularly of historians, is long and revealing of Kiwi contributions to Australian, Pacific and international historiographies: Patrick O'Farrell, Trevor Wilson, Patricia Grimshaw, David Hilliard, Len Richardson, among many.
76. Miles Fairburn, 'Is There a Good Case for New Zealand Exceptionalism?' in Tony Ballantyne and B. Moloughney (eds), *Disputed Histories*, Dunedin, 2006, pp. 143–67. For an earlier coverage of cultural relations see Terry Sturm's 'A Dinkum Bluey and Curly Kind of Culture', *Auckland Star*, 16 September 1981.
77. Robin and Griffiths, 'Environmental History', p. 439.
78. *Canberra Times*, 24 May 1979.

79. The latest in a long line: *Press*, 24 June 2006, D13: from Australia: 'We may have embraced its film and music, often to the extent of claiming it as our own, but New Zealand writing rarely gets the run it deserves in this country. When it comes to fiction we either look for our own or venture further afield rather than peering over the fence.' Historians too have bemoaned the lack of learning from one another provoked by the 'History wars' in Australia and New Zealand's Waitangi Tribunal debates. See *New Zealand Historical Association Newsletter*, April 2004.

Chapter Eight

1. See Martin Crotty, *Making the Australian Male: Middle class masculinity 1870–1920*, Melbourne, 2001; J. A. Mangan and John Nauright (eds), *Sport in Australasian Society: Past and present*, London, 2000. School histories are rife with records of deeds on the sporting fields. For a particularly fine analysis see Greg Dening, *Xavier: A centenary portrait*, Kew, 1978.
2. Len Richardson and Shelley Richardson, *Anthony Wilding: A sporting life*, Christchurch, 2005, p. 201; see also p. 98.
3. S. Fagan, *The Rugby Rebellion: The divide of league and union*, Kellyville NSW, 2005, p. 169.
4. J. Haynes, *From All Blacks to All Golds: New Zealand's rugby league pioneers*, Christchurch, 1996, pp. 61–62.
5. Haynes, *From All Blacks to All Golds*, pp. 36, 37, 41, 155, 45.
6. Jo Smith, '"All that Glitters": The All Golds and the advent of rugby league in Australasia', MA thesis, University of Canterbury, 1998, p. 50.
7. Haynes, *From All Blacks to All Golds*, p. 63.
8. Fagan, *The Rugby Rebellion*, pp. 180–82.
9. Haynes, *From All Blacks to All Golds*, p. 145.
10. G. Moorhouse, *A People's Game: The centenary history of rugby league football 1895–1995*, London, 1995, p. 145.
11. T. Collins, *Rugby's Great Split: Class, culture, and the origins of rugby league football*, London, 1998, p. 224.
12. Smith, '"All that Glitters"', pp. 112, 124.
13. R. Becht, *A New Breed Rising: The Warriors Winfield Cup challenge*, Auckland, 1994, pp. 10–13, 23–24.
14. P. Leitch and R. Becht, *The Year the Kiwis Flew: From wooden spooners to winners*, Auckland, 2006, pp. 12, 13, 28, 58.
15. T. Collins, 'Ahr Waggy' : *Harold Wagstaff and the making of Anglo-Australian rugby league culture*, Sydney, 2004, p. 4.
16. Smith, '"All that Glitters"', pp. 31–32.
17. C. Little, *The Northern Game in the South: The rise and fall of rugby league in Otago, 1924–1935*, History Hons essay, University of Otago, 1994, pp. 30–31.
18. For example, the NZRFU, after failing to halt the tour of All Golds, worked with other sporting organisations to try to make professional sport illegal. They started the Federation of Sport, held a conference in Wellington and invited MPs to attend, all with the aim of destroying any future professional tours. Haynes, *From All Blacks to All Golds*, pp. 20–23, 87.

19. R. Manning, 'The Two Rugbies', in B. Whimpress (ed.), *The Imaginary Grandstand: Identity and narrative in Australian sport*, Kent Town, 2002, pp. 98–99.
20. Robert Gate, *Rugby League: An illustrated history*, London, 1989, p. 44.
21. Ian Heads, *True Blue: The story of the NSW rugby league*, Randwick, NSW, 1992, p. 162.
22. D. Sanders, *Simply the Best: Celebrating 90 years of New Zealand league*, Auckland, 1997, pp. 101–04.
23. Moorhouse, *A People's Game*, p. 105.
24. S. B. Zavos and G. Bray, *Two Mighty Tribes: The story of the All Blacks vs. the Wallabies*, Auckland, 2003, p. 98. After the First World War only New South Wales still had a rugby union. Queensland and Victoria did not re-form until the 1920s and 1930s respectively. Zavos and Bray, p. 44.
25. Fagan, *The Rugby Rebellion*, pp. 10–11.
26. Zavos and Bray, *Two Mighty Tribes*, pp. 37–38.
27. P. Jenkins and M. Alvarez, *Wallaby Gold: 100 years of Australian test rugby*, Sydney, 1999, p. 49.
28. Zavos and Bray, *Two Mighty Tribes*, p. 102.
29. J. McCrystal, *The Originals: 1905 All Black rugby odyssey*, Auckland, 2005, pp. 43, 88.
30. G. T. Vincent, 'A Tendency to Roughness: Anti-heroic representations of New Zealand rugby football 1890–1914', in G. Ryan (ed.), *Tackling Rugby Myths: Rugby and New Zealand society 1854–2004*, Dunedin, 2005, pp. 67–68.
31. Zavos and Bray, *Two Mighty Tribes*, p. 45.
32. M. L. Howell, X. Lingyu and P. Horton, *Bledisloe Magic*, Auckland, 1995, p. 26.
33. Zavos and Bray, *Two Mighty Tribes*, pp. 108, 135, 154.
34. R. Palenski, *The Jersey*, Auckland, 2001, p. 203.
35. B. Howitt and D. Haworth, *Rugby Nomads*, Auckland, 2002, pp. 12–15, 20, 21–22.
36. Peter FitzSimons, *The Rugby War*, Sydney, 2003, pp. 1, 9, 15, 57, 38–41.
37. C. Obel and T. Austrin, 'The End of "Our National Game"? Romance, mobilities and the politics of organisation', in Ryan (ed.), *Tackling Rugby Myths*, p. 183; B. Howitt, *SANZAR Saga*, Auckland, 2005, p. 27.
38. Zavos and Bray, *Two Mighty Tribes*, p. 235.
39. See J. Romanos, *The Judas Game: The betrayal of New Zealand rugby*, Wellington, 2002.
40. P. Thomas, *A Whole New Ball Game: Confronting the myths and realities of New Zealand rugby*, Auckland, 2003, pp. 11, 14, 16.
41. G. Ryan, 'The Paradox of Maori Rugby 1870-1914', in Ryan (ed.), *Tackling Rugby Myths*, p. 90.
42. Zavos and Bray, *Two Mighty Tribes*, pp. 29–30.
43. M. MacLean, 'Of Warriors and Blokes: The problem of Maori rugby for Pakeha masculinity in New Zealand', in T. J. L. Chandler and J. Nauright (eds), *Making the Rugby World: Race, gender, commerce*, London, 1999, p. 9.
44. Zavos and Bray, *Two Mighty Tribes*, p. 201.
45. Jenkins and Alvarez, *Wallaby Gold*, p. 20.
46. M. G. Phillips, 'Rugby', in W. Vamplew and B. Stoddart (eds), *Sport in Australia: A social history*, Cambridge, 1994, p. 206.

47. Manning, 'The Two Rugbies', pp. 98–99.
48. Obel and Austrin, 'The End of "Our National Game"?', p. 178.
49. Ibid., pp. 21, 59.
50. Palenski, *The Jersey*, p. 46.
51. Zavos and Bray, *Two Mighty Tribes*, p. 105; Howell, Lingyu and Horton, *Bledisloe Magic*, pp. 120–21.
52. Howell et al., ibid., pp. 7, 11, 12.
53. S. B. Zavos, *The Gold & the Black: The rugby battles for the Bledisloe Cup: New Zealand vs Australia 1903–94*, St Leonards NSW, 1995, p. 135.
54. Zavos and Bray, *Two Mighty Tribes*, p. 246.
55. Ibid., pp. 50, 69.
56. D. O. Neely, R. King and F. Payne, *Men in White: The history of New Zealand international cricket, 1894–1985*, Auckland, 1986, p. 23.
57. G. Ryan, *The Making of New Zealand Cricket, 1832–1914*, London, 2004, p. 71.
58. G. Ryan, 'New Zealand', in B. Stoddart and K. A. P. Sandiford (eds), *The Imperial Game: Cricket, culture and society*, Manchester, 1998, p. 104.
59. J. P. Carr, 'The First Golden Age? A social history of New Zealand cricket 1914–1939', MA thesis, University of Canterbury, 2001, p. iv.
60. Ryan, 'New Zealand', p. 93.
61. R. Cashman, *Sport in the National Imagination: Australian sport in the federation decades*, Sydney, 2002, p. 139.
62. On the Bodyline tour the English employed fast bowling in line with the batsman's body that bounced high. The English placed fielders close by to catch shots played in self-defence. Australian players took body blows in order to stand their ground without risking shots. These tactics caused a furore among Australia's general population, media and politicians. The ACB sent complaints to the MCC and British government. The event remains vivid in Australia's collective memory; even to this day books are published about the tour. R. Sissons and B. Stoddart, *Cricket and Empire: The 1932–33 Bodyline tour of Australia*, London, 1984, p. 4.
63. G. Ryan, '"Extravagance of Thought and Feeling"': New Zealand reactions to the 1932/33 Bodyline controversy', *Sporting Traditions*, Vol. 13, November 1996, pp. 49, 41–42, 52, 54.
64. See Chris Harte, *A History of Australian Cricket*, London, 1993, p. 669; R. Cashman et al., *The Oxford Companion to Australian Cricket*, Melbourne, 1996, p. 403; Ryan, 'New Zealand', p. 111.
65. Cashman, *Sport in the National Imagination*, pp. 19, 24.
66. R. Cashman, 'Australia', in Stoddart and Sandiford, *The Imperial Game*, pp. 44–46.
67. B. Stewart, 'The Crisis of Confidence in Australian First-class Cricket in the 1950s', *Sporting Traditions*, Vol. 20, November 2003, pp. 45, 47–51, 53–54, 57–58.
68. Cashman, 'Australia', p. 43.
69. E. Bairam, J. M. Howells and G. Turner, *Production Functions in Cricket: The Australian and New Zealand experience*, Dunedin, 1989, pp. 11–12.
70. Cashman, *The Oxford Companion*, p. 75.
71. Carr, 'First Golden Age?', p. 141.
72. Cashman, *Sport in the National Imagination*, pp. 107–08.

73. Cashman, 'Australia', p. 50.
74. Carr, 'First Golden Age?', p. 129.
75. Ibid., pp. 140–41.
76. J. Pollard, *From Bradman to Border: Australian cricket 1948–89*, North Ryde, 1989, p. 227.
77. Ryan, *The Making of New Zealand Cricket*, p. 230.
78. Cashman, *The Oxford Companion*, p. 386.
79. A similar change occurred around the Anzus crisis of 1985 (see Chapter 9).
80. T. Taylor, Netball in Australia: A social history, Sydney, 2001: www.business.uts. edu.au/1st/downloads/WP02_Taylor.pdf
81. P. Hawes and L. Barker, *Court in the Spotlight: History of New Zealand netball*, Auckland, 1999, p. 13.
82. G. Andrew, ' "A Girl's Game, and a Good One Too": A critical analysis of New Zealand netball', MA thesis, University of Canterbury, 1997, pp. 109–22.
83. Hawes and Barker, *Court in the Spotlight*, pp. 23–24.
84. I. Jobbling and P. Barham, 'The Development of Netball and the All-Australia Women's Basketball Association (AAWBBA) 1891–1939', *Sporting Traditions*, Vol. 8, November 1991, p. 40.
85. Andrew, ' "A Girl's Game, and a Good One Too" ', p. 42.
86. Jobbling and Barham, 'The Development of Netball', p. 41.
87. Andrew, ' "A Girl's Game, and a Good One Too" ', p. 43.
88. C. Macdonald, 'Netball New Zealand', in A. Else (ed.), *Women Together: A history of women's organisations in New Zealand*, Wellington, 1993, p. 432.
89. Hawes and Barker, *Court in the Spotlight*, p. 54.
90. Ibid., pp. 62–65.
91. Netball Australia claimed they used these names because other sporting codes had not overexposed bird names, but this argument is difficult to substantiate. There are Sydney Swans, Adelaide Crows, Wollongong Hawks, Gippsland Falcons in men's Aussie rules, rugby league, soccer and basketball professional competitions.
92. Taylor, *Netball in Australia*.
93. T. Taylor, 'Women, Sport and Ethnicity: Exploring experiences of difference in netball', in Whimpress, *The Imaginary Grandstand*, pp. 42, 44.
94. J. Nauright and J. Broomhall, 'A Woman's Game: The development of netball and a female sporting culture in New Zealand 1906–70', *International Journal of the History of Sport*, Vol. 11, No. 3, December 1994, p. 401.
95. Andrew, ' "A Girl's Game, and a Good One Too" ', pp. 67–68.
96. Hawes and Barker, *Court in the Spotlight*, pp. 87, 91, 93, 104–06.

Chapter Nine
1. 'Defence' here means military strategy, planning and materiel.
2. Paul Keating, *Engagement: Australia faces the Asia–Pacific*, Sydney, 2000, pp. 218–19.
3. Hugh White, 'Living without Ilusions: Where our defence relationship goes from here', in Bob Catley (ed.), *NZ–Australia Relations: Moving together or drifting apart?* Papers from the 36th Otago Foreign Policy School, p. 129.
4. White, 'Living without Illusions', p. 138.

5. Transcript of Helen Clark's answers to questions at the end of a talk to the Trans-Tasman Business Circle, Sydney, 8 July 2004. Words have been omitted as indicated because of a break in the tape.
6. Keating, *Engagement,* pp. 219–20.
7. An authoritative recent treatment is Malcolm Templeton, *Standing Upright Here: New Zealand in the nuclear age, 1945–1990,* Wellington, 2006, especially pp.385–481. See also Stuart McMillan, *Neither Confirm Nor Deny: The nuclear ships debate between New Zealand and the United States,* Wellington & Sydney, 1987, especially pp. 79–87.
8. Senior official sources.
9. See Denis McLean, *The Prickly Pair: Making nationalism in Australia and New Zealand,* Dunedin, 2003, pp. 261–63. Also comments made by former US administration officials to the present writer.
10. Although calculating the percentage of GDP spent on defence is notoriously difficult, it is estimated that New Zealand spends a bit under 1 per cent in this area. Australia spends 1.9 per cent. In New Zealand under the National-led government of 1990 to 1999 there was no adjustment for inflation for nine years, which amounts to an effective cut of 3 per cent to 5 per cent each year. Although spending increased under the Labour-led government in the first years of the 21st century, it did not increase as a percentage of GDP, because GDP keeps growing. There is still a considerable gap between Australia's spending as a percentage of GDP and New Zealand's.
11. The F16 decision was taken in 2000; the decision to abandon the air combat wing, which consisted of A4 Skyhawks, was in 2001; a National-led government had already decided not to take up an option for a third frigate under the Anzac frigate programme in 1999. An earlier plan under the Labour government had been for New Zealand to take four frigates.
12. Email to the author, 18 July 2006.
13. New Zealand Ministry of Defence and New Zealand Defence Force, *The Defence of New Zealand 1991: A policy paper,* Wellington, 1991, p. 17.
14. The 'White New Zealand' policy from the 1880s to the 1960s was more covert than the White Australia policy.
15. For a setting of this situation within the context of the Vietnam War and afterwards see Roberto Rabel, *New Zealand and the Vietnam War: Politics and diplomacy,* Auckland, 2005, especially pp. 361–65. For a setting within the general history of New Zealand see Philippa Mein Smith, *A Concise History of New Zealand,* Cambridge, New York & Melbourne, 2005, especially pp. 216–25. Australia had conscription for the Vietnam War. New Zealand did not and the New Zealand contribution was grudgingly made as Rabel makes clear.
16. For a discussion on the role of attitudes to the United States in Australian politics see Richard Herr, 'The American Impact on Australian Defence Relations with the South Pacific Islands,' *Australian Outlook,* Vol. 38, December 1984, pp. 184–90.
17. Comment made by Derek Quigley to the present writer.
18. A good account of the effect of this on New Zealand–Britain relations and Muldoon's calculation is given in Gerald Hensley, *Final Approaches: A memoir,* Auckland, 2006, pp. 247–48.

19. Professor Ball is still in the Strategic and Defence Studies Centre at the Australian National University as is Coral Bell, who is a visiting fellow. Professor Mack is now at the University of British Columbia.

20. Denis Healey, *The Time of My Life*, London, 1989, p. 292. (The air marshal Healey is referring to in particular is probably Sam Elworthy, a New Zealander who was Chief of Air Staff in Britain and later Chief of Defence Staff.)

21. New Zealand Ministry of Defence and New Zealand Defence Force, *The Defence of New Zealand 1991*, p.18.

22. For an interesting discussion of Australia's stance on this issue compared with other countries see Hugh White, 'Australian Defence Policy and the Possibility of War', *Australian Journal of International Affairs*, Vol. 56, No. 2, 2002, pp. 253–64.

23. Winston Peters raised this point in a press conference after presenting a talk to the New Zealand Institute of International Affairs in Wellington on 21 February 2006.

24. Comment made by Hugh White to the present writer.

25. Message in a telegram from Fraser to Churchill, 26 March 1942, held in the National Archives, Kew.

26. New Zealand Ministry of Defence and New Zealand Defence Force, *The Defence of New Zealand 1991*, p. 19.

27. Communiqué of the Australia–New Zealand Defence Ministers' Talk, 27 March 1998.

28. Address to the NZ Institute of International Affairs, Wellington, 12 February 2004.

29. McLean, *Prickly Pair*.

30. Government of New Zealand, *Defence Policy Framework*, June 2000, p. 3.

31. The term 'intervention', which will be used to describe the actions in the region, is being used in a way that is as neutral as possible. It is not intended to confer on those who acted militarily a right to take military action. For a discussion about the sensitivities associated with the use of the term see Daniel Flitton, 'Issues in Australian Foreign Policy: July to December 2003', *Australian Journal of Politics and History*, Vol. 50, No. 2, 2004, p. 235.

32. Alexander Downer made this point, regretting that the Peace Monitoring Group has not been sufficiently recognised in Australia. *The Bougainville Crisis: An Australian perspective*, Canberra, 2001, p. 21.

33. For an interesting Australian perspective on the relationship see General Peter Cosgrove, *My Story*, Sydney, 2006, pp. 214–16.

34. A good discussion of the justifications for Australia's joining the coalition of the willing is to be found in Brendon O'Connor, 'Perspectives on Australian Foreign Policy 2003', *Australian Journal of International Affairs*, Vol. 58, No. 2, 2004, especially pp. 207–12.

35. E. McElhatton discusses different attitudes in New Zealand and Australia towards the United Nations in 'Australia and New Zealand: Like-minded partners?', *New Zealand International Review*, July/August 2006, pp. 18–21.

36. Interview in 2006 with Phil Goff, by then Minister of Defence.

37. 'Our Failing Neighbour: Australia and the future of Solomon Islands', ASPI report, prepared by Elsina Wainwright, 2003.

38. ASPI report, p. 19.

39. Flitton, 'Issues in Australian Foreign Policy', p. 237.
40. Rosemary Baird, 'Anzac Peacekeeping: Trans-Tasman responses to the Bougainville crisis in 1997 and the subsequent evolution of Australia's and New Zealand's regional peacekeeping', MA thesis, University of Canterbury, 2008.
41. Ibid., ch. 5.
42. 'Inquiry into Defence beyond 2000, Report of the Foreign Affairs, Defence and Trade Committee', Hon. Derek Quigley Chairperson, August 1999, *Appendix to the Journal of the House of Representatives of New Zealand*, Vol. 58, 1996–99.
43. Australian Department of Foreign Affairs and Trade website: www.dfat.gov.au (September 2006).
44. For a reflective discussion of this issue see Roger Mortlock, 'The Role of the Military', in John Henderson and Greg Watson (eds), *Securing a Peaceful Pacific*, Christchurch, 2005.
45. One of the most enlightening discussions on this issue has been written by Nigel Alwyn-Foster, 'Changing the Army for Counterinsurgency Operations', *Military Review*, November–December 2005. Nigel Alwyn-Foster is a British Army brigadier who served in Iraq.

Chapter Ten
1. In this sense, this book is a sequel to Donald Denoon and Philippa Mein Smith, with Marivic Wyndham, *A History of Australia, New Zealand and the Pacific*, The Blackwell History of the World, Oxford, 2000.
2. A useful introduction is the 'AHR Conversation: On transnational history', *American Historical Review*, Vol. 111, No. 5, December 2006, pp. 1441–64, involving C. A. Bayly, Sven Beckert, Matthew Connelly, Isabel Hofmeyr, Wendy Kozol and Patricia Seed.
3. Joan Hughes (ed.), *The Concise Australian National Dictionary*, Melbourne, 1992, p. 15; Tony Deverson and Graeme Kennedy (eds), *The New Zealand Oxford Dictionary*, Melbourne, 2005, p. 68.
4. Ian Britain, 'Australasian?', *Meanjin*, Vol. 63, No. 2, 2004, p. 2.
5. J. G. A. Pocock, *The Discovery of Islands*, Cambridge, 2005, p. 272.
6. Denis McLean, *Prickly Pair: Making nationalism in Australia and New Zealand*, Dunedin, 2003, p. 304.
7. J. Olick, 'On the Hermeneutics of Historical Analogy', Governing by Looking Back Conference, ANU, 12 December 2007.
8. 'Kiwis and Aussies: Appreciate the distinctions', *Sydney Morning Herald*, 19 August 2004.
9. 'Geoffrey Bolton in Conversation with Jill Roe', *Australian Historical Association Bulletin*, No. 93, December 2001, p. 49. Bolton spent his professional life in Brisbane and Perth.
10. *Sydney Morning Herald*, 19 August 2004.
11. Silence followed the publication of McLean's *Prickly Pair*.
12. *The Shorter Oxford English Dictionary*, 3rd edn, Vol. 1, Oxford, 1965, p. 1088.
13. See David Gerber, 'Theories and Lives: Transnationalism and the conceptualization of international migrations to the United States', *IMIS Beiträge (Institut für*

Migrationsforschung und interkulturelle Studien Universität Osnabrück), No. 15, 2000, pp. 31–35.

14. Cf. Murray McCaskill, 'The Tasman Connection: Aspects of Australia–New Zealand relations', *Australian Geographical Studies*, Vol. 20, April 1982.

15. Philippa Mein Smith, 'The Tasman World', in Giselle Byrnes (ed.), *The New Oxford History of New Zealand*, Oxford and Melbourne, forthcoming, ch. 16.

16. David Goddard QC, 'Case Study: Trans-Tasman Court proceedings and regulatory enforcement', Whose Law is it Anyway?, Legal Research Foundation, Harmonising Australian and New Zealand Business Laws Conference, Wellington, 9 March 2007; term 'plumbing' from Goddard.

17. www.finance.gov.au/publications/docs/ttpaper.pdf (December 2007).

18. New Zealand Government, Submission No. 9, Australia's Trade and Investment Relations under the Australia–New Zealand Closer Economic Relations Trade Agreement, Joint Standing Committee on Foreign Affairs, Defence and Trade, 2006: www.aph.gov.au/house/committee/jfadt/nz_cer/subs.htm (2 August 2006).

19. Fonterra, Submission No. 2, ibid..

20. A good survey of the ponderables and imponderables is Colin James' address, 'The Elusive Single Economic Market', Whose Law is it Anyway? Legal Research Foundation, Harmonising Australian and New Zealand Business Laws Conference, Wellington, 9 March 2007; See also Karyn Scherer, 'Australia: So close, yet so far', *New Zealand Herald*, 17 December 2007. On trade and the Pacific see Phil Goff, 'Making Globalisation Work for the Pacific', *Pacific Connection*, Issue 13, September–November 2007, pp. 3–4.

21. Economists have carefully analysed the idea of a single currency. See Arthur Grimes and Frank Holmes with Roger Bowden, *An ANZAC Dollar? Currency union and business development*, Wellington, 2000; Arthur Grimes, 'Trans-Tasman Transaction Costs, Terms of Trade and Currency Union', *(Australian) Economic Papers*, special issue, 2001, pp. 52–63, and Arthur Grimes, 'Regional and Industry Cycles in Australasia: Implications for a common currency', *Journal of Asian Economics*, Vol. 16, No. 3, 2005, pp. 380–97.

22. 'Australia's Treasure Island', *Press*, 2–3 October 2004, p. C1.

23. China may well experience a smooth transition into predominance in the region and cause less trauma than doomsayers predict. See W. W. Keller and T. G. Rawski (eds), *China's Rise and the Balance of Influence in Asia*, Pittsburgh, 2007.

24. *Pacific Connection*, Issue 13, September–November 2007, pp. 3–4.

25. Colin James, 'Three-step with Matilda: Trans-Tasman relations', in Roderic Alley (ed.), *New Zealand in World Affairs IV: 1990–2005*, Wellington, 2007, p. 46.

26. Phrasing from John Henderson and Greg Watson (eds), *Securing a Peaceful Pacific*, Christchurch, 2005.

27. Concept of oceanic perspective from Pocock, *Discovery of Islands*.

28. Australia 2020 Summit, *Initial Summit Report*, April 2008, p. 35: www. australia2020.gov.au/report/index.cfm (April 2008).

29. Shaun Goldfinch, 'Australia, New Zealand and the Pacific Island Nations', *Otemon Bulletin of Australian Studies*, Vol. 31, 2005, pp. 37–41.

30. See census at Statistics New Zealand: www.stats.govt.nz (16 June 2008).

31. Colin James, 'The Pacific-ation of New Zealand', in Anne Henderson (ed.), *Sydney Papers*, Vol. 17, Issue 1, summer 2005, pp. 138–45.
32. See the Australian Government's *Australia's Demographic Challenges*, Canberra, 2004, which estimates that by 2050 the proportion of the population over 65 years will double to around 25 per cent.
33. Graeme Hugo, 'Future Immigration Policy Development in Australia and New Zealand', *New Zealand Population Review*, Vol. 30, Nos 1 & 2, 2004, pp. 23–42.
34. Jacques Poot, 'Twenty Years of Econometric Research on Trans-Tasman Migration', MOTU seminar paper, Wellington, 8 November 2007.
35. Mark Geenty, 'Australia Magnet for NZ Talent', *Press*, 8 March 2008, p. F4.
36. Denoon and Mein Smith, *A History of Australia, New Zealand and the Pacific*, p. 468.
37. Geoffrey Sawyer, *Australia–New Zealand Association: Some constitutional problems*, NZ Institute of International Affairs, Auckland, Occasional Papers No. 1, 1968, p. 26.
38. Brian Galligan, 'Closer Political Association: Australia and New Zealand', in Arthur Grimes, Lydia Wevers and Ginny Sullivan (eds), *States of Mind: Australia, New Zealand 1901–2001*, pp. 299–300.
39. Australia 2020 Summit, *Initial Summit Report*, pp. 32–33.
40. Phrase from Tim Fischer; Australia 2020 Summit, pp. 17–18.
41. Australia 2020 Summit, p. 10.
42. Howard Dick, 'Big Questions in Australian Economic History: From the outside looking in', *Australian Economic History Review*, Vol. 47, No. 3, November 2007, p. 317.
43. Peter Beilharz, *Imagining the Antipodes: Culture, theory and the visual in the work of Bernard Smith*, Melbourne, 1997, p. 189.
44. As New Zealand's Captain Russell imagined in the late 19th century; Philippa Mein Smith, 'New Zealand Federation Commissioners in Australia: One past, two historiographies', *Australian Historical Studies*, Vol. 34, No. 122, October 2003, p. 312.
45. Grimes puts Queensland, Western Australia, and the Northern Territory in the same category. Arthur Grimes, 'Intra and Inter-regional Industry Shocks: A new metric with application to Australasian currency union', *New Zealand Economic Papers*, Vol. 40, No. 1, 2006, pp. 23–44.
46. Donald Denoon, 'Re-Membering Australasia: A repressed memory', *Australian Historical Studies*, Vol. 34, No. 122, October 2003.
47. Teresia Teaiwa, 'On Analogies: Rethinking the Pacific in a global context', *The Contemporary Pacific*, Vol. 18, No. 1, 2006, p. 72.
48. Idea assisted by personal communication, Pocock to Mein Smith, 4 August 2006.
49. These thoughts derive from two workshops on antipodean research held by the NZAC Research Centre, University of Canterbury and the Thesis Eleven Centre, La Trobe University, in Melbourne in April 2005 and Christchurch in April 2006.
50. Niall Ferguson, *The War of the World: History's age of hatred*, London, 2006.
51. John Darwin, *After Tamerlane: The global history of empire since 1405*, London, 2007, p. 6.

BIBLIOGRAPHY

Published Sources

'2007 CER Ministerial Forum', 31 July 2007: www.beehive.govt.nz/release/ 2007+cer+ministerial+forum (16 June 2008)

ACIL Tasman, 'New Zealand–Australia Economic Interdependence', prepared for Ministry of Economic Development, 4 May 2004

'AHR Conversation: On transnational history', American Historical Review, Vol. 111, No. 5, December 2006, pp. 1441–64

Allan, Stella M., 'New Zealand and Federation', United Australia, October 1900, pp. 9–11

Alwyn-Foster, Nigel, 'Changing the Army for Counterinsurgency Operations', Military Review, November–December 2005

Anderson, Benedict, Imagined Communities: Reflections on the origin and spread of nationalism, revised edn, London & New York, Verso, 1991

Anderson, Warwick, The Cultivation of Whiteness: Science, health and racial destiny in Australia, Melbourne, Melbourne University Press, 2002

Andre, Pamela, Stephen Payton and John Mills (eds), The Negotiation of the Australia New Zealand Closer Economic Relations Trade Agreement 1983, Canberra & Wellington, Australian Department of Foreign Affairs and Trade/New Zealand Ministry of Foreign Affairs and Trade, 2003

Andrew, G., '"A Girl's Game, and a Good One Too": A critical analysis of New Zealand netball', MA thesis, University of Canterbury, 1997

Anthony, Doug, '20 Years of Trans-Tasman CER: Where to now?', speech at CER 20th anniversary luncheon, Sydney, Trans-Tasman Business Circle, 28 August 2003

Arnold, Rollo, 'New Zealand in Australasia 1890–1914', MA (Hons) thesis, University of Melbourne, 1952

Arnold, Rollo, 'Some Australasian Aspects of New Zealand Life, 1890–1913', New Zealand Journal of History, Vol. 4, No. 1, April 1970, pp. 54–76

Arnold, Rollo, 'The Dynamics and Quality of Trans-Tasman Migration 1885–1910', Australian Economic History Review, Vol. 26, No. 1, March 1986, pp. 1–20

'Artist Profiles: Reg Mombassa': www.mambo.com.au/artists (September 2003); www. regmombassa.com (February 2008)

Ashkanasy, Neal, Edwin Trevor-Roberts and Louise Earnshaw, 'The Anglo Cluster: Legacy of the British Empire', Journal of World Business, Vol. 37, 2002, pp. 28–39

Attwood, Bain and Fiona Magowan (eds), Telling Stories: Indigenous history and memory in Australia and New Zealand, Wellington, Bridget Williams Books, 2001

Australia 2020 Summit, Initial Summit Report, April 2008: www.australia2020.gov. au/report/index.cfm (April 2008)

Australia–New Zealand: Aspects of a relationship, proceedings of the Stout Research Centre 8th annual conference, 6–8 September 1991, Wellington, Stout Research Centre, Victoria University of Wellington, 1991

Australian Bureau of Statistics, 'International Investment Position, Australia: Supplementary country statistics (cat. No 5352.0)': www.abs.gov.au/AUSSTATS/abs (2006)

Australian Department of Finance and Administration and New Zealand Ministry of Economic Development, 'Arrangements for Facilitating Trans-Tasman Government Institutional Co-operation': www.finance.gov.au/publications/docs/ttpaper.pdf (December 2007)

Australian Department of Foreign Affairs and Trade, *The Bougainville Crisis: An Australian perspective*, Canberra, Department of Foreign Affairs and Trade, 2001

Australian Department of Foreign Affairs and Trade website: www.dfat.gov.au (September 2006)

Australian Dictionary of Biography: www.adb.online.anu.edu.au (16 June 2008)

Australian Government, *Australia's Demographic Challenges*, Canberra, Treasury, 2004

Australian Government, *House Hansard*, Canberra, 1998, 2005

Australian Tourist Commission, *Annual Report 1967–68*, Melbourne, Australian Tourist Commission, 1968

Backhouse, Alfred P., *Report of Royal Commission of Inquiry into the Working of Compulsory Conciliation and Arbitration Laws*, Sydney, New South Wales Legislative Assembly, 12 July 1901

Bade, James N. (ed.), *Out of the Shadow of War: The German connection with New Zealand in the 20th century*, Melbourne, Oxford University Press, 1998

Bairam, E., J. M. Howells and G. Turner, *Production Functions in Cricket: The Australian and New Zealand experience*, Dunedin, University of Otago, 1989

Baird, Rosemary, 'Anzac Peacekeeping: Trans-Tasman responses to the Bougainville crisis in 1997 and the subsequent evolution of Australia's and New Zealand's regional peacekeeping', MA thesis, University of Canterbury, 2008

Barcan, Alan, *A History of Australian Education*, Melbourne, Oxford University Press, 1980

Bayly, C. A., *The Birth of the Modern World 1780–1914*, The Blackwell History of the World, Oxford & Malden, Mass., Blackwell Publishers, 2004

Beaglehole, J. C., 'The Development of New Zealand Nationality', *Journal of World History*, Vol. 2, No. 1, 1954, pp. 110–22

Bean, C. E. W., *The Official History of Australia in the War of 1914–1918*, Vol. 1, *The Story of Anzac: From the outbreak of war to the end of the first phase of the Gallipoli campaign, May 4, 1915*, Brisbane, University of Queensland Press/Australian War Memorial, 1981 (first pub. 1921)

Becht, R., *A New Breed Rising: The Warriors Winfield Cup challenge*, Auckland, HarperCollins, 1994

Bedford, R., R. Didham, E. Ho and G. Hugo, 'Maori Internal and International Migration at the Turn of the Century: An Australasian perspective', *New Zealand Population Review*, Vol. 30, Nos 1 & 2, 2004, pp. 131–41

Bedford, Richard and Elsie Ho, 'Migration from Australia to New Zealand: Who are these trans-Tasman migrants?', paper, University of Waikato, 2005

Beilharz, Peter, *Imagining the Antipodes: Culture, theory and the visual in the work of Bernard Smith*, Melbourne, Cambridge University Press, 1997

Beilharz, Peter, 'The Antipodes: Another civilization, between Manhattan and the Rhine?', *New Zealand Sociology*, Vol. 17, No. 2, 2002, pp. 164–78

Beilharz, Peter, 'Australia and New Zealand: Looking backward, looking forward and the parting of ways', *New Zealand Sociology*, Vol. 22, No. 2, 2007, pp. 315–24.

Beilharz, Peter, 'From Sociology to Culture, via Media: Thoughts from the Antipodes', address, American Sociological Association Conference, New York, 11 August 2007, 4 pp

Belich, James, *Paradise Reforged: A history of the New Zealanders from the 1880s to the year 2000*, Auckland, Allen Lane/Penguin, 2001

Bennett, James, 'Social Security, the "Money Power" and the Great Depression: The international dimension to Australian and New Zealand Labour in office', *Australian Journal of Politics and History*, Vol. 43, No. 3, 1997, pp. 312–30

Bennett, James, *'Rats and Revolutionaries': The labour movement in Australia and New Zealand 1890–1940*, Dunedin, University of Otago Press, 2004

Blainey, Geoffrey, *The Rush that Never Ended: A history of Australian mining*, Melbourne, Melbourne University Press, 1963

Blainey, Geoffrey, *The Tyranny of Distance: How distance shaped Australia's history*, revised edn, Sydney, Macmillan, 2001 (first pub. 1966)

Bisman, Ron, *A Salute to Trotting: A history of harness racing in New Zealand*, Auckland, Moa Publications, 1983

Bolitho, D. G., 'Some Financial and Medico-political Aspects of the New Zealand Medical Profession's Reaction to the Introduction of Social Security', *New Zealand Journal of History*, Vol. 18, No. 1, 1984, pp. 34–49

Bollard, Alan and Darcy McCormack assisted by Mark Scanlan, *Closer Economic Relations: A view from both sides of the Tasman*, Wellington & Melbourne, Committee for Economic Development of Australia and New Zealand Institute of Economic Research, 1985

Bowen, Ian, 'De Gaulle's Europe and Australia', Committee for Economic Development of Australia, *Growth*, No. 4, May 1963, Melbourne, Committee for Economic Development of Australia, 1963

Brabazon, Tara, *Tracking the Jack: A retracing of the Antipodes*, Sydney, University of New South Wales Press, 2000

Brassel, S., *A Portrait of Racing: Horseracing in Australia and New Zealand since 1970*, Brookvale, Simon and Schuster, 1990

Brayshay, M., M. Cleary and J. Selwood, 'Interlocking Directorships and Trans-national Linkages within the British Empire, 1900–1930', *Area*, Vol. 37, No. 2, 2005, pp. 209–22

Brawley, Shaun, *The White Peril: Foreign relations and Asian immigration to Australasia and North America 1919–78*, Sydney, University of New South Wales Press, 1995

Brennan, Geoffrey and Francis G. Castles (eds), *Australia Reshaped: 200 years of institutional transformation*, Cambridge & Melbourne, Cambridge University Press, 2002

Breward, Ian, *A History of the Churches in Australasia*, Oxford, Oxford University Press, 2001

'Brief History': www.harness.org.au/inter/history.htm (16 June 2008)

Britain, Ian, 'Australasian?', *Meanjin*, Vol. 63, No. 2, 2004, pp. 1–2

Brown, Bruce (ed.), *New Zealand and Australia: Where are we going?* NZ Institute of International Affairs seminar, Wellington, NZ Institute of International Affairs, 2001

Brown, Nicholas, 'Born Modern: Antipodean variations on a theme', *Historical Journal*, Vol. 48, No. 4, 2005, pp. 1139–54

Bryder, Linda, *A Voice for Mothers: The Plunket Society and infant welfare, 1907–2000*, Auckland, Auckland University Press, 2003

Burnett, Alan and Robin Burnett, *The Australia and New Zealand Nexus*, Canberra, Australian Institute of International Affairs/NZ Institute of International Affairs, 1978

Butchers, A. G., *Education in New Zealand*, Dunedin, Coulls, Somerville Wilkie, 1930

Cain, P. J. and A. G. Hopkins, *British Imperialism: Crisis and deconstruction, 1914–1990*, London & New York, Longman, 1993

Campbell, Colin, 'Juggling Inputs, Outputs and Outcomes in the Search for Policy Competence: Recent experience in Australia', *Governance*, Vol. 14, 2001, pp. 253–82

Capling, Ann and Brian Galligan, *Beyond the Protective State*, Cambridge & Melbourne, Cambridge University Press, 1992

Carmichael, Gordon A. (ed.), *Trans-Tasman Migration: Trends, causes and consequences*, Canberra, Australian Government Publishing Service, 1993

Carr, J. P., 'The First Golden Age? A social history of New Zealand cricket 1914–1939', MA thesis, University of Canterbury, 2001

Cashman, R. et al., *The Oxford Companion to Australian Cricket*, Melbourne, Oxford University Press, 1996

Cashman, R., *Sport in the National Imagination: Australian sport in the federation decades*, Sydney, Walla Press/Centre for Olympic Studies, University of New South Wales, 2002

Castles, Francis G., *The Working Class and Welfare: Reflections on the political development of the welfare state in Australia and New Zealand, 1890–1980*, Wellington & Sydney, Allen & Unwin: Port Nicholson Press, 1985

Castles, Francis G., *Australian Public Policy and Economic Vulnerability: A comparative and historical perspective*, Sydney, Allen & Unwin, 1988

Castles, Francis G. (ed.), *Families of Nations: Patterns of public policy in western democracies*, Dartmouth, Aldershot, 1993

Castles, Francis, Rolf Gerritsen and Jack Vowles (eds), *The Great Experiment: Labour parties and public policy transformation in Australia and New Zealand*, Auckland, Auckland University Press, 1996

Castles, Francis G., Jennifer Curtin and Jack Vowles, 'Public Policy in Australia and New Zealand: The new global context', *Australian Journal of Political Science*, Vol. 41, No. 2, June 2006, pp. 131–43

Catley, Bob, *Waltzing with Matilda: Should New Zealand join Australia?*, Wellington, Dark Horse Publishing, 2001

Catley, Bob (ed.), *NZ–Australia Relations: Moving together or drifting apart?*, Papers from the 36th Otago Foreign Policy School, Wellington, Dark Horse Publishing, 2002

Chapman, Valerie and Peter Read (eds), *Terrible Hard Biscuits: A reader in Aboriginal history*, Sydney, Allen & Unwin, 1996

Christian Brothers, *History of Australia and New Zealand for Catholic Schools*, Strathfield, Christian Brothers Australia, 1938 (c. 1929)

Coghlan, T. A., *A Statistical Account of the Seven Colonies of Australasia, 1901–1902*, Sydney, Government Printer, 1902

Coldrey, Barry, 'The Christian Brothers and School Discipline', *History of Education*, Vol.

21, No. 3, 1992, pp. 277–89

Coleman, P. J., 'New Zealand Liberalism and the Origins of the American Welfare State', *Journal of American History*, Vol. 69, No. 2, 1982, pp. 372–91

Collins, T., *Rugby's Great Split: Class, culture, and the origins of rugby league football*, London, Frank Cass, 1998.

Collins, T., *'Ahr Waggy' Harold Wagstaff and the Making of Anglo–Australian Rugby League Culture*, Sydney, Tom Brock Bequest Committee & Australian Society for Sports History, 2004.

Conference of Government Statists, *Report of the Conference of Government Statists held in Tasmania, January 1875*, Victoria Parliamentary Papers, No. 11, 1875

Conference of Statists, 'Census of Australasia, 1891 (Report of)', in *Conference of Statists*, Hobart, 1890

Connelly, Matthew, 'Seeing Beyond the State: The population control movement and the problem of sovereignty', *Past and Present*, No. 193, November 2006, pp. 197–233

Cookson, J. and G. Dunstall (eds), *Southern Capital: Christchurch: Towards a city biography 1850–2000*, Christchurch, Canterbury University Press, 2000

Cosgrove, General Peter, *My Story*, Sydney, HarperCollins Publishers, 2006

Costello, John and Pat Finnegan, *Tapestry of Turf: The history of New Zealand racing, 1840–1987*, Auckland, Moa Publications, 1988

Council of Australian Governments, *Commonwealth–State Ministerial Councils: A compendium*, July 2006

Crawford, J. G. (ed.), *Australian Trade Policy 1942–1966: A documentary history*, Canberra, ANU Press, 1968

Crotty, Martin, *Making the Australian Male: Middle class masculinity 1870–1920*, Melbourne, Melbourne University Press, 2001

Cuervo-Cazurra, A., 'Who Cares about Corruption?', *Journal of International Business Studies*, Vol. 37, 2006, pp. 807–22

Cullen, M., Address to NZ Gala Day Dinner, Sydney Foundation Hall, Museum of Contemporary Art, 10 March 2005

Cumming, Ian, *Glorious Enterprise: History of the Auckland Education Board 1857–1957*, Christchurch, Whitcombe & Tombs, 1959

Curnow, G. R. and R. L. Wettenhall (eds), *Understanding Public Administration: Essays in honour of R .S. Parker & R. N. Spann*, Sydney, Allen & Unwin, 1981

Darwin, John, *After Tamerlane: The global history of empire since 1405*, London, Allen Lane, 2007

Davidson, A. K. and P. Lineham, *Transplanted Christianity*, Palmerston North, Dunmore Press, 1997

Davidson, Jim, 'Dominion Culture', *Meanjin*, Vol. 63, No. 3, 2004, pp. 75–83

Davis, R. P., 'New Zealand Liberalism and Tasmanian Labor, 1891–1916', *Labour History*, Vol. 21, November 1971, pp. 24–35

Davis, R. P., '"A real and quite unique affinity": New Zealand and Tasmanian Labor, 1939–1949', *Labour History*, No. 40, May 1981, pp. 68–76

Davis, Richard, 'New Zealand Labour Government and the ALP 1939–40: An image of independence', *Electronic Journal of Australian and New Zealand History*, October 1996

Davison, Graeme, 'Australia: The first suburban nation?', *Journal of Urban History*, Vol. 22, No. 1, November 1995, pp. 40–74 de Brosses, Charles, *Histoire des Navigations aux Terres Australes*, Paris, Durand, 1756; Engl. trans. by J. Callander (without acknowledgment), Edinburgh, 1766–68

Dening, Greg, *Xavier: A centenary portrait*, Kew, Old Xaverians, 1978

Denoon, Donald and Philippa Mein Smith, with Marivic Wyndham, *A History of Australia, New Zealand and the Pacific*, The Blackwell History of the World, Oxford & Malden, Mass., Blackwell Publishers, 2000

Denoon, Donald, 'Re-Membering Australasia: A repressed memory', *Australian Historical Studies*, Vol. 34, No. 122, October 2003, pp. 290–304

Department of Foreign Affairs and Trade, *The Big End of Town and Australia's Trading Interests*, Canberra, Commonwealth of Australia, 2002

Department of Transport and Regional Services, Australia's trade and investment relations under ANZCER, Joint Standing Committee on Foreign Affairs, Defence and Trade, Trade Sub-Committee, submission No. 5, Canberra, April 2006

Deverson, Tony and Graeme Kennedy (eds), *The New Zealand Oxford Dictionary*, Melbourne, Oxford University Press, 2005

Dick, Howard, 'Big Questions in Australian Economic History: From the outside looking in', *Australian Economic History Review*, Vol. 47, No. 3, November 2007, pp. 316–22

Dilke, Charles W., *Problems of Greater Britain*, 2nd edn, London, Macmillan, 1890

Dix, John, *Stranded in Paradise: New Zealand rock 'n' roll 1955–1988*, Auckland, Paradise Publications, 1988

Dolowitz, D. and D. Marsh, 'Learning from Abroad: The role of policy transfer in contemporary policy-making', *Governance*, Vol. 13, 2000, pp. 5–24

Dowie, J. A., 'Studies in New Zealand Investment 1871–1900', PhD thesis, ANU, 1965

Dunstall, Graeme, *A Policeman's Paradise? Policing a stable society, 1918–1945: The history of policing in New Zealand*, Vol. 4, Palmerston North, Dunmore Press/ Historical Branch, 1999

Editorial Introduction, *New Zealand Journal of History*, Vol. 34, No. 1, April 2000

Emilsen, S. and W. W. Emilsen (eds), *Mapping the Landscape: Essays in Australian and New Zealand Christianity*, New York, Peter Lang, 2000

Evans, Lewis, Arthur Grimes, Bryce Wilkinson and David Teece, 'Economic Reform in New Zealand 1984–95: The pursuit of efficiency', *Journal of Economic Literature*, Vol. 34, 1996, pp. 1856–1902

Fagan, S., *The Rugby Rebellion: The divide of league and union*, Kellyville NSW, RL1908, 2005.

Fairburn, Miles, *The Ideal Society and Its Enemies*, Auckland, Auckland University Press, 1989

Fairburn, Miles, 'Is There a Good Case for New Zealand Exceptionalism?' in Tony Ballantyne and Brian Moloughney (eds), *Disputed Histories: Imagining New Zealand's Pasts*, Dunedin, University of Otago Press, 2006, pp. 143–67

Fairburn, Miles, 'Is There a Good Case for New Zealand Exceptionalism?', *Thesis Eleven*, Vol. 92, No. 1, 2008, pp. 29–49 [shorter, revised version]

Ferguson, Niall, *The War of the World: History's age of hatred*, London, Allen Lane, 2006

Finn, Jeremy, 'New Zealand Lawyers and "Overseas" Precedent 1874–1973: Lessons from the Otago District Law Society Library', *Otago Law Review*, Vol. 11, No. 2, 2006, pp. 1–26

FitzSimons, Peter, *The Rugby War*, Sydney, HarperSports, 2003

Flannery, Tim, *The Future Eaters: An ecological history of the Australasian lands and people*, Sydney, Reed Books, 1994

Flitton, Daniel, 'Issues in Australian Foreign Policy: July to December 2003', *Australian Journal of Politics and History*, Vol. 50, No. 2, 2004, pp. 229–46

Foley, John, *Queensland Harry*, Waimate, John Foley, 2005

Fonterra, Submission No. 2, Australia's Trade and Investment Relations under the Australia–New Zealand Closer Economic Relations Trade Agreement, Joint Standing Committee on Foreign Affairs, Defence and Trade, 2006: www.aph.gov. au/house/committee/jfadt/nz_cer/subs.htm (2 August 2006)

Forster, Colin and Cameron Hazelhurst, 'Australian Statisticians and the Development of Official Statistics', *Yearbook Australia*, Vol. 71, 1988, pp. 24–26

Foster, S. G. and Margaret Varghese, *The Making of the Australian National University*, St Leonards, NSW, Allen & Unwin, 1996

Fountain, H., 'Technology Acquisition, Firm Capability and Sustainable Competitive Advantage: A case study of Australian Glass Manufacturers Ltd, 1915–39', *Business History*, Vol. 42, No. 3, 2000, pp. 89–108

Frances, Raelene and Melanie Nolan, 'Gender and Labour in "a Manzone Country" and "a Man's Country": National, transnational, international and comparative labour history', *Labour History*, Vol. 95, November 2008 (forthcoming)

Freeman, M., 'Australian Universities at War', in Roy Macleod (ed.), *Science and the Pacific War: Science and survival in the Pacific 1939–45*, Dordrecht, Kluwer, 2000

Freestone, Robert, 'An Imperial Aspect: The Australasian town planning tour of 1914–15', *Australian Journal of Politics and History*, Vol. 44, No. 2, 1998, pp. 159–76

Fry, Eric (ed.), *Common Cause: Essays in Australian and New Zealand labour history*, Wellington, Allen & Unwin/Port Nicholson Press, 1986

Galbraith, John Kenneth, *The World Economy since the Wars: A personal view*, London, Sinclair-Stevenson, 1994

Galligan, Brian and Richard Mulgan, 'Asymmetric Political Association: The Australasian experiment', in Robert Agranoff (ed.), *Accommodating Diversity: Asymmetry in federal states*, Baden-Baden, NOMOS Publishing, 1999, pp. 57–72

Gammage, Bill, *The Broken Years: Australian Soldiers in the Great War*, Canberra, ANU Press, 1974

Gate, Robert, *Rugby League: An illustrated history*, London, A. Barker, 1989

Gauld, Robin, *Revolving Doors: New Zealand's health reforms*, Wellington, Institute of Policy Studies/Health Services Research Centre, Victoria University of Wellington, 2001

'Geoffrey Bolton in Conversation with Jill Roe', *Australian Historical Association Bulletin*, No. 93, December 2001, pp. 40–53

Gerber, David, 'Theories and Lives: Transnationalism and the Conceptualization of International Migrations to the United States', *IMIS Beiträge (Institut für Migrationsforschung und interkulturelle Studien Universität Osnabrück)*, No. 15, 2000, pp. 31–51

Gilbert, Alan D., K. S. Inglis and S. G. Foster (gen. eds), *Australians: A historical library*, 10 Vols, Sydney, Fairfax, Syme & Weldon, 1987

Glass, Margaret, *Charles Cameron Kingston: Federation father*, Melbourne, Miegunyah Press at Melbourne University Press, 1997

Goddard, David QC, 'Case Study: Trans-Tasman court proceedings and regulatory enforcement', Whose Law is it Anyway? Legal Research Foundation, Harmonising Australian and New Zealand Business Laws Conference, Wellington, 9 March 2007

Goff, Phil, 'Making Globalisation Work for the Pacific', *Pacific Connection*, issue 13, September–November 2007, pp. 3–4

Goldfinch, Shaun, 'Evaluating Public Sector Reform in New Zealand: Have the benefits been oversold?', *Asian Journal of Public Administration*, Vol. 20, 1998, pp. 203–32.

Goldfinch, Shaun, *Remaking New Zealand and Australian Economic Policy*, Wellington & Washington DC, Victoria University Press/Georgetown University Press, 2000

Goldfinch, Shaun, 'The Old Boys' Network? Social ties and policy consensus amongst Australian and New Zealand economic policy elites', *Policy, Organisation and Society*, Vol. 21, No. 2, 2002, pp. 1–25

Goldfinch, Shaun, 'Economic Reform in New Zealand: Radical liberalisation in a small economy', *Otemon Bulletin of Australian Studies*, Vol. 30, 2004, pp. 75–98

Goldfinch, Shaun, 'Australia, New Zealand and the Pacific Island Nations: Interweaved histories, shared futures', *Otemon Bulletin of Australian Studies*, Vol. 31, 2005, pp. 29–45

Goldfinch, Shaun and Daniel Malpass, 'The Polish Shipyard: Myth, economic history and economic reform in New Zealand', *Australian Journal of Politics and History*, Vol. 53, No. 1, 2007, pp. 118–37

Goldfinch, Shaun and Philippa Mein Smith, 'Compulsory Arbitration and the Australasian Model of State Development: Policy transfer, learning and innovation', *Journal of Policy History*, Vol. 18, No. 4, 2006, pp. 419–45

Golding, Peter, *Black Jack McEwen: Political Gladiator*, Melbourne, Melbourne University Press, 1996

Goldstone, Ross, 'Opportunism in Evangelism 1919–1939', in A. J. Ferch (ed.), *Journey of Hope: Seventh Day Adventist history in the South Pacific 1919–1950*, Wahroonga, South Pacific Division of Seventh Day Adventists, 1991, pp. 93–99

Gould, J. D., *The Muldoon Years: An essay on New Zealand's recent economic growth*, Auckland, Hodder & Stoughton, 1985

Goyen, Peter, *A Report to the Otago Education Board on State Education in Three Australian States and New Zealand*, Dunedin, Coulls, Culling & Co., 1902

Grant, D., *On a Roll: A history of gambling and lotteries in New Zealand*, Wellington, Victoria University Press, 1994

Grant, Ian F., *The Other Side of the Ditch: A cartoon century in the New Zealand–Australia relationship*, Wellington, New Zealand Cartoon Archive/Tandem Press, 2001

Grant, Kevin, Philippa Levine and Frank Trentmann (eds), *Beyond Sovereignty: Britain, Empire and transnationalism, c. 1880–1950*, Houndmills, Basingstoke, Palgrave, 2007

Grimes, Arthur, 'Trans-Tasman Transaction Costs, Terms of Trade and Currency Union', *(Australian) Economic Papers*, special issue, 2001, pp. 52–63

Grimes, Arthur, 'Regional and Industry Cycles in Australasia: Implications for a common currency', *Journal of Asian Economics*, Vol. 16, No. 3, 2005, pp. 380–97

Grimes, Arthur, 'Intra and Inter-regional Industry Shocks: A new metric with application to Australasian currency union', *New Zealand Economic Papers*, Vol. 40, No. 1, 2006, pp. 23–44

Grimes, Arthur and Frank Holmes with Roger Bowden, *An ANZAC Dollar? Currency union and business development*, Wellington, Institute of Policy Studies, Victoria University of Wellington, 2000

Grimes, Arthur, Lydia Wevers and Ginny Sullivan (eds), *States of Mind: Australia and New Zealand 1901–2001*, Wellington, Institute of Policy Studies, Victoria

University of Wellington, 2002

Guest, Morris and John Singleton, 'The Murupara Project and Industrial Development in New Zealand 1945–65', *Australian Economic History Review*, Vol. 39, No. 1, March 1999, pp. 52–71

Haines, Nicolas (ed.), *The Tasman: Frontier and freeway?*, Proceedings of the Second Conference on 'Australia's World', Canberra, Centre for Continuing Education, ANU, 1972

Hamer, Paul, *Maori in Australia: Nga Maori i te Ao Moemoea*, Wellington, Te Puni Kokiri, 2007

Hancock, W. K., *Australia*, London, Ernest Benn, 1930

Hanson, Elizabeth, *The Politics of Social Security: The 1938 Act and some later developments*, Auckland, Auckland University Press, 1980

Harford, Shelley, 'A Trans-Tasman Community: Organisational links between the ACTU and NZFOL/NZCTU, 1970–1990', MA thesis, University of Canterbury, 2006

Harrigan, Nicholas, 'Political Power and Political Divisions within Australian and New Zealand Business', paper, Politics and Interlocking Directorates Conference, University of Barcelona, 28–29 September 2006

Harte, Chris, *A History of Australian Cricket*, London, Andre Deutsch, 1993

Hartley Grattan, C., *The Southwest Pacific since 1900: A modern history: Australia, New Zealand, the Islands, Antarctica*, The University of Michigan History of the Modern World, Ann Arbor, University of Michigan Press, 1963

Hawes, P. and L. Barker, *Court in the Spotlight: History of New Zealand netball*, Auckland, Netball New Zealand, 1999

Hawke, Allan, Address to the New Zealand Institute of International Affairs, Wellington, 12 February 2004

Hawke, Allan, 'From CER to One Market', Speech to CPA Australia New Zealand Branch, Wellington 30 June 2004

Hawke, Allan, 'The Anzacs', unpub. seminar paper, University of Canterbury, 21 April 2005

Hawke, G. R., *Between Governments and Banks: A history of the Reserve Bank of New Zealand*, Wellington, Government Printer, 1973

Hayburn, Ralph (ed.), *Foreign Policy School 1978: Australia and New Zealand relations*, Dunedin, University of Otago, 1978

Haynes, J., *From All Blacks to All Golds: New Zealand's rugby league pioneers*, Christchurch, Ryan and Haynes, 1996

Hayter, H. H., *Notes of a Tour in New Zealand*, Melbourne, 1874 (printed for private circulation)

Hazledine, Tim and John Quiggin, 'No More Free Beer Tomorrow? Economic policy and outcomes in Australia and New Zealand since 1984', *Australian Journal of Political Science*, Vol. 41, No. 2, 2006, pp. 145–59

Heads, Ian, *True Blue: The story of the NSW rugby league*, Randwick NSW, Ironbark Press, 1992

Healey, Denis, *The Time of My Life*, London, Michael Joseph, 1989

Hempenstall, Peter, 'The Australia New Zealand Leadership Forums': www.nzac.canterbury.ac.nz/docs/leadershipforums

Hempenstall, Peter, 'Overcoming Separate Histories: Historians as 'Ideas Traders' in a trans-Tasman world', *History Australia*, Vol. 4, No. 1, June 2007, pp. 4.1–4.16

Henderson, John and Greg Watson (eds), *Securing a Peaceful Pacific*, Christchurch, Canterbury University Press, 2005

Hensley, Gerald, *Final Approaches: A memoir*, Auckland, Auckland University Press, 2006

Herr, Richard, 'The American Impact on Australian Defence Relations with the South Pacific Islands', *Australian Outlook*, Vol. 38, December 1984, pp. 184–90

Hirst, John, *The Sentimental Nation: The making of the Australian Commonwealth*, Melbourne, Oxford University Press, 2000

Hoadley, Steve, *New Zealand and Australia: Negotiating closer economic relations*, Wellington, NZ Institute of International Affairs, 1995

Hofstede, G. and G. J. Hofstede, *Cultures and Organizations: Software of the mind*, New York, McGraw Hill, 2005

Holmes, Frank, 'The Rocky Road to CER', *IPS Policy Paper*, No. 17, 2003, pp. 1–27, Institute of Policy Studies, Victoria University of Wellington

Holt, James, *Compulsory Arbitration in New Zealand: The first forty years*, Auckland, Auckland University Press, 1986

Hook, Milton, *Avondale: Experiment on the Dora*, Cooranbong, Avondale Academic Press, 1998

Howard, John, 'Transcript of the Prime Minister the Hon. John Howard PM Joint Press Conference with the Prime Minister of New Zealand Helen Clark, Parliament House, Canberra', 8 February 2006: www.pm.gov.au/news/interviews/ Interview1767.html

'Howard Morrison': www.sergent.com.au/howardmorrison.html (16 June 2008)

Howe, K. R., *Race Relations Australia and New Zealand: A comparative survey 1770s– 1970s*, Wellington & Sydney, Methuen, 1977

Howell, M. L., X. Lingyu and P. Horton, *Bledisloe Magic*, Auckland, Rugby Publishing, 1995

Howitt, B., *SANZAR Saga*, Auckland, HarperCollins, 2005

Howitt, B. and D. Haworth, *Rugby Nomads*, Auckland, HarperSports, 2002

Hughes, Joan (ed.), *The Concise Australian National Dictionary*, Melbourne, Oxford University Press, 1992

Hugo, Graeme, 'Future Immigration Policy Development in Australia and New Zealand', *New Zealand Population Review*, Vol. 30, nos 1 & 2, 2004, pp. 23–42

Hugo, Graeme, 'New Zealanders in Australia in 2001', *New Zealand Population Review*, Vol. 30, Nos 1 & 2, 2004, pp. 61–92

Hutchinson, G., *They're Racing: The complete story of New Zealand and Australian racing*, Melbourne, Penguin, 1999

Hutchinson, Mark, '"… Goes without Saying": Themes for trans-Tasman religious research', *Australasian Pentecostalist Studies*, No. 5–6, March–October 2001, pp. 53–62

Inglis, K. S., *Sacred Places: War memorials in the Australian landscape*, Melbourne, Miegunyah Press at Melbourne University Press, 1998

'Inquiry into Defence beyond 2000, Report of the Foreign Affairs, Defence and Trade Committee', Hon. Derek Quigley Chairperson, August 1999, *Appendix to the Journal of the House of Representatives of New Zealand*, Vol. 58, 1996–99

International Monetary Fund, *Manual on Fiscal Transparency*, Washington DC, 2001

Ip, Manying, *Dragons on the Long White Cloud: The making of Chinese New Zealanders*, Auckland, Auckland University Press, 1996

Jackson, H. R., *Churches and People in Australia and New Zealand 1860–1930*, Wellington, Allen & Unwin/Port Nicholson Press, 1987

Jackson, Margaret, 'It's Time for the Tasman Economic Area (TEA)', Address to Trans-Tasman Business Council, 12 May 2004

James, Colin, *A New Path: The Tasman connection*, Wellington, Australia–New Zealand Foundation, January 1982, 67 pp

James, Colin, 'The Pacific-ation of New Zealand', in Anne Henderson (ed.), *Sydney Papers*, Vol. 17, issue 1, summer 2005, pp. 138–45

James, Colin, 'The Elusive Single Economic Market', Whose Law is it Anyway? Legal Research Foundation, Harmonising Australian and New Zealand Business Laws Conference, Wellington, 9 March 2007, 8 pp

James, Colin, 'Three-step with Matilda: Trans-Tasman relations', in Roderic Alley (ed.), *New Zealand in World Affairs IV: 1990–2005*, Wellington, Victoria University Press/NZ Institute of International Affairs, 2007, pp. 23–53

Jenkins, P. and M. Alvarez, *Wallaby Gold: 100 years of Australian test rugby*, Sydney, Random House, 1999

Jobbling, I. and P. Barham, 'The Development of Netball and the All-Australia Women's Basketball Association (AAWBBA) 1891–1939', *Sporting Traditions*, Vol. 8, November 1991, pp. 29–48

Johanson, J. and F. Wiedersheim-Paul, 'The Internationalization Process of a Firm: Four Swedish case studies', *Journal of Management Studies*, Vol. 12, 1975, pp. 305–22

Joint Committee of Public Accounts, Parliament of the Commonwealth of Australia, *Financial Reporting for the Commonwealth: Towards greater transparency and accountability*, Canberra, 1995

Kay, Robin (ed.), *The Australian–New Zealand Agreement 1944*, Wellington, Government Printer/Historical Publications Branch, 1972

Keating, Paul, *Engagement: Australia faces the Asia–Pacific*, Sydney, Macmillan, 2000

Keith, Hamish, *The Big Picture: A history of New Zealand art from 1642*, Auckland, Godwit, 2007

Keller, W. W. and T. G. Rawski (eds), *China's Rise and the Balance of Influence in Asia*, Pittsburgh, University of Pittsburgh Press, 2007

Kelly, Paul, *The End of Certainty: The story of the 1980s*, Sydney, Allen & Unwin, 1992

Kelly, Veronica, 'A Complementary Economy? National markets and international product in early Australian theatre managements', *New Theatre Quarterly*, Vol. 21, No. 1, February 2005, pp. 77–95

Kelsey, Jane, *Economic Fundamentalism*, London, Pluto Press, 1995

Knowles, Brett, *The History of a New Zealand Pentecostal Movement: The New Life churches of New Zealand from 1946 to 1979*, Lewiston, Edwin Mellen Press, 2000

Lake, Marilyn and Henry Reynolds, *Drawing the Global Colour Line: White men's countries and the question of racial equality*, Melbourne, Melbourne University Press, 2008

Lange, David, *Nuclear Free: The New Zealand way*, Auckland, Penguin, 1990

Laracy, H., 'The Catholic Church in New Zealand: A historical perspective', in H. Bergin and S. Smith (eds), *He Kupu Whakawairua: Sprituality in Aotearoa New Zealand: Catholic voices*, Auckland, Accent, 2002

Le Rossignol, James E. and William Downie Stewart, *State Socialism in New Zealand*, New York, Harrap, 1910

Leach, Helen, *The Pavlova Story: A slice of New Zealand's culinary history*, Dunedin, Otago University Press, 2008

Leitch, P. and R. Becht, *The Year the Kiwis Flew: From wooden spooners to winners*,

Auckland, HarperSports, 2006

Litster, G., 'The SDA School System in New Zealand', in Peter Ballis (ed.), *In and Out of the World: Seventh Day Adventists in New Zealand*, Palmerston North, Dunmore Press, 1985, pp. 109–30

Litster, W. G., 'Factors Influencing the Development of the Curriculum in Seventh Day Adventist Schools in Australia and New Zealand 1892–1977', PhD thesis, University of Newcastle, 1982

Little, C., *The Northern Game in the South: The rise and fall of rugby league in Otago, 1924–1935*, History Hons essay, University of Otago, 1994

Livingston, W. S. and Wm. R. Louis (eds), *Australia, New Zealand and the Pacific Islands since the First World War*, Canberra, ANU Press, 1979

Lloyd, Henry Demarest, *A Country without Strikes: A visit to the compulsory Arbitration Court of New Zealand*, New York, Doubleday, 1900 (also London, Gay & Bird, 1901)

Lloyd, Henry Demarest, *Newest England: Notes of a democratic traveller in New Zealand, with some Australian comparisons*, New York, Doubleday, 1900

Lloyd, Trevor, 'Church Schools', in Noel Clapham (ed.), *Seventh Day Adventists in the South Pacific 1885–1985*, Warburton, Vic., Signs Publishing, 1986, pp. 168–85

Lynch, Brian (ed.), *New Zealand and the World: The major foreign policy issues, 2005–2010*, Wellington, NZ Institute of International Affairs, 2006

McAloon, Jim, *No Idle Rich: The wealthy in Canterbury and Otago 1840–1914*, Dunedin, University of Otago Press, 2002

McAloon, Jim, 'New Zealand on the Pacific Frontier: Environment, economy and culture', *History Compass*, Vol. 4, No. 1, 2006, pp. 36–42

McAloon, Jim, 'Unsettling Recolonisation: Labourism, Keynesianism and Australasia from the 1890s to the 1950s', *Thesis Eleven*, No. 92, February 2008, pp. 50–68

McArthur, M., 'Luck and the Unexpected Vacancy', *Research School of Pacific and Asian Studies Quarterly Bulletin*, Vol. 2, No. 4, December 2001, pp. 12–14

McCaskill, Murray, 'The Tasman Connection: Aspects of Australia–New Zealand relations', *Australian Geographical Studies*, Vol. 20, April 1982, pp. 3–23

McCrystal, J., *The Originals: 1905 All Black rugby odyssey*, Auckland, Random House, 2005

Macdonald, C., 'Netball New Zealand', in A. Else (ed.), *Women Together: A history of women's organisations in New Zealand*, Wellington, Historical Branch, Department of Internal Affairs, 1993

McElhatton, E., 'Australia and New Zealand: Like-minded partners?', *New Zealand International Review*, July/August 2006, pp. 18–21

McEwen, John, *Australia's Overseas Economic Relationships*, Sixteenth Roy Milne Memorial Lecture, Brisbane, 5 July 1965, Brisbane, Australian Institute of International Affairs, 1965

McEwen, John and Don Veitch, *McEwen's Way*, Melbourne, David Syme College of National Economics, Public Administration & Business, c. 1996

McGeorge, Colin, 'The Moral Curriculum: Forming the Kiwi character', in Gary McCulloch (ed.), *The School Curriculum in New Zealand: History, theory, policy and practice*, Palmerston North, Dunmore Press, 1992, pp. 40–52

McGibbon, Ian (ed.), *The Oxford Companion to New Zealand Military History*, Auckland, Oxford University Press, 2000

McGlade, J. A., 'Australia's Debt to New Zealand', *Christian Brothers Studies*, Vol. 50,

No. 2, 1977, pp. 1–5

Macintyre, Stuart, *A Colonial Liberalism: The lost world of three Victorian visionaries*, Oxford & Melbourne, Oxford University Press, 1991

Macintyre, Stuart, *A History for a Nation: Ernest Scott and the making of Australian history*, Melbourne, Melbourne University Press, 1994

Macintyre, S. and R. Mitchell (eds), *Foundations of Arbitration: The origins and effects of state compulsory arbitration 1890–1914*, Melbourne, Oxford University Press, 1989

McIntyre, W. David, 'From Dual Dependency to Nuclear Free', in Geoffrey W. Rice (ed.), *The Oxford History of New Zealand*, 2nd edn, Auckland, Oxford University Press, 1992, ch. 20

McIntyre, W. David, 'Australia, New Zealand, and the Pacific Islands', in Judith M. Brown and Wm. Roger Louis (eds), *The Oxford History of the British Empire*, Vol. 4, Oxford & New York, Oxford University Press, 1999, ch. 29

McKinnon, Malcolm, *Treasury: The New Zealand Treasury, 1840–2000*, Auckland, Auckland University Press/Ministry for Culture and Heritage, 2003

McLaren, Ian, *Whitcombe's Story Books: A trans-Tasman survey*, Parkville, University of Melbourne Library, 1984

McLean, Denis, *The Prickly Pair: Making nationalism in Australia and New Zealand*, Dunedin, University of Otago Press, 2003

McLean, Ian, 'Trans-Tasman Relations: Decline and rise', in Richard Pomfret (ed.), *Australia's Trade Policies*, Melbourne, Oxford University Press, 1995

MacLean, M., 'Of Warriors and Blokes: The problem of Maori rugby for Pakeha masculinity in New Zealand', in T. J. L. Chandler and J. Nauright (eds), *Making the Rugby World: Race, gender, commerce*, London, Frank Cass, 1999

Macleod, Jenny, *Reconsidering Gallipoli*, Manchester, Manchester University Press, 2004

McLeod, Roy (ed.), *The Commonwealth of Science: ANZAAS and the scientific enterprise in Australasia, 1888–1988*, Melbourne, Oxford University Press, 1988

McMillan, Nancy, 'Pressures for Change to the Trans-Tasman Travel Arrangements', MA thesis, University of Canterbury, 1989

McMillan, Stuart, *Neither Confirm Nor Deny: The nuclear ships debate between New Zealand and the United States*, Wellington & Sydney, Allen and Unwin/Port Nicholson Press, also New York, Praeger Publishers, 1987

McNab, Robert, *Murihiku and the Southern Islands*, Christchurch, Kiwi Publishers, 1996 (1st pub.1907)

McNeish, James, *Dance of the Peacocks: New Zealanders in exile in the time of Hitler and Mao Tse-Tung*, Auckland, Vintage, 2003

Mambo, 'In Reg's Own Words': www.mwk16.com/perfectstrangers/GRUV/mambo/mbohome.htm (21 February 2008)

Mangan, J. A. (ed.), *The Imperial Curriculum: Racial images and education in the British colonial experience*, London, Routledge, 1993

Mangan, J. A. and John Nauright (eds), *Sport in Australasian Society: Past and present*, London, Frank Cass, 2000

Manning, R., 'The Two Rugbies', in B. Whimpress (ed.), *The Imaginary Grandstand: Identity and narrative in Australian sport*, Kent Town, Australian Society for Sports History, 2002

March, J. G. and J. P. Olsen,' Institutional Perspectives on Political Institutions', *Governance*, Vol. 9, 1996, pp. 247–64

Marshall, John, *Memoirs Volume Two: 1960 to 1988*, Auckland, Collins, 1989

Martens, Jeremy, 'A Transnational History of Immigration Restriction: Natal and New South Wales, 1896–97', *Journal of Imperial and Commonwealth History*, Vol. 34, No. 3, September 2006, pp. 323–44

Mathews, Russell and Bhajan Grewel, *The Public Sector in Jeopardy: Australian fiscal liberalism from Whitlam to Keating*, Melbourne, Centre for Strategic Economic Studies, Victoria University, 1997

Mein Smith, Philippa, *Mothers and King Baby: Infant survival and welfare in an imperial world: Australia 1880–1950*, Houndmills, Basingstoke, Macmillan, 1997

Mein Smith, Philippa, 'New Zealand', in Helen Irving (ed.), *The Centenary Companion to Australian Federation*, Cambridge, New York & Melbourne, 1999, pp. 400–05

Mein Smith, Philippa, 'New Zealand Federation Commissioners in Australia: One past, two historiographies', *Australian Historical Studies*, Vol. 34, No. 122, October 2003, pp. 305–25

Mein Smith, Philippa, *A Concise History of New Zealand*, Cambridge, New York & Melbourne, Cambridge University Press, 2005

Mein Smith, Philippa, 'Did Muldoon Really "go too slowly" with CER?', *New Zealand Journal of History*, Vol. 41, No. 2, October 2007, pp. 161–79

Mein Smith, Philippa, 'The Tasman World', in Giselle Byrnes (ed.), *The New Oxford History of New Zealand*, Oxford & Melbourne, Oxford University Press, 2009, ch. 16 (in press)

Mein Smith, Philippa and Peter Hempenstall, 'Australia and New Zealand: Turning shared pasts into a shared history', *History Compass*, Vol. 1, No. 1, January 2003, AU 031, pp. 1–8

Mein Smith, Philippa and Peter Hempenstall, 'Changing Community Attitudes to the New Zealand–Australia Relationship', paper prepared for Australia–New Zealand Leadership Forum, 2004

Mein Smith, Philippa and Linda Moore, 'Statisticians Making Settler States and Economies in Australasia, 1870–1930', in M. Lyons (ed.), *History in Global Perspective: Proceedings of the 20th International Congress of Historical Sciences, Sydney 2005*, Sydney, Faculty of Arts and Social Sciences, University of New South Wales Press, 2006

Merrett, D., 'Australian Firms Abroad before 1970: Why so few, why those, and why there?' *Business History*, Vol. 44, No. 2, April 2002, pp. 65–87

Métin, Albert, *Le Socialisme sans Doctrines*, 2nd edn, Paris, F. Alcan, 1910

Miller, Caroline, 'The Origins of Town Planning in New Zealand 1900–1926: A divergent path?', *Planning Perspectives*, Vol. 17, 2002, pp. 209–25

Moloney, Pat, 'State Socialism and Willliam Pember Reeves: A reassessment', in Pat Moloney and Kerry Taylor (eds), *On the Left: Essays on socialism in New Zealand*, Dunedin, University of Otago Press, 2002

Moorhouse, G., *A People's Game: The centenary history of rugby league football 1895–1995*, London, Hodder & Stoughton, 1995

Morgan, Jan, *Speaking for Themselves: Ex-pats have their say*, Auckland, Cape Catley, 2008

Morris, Edward E., *Austral English: A dictionary of Australasian words phrases and usages*, London, Macmillan, 1898

Moses, John A. (ed.), *Historical Disciplines and Culture in Australasia: An assessment*, Brisbane, University of Queensland Press, 1979

Muldoon, Robert, *New Zealand Financial Statement: 1979*, Wellington, Government

Printer, 1979

Muldoon, Robert, *My Way*, Wellington, A. H. & A. W. Reed, 1981

Muldoon, Robert, *The New Zealand Economy: A personal view*, Auckland, Endeavour Press, 1985

Munz, Peter (ed.), *The Feel of Truth: Essays in New Zealand and Pacific history*, Wellington, A. H. & A. W. Reed, 1969

Murray, Colin, 'The New Zealand Trade Commissioner Service', 1961, copy courtesy of Paul Cotton

Nash, Walter, *New Zealand Financial Statement: 1946*, Wellington, Government Printer, 1946

National Commission of Audit, *Report to the Commonwealth Government*, Canberra, 1996

Nauright, J. and J. Broomhall, 'A Woman's Game: The development of netball and a female sporting culture in New Zealand 1906–70', *International Journal of the History of Sport*, Vol. 11, No. 3, December 1994, pp. 387–407

Neely, D. O., R. King and F. Payne, *Men in White: The history of New Zealand international cricket, 1894–1985*, Auckland, Moa, 1986

Neumann, Klaus, Nicholas Thomas and Hilary Ericksen (eds), *Quicksands: Foundational histories in Australia and Aotearoa New Zealand*, Sydney, University of New South Wales Press, 1999

New Zealand Dictionary of Biography: www.dnzb.govt.nz (16 June 2008)

New Zealand Government, Submission No. 9, Australia's Trade and Investment Relations under the Australia–New Zealand Closer Economic Relations Trade Agreement, Joint Standing Committee on Foreign Affairs, Defence and Trade, 2006: www.aph.gov.au/house/committee/jfadt/nz_cer/subs.htm (2 August 2006)

New Zealand Historical Association Newsletter, April 2004

New Zealand Institute of International Affairs, *New Zealand in World Affairs*, Vol. 1, Wellington, Price Milburn/NZ Institute of International Affairs, 1977

New Zealand Ministry of Defence and New Zealand Defence Force, *The Defence of New Zealand 1991: A Policy paper*, Wellington, GP Print, 1991

New Zealand Ministry of Foreign Affairs and Trade, *Critical Paths in Trans Tasman Economic Relations: Selected documents*, Wellington, Australia Division Ministry of Foreign Affairs and Trade, 2003

New Zealand Official Year-Book 1938, Wellington, Government Printer, 1937

New Zealand Official Year-Book 1951–52, Census and Statistics Department, Wellington, Government Printer, 1952

New Zealand Parliament, House of Representatives: Recess Education Committee, Wellington, Government Printer, 1930

New Zealand Treasury, 'Progress on the Single Economic Market', Discussion Paper for Australia–New Zealand Leadership Forum, 2005

Nicholson, I. H., *Shipping Arrivals and Departures Sydney, 1826–1840*, Roebuck Series, Roebuck Society Publication No. 23, Canberra, Roebuck, 1964 (reprinted 1981)

Nolan, Melanie, 'The High Tide of a Labour Market System: The Australasian male breadwinner model', *Labour & Industry*, Vol. 13, No. 3, April 2003, pp. 73–92

O'Brien, Anne, 'Masculinism and the Church in Australian History', *Australian Historical Studies*, Vol. 25, No. 100, April 1993, pp. 437–57

O'Connor, Brendon, 'Perspectives on Australian Foreign Policy 2003', *Australian Journal of International Affairs*, Vol. 58, No. 2, 2004, pp. 207–20

OECD, *OECD Economic Surveys 1995–1996: New Zealand*, Paris, 1996

OECD, *OECD Best Practices for Budget Transparency*, Paris, 2001

Official Record of the Proceedings and Debates of the Australasian Federation Conference, Melbourne, 1890, and *Official Report of the National Australasian Convention Debates*, Sydney, 1891, Australian Federation Full Text Database: http://setis.library.usyd.edu.au/oztexts/fed.html (22 July 2005)

O'Hara, J., *A Mug's Game: A history of gaming and betting in Australia*, Sydney, University of New South Wales Press, 1988

Olick, J., 'On the Hermeneutics of Historical Analogy', Governing by Looking Back Conference, Australian National University, 12 December 2007

Ollivier, Maurice, *The Colonial and Imperial Conferences from 1887 to 1937*, Ottawa, E. Cloutier, 1954

Olssen, Erik, *Building the New World: Work, politics and society in Caversham 1880s–1920s*, Auckland, Auckland University Press, 1995

Olssen, Erik, 'New Zealand–Australian Relations', in G. Davison, J. Hirst and S. Macintyre (eds), *The Oxford Companion to Australian History*, Oxford, Oxford University Press, 2001, *Oxford Reference Online*, Oxford University Press: www.oxfordreference.com (22 November 2004)

O'Malley, Rory, 'The Eclipse of Mateship: The "wide comb dispute" 1979–85', *Labour History*, No. 90, May 2006, pp. 155–76

Osborne, David and Ted Gaebler, *Reinventing Government: How the entrepreneurial spirit is transforming the public sector*, Reading, Mass., Addison-Wesley Pub. Co., 1992

Osborne, G. and W. F. Mandle (eds), *New History: Studying Australia today*, Sydney, Allen & Unwin, 1982

O'Toole, A. L., *Challenged: The story of Edmund Rice and the Christian Brothers in Australia and New Zealand since 1825*, Bristol, Burleigh Press, 1975

'Our Failing Neighbour: Australia and the future of Solomon Islands', Australian Strategic Policy Institute report, prepared by Elsina Wainwright, 2003

Palenski, Ron, *The Jersey*, Auckland, Hodder Moa Beckett, 2001

Palmer, G., 'New Zealand and Australia: Beyond CER', *New Zealand International Review*, Vol. 15, No. 4, 1990, pp. 2–7

Park, Ruth, *A Fence Around the Cuckoo*, Ringwood, Vic, Penguin, 1993

Park, Ruth, *Fishing in the Styx*, Ringwood, Vic, Penguin, 1994

Pawson, Eric and Tom Brooking (eds), *Environmental Histories of New Zealand*, South Melbourne & Auckland, Oxford University Press, 2002

Pearson, W. H., *Henry Lawson among Maoris*, Wellington, A.H. & A.W. Reed, 1968

Pervan, Ralph, 'Policy Formulation and Implementation: The W. A. Branch of the A.L.P. in the 'thirties', *Labour History*, No. 20, May 1971, pp. 25–45

Peters, Mahora with James George, *Showband! Mahora and the Maori Volcanics*, Wellington, Huia, 2005

Phillips, J. O. C., 'Musings in Maoriland – or was there a *Bulletin* School in New Zealand?', *Historical Studies*, Vol. 20, No. 81, October 1983, pp. 520–35

Phillips, Jock, *A Man's Country?*, Auckland, 1987

Phillips, Jock, Nicholas Boyack and E. P. Malone (eds), *The Great Adventure: New Zealand soldiers describe the First World War*, Wellington, Allen & Unwin/Port Nicholson Press, 1988

Phillips, M. G., 'Rugby', in Wray Vamplew and Brian Stoddart (eds), *Sport in Australia:*

A social history, Cambridge, Cambridge University Press, 1994

Pickles, Katie, 'Colonial Sainthood in Australasia', *National Identities*, Vol. 7, No. 4, December 2005, pp. 389–405

Pocock, J. G. A., *The Discovery of Islands*, Cambridge, Cambridge University Press, 2005

Pollard, J., *From Bradman to Border: Australian cricket, 1948–89*, North Ryde, Angus & Robertson, 1989

Poot, Jacques, 'Twenty Years of Econometric Research on Trans-Tasman Migration', MOTU seminar paper, Wellington, 8 November 2007

Poot, Jacques and Lynda Sanderson, 'Changes in Social Security Eligibility and the International Mobility of New Zealand Citizens in Australia', *Population Studies Centre Discussion Papers*, No. 65, June 2007

Potter, S. J., 'Communication and Integration: The British and dominions press and the British world, c. 1876–1914', *Journal of Imperial and Commonwealth History*, Vol. 31, 2003, pp. 190–206

Powell, Graeme, 'A Diarist in the Cabinet: Lord Derby and the Australian colonies 1882–85', *Australian Journal of Politics and History*, Vol. 51, No. 4, 2005, pp. 481–95

Preferential and Reciprocal Trade Bill, speech by R. J. Seddon, 18 November 1903, *New Zealand Parliamentary Debates*, 1903, pp. 715–25

Prentis, Malcolm, 'Minister and Dominie: An Australasian Scottish world?', New Zealand Historical Association Conference, Dunedin, 30 November 2003, 13 pp

Pugsley, Christopher, *Gallipoli: The New Zealand story*, Auckland, Hodder & Stoughton, 1984

Pugsley, Christopher, *Anzac: The New Zealanders at Gallipoli*, Auckland, Hodder Moa Beckett, 1995

Rabel, Roberto, *New Zealand and the Vietnam War: Politics and diplomacy*, Auckland, Auckland University Press, 2005

Reeves, William Pember, *The Long White Cloud: Ao tea roa*, 2nd edn, London, H. Marshall, 1899

Reeves, William Pember, 'Attitude of New Zealand', *Empire Review*, February 1901, pp. 111–15

Reeves, William Pember, *State Experiments in Australia and New Zealand*, 2 Vols, London, George Allen & Unwin, 1902

Reid, Michael, 'But by my Spirit: A history of the charismatic renewal in Christchurch 1960–1985', PhD thesis, University of Canterbury, 2003

Reserve Bank of New Zealand, 'Review of the Regulation and Performance of New Zealand's Major Financial Institutions': www.rbnz.govt.nz/finstab/banking/supervision/1498932.htm (6 November 2006)

Richardson, Len and Shelley Richardson, *Anthony Wilding: A sporting life*, Christchurch, Canterbury University Press, 2005

Rickard, John, *Australia: A cultural history*, 2nd edn, New York, Longman, 1996 (1st pub. 1988)

Roberts, Vanessa, 'The Origin of Victoria's Public Sector Reforms: Policy transfer from New Zealand?', MA thesis, University of Canterbury, 2005

Robertson, P. and J. Singleton, 'The Old Commonwealth and Britain's First Application to Join the EEC, 1961–3', *Australian Economic History Review*, Vol. 40, No. 2, 2000, pp. 153–77

Robin, Libby and Tom Griffiths, 'Environmental History in Australasia', *Environmental*

History, Vol. 10, No. 4, 2004, pp. 439–74

Rodgers, Daniel T., *Atlantic Crossings: Social politics in a progressive age*, Cambridge, Mass. & London, Belknap Press of Harvard University Press, 1998

Romanos, J., *The Judas Game: The betrayal of New Zealand rugby*, Wellington, Darius Press, 2002

Rose, R., 'What is Lesson Drawing?', *Journal of Public Policy*, Vol. 11, 1991, pp. 3–30

Rowland, J., G. W. Jones and D. Broers-Freeman, *The Founding of Australian Demography: A tribute to W. D. Borrie*, Research School of Social Sciences, Australian National University, Canberra, 1993

Rowley, C. D., *The Destruction of Aboriginal Society*, Canberra, Australian National University Press, 1970

Royal Commission on Federation [New Zealand], *Report of the Royal Commission on Federation, Together with Minutes of Proceedings and Evidence, and Appendices, Appendices to the Journals of the House of Representatives [AJHR]*, 1901, A-4

Royal Commission on Strikes [New South Wales], *Report of the Royal Commission on Strikes (New South Wales)*, Sydney, Government Printer, 1891

Royal Commission on University Education in New Zealand, *Report of Royal Commission on University Education in New Zealand*, Wellington, Government Printer, 1925

Ryan, Greg, '"Extravagance of Thought and Feeling": New Zealand reactions to the 1932/33 bodyline controversy', *Sporting Traditions*, Vol. 13, November 1996, pp. 41–58

Ryan, Greg, 'New Zealand', in B. Stoddart and K. A. P. Sandiford (eds), *The Imperial Game: Cricket, culture and society*, Manchester, Manchester University Press, 1998

Ryan, Greg, *The Making of New Zealand Cricket, 1832–1914*, London, Frank Cass, 2004

Ryan, Greg (ed.) *Tackling Rugby Myths: Rugby and New Zealand society 1854–2004*, Dunedin, University of Otago Press, 2005

Sanders, D., *Simply the Best: Celebrating 90 years of New Zealand league*, Auckland, Celebrity Books, 1997

Sawyer, Geoffrey, *Australia–New Zealand Association: Some constitutional problems*, New Zealand Institute of International Affairs, Auckland Branch, Occasional Papers No. 1, 1968

Schama, Simon, *Landscape and Memory*, London, HarperCollins, 1995

Segal, Naomi, 'Compulsory Arbitration and the Western Australian Gold-mining Industry: A re-examination of the inception of compulsory arbitration in Western Australia', *International Review of Social History*, Vol. 47, 2002, pp. 59–100

Selby, Wendy, 'Motherhood in Labor's Queensland 1915–1957', PhD thesis, Griffith University, 1992

Selby, Wendy, 'Social Evil or Social Good? Lotteries and state regulation in Australia and the United States', in Jan McMillen (ed.), *Gambling Cultures: Studies in history and interpretation*, London, Routledge, 1996

Simms, Marian, 'Australia and New Zealand: Separate states but path-dependent', *Round Table*, Vol. 95, No. 387, October 2006, pp. 679–92

Sinclair, Keith, *William Pember Reeves: New Zealand Fabian*, Oxford, Clarendon Press, 1965

Sinclair, Keith, 'The Past and Future of Australia–New Zealand Relations', *Australian Outlook*, Vol. 22, 1968, pp. 29–38

Sinclair, Keith, 'Why are Race Relations in New Zealand Better Than in South Africa,

South Australia or South Dakota?', *New Zealand Journal of History*, Vol. 5, No. 2, October 1971, pp.121–27

Sinclair, Keith, 'Fruit Fly, Fireblight and Powdery Scab: Australia–New Zealand trade relations, 1919–39', *Journal of Imperial and Commonwealth History*, Vol. 1, No. 1, October 1972, pp. 27–48

Sinclair, Keith, *A Destiny Apart: New Zealand's search for national identity*, Wellington, Allen & Unwin/Port Nicholson Press, 1986

Sinclair, Keith (ed.), *Tasman Relations: New Zealand and Australia, 1788–1988*, Auckland, Auckland University Press, 1987

Singleton, John, 'Introduction', *Australian Economic History Review*, Vol. 41, No. 3, 2001, pp. 233–40

Singleton, John and Paul L. Robertson, *Economic Relations between Britain and Australasia 1945–1970*, Houndmills, Basingstoke, Palgrave, 2002

Sissons, R. and B. Stoddart, *Cricket and Empire: The 1932–33 bodyline tour of Australia*, London, Allen & Unwin, 1984

Smith, Bernard (with Terry Smith), *Australian Painting 1788–1990*, 3rd edn, Melbourne, Oxford University Press, 1991

Smith, Jo, '"All that Glitters": The All Golds and the advent of rugby league in Australasia', MA thesis, University of Canterbury, 1998

Smithies, James, 'The Trans-Tasman Cable, the Australasian Bridgehead and Imperial History', *History Compass*, Vol. 6, April 2008: www.blackwell-compass.com (4 April 2008)

Snape, Richard H., Lisa Gropp and Tas Luttrell, *Australian Trade Policy 1965–1997: A documentary history*, St Leonards, NSW, Allen & Unwin, 1998

Statistics New Zealand: www.stats.govt.nz (16 June 2008)

Stenhouse, John and Brett Knowles (eds), *The Future of Christianity: Historical, sociological, political and theological perspectives*, Adelaide, ATF Press, 2004

Stewart, B., 'The Crisis of Confidence in Australian First-class Cricket in the 1950s', *Sporting Traditions*, Vol. 20, November 2003, pp. 43–62

Strevens, Diane, *In Step with Time: A history of the Sisters of St Joseph of Nazareth, Wanganui, New Zealand*, Auckland, David Ling Publishing, 2001

Studlar, D. T., 'The Political Dynamics of Tobacco Control in Australia and New Zealand: Explaining policy problems, instruments, and patterns of adoption', *Australian Journal of Political Science*, Vol. 40, 2005, pp. 255–74

Supski, Sian, 'Anzac Biscuits: A culinary memorial', *Journal of Australian Studies*, No. 87, 2006, pp. 51–59

Sutch, W. B., *Colony or Nation? Economic crises in New Zealand from the 1860s to the 1960s*, Sydney, Sydney University Press, 1966

Sweetman, Rory, 'A Fair and Just Solution'? A history of the integration of private schools in New Zealand*, Palmerston North, Dunmore Press, 2002

Tapp, E. J., 'Australian and New Zealand Relations', *Australian Outlook*, Vol. 5, 1951, pp. 165–74, 231–35

Tapp, E. J., *Early New Zealand: A dependency of New South Wales, 1788–1841*, Melbourne, Melbourne University Press, 1959

Tapp, E. J., 'New Zealand: The seventh state of Australia?', *Australian Quarterly*, Vol. 34, December 1962, pp. 74–81

Tate, Frank, *Investigation into Certain Aspects of Post-primary Education in New Zealand*, Wellington, Government Printer, 1926

Taylor, T., *Netball in Australia: A social history*, Sydney, University of Technology, 2001

Taylor, T., 'Women, Sport and Ethnicity: Exploring experiences of difference in netball', in B. Whimpress (ed.), *The Imaginary Grandstand: Identity and narrative in Australian sport*, Kent Town/Australian Society for Sports History, 2002

Teaiwa, Teresia, 'On Analogies: Rethinking the Pacific in a global context', *The Contemporary Pacific*, Vol. 18, No. 1, 2006, pp. 71–83

Templeton, Hugh, *All Honourable Men: Inside the Muldoon Cabinet 1975–1984*, Auckland, Auckland University Press, 1995

Templeton, Malcolm, *Standing Upright Here: New Zealand in the nuclear age, 1945–1990*, Wellington, Victoria University Press/NZ Institute of International Affairs, 2006

Thomas, P., *A Whole New Ball Game: Confronting the myths and realities of New Zealand rugby*, Auckland, Hodder Moa Beckett, 2003

Thompson, John, 'British Roots, Australian Fruits', *Meanjin*, Vol. 63, No. 3, 2004, pp. 85–93

Tolich, M., 'Against the Odds: The TAB and the sunset of the horse racing industry', in Bruce Curtis (ed.), *Gambling in New Zealand*, Palmerston North, Dunmore Press, 2002

Tranter, B. and M. Western, 'Postmaterial Values and Age: The case of Australia,' *Australian Journal of Political Science*, Vol. 38, 2003, pp. 239–57

Tsokhas, Kosmas, 'The Matson Line, Australian Shipping Policy and Imperial Relations 1935–1939', *Australian Journal of Politics and History*, Vol. 40, No. 3, 1994, pp. 364–78

Umetsu, Hiroyuki, 'The Birth of ANZUS: America's attempt to create a defense linkage between Northeast Asia and the Southwest Pacific', *International Relations of the Asia–Pacific*, Vol. 4, No. 1, February 2004, pp. 171–96

Ville, Simon P., *The Rural Entrepreneurs: A history of the stock and station agent industry in Australia and New Zealand*, New York & Melbourne, Cambridge University Press, 2000

Wade, R. H., 'Recollections of Australia/New Zealand Relations in the 1940s', handwritten ms, November 1995, copy courtesy of Paul Cotton

Walker, David, *Anxious Nation: Australia and the rise of Asia 1850–1939*, Brisbane, University of Queensland Press, 1999

Walker, Gordon, 'The CER Agreement and Trans-Tasman Securities Regulation: Part 1', *Journal of International Banking Law*, issue 10, 2004, pp. 390–7, and 'Part 2', *Journal of International Banking Law*, issue 11, 2004, pp. 440–6

Wanna, John, Joanne Kelly and John Forster, *Managing Public Expenditure in Australia*, St Leonards, NSW, Allen & Unwin, 2000

Ward, Alan, 'Exporting the British Constitution: Responsible government in New Zealand, Canada, Australia and Ireland', *The Journal of Commonwealth and Comparative Studies*, Vol. 25, 1987, pp. 3–25

Ward, R. Gerard, 'Taupo Country, New Zealand: On place, naming and identity', in Brij Lal (ed.), *Pacific Places, Pacific Histories*, Honolulu, University of Hawai'i Press, 2004

Ward, Russel, *The Australian Legend*, Melbourne, Oxford University Press, 1958

Waters, W. J., 'Australian Labor's Full Employment Objective, 1942–45', *Australian Journal of Politics and History*, Vol. 16, No. 1, 1970, pp. 48–64

Watson, Don, *Recollections of a Bleeding Heart: A portrait of Paul Keating PM*, Sydney, Knopf, 2002

Webb, L. C., *The Control of Education in New Zealand*, Wellington, NZ Council for Educational Research, 1937

White, Colin, *Mastering Risk: Environments, markets and politics in Australian economic history*, Melbourne, Oxford University Press, 1992

White, Hugh, 'Australian Defence Policy and the Possibility of War', *Australian Journal of International Affairs*, Vol. 56, No. 2, 2002, pp. 253–64

Whitwell, Greg, 'The Power of Economic Ideas? Economics policies in post-war Australia', in Stephen Bell and Brian Head (eds), *State, Economy and Public Policy in Australia*, Melbourne, Oxford University Press, 1994

Winks, Robin, *These New Zealanders*, Christchurch, Whitcombe & Tombs, 1954

Winton, Ronald, *Why the Pomegranate? A history of the Royal Australasian College of Physicians*, Sydney, Royal Australasian College of Physicians, 1988

Wood, F. L. W., *New Zealand and the Big Powers: Can a small nation have a mind of its own?* Sir Sidney Holland Memorial Lecture, Wellington, 1967

World Values Survey, 2006: www.worldvaluessurvey.org (17 June 2008)

Young, Angus, 'Two Countries, One Currency? Evolution in trans-Tasman trade and monetary relations', MCA thesis, Victoria University of Wellington, 2002

Young, Grant, '"The War of Intellectual Independence"? New Zealand historians and their History, 1945–1972', MA thesis, University of Auckland, 1998

Young, John M. R. (ed.), *Australia's Pacific Frontier*, Melbourne, Cassell Australia, 1967

Zavos, S. B., *The Gold & the Black: The rugby battles for the Bledisloe Cup: New Zealand vs Australia 1903–94*, St Leonards, NSW, Allen & Unwin, 1995

Zavos, S. B. and G. Bray, *Two Mighty Tribes: The story of the All Blacks vs. the Wallabies*, Auckland, Penguin, 2003

Archival records

Alexander Turnbull Library, Wellington

Holland, (Sir) Sidney George: MS-Papers-1624
MS-Papers-1624-078/5
MS-Papers-1624-079/1
MS-Papers-1624-079/2
MS-Papers-1624-079/3
Marshall, (Sir) John Ross: Political papers, MS-Papers-1403
MS-Papers-1403-139/4 NAFTA
Reeves, William Pember: MS-Papers-0129
MS-Papers-0129-32
Scrapbooks of Newspaper Clippings, qMS-1683-1685
Seddon family: MS-Papers-1619
MS-Papers-1619-020
MS-Papers-1619-021
MS-Papers-1619-048

Archives New Zealand, Wellington

Colonial Secretary, IA 1 1874/342
Department of Agriculture, AG
Series 40 Australia–NZ Trade Relations

Department of Customs
Box 92 22.22/8 Trade Agreement with Australia and New Zealand
Box 93 22.22/8
Box 96 22.22/244 Australia–New Zealand Free Trade Proposals
Box 97 22.22/244 Tariff – NAFTA
Department of External Affairs and Ministry of Foreign Affairs, EA 1
Series 58/4 Australia – Trade Relations
Series 59 Visits
Series 64/1/6 New Zealand – External Relations – New Zealand–Australia
[Archway code ABHS 18069 W5402 Box 119 BRU 64/1/6]
Series 64/5 Publicity – Australia
Series 104/203 Economic Affairs – Australia
Series 203/4 Australia – Economic Affairs, 203/9 Australia – External Relations
Department of Health, H 1 139/87
Department of Industries and Commerce, IC 1
Series 12 Fruit and Vegetables
Series 22 Australia/New Zealand Trade Discussions
Series 56 New Zealand Overseas Trade
Series 107 NZ/Australia Free Trade Area
W1842/1958 107/4/1/1 GATT – NZ/Australia Free Trade Area
W2458, record 125, Australia/New Zealand Consultative Committee on Trade
Box 5 422A NAFTA Review
Box 8 484 NAFTA Review
W2968/5–8 NAFTA Review
Department of Tourist and Publicity, TO 1
Series 1/39, 1/98
Series 6 Agencies
Series 28 Exhibitions
Series 40 Visits
Series 53 Tourist Development
New Zealand Forest Service, F 1 W3129 339 de 80.004
Prime Minister's Department, PM
PM 11, Keith Holyoake, official visit to Australia, 1970
Registrar–General New Zealand, BDM 1 RG1874/414
Treasury, T 79 36

Australian National University Archives, Canberra
Leicester Webb Papers

Christian Brothers Archives, St Mary's Province, NSW, Balmain, Sydney
Miscellaneous, File 2: Brothers trained in St Mary's Province for St Joseph's Province
(NZ), 1960–1970
Miscellaneous, Files 3 & 4: Statistics, Correspondence
Item 310: Book of Foundations, 1907–1976
Item 03461: St Josephs Province (NZ)
Items 03462–03467: Correspondence 1954–1980
Item 03468: St Joseph's Province, Report to Provincial Chapter 1983

Item 03469: Newsletters and Circulars
Item 03470: Provincials Reports
Our Studies, Vol. 2, No. 2, 1930 – Vol. 24, No. 2, 1952

National Archives of Australia, Canberra

Microfilm, Lyons government, 1934/12/31, CRS A6006
Department of Health
Potatoes from New Zealand (Powdery Scab) Section 4, A1928/1 820/3
Department of Trade and Customs
Department of Commerce
Potatoes New Zealand Part 1, A458 Q500/14
Potatoes New Zealand Parts 2–4, A461/9 G325/1/10
Embargo on New Zealand Potatoes, A601 878/10/2, 878/10/3, 878/10/4
New Zealand: Australian Trade Commissioner in New Zealand, 1935–1945, A1667
    277/B/5A
Trade: Commercial Relations between Australia and New Zealand, A981/4 TRAD96
New Zealand–Australia. Foreign Policy – Ministerial visits to New Zealand –
    Minister for Trade and Customs, 1944/630/5/1/12/2, A989/1

National Library of Australia, Canberra

John Passmore Papers
R. S. Parker Papers

State Library of South Australia, Adelaide

Kingston, C. C., 'Memorandum re Conciliation Bill', October 1892, PRG 1039/2

Databases

Baird, Rosemary, 'Sporting Cultures in the Trans-Tasman World', NZAC/Social
    Science Research Centre Summer Project, University of Canterbury, 2006–2007
Dann, Claire, 'A Continuing Community of Interests: a database of Australasian organisa-
    tions 1880–2003', Social Science Research Centre Summer Project, University of
    Canterbury, 2003. Copy held at NZARC, University of Canterbury
Harrigan, Nicholas, Dataset on Australian and New Zealand Business, used by Shaun
    Goldfinch
Macdonald, Julia, 'Gambling as a Major Trans-Tasman Enterprise', Social Science
    Research Centre Summer Project, University of Canterbury, 2004–2005,
    NZARC, University of Canterbury
McGeorge, Colin, 'Notes on Some Australia–New Zealand Links in Education', 2005.
    In possession of P. J. Hempenstall
Whitcher, Gary, UC Summer Scholarship Project on New Zealand and American
    Influences, 2007, NZARC, University of Canterbury

Interviews

By Shaun Goldfinch, Sydney and Canberra, October–November 2004
By Peter Hempenstall
    R. Barwick, Canberra, 8 July 2003

W. N. Gunson, Canberra, 27 September 2002
A. D. Ward, Christchurch, 8 and 21 September 2002
R. G. Ward, Canberra, 28 November 2002
By Philippa Mein Smith, Sydney, 24–28 August 2003

Newspapers, journals and magazines

Canterbury College Review, 1908–1909
Journal of the Statistical Society of London, Vol. 24, No. 2, 1861
Money Management, March 2000
New Zealand Foreign Affairs Review
New Zealand Management, May 2003
New Zealand Memories, August/September 2002
Auckland Star
Australian
Bulletin
Canberra Times
Christchurch Star
Dominion Post
New Zealand Herald
Press, Christchurch
Sunday Star-Times
Sydney Morning Herald

INDEX

Commonwealth 52, 58, 83, 86–87, 88–91, 94,
114, 186–87, 202
states 75, 87
Labor Party (Aust.) 74–75, 83, 102
labour flows 21, 24–25, 70–71, 144, 152,
156, 213 *see also* migration flows; personnel
interchange
Labour governments (NZ) 21–23, 52, 87, 88, 94,
104, 109, 114, 186–88, 190, 194–95, 202
labour movement 15, 21, 44, 58
Labour Party (NZ) 75, 87, 186, 191
Labour History 15
labour policies 83, 90–91, 129 *see also* employment
policies
land policies 82, 83, 143
Lane, William 70
Lang, Jack 102
Lange, David 23, 52, 54, 96 *see also* Labour
governments
law 81, 86, 92, 93, 126, 127, 129, 136–37, 210, 211
Lawrence, Bruno 74
Lawson, Henry 156
leadership forums 25–26, 128–29, 161, 212
Leunig, Michael 49, 50
Liberal government
NZ 84, 99
Victoria 92
Liberal Party (Aust.) 94
Liberal–Country Party coalition government
(Aust.) 108
Liberal–National coalition governments (Aust.) 37,
64, 65, 89, 91, 94, 191
Liberal–National Country Party coalition
government (Aust.) 114
Lindsay, Norman 145
Lion Nathan 134
literature 14, 40, 125, 161
Lloyd, Henry Demarest 83
Lloyd, P. J. 113
Lloyd, Trevor *104*
Lloyds 132
Lochinvar 149
Lodge, Nevile 76, *167*
London 82, 100
Longburn (NZ) 153
Lonsdale, Neil 66
Lottery Commission (NZ) 76–77
Lowe, Graeme 165
Lyons, Joe 101–103

Mack, Andrew 192
magazines 26–27, 73, 88
Mahora and the Volcanics 71–72

Malaysia 79, 156
Malone, W. G. 48
Mambo art 36–37, 60
Mandle, Bill 14, 175
manufacturing industry 101, 104, 110, 112, 113,
116, 117–19, 133 *see also* motor industry
Maori 18, 20, 29, 38–39, 62–63, 146, 149, 200, 215
in Australia 27, 28, 69–70, 207
in sport 164, 167, 171, 181, 183, 215
show bands 28, 71–72
see also race relations
Maori Women's Welfare League (Aust., NZ) 70
March, J. G. 126
Marists 148, 149, 151
Marlow, Christopher Claver 150, 152
Marsden, Samuel 20, 69
Marshall, Benji 165
Marshall, John (Jack) 64, 96, 109–11, 115 *see also*
National governments
Martin, Larry 191
Marylebone Cricket Club *see* MCC
mass media 88
Massy Greene, Walter 103–04
Masters, Harold 169
Matamata 78
Matangi, Meg 181
mateship 46, 49, 70, 201, 209
Max Merritt and the Meteors 74
May, Ricky 72
Mazengarb committee 88
McAloon, Jim 20
MCC 174
McCahon, Colin 116
McCaskill, Murray 159
McCullough, Jack 42
McDonald, Kerry 129
McDowell, Ernest Gordon 153
McEwen, John 96, 104–105, 108–15, 121
McKechnie, Brian 178
McKenzie, J. R. 105
McKillop, Mary 148–49
McKinnon, Don 196
McLean, Denis 16, 28, 195, 207
Mead, Margaret 27
Meads, Colin 168
media 82, 88, 120, 133, 192
coverage by 53, 65, 96, 129, 164, 173, 174–75,
177, 180, 181–82
Medical Journal of Australia 156
Medsafe 211
Mein Smith, Philippa 16
Melbourne 33, 68, 80, 126, 149, 151
Melbourne Cup 35, 74, 75, 78